AF505828

Southampton Studies in International Policy

Published in association with the Mountbatten Centre for International Studies, University of Southampton

General Editor: **Dilys M. Hill**

Other academic members of the editorial board: Ralph Beddard, John Oldfield, Kendrick Oliver, John Simpson

This series was established in 1986 to encourage the publication of multi-disciplinary studies of those public policies with significant international components or implications. Areas of special interest include arms control and defence policies, environmental policies, human rights, maritime and space issues, Third World development questions and the European Union.

Selected titles:

Lisbeth Aggestam and Adrian Hyde-Price (*editors*)
SECURITY AND IDENTITY IN EUROPE
Exploring the New Agenda

Wyn Q. Bowen
THE POLITICS OF BALLISTIC MISSILE NONPROLIFERATION

Andrew Dorman
DEFENCE UNDER THATCHER

David H. Dunn
THE POLITICS OF THREAT
Minutemen Vulnerability in American National Security Policy

Tony Evans
US HEGEMONY AND THE PROJECT OF UNIVERSAL HUMAN RIGHTS

Paul S. Herrnson and Dilys M. Hill (*editors*)
THE CLINTON PRESIDENCY
The First Term, 1992–96

Dilys M. Hill, Raymond A. Moore and Phil Williams (*editors*)
THE REAGAN PRESIDENCY
An Incomplete Revolution?

Dilys M. Hill and Phil Williams (*editors*)
THE BUSH PRESIDENCY
Triumphs and Adversities

Stephen M. Hill
UNITED NATIONS DISARMAMENT PROCESSES IN INTRA-STATE CONFLICT

Mark F. Imber
THE USA, ILO, UNESCO AND IAEA
Politicization and Withdrawal in the Specialized Agencies

John Simpson and Darryl Howlett (*editors*)
THE FUTURE OF THE NON-PROLIFERATION TREATY

Joanna Spear
CARTER AND ARMS SALES

Antonio Varsori (*editor*)
EUROPE, 1945–1990s
The End of an Era?

Southampton Studies in International Policy
Series Standing Order ISBN 0–333–71493–8
(*outside North America only*)

You can receive future titles in this series as they are published by placing a standing order.
Please contact your bookseller or, in case of difficulty, write to us at the address below with your
name and address, the title of the series and the ISBN quoted above.

Customer Services Department, Macmillan Distribution Ltd, Houndmills, Basingstoke,
Hampshire RG21 6XS, England

United Nations Disarmament Processes in Intra-State Conflict

Stephen M. Hill
Department of Political Science
University of Wisconsin – Eau Claire
USA

First published 2004 by
PALGRAVE MACMILLAN
Houndmills, Basingstoke, Hampshire RG21 6XS and
175 Fifth Avenue, New York, N. Y. 10010
Companies and representatives throughout the world

PALGRAVE MACMILLAN is the global academic imprint of the Palgrave Macmillan division of St. Martin's Press, LLC and of Palgrave Macmillan Ltd. Macmillan® is a registered trademark in the United States, United Kingdom and other countries. Palgrave is a registered trademark in the European Union and other countries.

ISBN 0–333–94716–9

This book is printed on paper suitable for recycling and made from fully managed and sustained forest sources.

A catalogue record for this book is available from the British Library.

Library of Congress Cataloging-in-Publication Data
Hill, Stephen M.
    United Nations disarmament processes in intra-state conflict / Stephen M. Hill.
        p. cm. (Southampton studies in international policy)
    Includes bibliographical references and index.
    ISBN 0–333–94716–9 (cloth)
      1. Peacekeeping forces–History–20th century. 2. United Nations–Armed Forces–History–20th century. I. Title. II. Series.

JZ6374.H549 2004
341.5′84–dc22   2004051683

10   9   8   7   6   5   4   3   2   1
13   12   11   10   09   08   07   06   05   04

Printed and bound in Great Britain by
Antony Rowe Ltd, Chippenham and Eastbourne

To Polly and the memory of Paul Ormerod

Contents

Acknowledgements

This book represents the latest stage in an intellectual journey that has brought me into contact with a number of wonderful people. Without them I could never have accomplished this project, nor any that have preceded it. My greatest thanks must go to Stuart Croft, who having adopted me as his PhD student many years ago, has continued to fulfill his role as a mentor far beyond the call of duty. Similarly, as a fledgling Masters student, I was inspired by the enthusiasm and intellectual rigor of David Dunn, whose support and encouragement has been critical throughout my academic career. Ali Abootalebi, John Duffield, Alan James, Steve Majstorovic and Terry Terriff, have also provided me with invaluable help and guidance. I can only hope to become half the academic that each of these great scholars represent.

Of course, on any journey it helps to have good companions and I am fortunate enough to have had the best. My thanks must therefore go to Stuart Griffin, Robert Shaw, Barry Thomas and Adrian Treacher. Without the heady intellectual atmosphere they generated in Room 632 my academic goals could never have become so lofty. In addition, although it is impossible to mention all the great friends I have made throughout my lifetime, I do want to pay particular gratitude to Michael Booth, Grant Breheny, Martin and Alison Brown, Pauline Gleave, Marcus Crepaz, Sr. Gabriel, Stephen Hedderman, Anne-Marie Heggarty, Ian Kelly, Mary Ledwick, Bernadette and Francois Letissier, Steve Lewis, Philip Loy, Guy Mortenson, Nicoletta Pisa and Simon Stafford. I only wish Paul Ormerod was around to appreciate his contribution.

I am also extremely fortunate to possess such a loving family. My parents are the foundation on which my success has been built and together with my siblings, Terry, Angela, Kathleen and Margaret, they have continued to provide me with unconditional love and support. So too have their spouses Elizabeth, John, Robert and Keith and my in-laws, the Hashmi family. And how could I forget my nephews and nieces, Jason, Nicholas, Christopher, Emma, Laura and Rebecca. Of course, neither these acknowledgements, nor my life, would be complete without my loving wife, Polly. I could not have hoped to marry someone more caring, intelligent and fun. She is an amazing person and I will be forever grateful that she has blessed my life with such happiness.

Lastly, I would like to thank Dilys Hill and John Simpson for accepting my manuscript as part of their *Southampton Studies in International Policy Series* and Alison Howson and Guy Edwards at Palgrave for their patience in seeing it through to completion. I would also like to thank Shirley Tan and Wang Hui Guan for their copy-editing expertise.

Abbreviations

ADEFAES	Association of Former Members of the Armed Forces (El Salvador)
AEC	Angolan Electoral Council
ANC	African National Congress
ANDA	National Administration of Water and Sewers (El Salvador)
ANP	Angolan National Police Force
ANTEL	National Administration of Telecommunications (El Salvador)
ARENA	Aliaza Republican Nationalista (El Salvador)
ASEAN	Association of Southeast Asian Nations
AWSS	Authorized Weapons Storage Sites (Somalia)
BIRI	El Salvadoran Rapid Deployment Infantry Battalions (El Salvador)
CAC	Cessation of the Armed Conflict Period (El Salvador)
CCF	Joint Cease-fire Commission (Mozambique)
CCFA	Joint Commission for the Formation of the Armed Forces (Angola)
CCFADM	Joint Commission for the Formation of the Mozambican Defense Force
CCPM	Joint Political and Military Commission (Angola)
CGDK	Coalition Government of Democratic Kampuchea
CIAV	International Support and Verification Mission (El Salvador)
CID	Criminal Investigation Division (El Salvador)
CIVPOL	United Nations Civilian Police Observers
CMF	Commonwealth Monitoring Force (Rhodesia/Zimbabwe)
CMVF	Joint Verification and Monitoring Commission (Angola)
CNA	National Commission on Administration (Mozambique)
CNE	National Election Commission (Angola)/National Election Commission (Mozambique)
CSC	Supervisory and Control Commission (Mozambique)
COMINFO	National Information Commission (Mozambique)
COMPOL	National Police Affairs Commission (Mozambique)
COPAZ	National Commission for the Consolidation of Peace (El Salvador)
CORE	Commission for the Reintegration of Demobilized Personnel (Mozambique)
CPAF	Cambodian People's Armed Forces
CPP	Cambodian People's Party
CPSC	Comprehensive Political Settlement of Cambodia
DDA	United Nations Department of Disarmament Affairs

DF	Frontiers Division (El Salvador)
DPA	United Nations Department of Political Affairs
DPKO	United Nations Department of Peacekeeping Operations
DRO	Demobilization and Reintegration Office (Angola)
ECOWAS	Economic Community of West African States
ERP	Ejercito Revolucionario del Pueblo (El Salvador)
EC	European Community
EU	European Union
FAA	Angolan Armed Forces
FADM	Mozambican Defense Force
FAES	Armed Forces of El Salvador
FAM	Mozambican Armed Forces
FAO	Food and Agricultural Organization
FARN	Fuerzas Armadas de Resistencia Nacional (El Salvador)
FDR	Frente Democratico Revolucionario (El Salvador)
FENESTRAS	National Federation of Salvadoran Workers Union (El Salvador)
FMLN	Frente Farabundo Marti para la Liberacion Nacional (El Salvador)
FPL	Fuerzas Populares de Liberacion-Farabundo Mari (El Salvador)
FRELIMO	Frente da Libertacao de MoZambique
FUNCINPEC	Front Uni National Pour UN Cambodge Independent, Neutre, Pacifique et Cooperatif (Cambodia)
GN	National Guard (El Salvador)
GPA	General Peace Agreement (Mozambique)
GURN	Government of National Unity (Angola)
HRS	Humanitarian Relief Sector (Somalia)
ICFY	International Conference on the Former Yugoslavia
ICRC	International Committee of the Red Cross
IMF	International Monetary Fund
IO	International Organization
IOM	International Organization for Migration
JAP	Joint Action Plan (former Yugoslavia)
JC	Joint Commission (Angola)
JIM	Jakarta Informal Meeting
JNA	Yugoslav People's Army
JVC	Joint Verification Commission (Mozambique)
KPNLF	Khmer People's National Liberation Front (Cambodia)
MERCOSUR	Common Market of the Southern Cone
MINUGUA	United Nations Verification Mission in Guatemala
MINURCA	United Nations Mission in Central African Republic
MINUSAL	United Nations Mission in El Salvador
MONUA	United Nations Observer Mission in Angola
MPLA	Movimento Popular de Liergao de Angola

NATO	North Atlantic Treaty Organization
NGC	National Government of Cambodia
NGO	Non-Governmental Organization
NRP	National Reconstruction Plan (El Salvador)
OAS	Organization of American States
OAU	Organization of African Unity
ONUCA	United Nations Observer Group in Central America
ONUMOZ	United Nations Operation in Mozambique
ONUSAL	United Nations Operation in El Salvador
ONUV	United Nations Office of Verification in El Salvador
ONUVEN	United Nations Observer Mission to Verify the Electoral Process in Nicaragua
OSCE	Organization for Security and Cooperation (Europe)
PAHO	Pan American Health Organization
Paris	Paris Conference on Cambodia
PAT	Auxiliary Transitory Police (El Salvador)
PCN	Partido de Conciliacion Nacional (El Salvador)
PDC	Christian Democratic Party (El Salvador)
PDD25	United States Presidential Decision Directive 25
PDK	Party of Democratic Kampuchea
PNC	National Civil Police (El Salvador)
PNSA	National Public Security Academy (El Salvador)
PRK	People's Republic of Kampuchea
PRM	Police Force (Mozambique)
PT	Treasury Police (El Salvador)
RDP	Rapid Demobilization Plan (Angola)/Rapid Demobilization Plan (Mozambique)
RENAMO	Resistencia Nacional Mozambicana
RRF	United Nations Rapid Reaction Force (former Yugoslavia)
RRP	Rapid Reaction Police (Angola)
RSK	Republic of Serbian Krajina
RSS	Reintegration Support Scheme (Mozambique)
SAA	Sarajevo Airport Agreement
SADC	South African Development Community
SDC	Swiss Agency for Development and Cooperation (Mozambique)
SDC	Selection and Demobilization Centers (Angola)
SISE	State Information and Security Service (El Salvador)
SNA	Somali National Alliance
SNC	Supreme National Council (Cambodia)
SNM	Somali National Movement
SoC	State of Cambodia
SIU	Special Investigative Unit (El Salvador)
SRSG	Special Representative of the Secretary-General

TO	Territorial Defense Forces (former Yugoslavia)
TSE	Supreme Electoral Tribunal (El Salvador)
TWGDR	Technical Working Group for Demobilization and Reintegration
UCAH	United Nations Humanitarian Assistance Coordination Unit (Angola)
UEA	Executive Anti-Narcotics Unit (El Salvador)
UN	United Nations
UNAMIC	United Nations Advance Mission in Cambodia
UNAMSIL	United Nations Assistance Mission for Sierra Leone
UNAVEM	United Nations Verification Mission in Angola
UNCDA	United Nations Center for Disarmament
UNCRO	United Nations Confidence Restoration Operation (former Yugoslavia)
UNDP	United Nations Development Program
UNESCO	United Nations Education and Science Council
UNHCR	United Nations High Commission for Refugees
UNICEF	United Nations Children's Fund
UNIDIR	United Nations Institute of Disarmament Research
UNITA	Uniao Nacional para a Independencia Total de Angola
UNITAF	Unified Task Force (Somalia)
UNMOT	United Nations Mission of Observers in Tajikistan
UNOHAC	United Nations Office for the Coordination of Humanitarian Assistance
UNOMIL	United Nations Operation in Liberia
UNOSOM	United Nations Operation in Somalia
UNPROFOR	United Nations Protection Force (former Yugoslavia)
UNPA	United Nations Protected Area (former Yugoslavia)
UNSA	United Nations Safe Area (former Yugoslavia)
UNSAS	United Nations Stand-By Arrangements System
UNSC	United Nations Security Council
UNTAC	United Nations Transitional Authority in Cambodia
UNTAES	United Nations Transitional Administration for Eastern Slavonia, Baranja and Western Sirmium
USAID	United States Agency for International Development
USC	United Somali Congress
USSR	Union of Soviet Socialist Republics
VOPP	Vance-Owen Peace Plan (former Yugoslavia)
WB	World Bank
WFP	World Food Program
WHO	World Health Organization

Introduction

As the 1980s began few people could have predicted the dramatic changes that were to take place within the international system by the end of the decade. The election of Mikhail Gorbachev as General Secretary of the USSR in 1985 heralded an end to over four decades of ideological confrontation and effectively eradicated the risk of military conflict. Spurred on by domestic pressures, both superpowers began to seek peace dividends by ending overtly expensive support for regimes in areas of the world that were no longer deemed to affect their national interest. The international community, euphoric in its anticipation of a new peaceful age, hoped that all that would be required was a method of overseeing the conclusion of conflicts, which had resulted from, and been sustained by, a now defunct global rivalry.

However, expectations that the proxy wars being fought on behalf of the superpowers would dry up, along with the financial and military support they had provided, were to be sadly misguided. Rather, the retreat of superpower hegemony simply uncovered a Pandora's box of cultural, ethnic, religious and nationalistic disagreements, which were all too ready to fill the vacuum left behind and which possessed a force and momentum of their own. With the fog of Cold War antagonism lifting, public attention began to focus on the ability of the major international powers to resolve these conflicts, which through war and famine were claiming hundreds of thousands of victims every year. With a consensus never before attained the international community turned to the United Nations (UN), not only to oversee the withdrawal of the superpowers themselves, but also to attempt increasingly ambitious methods of bringing seemingly intractable conflicts to a peaceful conclusion.

The dilemma facing the UN in its attempts to reconcile warring parties and reconstruct these so-called 'failed states' was apparent. As Roy Licklider expressed it:

> Ending international war is hard enough, but at least there the opponents will presumably eventually retreat to their own territories...But in civil wars the members of the two sides must live side by side and work together in a common government to make the country work...How do groups of people who have been killing one another with considerable enthusiasm and success come together to form a common government.[1]

What is more, it was clear that any strategy designed to reconstruct wartorn states would have to involve disarmament, for without it the new state's monopoly over the domestic use of force would not be complete. Further, without disarmament it was believed that there could be no reconciliation, and thus no recreation of social cohesion and economic well being within society itself.[2] This book is therefore concerned with the relationship between these two objectives and the UN's ability to achieve them.

In writing this book my aims are thus two-fold. The first is to provide an historical account of the major disarmament processes conducted by the UN in intra-state conflicts during the 1990s. This decade, which spans the period between the end of the Cold War and the beginning of the new millennium, represents one of the most tumultuous in the UN's history. Not only did it witness the unprecedented expansion of the UN's peacekeeping commitments, but it also saw its first significant involvement in small arms control. An overview of both of these developments is therefore provided at the beginning of Chapter 1.

My second aim is to provide an explanation for the variation in success that the UN has experienced in implementing its disarmament processes. Thus, from a Constructivist theoretical perspective I utilize developing approaches in conflict mediation to create an analytical framework, which I then use to conduct a structured, focused, case comparison.[3] The analytical framework (the theoretical foundation for which is explained in the latter half of Chapter 1) posits that the UN's success in disarmament depends on its ability to transform the social structures of war-torn societies through the application of a twin-track approach to the provision of security at three levels of society; the warring parties, ex-combatants and the general population.

In order to accomplish both these aims, Chapters 2 through 7 will consist of seven case studies involving UN disarmament processes conducted in intra-state conflict in six countries. These are Angola, Cambodia, Mozambique, Somalia, El Salvador and the former Yugoslavia. As well as providing an historical account, it is hoped that by dealing with them in the best sequential manner possible that a process tracing approach can be taken to the UN's learning (or not) over a ten-year period.

Though chosen principally for their historical relevance, the case studies also incorporate a number of variables that will help to demonstrate the utility of the analytical framework. The first is the size of the operation undertaken (measured by the size of its deployment and the nature of its mandate). In this respect the cases range from the deployment of a few hundred UN personnel to literally tens of thousands and from relatively peripheral mandates to highly intrusive and encompassing ones. Secondly, as the cases covered include countries spread over four continents (Northern and Southern Africa, South-East Asia, Central America and South-Eastern Europe) their geographical distribution will help account for cultural variance.

Thirdly, though the majority of the cases involve peacekeeping operations established to assist in the implementation of 'comprehensive agreements' negotiated between former warring parties, those of Somalia and the former Yugoslavia are obvious exceptions. In both these cases the UN's initial involvement was designed principally to ensure the delivery of humanitarian aid and to help foster conditions for the achievement of a negotiated settlement. Their exceptionality is reinforced by the fact that they are also the only cases in which the UN became involved in coercive disarmament.

Finally, the conclusion of the book will espouse the major lessons of the UN's experiences in disarmament during the 1990s and assess the utility of the analytical framework it purports. On this basis it will also proffer recommendations for the UN's future disarmament strategies.

1

United Nations Peacekeeping, Disarmament and Conflict Resolution

Men do not fight because they have their arms. They have arms because they deem it necessary to fight. Take away their arms, and they will either fight with their bare fists or get themselves new arms with which to fight. What makes for war are the conditions in the minds of men which make war appear the lesser of two evils. In those conditions must be sought the disease of which the desire for, and possession of, arms is but a symptom.

Hans J. Morgenthau, *Politics Among Nations*, 1948[1]

[T]he level of arms can be reduced only when they are no longer felt to be needed. The problems of perceived threat and of conflict have to be resolved first.

Edward E. Azar, 'Protracted International Conflict: Ten Propositions', 1999[2]

Weapons are never the cause of war, they are the instruments...My primary objective was to create the conditions for a stable political environment that would render the weapons irrelevant.

Aldo Ajello, Former Special Representative of the UN Secretary-General in Mozambique, 1999[3]

1 The evolution of United Nations peacekeeping

Peacekeeping, as we recognize it today, was unforeseen when the United Nations (UN) was created in 1945. For this reason neither the term nor the concept appears anywhere in the organization's Charter. Instead, through their powers as permanent members on the UN Security Council (UNSC), the post-war victors were expected to police the world with the consensus inherent in Chapter VII (enforcement) resolutions and the might of their combined militaries. Unfortunately, post-war collaboration was soon replaced with Cold War standoff and the UN itself became simply another means to manage the relationships of the great powers rather than a means to organize their combined efforts. It was in this highly charged political atmosphere that UN peacekeeping was first developed and its primary objective was to prevent the USA and USSR from becoming embroiled in localized disputes that might otherwise have escalated into global conflict. Initially seen for this reason as a method of preventive diplomacy, peace-keeping developed its own set of principles and operational norms that enabled UN 'blue helmet' forces to be perceived as both non-coercive and neutral. By the end of the Cold War the UN itself was defining its peace-keeping operations as those that involved:

> ...military personnel, but without enforcement powers, undertaken by the United Nations to help maintain or restore international peace and security in areas of conflict. These operations are voluntary and are based on consent and co-operation. While they involve the use of military personnel, they achieve their objectives not by force of arms, thus contrasting them with the 'enforcement action' of the United Nations under Article 42.[4]

With the exception of the operation in the Congo (1960–64), these principles and operational norms were maintained throughout the 13 UN operations conducted during the Cold War.[5] This less than pro-active style of peacekeeping was generally the result of the sensitivity of the superpowers to the UN assuming any more responsibility than was absolutely necessary. The 279 Security Council vetoes cast before mid-1990 stand as testimony to the deep mistrust that prevailed throughout this tense period.[6]

The unexpected end of the Cold War thus heralded a new era for the UN. In searching for ever greater peace dividends, both superpowers began to terminate their support for various governments and rebel groups that continued to fight proxy wars on their behalf. The international community, caught up in the euphoria of the moment and naively assuming that these civil wars were being fought solely because of the Cold War, simply expected them to wind down along with the financial and military aid on which they apparently depended. Unfortunately, this was not to be the case. Instead, the retreat of superpower hegemony uncovered a Pandora's box of cultural, ethnic, religious and nationalistic disagreements that were all too ready to fill the vacuum left behind and that evidently possessed a life of their own. Thus, with public attention increasingly focusing on the ability of the major international powers to resolve these conflicts (which through war and famine were continuing to claim hundreds of thousands of victims every year) the international community turned to the UN, not only to oversee the withdrawal of the superpowers themselves, but also to attempt ever more ambitious methods of bringing these seemingly intractable conflicts to a peaceful conclusion.

It was therefore in the embryonic years of the post-Cold War era that UN peacekeeping was to experience its greatest ever expansion. Between 1988 and 1994 the UN established a total of 16 new operations, thereby surpassing the number it had conducted throughout the previous 40 years. These new operations included those in Cambodia, Somalia and the former Yugoslavia, the three largest in the UN's history. By the mid-1990s there were over 70,000 peacekeepers in the field and the annual cost of peacekeeping had rocketed to nearly $4 billion. However, UN peacekeeping was not only experiencing significant changes in the number, size and cost of its operations, but also in the nature of its goals. In this respect the traditional role of UN peacekeeping as a 'thin blue line' separating antagonistic States was no longer applicable to the emerging conflicts of the post-Cold War era. Instead, the civil wars, secessions, partitions, ethnic clashes and tribal warfare that were now characteristic of military conflict, were forcing the UN 'once again...to adapt to the violent evolution of the world'. No longer confined to simply containing a situation pending a political settlement, the UN's new peacekeeping operations were seeking to 'restore, or even build peace'.[7] This required the UN to perform a 'growing litany of new responsibilities other than the traditional military aspects of peacekeeping'. These involved amongst others, organizing and supervising the conduct of elections; arranging the return of refugees; maintaining law and order; disarming and demobilizing former soldiers; the protection of humanitarian assistance in volatile areas; and assisting with economic reconstruction and rehabilitation.[8]

The size and complexity of these new UN peacekeeping operations incited some analysts to talk of a 'second generation' of peacekeeping. This was especially the case after the UN Secretary-General Boutros Boutros-Ghali, defined peacekeeping in his seminal text of 1992, *Agenda for Peace,* as a UN 'presence in the field, *hitherto* with the consent of all the parties concerned'. He also included a suggestion for 'peace-enforcement units' that, under his command, might enforce a cease-fire where one was not already present.[9] Nevertheless, for Alan James the 'second generation' title remained a misnomer for three reasons. Firstly, although most of the UN's post-Cold War peacekeeping operations had displayed aspirations of peace-building to an extent that their Cold War predecessors had not, none of them, except for the operations in Somalia and Yugoslavia, had operated outside the principles and operational norms of traditional peacekeeping. Secondly, once force had been used in Somalia and Yugoslavia the UN's actions could no longer be classed as peacekeeping, as it had henceforth failed to comply with the essential tenets of peacekeeping; consent and impartiality. 'In principle, therefore, if an operation's *modus operandi* goes beyond behavior which is characteristic of peacekeeping, it cannot be a form of the latter, such as a second generation of it'. Finally, James also rejected a distinction based on the predominance of intra-state peacekeeping operations in the post-Cold War period, arguing that the UN's operations during the Cold War had at least displayed something in the nature of a numerical balance between an internal and border focus.[10]

Certainly, as this text will attest, the UN's experiences in places such as Somalia and Yugoslavia have forced the Organization and its member States to reassess the importance of consent and its theoretical and practical relationship to peacekeeping.[11] Nevertheless, influential analysts in the UN system, including Assistant Secretary-General Michael Doyle, continue to organize the UN's peacekeeping activities into generational categories, with multidimensional operations involving the implementation of complex, multidimensional peace agreements forming a 'second generation'. For Doyle such operations take 'a substantial step beyond first-generation operations because (despite being based on the consent of the parties) the nature of consent and the purposes for which it is granted are qualitatively different than in traditional peacekeeping'. In particular this type of operation may have been awarded 'strategic consent' through the parties' acceptance of the UN's mandate, but the 'tactical consent' of individuals and groups on the ground may still be absent.[12] The defining characteristic of peace-enforcement operations, on the other hand, is the lack of consent by one or more of the parties to some, or all, of the UN's mandate. As they therefore lack strategic consent they constitute a 'third generation' of peacekeeping.[13] Though mindful of the conceptual stretching being undertaken by Doyle and others, this text will adopt the first, second and third generation typologies.

2   The new disarmament agenda

2.1   Changing global markets

Just as the global confrontation of the superpowers had masked the indigenous sources of conflict that were now fuelling the civil wars of the post-Cold War era, the simultaneous preoccupation of the international community with the reduction of nuclear and heavy conventional weapons had masked an equally sinister development: the proliferation of small arms and light weapons.[14] Although there exist various definitions for this category of weapon, as Lawrence identifies, one need only analyze the weapons actually been used in conflicts around the world to gain an empirical answer to the question of what they are. In this sense small arms and light weapons include handguns, carbines, assault rifles, submachine guns, machine guns, rocket-propelled grenades, light anti-tank missiles, small caliber mortars, shoulder-fired anti-aircraft missiles and hand placed landmines.[15] Despite pouring incalculable numbers of these weapons into areas of conflict both superpowers continued to relegate them to the margins of the Cold War disarmament agenda. An obvious manifestation of this was the omission of small arms and light weapons as a category in the UN Register of Conventional Weapons when it was established in 1992.[16]

Unfortunately, rather than helping to reduce the availability of small arms and light weapons through international markets, the end of the Cold War had the opposite effect. There were two principle reasons for this. Firstly, subsequent bilateral and multilateral disarmament agreements, combined with unilateral national decisions to reduce armed forces and weapons expenditure, resulted in the generation of large quantities of surplus weapons within a relatively short time period.[17] For example, the dissolution of the East German *Volksarmee* rendered surplus over 295,000 tons of weapons alone, including one million handguns and over 26,000 rocket propelled grenades. Many of these have subsequently disappeared, eventually finding their way to civil conflicts around the world.[18]

Secondly, the international market in small arms and light weapons has become increasingly permissive. Despite a dramatic downsizing of the arms industry since the end of the Cold War, existing stockpiles, an over-capacity for production and the fact that more than 300 companies in over 70 States are still involved in the manufacture of small arms and light weapons has encouraged ever more aggressive sales strategies.[19] This number includes countries like Brazil, China, India and Egypt, all of which have recently joined the more established weapons producers in seeking a slice of the $10–20 billion a year small arms sales pie.[20]

Faced with such intensified competition many States have loosened their export control policies in order to aid their own arms manufacturers.[21] One effect of this has been the erosion of the long established convention that arms should only be sold to governments, thereby allowing sub-state groups greater access to weapons supplies.[22] It has also induced States (some with ostensible ethical foreign policies) to curb their criticisms of international human rights abuses and to align themselves with disreputable governments.[23] There can be little surprise, therefore, that an estimated 639 million small arms and light weapons are now believed to be in circulation around the globe.[24]

A related, yet even more pernicious development in the post-Cold War era has been the expansion of the black market in these weapons. Civil wars, unstable States, terrorists and organized crime are all customers in this global second-hand arms bazaar.[25] The international drug trade, with an estimated turnover of over $400 billion a year, provides a lucrative market on its own.[26] Accounting for approximately 55 per cent of the total trade in small arms and light weapons, illegal trade is believed to generate between $1 billion and $10 billion dollars per annum depending on the health of the market.[27] The easy availability of these weapons is reflected in their price. Whilst bartering for an AK-47 in Mozambique at the height of its civil war required little more than a chicken or two boxes of maize, buying one in its capital, Maputo, still cost as little as $15 to $20 whilst the UN peacekeeping operation was deployed there in the mid 1990s.[28]

The manner in which small arms and light weapons are traded within and between states such as Mozambique has even led some analysts to reject 'proliferation' as an adequate adjective to capture the true dynamic of their spread throughout the international community. Instead, terms like 'circulation' and 'diffusion' are believed to more accurately describe the ways in which they are moved across national boundaries and recycled between belligerents, eventually permeating all strata of societies.[29]

2.2   The relationship of small arms and light weapons to intra-state conflict

Given the fact that 90 per cent of all deaths in civil wars throughout the 1990s (approximately 3 to 4 million) were attributable to small arms and light weapons, their relationship to conflict and violence would seem self-evident.[30] However, as Joanna Spear has astutely observed, most analysts of international arms transfers have neglected to discuss the precise nature of the relationship between arms and intra-state conflict, in most cases simply taking for granted 'that arms cause trouble'.[31]

The assumption that arms and their accumulation make conflict more likely is not, of course, a new one. It was essentially the argument made throughout the 20th Century by those who believed that the probability of future international wars was increased by nations continuing to retain and augment their conventional and nuclear arsenals. On the other hand, there were those who believed that arms were only a symptom, not a cause of conflict, and it was therefore the absence of reasons to fight that made war less likely, not the absence of weapons *per se*. Thus, while the former group pressed for complete disarmament, the latter concentrated on enhancing stability between States through arms control. In some cases arms control prescribed disarmament, but in others it required an increase in weapons levels and the introduction of new weapon systems to create parity and invulnerability (for example, to establish mutually assured destruction).[32]

Of those arms transfer analysts who have studied the relationship between light weapons and civil wars, the majority seem to agree with the advocates of arms control that the two are not directly related (Spear, 1996; Latham, 1996; Sislin and Pearson, 2001; Cooper, 2002). Even the United Nations Panel of Governmental Experts on Small Arms concluded in its 1997 report that 'accumulations of small arms and light weapons by themselves do not cause the conflicts in which they are used'.[33] Nevertheless, by making it easier for sub-state groups with grievances or predatory motives to choose violent forms of political action, accumulations of weapons (especially large acquisitions) do appear to act as at least a proximate cause of civil conflict, triggering violence that might not otherwise occur.[34] Changes (even anticipated changes) in arms balances between intra-state groups may also intensify feelings of insecurity that eventually find expression in preemptive attacks or State repression.[35] This is because such groups are essentially suffering from a condition known in modern international relations parlance as the security dilemma. With its antecedents in the writings of Thomas Hobbes, the concept of the security dilemma was first introduced to the study of international relations by John Herz in 1950, when he described a situation in which States in an anarchic international system:

> Striving to attain security from…attack, are driven to acquire more and more power in order to escape the impact of the power of others. This, in turn, renders the others more insecure and compels them to prepare for the worst. Since none can ever feel entirely secure in such a world of competing units, power competition ensues, and the vicious circle of security and power accumulation is on.[36]

Thus, the security dilemma and the spiraling effect it induces can intensify mistrust between States that hold no predatory intentions towards each other. Nevertheless, in the permissive atmosphere generated by the security dilemma even the most pacific of governments will be drawn to consider a preemptive attack as the best means of defense. Distinguishing between predatory and security driven States can therefore be extremely difficult, as both types of behavior manifest themselves in aggressive action.

This logic also applies in intra-state conflict. In the words of Barry Posen, the first scholar to use the concept to explain the outbreak of civil wars, when a government's authority and power begin to crumble the State becomes afflicted by an 'emerging anarchy' similar to that which exists in the international system. As sub-state groups in this scenario become increasingly responsible for their own security they are (just as States are) henceforth compelled to ask of proximate groups: '[are they] a threat? How much of a threat? Will [their] threat grow or diminish over time? Is there anything that must be done immediately?'[37] However, as pointed out by Hobbes himself, given the innate vulnerability of individuals relative to that of states, security dilemmas in the anarchic civil context are always going to be more intense than those in its international counterpart. Even a small influx of arms can therefore induce acute security dilemmas, thereby increasing the probability of violent civil conflict.

It is evident then that weapons do not have a direct causal relationship to violence. Nevertheless, they do appear to be a permissive cause, with their mere presence affecting the probability of conflict by firstly empowering sub-state groups with either predatory motives or significant grievances and secondly, by fuelling their security dilemmas. Though arms access cannot therefore be considered a sufficient condition for intra-state violence, it does appear to come close to being a necessary condition.[38]

Unfortunately, the pernicious effects of small arms and light weapons are not confined to increasing the probability of conflict *per se*. Through more or less complex causal pathways the easy availability of weapons is also believed to play a role in increasing the intensity and duration of civil wars. It is also believed to create 'cultures of violence' in which the possession of weapons connotes political power and non-coercive strategies for conflict resolution are marginalized. In these conditions the security of vulnerable groups (such as women, children and refugees) is diminished; developmental gains are eroded; the burden on public health resources is increased; good governance is undermined; and traditional and modern institutions of 'human security' are destroyed.[39]

2.3   The role(s) of the UN in international small arms control

With their increasing importance as international actors throughout the last century it was perhaps inevitable that the UN and other international organizations (IOs) would eventually become involved in arms control. Or as Stuart Croft more accurately expresses it, given that States have used arms control as a tool in their relations for literally thousands of years, it was perhaps inevitable that they would also seek to utilize it through IOs.[40]

In his comprehensive overview of developments in the area, *Strategies of Arms Control*, Croft also argues that the traditional narrow definition of arms control as a tool to create strategic stability between States needs to be broadened to take account of the actual breadth of arms control activity undertaken by both States and IOs in the modern world. In fact he believes that the new roles of IOs in arms control represent the most significant widening (in terms of the different types of arms control practiced throughout history) and deepening (in terms of the level of detail provided in arms control agreements, the nature of the provisions for verification and the provision for regime formation/continuation) of the concept in recent years.

In Croft's opinion one of the largest contributions to this horizontal and vertical conceptual expansion has been the developing role of IOs in the specific area of small arms control. In essence small arms control is no different to its larger counterpart, as it is designed to achieve the same objectives; to prevent the outbreak of war; to create post-war stability; to create and strengthen norms of behavior (in both the uses and targets of weapons); to legitimize the possession and non-possession of certain forms of weaponry; and to impose the interests of 'the international community' upon others.[41] However, as previously noted, small arms have been traditionally omitted from the arms control agenda of the international community and, therefore, present attempts by the UN to control these weapons represent a widening of the arms control concept not only in terms of the actors involved, but also in terms of the weapons being controlled.

One of the first attempts to conceptualize the UN's approach to small arms control was made by the former UN Secretary-General, Boutros Boutros-Ghali, in his 1995 document 'Supplement to an Agenda for Peace'. Noting that the end of the Cold War had encouraged the major powers to turn their attention, and that of the UN, to the problem of the proliferation of nuclear weapons (a policy he called macrodisarmament), Boutros-Ghali now called on them to apply equal energy to dealing with the destructive effects of the proliferation of small arms and light weapons. Despite the increased commercialization of the global arms market, the numerous and diverse sources of supply and the past reluctance of States to apply effective export controls, he was confident that by revealing where such weapons were produced, by tracking their transfer, by regulating their acquisition, and by finding ways to collect, control and destroy them, the international community could bring an effective 'microdisarmament' regime into being.[42]

Boutros-Ghali's vision was to be given a significant boost in December 1995 when the General Assembly requested him to prepare a report, with the assistance of a group of qualified governmental experts, outlining the 'nature and causes of the excessive and destabilizing accumulation and transfer of small arms and light weapons', as well as ways and means of dealing with them. The subsequent *Report of the Panel of Governmental Experts on Small Arms* of 1997 proffered a total of 24 recommendations based on an obvious preference for regional and sub-regional initiatives. The Panel's predilection in this regard had been influenced primarily by it own regional workshops, in which it had become apparent that there were effects and consequences of small arms proliferation that were unique to regions, sub-regions and individual States.[43]

Two years later and once again at the behest of the General Assembly, Boutros-Ghali's successor, Kofi Annan, produced a similar study, this time dedicated to detailing the progress that had been achieved in implementing the recommendations of the previous Panel's report, as well as making further recommendations. The new document, entitled the *Report of the Group of Governmental Experts on Small Arms,* noted that progress had been made at various levels through the efforts of the UN, regional and sub-regional organizations, other international forums and member states. Though the report found the degree of progress with respect to most of the recommendations encouraging, it did also note that the degree of implementation varied across the board, with some recommendations having been fully implemented and others having had no success at all.

The report also noted the significant developments that had occurred in the UN Secretariat in the interim, including the creation in June 1998 of a Coordinating Action on Small Arms mechanism for the purposes of consultation, information exchange and priority setting among the UN departments and agencies with a comparative advantage in pursuing agreed strategies on small arms. This office is located within the Secretariat's Department of Disarmament Affairs (DDA), the department designated as the focal point for the coordination of all efforts to deal with the problem of small arms within the UN system.[44]

At the regional and sub-regional levels, the report highlighted the continued work of organizations such as the Organization of American States (OAS), the Organization for Security and Cooperation in Europe (OSCE), the European Union (EU), the Common Market of the Southern Cone (MERCOSUR), the Organization of African Unity (OAU), the Economic Community of West African States (ECOWAS), and the Southern African Development Community (SADC), in their attempts to control and reduce the illicit and legal trade in small arms and light weapons. In many cases this work has been conducted in close cooperation with the UN. For example, since 1997 the DDA, the Department of Political Affairs (DPA) and the UN Development Program (UNDP) have worked with ECOWAS and other states providing developmental assistance to adopt and establish a Program for Coordination and Assistance on Security and Development in West Africa and to facilitate the October 1998 ECOWAS agreement for a Moratorium on the Importation Exportation and Manufacture of Small Arms and Light Weapons in West Africa.[45]

The UN's first sub-regional initiative had actually begun as early as 1994 in northwest Africa. During the previous year the President of Mali, Alpha Oumar Konare, had requested the UN's help in combating an uncontrollable escalation in the illicit small arms trade affecting his country. Although the UN initially believed the problem could be dealt with more efficiently and effectively on a sub-regional level, the difficulty of co-ordinating such action at that time convinced it to address the issue in Mali first, in the hope that it could be expanded later. The first UN mission was therefore sent to Mali in August 1994, whilst follow-on missions were sent to Burkina Faso, Chad, Cote D'Ivoire, Mauritania, Niger and Senegal in February and March 1995.[46] Furthermore, once the Malian government had reached a peace accord with its Tuareg rebels, in which the rebels had agreed to disarm, President Konare once again called on the UN to help with the collection and destruction of nearly 3,000 small arms.[47]

In its final report the UN mission to Mali made a number of recommendations, both to the UN and to regional governments. Perhaps the most significant (and certainly the most often quoted) of these recommendations was that Mali required a 'security first' approach. This conclusion had been reached as a result of the mission's identification of the Malian government's inability to provide a sufficient degree of law and order to its own citizens as the primary cause of the country's demand for small arms. As the Malian people could no longer rely on their government to provide them with security, they had simply begun to provide it for themselves. Thus, basic insecurity was fuelling the demand for weapons, whilst the subsequent easy availability of weapons was fuelling a cycle of banditry and violence. This, in turn, was impeding the government's attempts at structural development and halting any progress in socio-economic advancement.[48] The mission concluded, therefore, that the role of the UN should be to assist the Malian government in reconstructing its internal security forces so as to stem the tide of insecurity and provide essential space for socio-economic development. The 1997 *Report of the Panel of Governmental Experts on Small Arms* reiterated the mission's findings, recommending that the UN 'should adopt a proportional and integrated approach to security and development, including the identification of appropriate assistance for the internal security forces initiated with respect to Mali and other West African States and extend it to other regions of the world.'[49]

Perhaps the greatest evidence of the UN's success in coordinating international action on the problem of the diffusion of small arms and light weapons came with the holding of the UN Conference on the Illicit Trade in Small Arms and Light Weapons in All its Aspects between 9 and 21 July 2001. Though the final 'Program of Action' adopted by the conference did not go as far as many activists, academics, States and NGOs would have liked, it did nonetheless represent a milestone on the road to achieving a true global response to the issue.[50] A review conference will be held in 2006. At its own request the Security Council has already been furnished with a report from Annan outlining ways in which it can better contribute to the goals expressed by the 'Program of Action'. These recommendations include tightening the Council's arms embargoes (and considering the use of coercive measures against those who violate them); encouraging states to adopt appropriate national legislation as well as award end user certificates for weapons sold; and calling on all States to increase transparency in their arms dealings through universal and consistent participation in the UN Register of Conventional Arms.[51]

Lastly, as well as working with states on an international and regional level, the UN has also encouraged awareness of the small arms issue through the organization of workshops and the publication of official reports. For example, in collaboration with the UN regional centers for peace and disarmament in Africa and Latin America and the Caribbean, the DDA convened workshops in June and August 1999.[52] The UN also produced a *Report of the Secretary-General on Small Arms* in September 2002.[53]

2.4 Disarmament in UN peacekeeping operations

Mindful that all the measures outlined in the Conference's 'Program of Action' could still not eradicate the small arms and light weapons that already existed in areas of conflict, the Secretary-General also stressed the importance of Security Council support for post-conflict peacebuilding measures, such as disarmament, demobilization and reintegration.[54] Disarmament in the context of UN peacekeeping operations is defined as the collection of small arms and light and heavy weapons within a conflict zone. It frequently entails the assembly and cantonment of ex-combatants and may also include de-mining operations. Demobilization refers to the process by which parties to a conflict begin to disband their military structures and combatants begin their transformation to civilian life. During this process ex-combatants generally register for assistance towards reintegration, a process in which demobilized ex-combatants are adapted both economically and socially to productive civilian life.[55]

Between 1989 and the turn of the millennium the UN undertook 14 peacekeeping operations that included at least one of these three peace-building measures. These include seven covered by this text: the UN Transitional Authority in Cambodia (UNTAC); two UN Angolan Verification Missions (UNAVEM II and III) and a follow-on Angolan Observer Mission (MONUA); the UN Operation in Mozambique (ONUMOZ); the second UN Operation in Somalia (UNOSOM II); and the UN Operation in El Salvador (ONUSAL). Others include the UN Operation in Central America (ONUCA); the UN Observer Mission in Liberia (UNOMIL); the UN Transitional Administration for Eastern Slavonia, Baranja and Western Sirmium (UNTAES); the UN Verification Mission in Guatemala (MINUGUA); the UN Mission of Observers in Tajikistan (UNMOT); the UN observer Mission in Sierra Leone and the UN Assistance Mission for Sierra Leone (UNAMSIL); and the UN Mission in the Central African Republic (MINURCA).[56]

Since 1995 the United Nations Institute for Disarmament Research (UNIDIR) has also conducted a number of excellent studies into the issue of disarmament within the context of peacekeeping missions conducted by the UN and other organizations.[57] These studies have been used extensively in the case study chapters of this text. And in June 1999 the UN Department of Peacekeeping Operations (DPKO) produced its own report on the disarmament, demobilization and reintegration of ex-combatants in a peacekeeping environment.[58] This was followed in February 2000 by the 'Report of the Secretary-General on the Role of United Nations Peacekeeping in Disarmament, Demobilization and Reintegration'.[59]

3   Creating an analytical framework for disarmament in UN peacekeeping operations

Though it may not come as a surprise to find that the majority of scholarly attention during the Cold War was devoted to the settlement of inter-state conflict, the relative neglect of intra-state conflict at this time belied its frequency and destructive capacity. For example, of the 127 post-World War II conflicts listed in the *Correlates of War*, more than 72 per cent of them were some form of civil war, accounting for 63 per cent of the total battle deaths and 82.3 per cent of the nation months of war between 1945 and 1992.[60]

The apparent intractability of civil wars may go some way to explain this academic aversion. Whilst Stephen John Stedman has found that only 15 per cent of civil wars fought between 1900 and 1980 ended in negotiated settlements (compared with 50 per cent of inter-state wars during the same time period), Roy Licklider has found that figure rises to only 25 per cent for those fought between 1945 and 1993. Both studies found the remaining number to have ended with military victory for one or other of the warring parties. Equally as disheartening are the statistics for the relative stability of each civil war settlement type, with Licklider's study showing a 50 per cent chance of a retrogression to war in those cases ended through negotiated settlement, yet only a 15 per cent chance of a similar outcome for those ended by military victory.[61]

Despite this previous bias, a great deal of scholarly literature has been recently produced on the issues surrounding civil wars. The fact that 104 civil wars began between 1989 and 2000, compared to only seven inter-state wars during the same period, is undoubtedly a significant contributory reason. Rather than breaking new theoretical ground, however, the majority of this literature has concerned the application of theoretical approaches initially created to explain, understand and predict international relations. As the following sub-sections will explain, each of the main theoretical traditions in international relations has been applied to the issues of civil wars, including Classical Realism, Neo-Realism, Neo-Liberalism and Constructivism. Nevertheless, it is the argument of this text that only Constructivism comprehensively explains the dynamics of civil war settlement and resolution.

3.1   Classical realism, neo-realism and neo-liberalism

In the words of the most prominent Classical Realist of the 20th Century, Hans J. Morgenthau:

> So long as men seek to dominate each other and to take away each others' possessions, and so long as they fear and hate each other, they will try to satisfy their desires and to put their emotions to rest. Where an authority exists strong enough to direct the manifestations of those desires and emotions into nonviolent channels, men will seek only non-violent instruments for the achievements of those ends.[62]

In this short paragraph Morgenthau encapsulates two of the most basic assumptions of Classical Realism; that humans seek power and control over others (*animus dominandi*) and that nothing short of a powerful central authority will restrain them from using force to attain it. Applying the same theoretical assumptions Richard Betts and Edward Luttwak have both argued against the concept of impartial intervention in civil wars unless the third party is prepared to overawe the warring parties and impose a peace upon them. Short of this, they suggest, third parties should either let the warring parties fight it out or weigh in on the side of the most powerful.[63] As Luttwak states succinctly, '[if] the United Nations helped the strong defeat the weak faster and more decisively, it would actually enhance the peacemaking potential of war'.[64] The assumption of civil warring parties as power maximisers has been bolstered in recent years by the growing number of studies suggesting that competition over natural resources and other commodities controlled by the State has been a significant, if not primary, cause of civil wars and contributed considerably to their intract- ability (King, 1997; Keen, 1998; Berdal and Malone, 2000; Collier, 2001).

Whilst accepting that predation plays an important part in all civil wars to some extent, other scholars have argued that assuming all civil warring parties seek total power is simply too facile an analysis.[65] Instead, these scholars have concentrated on the question of why some parties that have signed peace agreements successfully implement them, yet others do not. This has led them to highlight the role played by the security dilemma during the implementation period after the parties have signed peace agreements (Walter, 1997, 2002; Walter and Snyder, 1999; Hartzell, 1999).

As noted earlier in Section 2.2, the security dilemma can lead to a spiral- ing effect as groups begin to arm themselves in fear that others may attack them in the 'emerging anarchy' of imploding states. Equally, however, the security dilemma can intensify when parties commit themselves to disarm and demobilize their armed forces or consolidate them into a single unified national army. This is because by doing so they forego their primary means of defense if their opponents either cheat during implementation or attempt to usurp power once the agreement has been implemented. In essence this scenario is captured by the prisoner's dilemma, in which co- operation between the parties leads to greater vulnerability for each of them unless they can be assured that their opponents will not abuse their trust. Jack Snyder and Robert Jervis assert the utility of these concepts when they state that:

> Using the framework of the security dilemma and the related prisoner's dilemma allows analysts, participants, and outsiders to tap into know- ledge of how they can increase cooperation in a situation in which both sides prefer to defect [from their agreements] while the other side cooperates, yet both sides also prefer mutual cooperation to mutual defection.[66]

Studies conducted to identify the most efficacious means to increase co- operation between parties caught in such a security dilemma have focused on two key methods. The first, represented by the work of Barbara Walter, advocates the provision of third party guarantees during the tensest stages of the implementation process, principally those involving the disarmament and demobilization of the parties' armed forces. Walter's argument is that the 'critical barrier' to peace that the security dilemma represents can only be overcome with the presence of a third party that is 'committed to peace' because such actors can:

> ...verify compliance with the terms of demobilization and warn of a surprise attack, they can guarantee that soldiers will be protected as they demobilize, and they can become involved if one or both sides resume the war. Third parties can thus ensure that the payoffs from cheating no longer exceed the payoffs from faithfully executing the settlement terms. Once cheating becomes difficult and costly, promises to co-operate should gain credibility and cooperation should become more likely. The success of civil war settlements, therefore, not only hinges on the ability of combatants to reach mutually agreeable political deals but also on outsiders' willingness to verify or enforce the process of demobilization.[67]

On the other hand, Caroline Hartzell (1999; Hartzell and Hoddie, 2003), having discounted the role of third party guarantees as insufficient in the explanation of implementation success rates in her study of civil wars fought between 1945 and 1997, proposes instead that the extent of institutional guarantees provided in the agreement is the key to successful implementation. She believes third-party guarantees to be inadequate for two reasons. Firstly, parties to agreements will always be reluctant to trust third parties, especially when they know they have so little control over their actions. Secondly, and most importantly, third party guarantees fail to address the thorny issue of who will control the coercive powers of the state once it has been restructured.[68] So, whereas Walter treats institutional guarantees as a secondary (though important) consideration, Hartzell believes them to be the primary means available for helping parties overcome their security fears as they head towards the consolidation of power in a single state. Hartzell therefore proposes a second method to deal with the 'cooperation problem': construct institutions that will either balance power among rival groups or prevent only one party from becoming dominant and exercising central authority. This requires institutions that will incorporate power sharing over the use of coercive force, the distribution of political power and the distribution of resources in the new state. Only when all three of these elements are combined in the peace agreement will the parties be convinced that their security concerns have been sufficiently allayed.[69]

So, despite the fact that both Walter and Hartzell's understanding of group behavior is based on rationalist assumptions, they nonetheless differ significantly in their answers to the 'cooperation problem' facing parties caught in the security dilemma. In prescribing the presence of a powerful and committed third-party to help security driven (not power driven) actors overcome their security dilemmas, Walter's Neo-Realist approach is evident. Hartzell, however, has more in common with the Neo-Liberal tradition in that she highlights the power of institutions and regimes to significantly affect the behavior of actors in conditions of anarchy. This is particularly the case in her latest study with Matthew Hoddie in which they analyze the relationship between successfully implemented military power sharing arrangements and the establishment of stable peace in post-war societies.

Having studied 16 cases in which civil wars were ended between 1980 and 1996 with peace agreements incorporating military power-sharing arrangements, Hoddie and Hartzell found that in eight of those cases in which such arrangements were successfully implemented (Bosnia 1992–1995, Chechnya 1994–1996, El Salvador 1979–92, Georgia-SO 1989–92, Mozambique1982–92, Nicaragua 1981–89, Philippines 1972–96, South Africa 1983–91) only one returned to war after five years (Chechnya). Of four that saw their arrangements only partially implemented (Angola 1989–91, Angola 1992–94, Chad 1989–96, Lebanon 1975–89), two returned to war within five years (Angola twice). The latter statistic was borne out again for those arrangements that failed completely (Azerbaijan 1989–94, Cambodia 1970–91, Rwanda 1990–93, Sierra Leone 1992–96; Both Rwanda and Sierra Leone returned to war).[70]

However, beyond the rather predictable conclusion that states ending civil wars are more likely to experience stable peace if the former warring parties actually fulfill their agreements (87.5 per cent compared to 50 per cent likely), the reasons cited by Hoddie and Hartzell for the importance of military arrangements helps illuminate their theoretical approach. For these scholars it is the process of committing themselves to military power sharing arrangements and then, most importantly, following through with their commitments that affects the perceptions of former combatants. Thus, the power of institutions and regimes to affect non-State actors' behavior is evident in their hypothesis that:

> By implementing the provisions of a peace agreement, signatories engage in costly signaling regarding their commitment to the peace, signals that serve to reassure opponents about the prospects for long-term co-existence…These costs are associated with a loss of power *vis-a-vis* a former enemy as well as a potential loss of credibility or stature within one's own group. It is the very fact that individuals are willing to absorb these unavoidable costs – to engage in costly signaling – that suggests a genuine commitment to peace and reassures all parties to the settlement that they will not be the future targets of their domestic competitors.[71]

For Hoddie and Hartzell, therefore, it is the reiterated non-bellicose interactions between the parties that take place within implementation timetables that convinces each of them to trust the other. The UN's role in this context is simply to act as an intermediary, communicating its findings as it monitors and verifies progress towards implementation. In fact, for the UN to act in any more of a coercive role would actually work to undermine the confidence built through voluntary interaction, as each party could not be sure that their adversary's previous compliance was not due more to the threat of sanctions than it was to their commitment to cooperation. Put simply, if the UN threatens parties with sanctions for non-compliance, then the value of the signal that comes with implementation will be lost and the establishment of trust between the parties will be less likely. This will increase the probability of a return to war once the UN leaves.[72]

3.2   Constructivism

As in international relations theory in general, the greatest challenge to the hegemony of the Neo-Realist/Neo-Liberal debate in the conflict settlement and resolution literature (as represented by the Walter/Hartzell debate above) has come from the Constructivist tradition. As in their international applications both Neo-Realism and Neo-Liberalism have continued to apply their basic assumptions to actors in the realm of domestic anarchy by treating civil warring parties as rational egoists (rationalism) in a domestic structure defined by the distribution of capabilities (materialism). Both these assumptions have been challenged by Constructivism, which in concerning itself with how politics is 'socially constructed' has made two basic claims: firstly, that the fundamental structures of societies are social rather than strictly material (a claim that opposes materialism); and secondly, that these 'social structures' constitute actors' identities and interests, rather than just their behavior (a claim that opposes rationalism).[73]

According to Alexander Wendt, 'social structures' have three elements: shared knowledge, material resources and practices.[74] Shared knowledge, or 'culture', is knowledge that is both common and connected between individuals within a society and can take many forms, including norms, rules, institutions, ideologies, organizations and patterns of enmity and amity.[75] Whereas rationalists take the interests of the actor as exogenously given and focus on causal effects on behavior, Constructivists seek to show that the actors themselves are socially constructed in that their interests and identities (sets of meanings that an actor attributes to itself while taking the perspective of others) are constituted by the culture in which they are embedded.[76] Wendt explains the limitations of the rationalist position in failing to understand the causal and constitutive effects of culture when he states:

> Rationalists tend not to be very interested in explaining interests, preferring to see how far they can get by focusing on behavior while holding interests constant. Still less are they interested in issues of identity. But

on both counts a dogmatic position rejecting the study of identity- and interest-formation altogether makes little sense. It may be that we can gain much insight into social life by taking interests as given, but this does not deny the fact that interests are socially constructed. To assume a priori that interests are never socially constructed is to assume that people are *born* with or make up entirely on their own all their interests, whether in gaining tenure, making war, or marrying their high school sweetheart. Clearly this is not the case. A rationalist neglect of identity seems equally misplaced.[77]

The process of identity and interest formation is known as 'socialization' and its effects can be measured by the degree to which an actor 'internalizes' the norms of the prevailing culture. The first degree represents the most superficial level of internalization, as the actor observes norms only because they are forced to do so. The second degree represents a deeper level of socialization; one in which the actor observes norms, not because of coercion, but because they perceive it to be in their self-interest to do so. The third and deepest degree of internalization connotes that an actor will observe norms because they have accepted them as legitimate. It is only when an actor reaches this third degree of internalization that one can speak of them as having been 'constructed' by culture.[78] It is important to note, however, that groups might initially conform to norms for self-interested (egoistic) reasons, but if sustained over time such action will erode their identities eventually creating collective ones.[79]

Wendt notes that these three explanations correspond roughly to the significance given to norms in the explanation of actor behavior by each of the Neo-Realist, Neo-Liberal and Constructivist traditions.[80] Whereas Neo-Realists provide little if any role for norms in their explanation, Neo-Liberals incorporate important roles for norms and institutions at both the domestic (when regime type is believed to have important effects on the formation and conduct of foreign policy) and systemic levels of explanation (when regimes can change the incentives for action, as in Hartzell's arguments that regimes can reduce uncertainty about others' intentions and behavior). Nevertheless, of the three traditions, only Constructivism accounts for the constitutive effects of culture.[81]

However, the existence of culture or 'intersubjective understanding' between sub-state groups does not imply that there exists any particular type of relationship. Nor does the degree of internalization. Rather, depending on the intersubjective understanding that exists between such groups at any one time, the culture could be one of aggression, competition or cooperation.[82] These ideal types correspond to Wendt's 'three cultures of anarchy', which he labels Hobbesian, Lockean and Kantian. A Hobbesian anarchy is one in which security competition is perceived as zero-sum, making concerns over relative gains paramount. Security dilemmas in such a fear-driven environment are particularly acute, as even benign groups will be compelled to act aggressively due to the malign intentions they have attributed to others.[83]

On the other hand, a Lockean anarchy is formed when groups acquire competitive social identities instead of aggressive ones. In this culture groups do not seek to eliminate other groups, but the possibility that force may be still used to settle disputes remains. As groups perceive each other as rivals, relative gains are still important. Nevertheless, because groups no longer fear for their survival, the security dilemmas generated in this culture are much less intense than in its Hobbesian counterpart.[84] Finally, a Kantian anarchy is one in which the groups have acquired cooperative 'friendly' social identities. As the use of force is no longer expected under any circumstances, groups in this culture can concentrate on positive-sum cooperation and absolute gains. As these three alternative cultures suggest, there is simply no 'logic of anarchy'. Rather 'anarchy is what [groups] make of it'.[85]

The second element of social structures is material resources, or the material capabilities of groups. By assuming that all groups holding material resources will view each other as potential threats to their survival, regardless of the relationship that exists between them, Neo-Realists have adopted a 'de-socialized' view of material capabilities. In contrast, Constructivists believe that such capabilities only acquire meaning for human action through the intersubjective understanding in which they are embedded. Thus, groups caught in a culture of aggression will, as Neo-Realists suggest, be compelled to view the material capabilities of other groups as threatening to their survival. However, groups with an intersubjective understanding of competition or cooperation will not. In simple terms a 'gun in the hands of a friend is a different thing from one in the hands of an enemy, and enmity is a social, not material, relation'.[86]

Lastly, social structures are composed of practices. These are the repeated interactions that take place between groups that contribute to the formation of social identities. As Went explains:

> [The] basic idea is that identities and their corresponding interests are learned and then reinforced in response to how actors are treated by significant Others. This is known as the principle of 'reflected appraisals' or 'mirroring', because it hypothesizes that actors come to see themselves as a reflection of how they think Others see or 'appraise' them, in the 'mirror' of Others' representations of the Self. If the Other treats the Self as though [they] were an enemy, then by the principle of reflected appraisals [they are] likely to internalize that belief in [their] role identity vis-à-vis the Other. Not all Others are equally significant, however, and so power and dependency relations play an important role in the story.[87]

Thus, whereas Hartzell's Neo-Liberal analysis holds the actor's identities and interests as constant throughout their interactions, Constructivism allows for the possibility of change. For Neo-Liberals this means that actors' learning is limited to realizing their interests more effectively as interaction progresses ('simple learning'), whereas Constructivists allow for the possibility that interaction might also have construction effects on their identities and interests ('complex learning').[88] This, in effect, means that Neo-Liberals do not accept the possibility of progression beyond the second degree of internalization. On the other hand, Constructivists exist because of their belief that actors can and do make the transition to the third degree.

The relationship between actors' identities and culture is therefore 'mutually constitutive'. In other words, whilst the identities of actors are formed by the culture in which they are embedded, the culture itself is formed by the interactions that take place between them. It is on the basis of this argument that Peter Katzenstein criticizes both Neo-Realism and Neo-Liberalism for overlooking 'the degree to which social environments and actors penetrate one another'.[89] Obviously, the major implication of this relationship is that once actors have been socialized in a particular culture, their subsequent behavior towards one another will further legitimize their expectations and thus reinforce the existing culture. Culture, in essence, becomes a self-fulfilling prophecy.[90] However, Constructivist recognition of the relative stability of culture does not preclude acceptance of the possibility of change, no matter how difficult that might be in some circumstances. As Wendt explains:

> It is actors' beliefs that make up shared knowledge over time. Culture is constantly in motion, even as it reproduces itself. It is what people make of it, even as it constrains what they do at any given moment. It is an on-going *accomplishment*. Despite having a conservative bias, therefore, culture is always characterized by more or less contestation among its carriers, which is a constant resource for structural change.[91]

There are a number of overlapping sources of change listed by Wendt, including the internal contradictions between different logics that exist within a culture ('cultures consist of many different norms, rules and institutions and the practices they induce will often be contradictory') and the fact that agents are never perfectly socialized (leaving all actors with private beliefs that motivate them to pursue personal projects that can change their environments).[92] A further source is the invention of new ideas from within a culture, or 'creativity'. Finally, there are exogenous shocks, such as revolutions, cultural imperialism, invasions and, perhaps, second and third-generation UN peacekeeping operations.[93] Nevertheless, acceptance of the inertia of cultural change is imperative to a full appreciation of why some groups that preexist the creation of a new state may defy attempts to change their identities and why conflicts between communal groups may seem so intractable.[94]

Finally, as this theoretical discussion has emphasized, the issue of rationality is an integral one to the on-going debate between rationalist and Constructivist traditions. Though both approaches accept that actors are rational beings, rationality to the former assumes egoism, whilst to the latter its character is defined by the shared knowledge in which it operates. This can be expressed as the difference between beliefs in 'universal' and 'contextual' rationality, the latter being situations in which:

> The overriding motivation has an intrinsically intersubjective or social character in that it expresses a recognizable orientation to the values of some community as they are manifested in some basic moral, religious or social norms. It is in this sort of orientation that we are often willing to consider even an action endangering self-preservation as possibly rational.[95]

3.3 Developing approaches in conflict mediation

Despite the usual bias towards the study of international conflict during the Cold War a significant body of literature on third party mediation of civil wars has been generated over the past 40 years.[96] Within this literature two main schools of thought have emerged, which in their purest form lie at either end of a scale of third party participation that stretches from light to heavy action.[97]

At the heavy end of the scale lies the Power-political (or bargaining) school, which along with its Realist theoretical foundations, locates itself within a positivist social scientific framework and advocates the mediation of international and civil conflicts through the exercise of power and influence.[98] It is based on the assumption of strategic rationality in which action is conceptualized as the 'intentional, self-interested behavior of individuals in an objectivated world, that is, one in which objects and other individuals are related to in terms of their possible manipulation'.[99] Thus conceived as a bargaining game in which all the participants are utility maximisers, the role of the third party 'mediator' in negotiations is to reduce the intensity of the violence or settle the conflict through the identification of a range of acceptable compromises between the conflicting parties. As Mark Hoffman explains:

> The aim [of the mediator] is to identify the range of an acceptable pay-off matrix or a zone of potential agreement for the conflicting parties. Using whatever leverage it has, the [mediator] can then attempt to move the parties towards an outcome within that range. The mediator may offer incentives to increase receptiveness to particular outcomes, or

'frame' the conflict in ways that increase the possibility of agreement, or coerce the parties into concessions, hopefully without loss of face...This approach sees the mediation process as an exercise in power and influence. It is directive and carried out within a defined structure of power relations in which the third party often becomes an 'outcome advocate' for a particular package.[100]

Two of the most prominent advocates of this approach have been Saadia Touval and I.W. Zartman, (1985, 1998; Zartman, 1989, 1993, 2000), whose understanding of mediation within the context of power-politics has led them to emphasize not only the leverage possessed by third parties, but also the timing of its application. The key to their approach is the concept of 'ripeness', which they define as those times when a conflict is most susceptible to settlement. The ripest moment of any conflict will occur when the warring parties are suffering in a mutually hurting stalemate (preferably combined with the perception that the continuation of war will only increase their pain significantly) and each of them is sufficiently convinced that their opponents are equally committed to the search for a peaceful solution.[101] Once this ripe moment is achieved (either by serendipity or the deliberate actions of the mediator) the challenge for the mediator lies in presenting 'an alternative to the conflicting parties that attains some of the goals of their first tracks [unilateral preferences] while eliminating or reconciling the more conflictual elements'.[102] The success of the mediator will therefore depend not on their impartiality, but on whether the mediator possess resources that either disputant values.[103]

Though Touval and Zartman's bargaining approach to mediation is concerned principally with bringing the warring parties to a peaceful settlement, it is also applicable to the post-settlement phase when international bodies like the UN attempt to help parties implement their agreement. However, though the interests of the parties and UN may not be affected by the transition from the pre-settlement to the implementation phase, their relative leverage is. This dynamic is captured well by Michael Doyle's (1996) description of peace agreements as 'obsolescing bargains', in which the sunk costs of each party and the UN increase as the implementation phase progresses. This is particularly the case in the initial phases of a UN operation when large quantities of peacekeeping personnel and equipment are deployed and the UN thereby invests a significant degree of its reputation in a successful outcome. As the parties to the agreement are cognizant of this, the UN's leverage over them is inevitably weakened.

This brings us to the second major approach to third party intervention and the one most compatible with the Constructivist viewpoint on the importance of shared knowledge: the facilitation (or interactive problem-solving) school. This approach lies at the opposite end of the scale of third-party participation to that of Power-political mediation, and has grown over the past 40 years in reaction to the perceived failure of the latter to either break stalemates or bring long lasting stable peace to conflicts. It is a social-psychological approach that aims to deal with the most intractable societal and inter-societal conflicts (commonly referred to as 'deep-rooted' or 'protracted social conflicts'), the source of which is believed to be the frustration of a number of basic human needs, such as identity, security and recognition, that individuals often express collectively through identity (ethnic) groups.[104]

As with Constructivist theory, Facilitation 'takes as its starting point a recognition that our identities are socially and historically constructed and that such identity-frames are central to the causes and dynamics of conflicts'.[105] It thus focuses on the structural, social, attitudinal and inter-personal dimensions of conflict relationships, hoping to perform a 'transformative function'.[106] This function can be performed through interactive conflict resolution processes (referred to as Track 2 diplomacy), such as problem-solving workshops involving unofficial representatives of the conflicting groups in order that they might analyze the conflict and suggest their own solutions. These workshops are designed not only to transform the identities and interests of the participants, but also to promote change at the policy level.[107] Transformation can also be performed through the generation of critical social movements (or peace constituencies) that can promote both the deconstruction of existing social structures and the reconstruction of more cooperative ones.[108] As Vivienne Jabri explains:

> The role of constituencies of peace is directly linked to the transformation of and challenge to dominant discourses and normative expectations which surround a particular conflict. Such social movements direct their actions at the wider society by widening the role of the public sphere and the possibility of contestation of leadership positions, exclusionist discourses and identities, and support for violent conflict.[109]

There is then a significant difference between the Power-political and Facilitative approaches to third party interventions in civil conflicts. Whereas the Power-political school, with its emphasis on the creation of stability and order, seeks only to settle conflicts, the Facilitative school seeks to reveal the underlying sources of conflict and resolve them through the transformation of existing social structures. This enables a distinction to be made between the facilitator's goal of conflict *resolution* and the power-political mediator's goal of conflict *settlement*. This dichotomy has also been expressed as *positive* and *negative peacemaking*.[110]

However, though it may make sense to treat the Power-political and Facilitation approaches as distinct at a theoretical level, at the level of praxis they are more complimentary than antithetical. This argument is supported by a number of conflict resolution scholars who believe that mediator activity should best be conceptualized as moving along a continuum from one end of the scale of third party participation to the other, depending on the idiosyncratic character of the conflict and the timing of the intervention (Fisher and Keashley, 1991; Hoffman, 1992; Jabri, 1995, Stedman, 1996; Pruitt, 2000; Kelman, 2001). Even John Burton, the pioneer of interactive problem-solving approaches, acknowledges that institutions to maintain law and order will still be necessary, even though these are tools of the power-political approach, 'for there is always a need to protect the public interest and safety in the here-and-now'. Nevertheless, he also believes these tools of conflict suppression should be accompanied by a problem-solving approach, 'so as to resolve the antagonisms present in the system'. The holistic approach, therefore, is a twin-track approach. 'Track 1 is the formal one, the official one, the law and order one...Track 2 is the analytical track that explores options and feeds into the first Track'.[111]

3.4   Establishing the analytical framework

As already explained, it is a Constructivist proposition that weapons are given meaning through the social structures in which they exist. It is the argument of this text therefore that the success of UN disarmament processes will depend on the Organization's ability to transform existing social structures in war-torn societies through the application of the 'twin-track approach' outlined above. This will involve three levels of each society; the warring parties, ex-combatants and the general population. Only if this twin-track approach is applied to all three levels simultaneously will the UN be able to engender the security necessary for general disarmament to occur.

The type of Track 1 diplomacy required at the level of the warring parties will depend on the type of intersubjective understanding existing between them at the time of the intervention. If the warring parties are caught in an intersubjective understanding of *aggression* then external and internal security guarantees will have to be provided to overcome their relatively severe security dilemmas. In the cases analyzed by this text these guarantees will come in the form of a significant UN military presence and in institutional power-sharing arrangements. These institutional arrangements will provide the parties with the post-implementation security guarantees necessary for them to see the process through.

On the other hand, for parties caught in an intersubjective understanding of *competition* the need for external and internal guarantees will be lower as their security dilemmas are less acute. This will probably mean that the principal guarantees required by the parties will be negotiated institutional arrangements that allow for the satisfaction of an adequate degree of their political and economic aspirations. As security concerns still exist (especially at the beginning of the implementation phase), however, combinations of UN deployments and power-sharing arrangements may still be necessary.

These two cultures thus represent the first and second degrees of new norm socialization. In the first, the warring parties may only follow the new norms being introduced due to the threat of a significant third party. In the second culture they may follow them only because they perceive such behavior to be in their self-interest. Nevertheless, as already explained, parties entering into sustained prosocial behavior for self-interested reasons may still have their identities eroded and new ones constructed. The more socialized the parties become, therefore, the closer they will move from cultures of aggression and competition towards an intersubjective understanding of *cooperation* in which security guarantees are no longer required and the maintenance of armed forces will be perceived as unnecessary.

At the level of ex-combatants and the general population Track 1 diplomacy will involve the provision of public security. This will negate the need to possess a weapon for personal security and help ensure the protection of human rights. It will also dissuade those who have benefited economically from the violence and those who may prefer to enter a life of crime rather than contribute constructively to the reconstruction of their society. In many cases Western conceptions of human rights will be new norms that may initially only be followed due to the enforcement powers of an externally created criminal justice system. However, through socialization these norms will eventually be absorbed and acted on independently by the target society.

Given the nature of Track 2 diplomacy it can only take place at the lower levels of post conflict society: those of ex-combatants and the general population. Thus, for the former it will involve the provision of alternative economic opportunities, either in the form of training, education, civilian employment or participation in the armed forces of the newly unified state. For the latter it will involve nation-wide socio-economic development, including the generation of a vibrant civil society strong enough to challenge the hegemonic discourses of the ruling elites and thus contribute to societal reconciliation.

The interdependence of these three societal levels is therefore obvious. The general population will not relinquish its weapons whilst ex-combatants being reintegrated into society withhold theirs. Equally, demobilizing soldiers cannot be expected to relinquish their weapons when the society into which they are reintegrating is awash with similar weapons. And neither soldiers nor the general population will relinquish their weapons until the civil war has been resolved. Also, as the preceding discussions have made clear, the ability of the UN to apply this twin-track strategy will depend substantially on an appreciation of the 'contextual rationality' at work in distinct cultures.

Type of Mediation Societal Level	**Track 1**	**Track 2**
Former Warring Parties	External and internal security guarantees (dependent on type of intersubjective understanding between parties)	Not applicable
Ex-combatants	Public Security	Provision for demobilization and reintegration
General Population	Public Security	National socio-economic development

Figure 1
Source: compiled by author

2
Angola and Cambodia 1991–1993

1 Introduction

This chapter will analyze the UN's disarmament processes conducted in Angola and Cambodia between 1991 and 1993. Despite the concurrence of these operations the UN's commitments to each could hardly have been more contrasting. On the one hand, the United Nations Transitional Authority in Cambodia (UNTAC) involved the deployment of over 22,000 military and civilian personnel, consequently making it the largest UN peacekeeping operation to date. On the other, the second United Nations Angolan Verification Mission (UNAVEM II) was to consist of only 350 military observers, 90 police monitors and 400 civilian election observers. Commensurately, whilst UNTAC's operational budget exceeded $2 billion, UNAVEM II was forced to cope with only $132 million.

Despite this enormous discrepancy in size and funding both disarmament processes were to end in complete failure. To explain why, this chapter will utilize the twin-track framework outlined in Chapter 1. As with all the case studies in this text, this chapter will begin with an overview of the developments leading up to the signing of each country's peace agreements. Descriptions of the nature of the UN's mandates and their implementation will then be followed by a comparative analysis of their disarmament processes. Finally, the conclusion will assess the utility of the twin-track framework to account for the failure of both disarmament processes.

2 Background to the conflicts

2.1 Angola

The resistance groups that had fought to end Portuguese colonial rule had already turned on each other before Angola's independence was declared in 1975. For the following 16 years the nominal government of Angola, led by the *Movimento Popular de Liergao de Angola* (MPLA) and backed by the Soviet Union and Cuba, fought a bloody civil war with the US and South African supported resistance movement, *Uniao Nacional para a Independencia Total de Angola* (UNITA).

Only in the late 1980s were local and international events to produce an environment conducive to a settlement of the conflict. Locally, the protagonists had reached a stalemate on the battlefield. Although the approximately 130,000 members of the MPLA's armed forces were capable of defeating large UNITA troop concentrations, they still lacked the counter-insurgency experience necessary to clear rural areas of its guerillas. Conversely, though UNITA's 70,000 troops experienced significant success with small-scale guerilla tactics, they could not defeat their more numerous foes in conventional warfare.[1] UNITA's problems were further compounded by the heavy losses incurred by its forces at the infamous battle of Cuito Cuanavale in 1987.

Internationally, the thawing of the Cold War helped to engender greater superpower cooperation in the search for a settlement. The first major breakthrough came as a result of a regional peace agreement designed to bring independence to the South African protectorate of South West Africa (Namibia). Although a plan to bring democratic elections and independence to Namibia had been approved by the UN as far back as 1978, South African intransigence had prevented its implementation. Despite UN assertions that there existed no relationship between them, the US continued to link the prospect of Namibian independence with the removal of the approximately 50,000 Cuban troops stationed on Angolan territory.[2]

Although the South Africans had not initially made this linkage themselves, they soon realized they could stall negotiations by making it a prerequisite of their own acquiescence.[3] Therefore, only when a reduction in superpower tensions made the withdrawal of the Cuban troops politically feasible could negotiations proceed. This led to the signing of the Nambian Accords by Angola, South Africa and Cuba on 22 December 1988. Subsequently, as part of the regional peace agreement, the United Nations Verification Mission (UNAVEM) was established to verify the withdrawal of all Cuban troops from Angolan territory. This withdrawal was complete by June 1991.

With Namibia now independent and the Cuban presence in Angola removed, the superpowers turned their attention to energizing the Angolan peace process.[4] Having supplied the MPLA with massive military support throughout the 1980s, even increasing its arms supplies up until mid-1990 in the hope of ensuring an outright military victory, the USSR began to seek a negotiated settlement, seemingly at any cost.[5] America, for its part, was still willing to support UNITA to prevent its total defeat, but was no longer prepared to continue support for an all out military victory. Finding the costs of full-scale support for UNITA too costly in economic and domestic political terms, South Africa had also drastically cut is support for the rebels.[6]

Nevertheless, the initial diplomatic thrust towards a peace settlement was not to be provided by the superpowers, but by the President of Zaire, Mobuto Sese Seko. In June 1989 Mobuto managed to bring the Angolan President, Jose Eduardo dos Santos, and UNITA's leader, Jonas Savimbi, together for a summit with 21 other African Heads of State in his home down of Gbadolite.[7] The main goal of this summit was to discuss the peace plan that had been proffered by the Angolan government five months earlier in which it had offered UNITA members both a general amnesty and their integration into existing government structures. It also required Savimbi to go into temporary exile.

However, although Mobuto later announced that both sides had accepted the plan, a cease-fire established on 24 June was broken within five days when UNITA attempted to sabotage Luanda's electrical system. Savimbi then refused to exile himself and rejected both the existing constitution and the offer to integrate UNITA forces into government structures.[8] It soon became apparent that the confusion generated in the aftermath of the Gbadolite summit had been caused primarily by Mobuto's attempts to persuade both parties to accept the plan by presenting different versions of it to each of them. Although this tactic had been successful in gaining their initial acquiescence, it also had disastrous effects on the cease-fire and on Mobuto's own credibility as a mediator.

The second peacemaking initiative was to be driven by Portugal, the ex-colonial power in Angola. Although both parties had reason to be suspicious of its motives, a series of talks were held in Portugal between April and November 1990.[9] Initial talks in April and June, however, did little more than highlight the differences between the two sides on a number of issues, including the conditions for a cease-fire, the nature of the political system and the modalities for monitoring a settlement. Although, by the third round of talks in August, UNITA had dropped its demand for a transitional government, it nevertheless refused to accept a cease-fire until the MPLA (henceforth referred to as the Government) had recognized it as a political party. The Government, on the other hand, expressed support for a multi-party system, but wanted UNITA to renounce violence and adhere to a cease-fire first.[10]

Both parties remained intransigent over the sequence of political recognition and a cease-fire when they met for a fourth round of talks in late September. Despite this, they did manage to agree on the creation of a joint monitoring commission to oversee the implementation of an eventual settlement, which was to be composed of Government and UNITA representatives, with Portugal, the USSR and the US present as observers. By the time a fifth round of talks were held in November a cease-fire was reportedly close to being agreed, but differences still remained over the date for elections and over the nature of the prospective unified armed forces. Whilst the Government wanted UNITA guerillas to integrate into the existing

Angolan army, UNITA wanted to form a completely new national force. And whilst the Government wanted elections at least 36 months after an agreement, UNITA wanted them to be held within 12 months.[11]

With the superpowers continuing to apply diplomatic pressure, including personal meetings between Savimbi and US President Bush, an agreement on general principles for a settlement was reached by mid-December. These principles decreed that UNITA had the right to take part in a multi-party political system following a cease-fire; that the Government would seek proposals from all political parties with a view to major reform of the Angolan Constitution; that the international community would refrain from supplying war material to either side and support a cease-fire; that the cease-fire would be monitored by neutral foreign observers, with the UN invited to participate; that a national army would be formed by the time of elections; and lastly, that elections would be monitored by international observers.[12]

Although a sixth round of negotiations had been planned for mid-January, in which the parties had intended to build on these agreed principles, they were eventually cancelled due to UNITA's refusal to sign a cease-fire before political conditions had been agreed. Despite attempts to restart negotiations, the political impasse was not broken until US Assistant Secretary of State for African Affairs, Herman Cohen, suggested that elections be held within 15 to 18 months after an agreement. Once the Government accepted this, an agreement was reached by 1 May. A *de facto* cease-fire was subsequently established on 15 May, which became official on the signing by both parties of the *Accords de Paz para Angola* (Bicesse Accords) in Estoril on 31 May 1991.[13] Subsequently, pursuant to Security Council Resolution 696, UNAVEM was given a 17-month extension to its mandate and renamed UNAVEM II.

2.2 Cambodia

If the end of the Cold War and the proposed creation of a 'New World Order' heralded hope for any nation, Cambodia was it. Despite a population of only nine million, its perceived strategic importance was such that within 40 years, the French, the US, the Chinese and the Soviet Union had all attempted to control it through their respective puppet regimes. When the country finally gained its independence in 1953 Samdech Norodom Sihanouk was Head of State, a man the French had elevated to the Cambodian throne 12 years before. Prince Sihanouk's rule lasted until March 1970, when his monarchy was deposed by a military *coup d'etat*, led by the US backed General Lon Nol. However, the darkest period in Cambodian history was to begin in April 1975 with the defeat of the Lon Nol regime by the infamous Khmer Rouge (officially known as the *Party of Democratic Kampuchea* (PDK)). Supported by the Chinese, the Khmer Rouge renamed the country 'Democratic Kampuchea' and continued to implement a policy of mass communist collectivization and urban expulsions that left an estimated two million fatalities during their four-year tenure.

Ostensibly in self-defense (the Khmer Rouge had made incursions into disputed territory in south Vietnam), but also to protect ethnic Vietnamese from Khmer Rouge persecution, the Vietnamese invaded Cambodia in December 1978. Within a month they had installed a puppet regime led by ex-Khmer Rouge cadre, who had defected to Vietnam during purges within the Cambodian government. The new regime became known as the *People's Republic of Kampuchea* (PRK).[14] As was typical of the period, the Vietnamese invasion left the international community divided and diplomatically strained. The Chinese were so incensed they conducted a number of punitive offensives into northwestern Vietnam during February and March 1979. The USSR, on the other hand, vetoed a resolution in the UN Security Council that had sought to condemn the Vietnamese action the same year.[15]

Nevertheless, in order to create a more effective internal opposition to the PRK, China colluded with the states of the Association of Southeast Asian Nations (ASEAN) to arrange a marriage of convenience between the PDK and the two other existing parties in Cambodia, the *Front Uni National Pour UN Cambodge Independent, Neutre, Pacifique et Cooperatif* (FUNCINPEC), led by Prince Sihanouk and his son Norodom Ranariddh and the *Khmer People's National Liberation Front* (KPNLF), a pro-western group led by former prime minister, Sonn Sann. These three parties formed the *Coalition Government of Democratic Kampuchea* (CGDK) in 1982. Despite the active involvement of the Khmer Rouge, the CGDK was subsequently elected to the Cambodian seat at the UN.

For the rest of the decade the Cambodian conflict was to exist in a virtual stalemate. Whilst the USSR and Vietnam supplied the PRK with military assistance, the US, China and ASEAN did the same for their clients in the CGDK.[16] Although the forces of the PDK numbered almost three times that of the CGDK, the latter's ability to operate on both sides of the Thai-Cambodian border, together with their use of small-scale guerilla tactics, ensured neither side could achieve an outright victory. Of the three forces making up the CGDK, the Khmer Rouge was by far the largest, with around 45,000 members by 1989. However, only 25,000 of these were believed to be active soldiers, the rest being made up of porters.[17] Estimates of forces belonging to the KPNLF ranged between 3,000 and 10,000, whilst those for FUNCINPEC had increased to 22,000 by the end of the decade. However, neither of these forces possessed the system of porters that allowed the Khmer Rouge to conduct small-scale operations inside Cambodia. Factional quarreling, along with low morale, had also substantially reduced the combat readiness of many of their troops.[18] Despite their relative numbers, therefore, neither of them possessed the military strength or martial zeal to be a crucial factor in the war.[19]

The PRK had modeled its military forces on the three-tiered defense structure established by the Vietnamese government. At the top of the structure lay the regular army, known from 1989 as the *Cambodian People's Armed Forces* (CPAF). Despite receiving supplies from the USSR and Vietnam, the CPAF continued to suffer from a number of deficiencies, including a shortage of good commanders and a lack of discipline. It nonetheless numbered at least 50,000 by 1989. However, the CPAF was not intended to be the PRK's main line of defense. Rather, it was designed to act as a mobile reaction force in support of regional forces and local militia, which constituted the second layer in the defense structure. The bottom layer consisted of the local village militias, which were estimated to number between 100,000 and 300,000 (as Turley notes, however, these forces were poorly equipped, briefly trained and unevenly distributed). Therefore, even the lower estimates suggested that the PRK was still fielding at least 150,000 soldiers to the CGDK's 50,000.[20]

In such circumstances a prerequisite for the resolution of the Cambodian conflict was a thawing of relations between the international and regional players. The first real movement in this regard took place in 1986, when President Gorbachev outlined the USSR's new perspective on the Asia-Pacific region and called for the resolution of regional conflicts. Before the year's end, the USSR had also signaled its willingness to discuss the Cambodian situation with China, thereby removing the primary obstacle to the normalization of relations between the two countries. In anticipation of greater Sino-Soviet rapprochement, Vietnam began to reassess its own commitments in Cambodia. The elevation to political power of a number of political and economic reformers at the Sixth Congress of the Vietnamese Communist Party in 1986 also opened the possibility of improved relations between Vietnam and China.[21]

The first significant regional breakthrough was to follow an agreement in July 1987 between Vietnam and Indonesia (both of whom represented their respective political blocs) to hold informal talks in two phases. The first phase was to consist of an exchange of views between the Cambodian parties, whilst the second was to involve Vietnam, Laos and the ASEAN states. With this agreement the scene was set for private meetings to take place between Prince Sihanouk and the Prime Minister of Cambodia since 1985, Hun Sen. These meetings, held between December 1987 and January 1988, were the 'cocktail parties' that Prince Sihanouk had long called for and for which he had resigned temporarily from his position as President of the CGDK to facilitate. The mere possibility that Sihanouk might abandon the CGDK in return for a position in Phnom Penh helped make ASEAN, China and the US more flexible in their approaches to negotiations.[22]

As a result of these private talks Indonesia paid host to the first Jakarta Informal Meeting (JIM I) in July 1988. With all the Cambodian parties present, together with Vietnam, Laos and ASEAN, this meeting produced the first consensus document of the conflict. Included in the document was an explicit link between the withdrawal of Vietnamese forces from Cambodia and the cessation of external assistance to the internal parties. Subsequently, a JIM II was held in February 1989 that reiterated the consensus achieved at JIM I, but which also highlighted the remaining differences between the parties on the nature of potential power-sharing arrangements. As ASEAN insisted on the achievement of a comprehensive agreement before even JIM I could be implemented (including an internal settlement) the lack of consensus on power-sharing meant the deadlock seemed as great as ever.[23]

Meanwhile, following the talks between Sihanouk and Hun Sen, the UN Secretary-General, Javier Perez de Cuellar, had invited his Special Representative (SRSG), Rafeeudin Ahmed, to travel to South-East Asia to relay to the Cambodian parties and to regional governments, 'certain concrete ideas which might serve as a framework for a comprehensive settlement plan'. These ideas it was hoped would lead to the establishment of an 'independent, neutral and non-aligned Cambodian state' (the PRK changed its name to the State of Cambodia (SoC) in June 1989 and adopted a statement of permanent neutrality the following month).[24]

With Vietnam and the SoC continually spurning offers by the UN to hold a peace conference, due to their suspicions of its bias towards the CGDK, the responsibility of playing host subsequently fell to France. As Indonesia had played such a pivotal role during JIM I and JIM II, France also asked it to co-chair the inclusive conference it had invited all the parties to attend in Paris in July 1989. Although attended by 19 nations, the Paris Conference (PARIS I) was, as its predecessors had been, doomed to failure. The major disagreements between Vietnam and the Cambodian parties centered around the nature of an interim power-sharing arrangement; the role of the UN in an International Control Mechanism that would supervise any agreement (proposed initially by the UN Security Council's Permanent Five); the use of the term 'genocide' to describe the actions of the PDK during their four-year rule; the question of the number of Vietnamese settlers and what to do with them; and the modalities of a cease-fire.[25]

Although the parties seemed most divided over the issue of power-sharing, at least one PARIS I committee chairman believed the real reason the conference failed was the PDK's insistence that the other participants accept its allegations that Vietnamese forces remained in Cambodia and that they help remove them.[26] In fact the CGDK had submitted a memo at the conference demanding the repatriation of 1,250,000 Vietnamese it believed had settled in Cambodia during the previous decade.[27]

Nevertheless, disagreements over the nature of future power-sharing arrangements had caused the failure of both JIM conferences and had now played a substantial part in the breakdown of PARIS I. The momentum of discussions was only to be renewed, therefore, following the presentation of an idea to address the issue by Australian Foreign Minister, Gareth Evans, in November 1989. First presented to Evans by US Congressman, Stephen Solarz (who had been touting the suggestion since before PARIS I), the idea was to create some form of UN management over Cambodia pending democratic elections. Once the Permanent Five of the Security Council adopted this idea in January 1990, two competing visions of a potential UN role emerged. The first, supported by the USSR, envisaged the UN monitoring the organization of two equivalent governments, the SoC and the CGDK's National Government of Cambodia (NGC). The second, backed by China, proposed the complete dismantling of the SoC and its replacement with the direct administration of the UN.[28]

In preparation for a substantial UN role, the Secretary-General sent four fact-finding missions to Cambodia whilst the Permanent Five continued to meet. Two of the missions were led by the United Nations Development Program (UNDP) and were sent to study the country's communication and transportation infrastructure, water supply, sanitation and housing. The third and fourth were sent to assess the Phnom Penh administration and the modalities for the repatriation of refugees.[29] Meanwhile, in February and June 1990 the Cambodian parties held their own talks in Jakarta and Tokyo, thus (in parallel with the Permanent Five meetings) enabling the international, regional and internal dimensions of the conflict to be addressed virtually simultaneously.[30]

At the Permanent Five's sixth meeting in August 1990 they released a 'Framework Document' proposing that the UN organize democratic elections and supervise the five key ministries within the 'administrative structures of the two opposing groups, the SoC (run by the Cambodian People's Party) and the NGC'. It was therefore envisaged that both organizations would remain intact whilst the UN ensured a 'neutral political environment'. The document also called for the creation of a Supreme National Council (SNC), a quadripartite body in which the sovereignty of Cambodia would be enshrined, but which otherwise would remain largely symbolic and advisory. As such, the Framework Document formed the blueprint of the final agreement signed 14 months later.[31] However, the initial reactions of Vietnam and the SoC were less than congenial. Both of them complained that the proposed UN mandate was too broad and that to disarm completely, as the document demanded, would be 'an invitation to commit suicide'.[32]

With negotiations nearing an end, heavy fighting resumed in February 1991 and continued until after a joint appeal for a cease-fire by the Secretary-General, France and Indonesia on 22 April. The subsequent cease-fire was the first in over 12 years and as it continued to be consolidated a number of meetings were held in Jakarta, Beijing, Pattaya, New York and

Paris, in order to reach agreement between the parties on outstanding issues.[33] These issues mainly concerned the nature of the relationship between the SNC and the proposed UN operation; the pace and nature of the disarmament process; and the continuing problem of how to express the atrocities perpetrated by the PDK in a manner the party itself could agree to.

By September all of these disagreements had been overcome. Significantly, the parties had now agreed to disarm only 70 per cent of their forces before elections were held, with the remaining 30 per cent to be cantoned under UN supervision pending demobilization. They had also agreed to avoid the use of the term 'genocide', deciding instead to call for 'effective measures to ensure that the policies and practices of the past [would] never be allowed to return'.[34] The Comprehensive Political Settlement of Cambodia (CPSC) was thus signed by 18 nations, together with Cambodia, at the end of the second Paris Conference (PARIS II) held from 21 to 23 October 1991.

3   The UN's disarmament mandates and the nature of the peace agreements

3.1   UNAVEM II

Despite being negotiated at the same time, the peace agreements for Angola and Cambodia envisaged vastly different roles for the UN in their implementation. Whilst its role in the latter was designed to be the most intrusive to date, its role in the former was expected to be far more peripheral. Consisting of seven main elements, the Angolan Accords began by officially establishing the cease-fire. At this stage the parties were to also to provide each other with complete information on their respective troop strengths.

Secondly, the Accords provided a monitoring role for the three main international monitors, the US, USSR and Portugal. Together with representatives of the two internal parties, these states were to compose the Joint Political and Military Commission (CCPM), which had 'the duty to see that the Peace Accords [were] applied, thereby guaranteeing strict compliance with all political and military understandings, and to make the final decision on possible violations of those Accords'.[35] Representatives of the UN could be invited to participate in meetings of the CCPM when requested by the parties. In order to provide the CCPM with the information it required a number of sub-commissions were also established, including a Joint Verification and Monitoring Commission (CMVF) and a Joint Commission for the Formation of the Armed Forces (CCFA).

The third element of the Accords concerned the disarmament and demobilization of the armed forces of both the MPLA and UNITA. This was to occur at 50 Assembly Areas that were to be built, protected and maintained by the parties themselves. All forces were expected to have arrived at their respective areas by 1 August (all paramilitary forces were to have been demobilized or integrated into the regular armies by the time of the cease-fire), where they were to occupy themselves with cultural and recreational activities, as well as helping to improve their own living conditions whilst they awaited demobilization. Demobilization itself received little attention in the Accords, except the recognition that it constituted a 'national problem that must be studied jointly by the two parties and submitted to CCPM for review and a decision'.

The fourth element of the Accords envisaged the creation of newly unified Angolan Armed Forces (FAA). Consisting principally of a 40,000 strong army drawn equally from the combatants of each party, it was to be formed in parallel with the disarmament and demobilization processes.[36] Responsibility for training the FAA was not, however, allocated to the UN, but rather to the states of Portugal, France and Britain. Its formation was to be complete by the time of the elections, as too was the disarmament and demobilization of those combatants not chosen to join it.

The organization of elections was to be the fifth element of the Accords. Elections were to be held for both the Presidency and the National Assembly (whether or not to hold them simultaneously was to be a matter for further discussion). While the President was to be elected 'through a majority system, with recourse to a second round, if necessary', the National Assembly was to be elected by proportional representation. As the parties could not agree on a specific date for the elections, the Accords stipulated only that they be held between 1 September and 30 November 1992.[37] Significantly, the Accords also referred simply to the possibility of asking the UN to provide electoral observation and assistance, thereby leaving open the question of whether other international organizations might play a monitoring role.

The final elements of the Accords established an arms embargo on Angola and provided a role for the UN in the verification and monitoring of the Angolan police.[38] This latter role involved the provision of an expert in police affairs to accompany monitoring teams composed of members of the parties themselves. Though the Accords stated that the inclusion of UNITA members in the police force would be 'guaranteed', the number to be incorporated was to be dependent on 'the availability of vacancies'.

In general, therefore, the UN's mandate in the Angolan peace process was simply to monitor the monitors; to 'verify the arrangements agreed by the two parties...for monitoring the cease-fire...and for monitoring the Angolan police during the cease-fire period'.[39] As such, UN military and police observers were to work alongside, but remain operationally distinct from the monitoring teams composed of UNITA and MPLA personnel. In the final analysis, this meant that the CCPM, not the UN, held responsibility for ensuring that both parties complied with their commitments.

Accordingly, the local monitoring system was to be established by 15 June, whilst the UN's verification system was to be fully operational 15 days later.

3.2   UNTAC

The role of the UN in the implementation of the CPSC was to be far greater than its role in the Angolan Accords. No more was this made evident than in the commitment of the UN to create a 'neutral political environment' in the transitional period between the signing of the CPSC and the formation of a new government. To achieve this, all 'administrative agencies, bodies and offices within the administrations of both the SoC and CGDK that could directly influence the outcome of elections' were to be placed 'under direct United Nations supervision or control'. Special attention was to be given to the five key ministries of 'foreign affairs, national defense, finance, public security and information'.[40]

To prevent the impression that Cambodia was to become a UN trustee-ship and to help form a unified Cambodian voice, the CPSC created the Supreme National Council (SNC). As noted in the previous section, the SNC was to be formed on a quadripartite basis from the four Cambodian parties and was to become the 'unique legitimate body and source of authority in which, throughout the transitional period, the sovereignty, independence and unity of Cambodia [was to be] enshrined'. It was there-fore the SNC's role to endow the UN with 'all powers necessary to ensure the implementation of [the] Agreement'. In recognition of its authority the UN also agreed to comply with any advice given to it by the SNC, unless that advice was believed to conflict with the objectives of the CPSC.[41]

The military aspects of the Agreements were to be completed in two phases. The first phase, which was to begin with the signing of the CPSC, required the parties to abide by the cease-fire. They were also required to provide UNTAC with complete information concerning the strengths of their respective military and police forces, as well as their locations of deployment.

The second phase (Phase II), whilst expecting the cease-fire to continue, was also to incorporate the disarmament and demobilization of the parties' forces. Only during Phase II was UNTAC to supervise, monitor and verify the implementation of the Agreements. Though a specific date for the start of Phase II was not included in the CPSC, it did stipulate that the UN's Military Commander and the Cambodian parties would have to agree on a date at least four weeks before it was due to commence. This four-week period was designed to provide time for the designation of locations for each party's regroupment and cantonment areas; for the UN to ensure the logistical suitability of these areas; and for the parties to disseminate in-formation to their forces concerning what was expected of them within the disarmament and demobilization processes.

In order to make adequate preparations for the arrival of the parties' forces, the UN agreed to establish the regroupment and cantonment areas at least one week before the beginning of Phase II. Similarly, the parties agreed to assemble their troops at the regroupment sites within two weeks of Phase II's initiation, after which the UN was to escort them to their respective cantonment areas. Once they had arrived the UN was to organize and verify the disarmament and demobilization of at least 70 per cent of them 'prior to the end of the process of registration for the elections'. The rest were to remain cantoned under UN supervision until they could be demobilized as soon as possible thereafter. The UN also stated its willingness to 'assist, as required' with the reintegration into civilian life of all forces demobilized before the elections.[42]

In the realm of public security the CPSC declared that all 'civil police [were to] operate under UNTAC supervision and control, in order that law and order [could be] maintained effectively and impartially, and that human rights and fundamental freedoms [would be] fully protected'. In consultation with the SNC, UNTAC was also to supervise Cambodia's law enforcement and judicial processes 'to the extent necessary to ensure the attainment of these objectives'. The supervision of public security was therefore to be an integral element of UNTAC's responsibility to '[foster] an environment in which respect for human rights [would] be ensured'. The parties also called upon the international community to provide economic and financial support for the rehabilitation and reconstruction of the country.

Finally, elections for a constituent assembly were to be held in May 1993 and on a specific date determined by the Special Representative of the Secretary-General. Once elected by proportional representation its members were to draft and adopt a new Cambodian Constitution and transform themselves into a legislative assembly. Although the UN had previously monitored elections, this was to be the first time it had been charged with directly organizing them. The UN was thus required to assume responsibility for the whole process, from the planning stages, through the writing of the electoral law, to the registration and conduct of the poll.[43]

4   Implementation

4.1   Angola

Although many of the major elements of the Accords were expected to be have been completed by the end of 1991, by this time very little had been achieved. Fears of UNITA subterfuge were heightened when it declared only 50,000 troops for demobilization, 20,000 fewer than it had claimed during the negotiations. Although Savimbi was believed to have exaggerated the number of troops he possessed in order to gain a more favorable bargaining position, concern persisted that he might also be hiding the remainder in the bush.[44] More optimistically, the UN accepted a request from the parties in November for it to observe elections still scheduled for the following year. However, only a month later President dos Santos felt sufficiently pessimistic about the whole peace process to state that the CCPM was not 'capable of resolving the problems the country [was] facing within the framework of pacification and national democratization'.[45]

Matters were only to get worse during the early months of 1992 as UNITA continued to prevent the extension of the Government's administration into the areas it controlled. The defection of two of its most prominent members in March 1992 did little to encourage further cooperation. One of the defectors, UNITA's 'Foreign Minister', Tony da Costa Fernandes, even accused Savimbi of fostering a personality cult; of assassinating his critics; of genocide of the Chingunji clan; and of hiding thousands of guerrillas and weapons in remote areas.[46]

It was not until April 1992, a full nine months after the originally scheduled date, that the disarmament and demobilization process was to begin. Even then it was to be slow and incremental. With insufficient numbers assembling and inadequate conditions at the assembly sites, the Portuguese military representative on the CCPM had already been forced to admit in May that neither the demobilization process nor the formation of a unified army could be complete by the time of the scheduled elections.[47] Imbalances were also becoming apparent in the assembly and demobilization processes. Although 85 per cent of UNITA's armed forces had officially assembled by the end of June, only 37 per cent of the Government's had done the same. However, only 4 per cent of UNITA troops had actually demobilized, compared to 18 per cent of the Government's.[48]

The security situation deteriorated even further in July when armed UNITA and Government supporters clashed in the northern town of Malarjie. Although this incident generated a number of calls for the UN to deploy armed peacekeepers, neither the peace guarantors nor the internal parties supported such action. Arguing that the setbacks so far did not represent a threat to the peace process as a whole, all parties to the Accords instead argued for the electoral process to proceed. Consequently, the elections were held on 29–30 September despite common knowledge that thousands of combatants remained outside of the disarmament process and that only 1,500 of the projected 40,000 troops for the new army had been sworn in.[49] On 5 October, in an ominous move, the UNITA generals and troops that had already joined the new army all began to withdraw to strategically encamped units outside the major urban centers. Savimbi also left Luanda, heading for the security of UNITA's headquarters in Huambo.[50]

In an effort to ward off impending trouble, the Security Council sent an *ad hoc* commission of ambassadors to meet with the leaders of both parties. At the same time, SRSG Margaret Anstee met with Savimbi in an attempt to persuade him to accept the pending election results. Although Savimbi agreed to do so, if the elections were found to be both transparent and free of corruption, he subsequently rejected the decision of the National Election Commission (CNE) when it declared the elections to have been free of fraud on 11 October. When the final results were announced by the CNE on 17 October, they showed a 91 per cent voter turnout and a parliamentary majority for the MPLA with 53.7 per cent of the vote. UNITA had won only 34.1 per cent. In the presidential elections, dos Santos had won 49.57 per cent, with Savimbi coming a close second with 40.07 per cent. As neither candidate had achieved an outright majority, a second run-off election was required within six weeks.[51]

UNITA's rejection of the elections was vociferous. When Anstee agreed with the CNE and declared the elections to have been 'generally free and fair', UNITA's radio station responded by accusing her of having 'sold her honor and dignity for diamonds, industrial mercury and US dollars given to her by the MPLA Government'.[52] When the Security Council endorsed Anstee's statement on 30 October and voted to extend UNAVEM II's mandate until the end of November, heavy fighting broke out within 24 hours.[53] Although the UN continued its diplomatic efforts, somewhat beyond its mandate, the fighting intensified.

By the time a UN brokered cease-fire came into effect on 2 November, the fighting had claimed approximately 2,000 lives, including those of two UN observers. Also included in the dead were a number of prominent UNITA officials who had been killed during riots ostensibly conducted in retaliation for a suspected UNITA organized *coup d'etat*.[54] Whilst denying any attempt to seize power, UNITA blamed its renewed offensives on the continued ethnic cleansing of its supporters from Luanda by Government supporters and police.[55] Thus, in true Angolan tradition, the 2 November cease-fire lasted only two days and the country was once again plunged into chaos.

4.2   Cambodia

Just as it was in Angola, the UN was facing mounting problems in Cambodia by the beginning of 1992. Unable to deploy UNTAC immediately, the UN hastily constructed a preparatory mission, the *United Nations Advance Mission in Cambodia* (UNAMIC), which it deployed in November 1991. However, UNAMIC was too small and inadequately funded to overcome the UN's planning problems and UNTAC's deployment was retarded as a result.

The political situation deteriorated seriously during May 1992 when the PDK effectively withdrew its cooperation and refused to allow UNTAC to deploy in areas it controlled. The PDK cited the UN's failure to dissolve the main institutions and structures of the Phnom Penh authorities, together with its failure to verify the withdrawal of Vietnamese forces, as the principal reasons for its actions. Secretary-General Boutros-Ghali responded by accusing the PDK of introducing 'its own interpretations of provisions of the Paris Agreements relating to the withdrawal of Vietnamese forces' as UNTAC's mandate was clearly to exercise control through the "existing administrative structures" of each of the four factions'.[56] The UN was not, therefore, authorized to dismantle any Government administrative structures. Besides which, the UN had neither the staff nor the expertise to run a transitional government itself.

In an attempt to overcome the PDK's objections an informal 'proposal for discussion' was drawn up at a Ministerial Conference on the Rehabilitation of Cambodia in Tokyo on 22 June. Although designed by a number of the participants to the conference, including the Permanent Five and SRSG Yasushi Akashi, the proposal failed. The Security Council's responded with Resolution 766 of 21 July demanding that the PDK (although not actually named) permit the deployment of UNTAC personnel in its areas of control. It also demanded that the PDK implement Phase II of the operation, which should already have begun on 13 June.

Relations between UNTAC and the PDK were not to improve. Although UNTAC attempted to reassure the PDK's concerns over the suspected presence of Vietnamese soldiers in Cambodia, even offering to establish a further ten border posts at which PDK representatives could be present, neither the UN's word nor its offer were accepted. However, the PDK's second bone of contention was not quite so easily refuted. Lacking the necessary funding, personnel or experience to either control or properly supervise the Government's administration, the UN was simply unable to create the 'neutral political environment' the Accords had stipulated. Although the PDK continued to demand measures that went far beyond those included in the Accords, it was evident to all that the Government's administration had not been sufficiently affected by the UN's presence.

Despite receiving assurances from FUNCINPEC and the KPNLF that they would both continue to demobilize without the PDK, Boutros-Ghali recognized that to do so would obviously provide the PDK with a distinct military advantage. He therefore concluded that the demobilization process should continue only temporarily without the reinstatement of the PDK.[57] With the PDK's refusal to participate, only 13,512 soldiers had been cantoned by 10 July, which represented barely 5 per cent of the 200,000 troops that had been expected to do so by 13 June.[58]

The PDK stated its conditions for reentering the peace process in a letter released in mid-July. In return for regrouping and cantoning its forces over a four-week period it demanded the 'de-politicization' of the Government's ministries and verification by UNTAC of the withdrawal of foreign forces. However, following discussions with the PDK's spokesperson on the SNC, Khieu Samphan, Akashi declared his belief that the replacement of certain Government Ministers and Vice-Ministers, as the letter demanded, would not satisfy the PDK. Rather, he believed the PDK was simply 'trying to gain what it could not get either in the battlefield or in the Paris negotiations, that is, to improve its political and military power to such an extent that the other parties will be placed at a distinct disadvantage when UNTAC leaves'. Akashi had already become 'selective and flexible' with the tempo of cantoning non-PDK affiliated troops in order to prevent this scenario from coming to fruition.[59]

Though UNTAC had still managed to canton some 52,000 troops belonging to the non-PDK affiliated parties by September 1992, around 38,000 of them were subsequently released on so-called 'agricultural leave'.[60] With the demobilization process therefore effectively suspended, the Secretary-General was faced with the dilemma of whether or not to continue with the operation. He personally rejected a withdrawal of UNTAC on the grounds that it would be 'unacceptable after so much [had] been achieved and so many hopes raised that Cambodia [would] at last achieve peace and democracy'. He also rejected a suspension of the operation in the belief that it 'would require the international community to maintain indefinitely a large and very costly operation, whose recurrent costs are now running at almost $100 million per month'.[61] Although Boutros-Ghali recognized that the elections due for May 1993 would 'clearly not be taking place in an environment as disarmed and politically neutral as was envisaged in the Paris Agreements and in the implementation plan', he courageously took the decision to proceed with the operation without the PDK's cooperation.

Despite attempts by the PDK to upset the elections with the threat of violence, 4,267,192 Cambodian citizens cast their ballots on 27–28 May. This represented 89.56 per cent of all registered voters. Although the Secretary-General was able to declare the poll both 'free and fair' on 29 May, a significant amount of violence in the preceding period meant he was unable to do the same for the electoral campaign.[62] When the final results were declared on 10 June, FUNCINPEC had won 45.47 per cent of the vote; the SoC's Cambodian People's Party (CPP) had won 38.23 per cent; and the 17 other parties that contested the elections shared the remainder.[63]

Unsurprisingly, the CPP began to question the credibility of the elections even before the final results had been declared. By 1 June it had challenged the election processes in four provinces, referring to procedural violations and irregularities. Even though SRSG Akashi assured the CPP that, even if true, none of their allegations could affect the outcome of the elections, a number of its candidates to the new assembly resigned in protest. In an attempt to avert an impending CPP led military coup Prince Sihanouk announced the formation of a new government with himself as Head of State and Hun Sen and Ranariddh as Vice-Ministers on 3 June.[64]

Although interventions by the US and UN led to the collapse of this power-sharing agreement three days later, pressure from the CPP (which still controlled the organs of state, including the military) and other ominous events, including Prince Norodom Chakrapong's (a son of Prince Sihanouk, half-brother of Prince Ranariddh and Deputy Prime Minister of the SoC) proclamation of an 'autonomous zone' of seven eastern provinces on 12 June, persuaded those in UNTAC and the international community reluctant to accept a compromise that the success of the whole operation might depend on it.[65]

Consequently, with the danger of secession threatening to drive the country back into chaos, Sihanouk brokered another power-sharing arrangement, this time with Ranariddh as First Prime Minister and Hun Sen as Second Prime Minister. Despite FUNCINPEC's retention of the most powerful position in the government, Hun Sen was still perceived as the power behind the throne.[66]

5   Analysis of the operations

5.1   Funding, administration and deployment

By the beginning of 1992 Boutros-Ghali had already recognized the chasm that was developing between the tasks entrusted to the UN and the financial means provided to it.[67] By the end of the year the UN had deployed over 50,000 peacekeepers in 13 peacekeeping operations, at an annual cost of $3 billion.[68] However, as of June 1992, only 25 per cent of the assessed contributions of that year's peacekeeping budget had been paid. By the same time 65 per cent of 1992's assessed contributions to the regular budget remained outstanding, together with 35 per cent of the year before. This meant that, as of mid-1992, the UN was short of an amount equivalent to at least a full year's funding.[69]

Faced with an increasing shortage of cash, the UN began to cut corners, riding its luck to an extreme. No more was this the case than in Angola. With a territorial expanse the size of Western Europe and with a practically non-existent infrastructure, the Angolan mandate would have been a daunting task even to a well equipped and properly manned operation. Nonetheless, the UN deployed only 400 observers to monitor the elections, despite the existence of nearly 6,000 polling stations. As a result, UNAVEM II was forced to resort to 'sample observation', in which teams of two observers would spend an average of 20 minutes at each station, enough time to observe approximately four votes.[70] Even with this hectic timetable the observers were only able to visit 4,480 of the polling stations.[71] And as the Electoral Law also required the votes to be counted at the polling stations themselves, the ratio of observers to stations meant that only a fraction of these counts could be observed.[72]

Both UNAVEM II and UNTAC were also to suffer from the inefficient manner in which the UN approves the budgets for peacekeeping operations. In the case of UNAVEM II, its budget was not approved for a period of nearly three months after the operation had begun, contributing to a slower than planned start and delaying the purchasing of essential equipment.[73] A similar scenario existed in Cambodia. The preparatory mission, UNAMIC, was still working on a minuscule budget of $45 million four months after it had been deployed. Most of this money was supposedly allocated to de-mining, which could have swallowed ten times that amount alone.[74] Only on 14 February 1992 did the General Assembly approve an emergency request by the Secretary-General for an advance appropriation of $200 million to help with the 'smooth and timely deployment of UNTAC'. However, the lack of an overall budget continued to prevent the deployment of UNTAC personnel. Even SRSG Akashi, who was himself not appointed until two months into the operation, stated quite bluntly that despite the problems evident in Cambodia itself, '...our main problems are not in Cambodia but here in New York over money and equipment'.[75]

So reluctant were the major contributing states to pay their dues that the leader of the SoC, Hun Sen, was compelled to visit the US personally in March 1992 to beg Congress to release the money required to put the Accords into effect. As he told a Washington forum during his visit, 'once the peace accord was signed, governments (which had pressed for a UN role) became reluctant to pay. They have placed the Cambodian people in a very dangerous situation.'[76] The nominal leader of the PDK, Khieu Samphan, had already cited the absence of UNTAC troops on the streets of Phnom Penh during the initial months of the operation as a danger to the peace process in itself.[77] Despite their warnings the US did not pay its initial start-up contribution of just $60 million until 7 May 1992.[78]

As a consequence of its delayed funding, UNTAC was able to deploy only 3,694 of its projected 15,900 troops by the beginning of the rainy season in late April 1992. Despite the obvious climatic and topographical barriers present, the UNTAC Force Commander, Lt. General John Sanderson, drew up plans for Phase II of the operation. These plans envisaged the deployment in their respective areas of at least eight battalions by 13 June, the prospective date for the beginning of Phase II. By this time, however, only four battalions had actually deployed. As these forces were responsible, amongst other things, for de-mining the regroupment and cantonment areas, as well as the construction of shelters and accommodation for demobilizing troops, their late deployment had obvious consequences.[79] Whilst the remaining four battalions reached Cambodia by early July, UNTAC's military component was still 800 troops short of its full quotient by the following September.[80]

Although, in James Schear's view, the delays in UNTAC's deployment did not affect adherence to the overall settlement timetable, it nevertheless:

> [denied] the operation early momentum, and it dampened the desired positive psychological impact upon domestic public opinion. It also, most damagingly, contributed to a sense of political drift and disarray

allowing the four Khmer factions, in particular the Khmer Rouge and the Hun Sen regime, to hedge positions on full compliance with the Accords.[81]

By failing to implement its authority in a more assertive and forceful manner, UNTAC failed to take advantage of the element of surprise arising from the unfamiliarity of the combatants with the workings of the UN, the deterrent effect of its technical capabilities and the moral and political authority inherent in its mandate.[82] It was hardly surprising then, that the Secretary-General called for a re-evaluation of the UN's budgetary and procurement processes in mid-1992, on the grounds that the 'experience of mounting a large and complex UN operation such as UNTAC may point to the possible need to reexamine the manner in which the existing financial and administrative rules and regulations of the [UN] are applied to such operations'.[83]

5.2   Planning and the nature of the peace agreements

Although a lack of funding was at the heart of most of the UN's problems, it could not explain all of the organizational inadequacies witnessed in Angola and Cambodia. It was evident that many of the complications that had arisen in both missions could have been averted with proper pre-operational planning. Yet, the UN system for planning and supporting field operations had seemingly remained largely unchanged since the end of the Cold War. As such, it continued to rely unduly on improvisation and *ad hoc* arrangements, both for organizing operations and for managing the working relationships between members of the Secretariat and between officers and civilians in the field.[84]

The need for the development and reorganization of UN planning capabilities was evident both in New York and in the operations themselves. As of 1992 the UN Secretariat simply did not possess the 'experience, resources and qualified personnel to organize a mission of [the] complexity, magnitude and novelty [of UNTAC] at such short notice'.[85] When Force Commander Sanderson visited UN Headquarters to help speed up the deployment of UNTAC troops, he discovered that it not only lacked maps of Cambodia (as had been the case in the Namibian operation), but also lacked any speakers of the Khmer language. Similarly, there was no operations room; no team of military advisers to brief him on the UN's plans; no one able to brief contributing countries on what was expected of them; and no concept of how UNTAC's mandate might be translated into operational military terms.[86] In an attempt to address these inadequacies a Department of Peacekeeping Operations (DPKO) was created at UN Headquarters in February 1992. The DPKO, it was hoped, would eventually 'serve as a center of institutional memory and…develop and maintain a ready capacity to act for future peacekeeping operations'.[87]

The UN's response to its lack of planning for the Cambodian operation was to create UNAMIC, a development that Sanderson believed lulled the Secretariat into a false sense of security. As Sanderson explained:

> The response to the deteriorating situation was to stick new pieces on to UNAMIC when it was not organized even to look after itself. UNAMIC, therefore, staggered from one crisis to another as it attempted to react to circumstances for which it was ill-prepared, leaving it unable to execute the important task of planning for UNTAC.[88]

Indeed, UNAMIC itself was only created once it was realized that the survey missions conducted by the UN in late 1991 were insufficient to begin concrete preparations for the implementation of the military aspects of UNTAC's mandate.[89]

Strategic planning was also hampered by the lack of cooperation between the different components of UNTAC. Each component began by conducting independent survey missions and formulating their own idiosyncratic plans. This resulted in ridiculous situations, such as the refugee repatriation program beginning before the military component had deployed in sufficient numbers to designate minefields and provide the necessary security.[90] Even in the field each component reported to their own headquarters rather than to UNTAC headquarters, a tendency that Sanderson argued caused 'considerable grief and disharmony in the operation'.[91] Joint coordination meetings were not organized until March 1993. This lack of strategic planning was exacerbated by the inadequacies in field management which, Warner observed, made it seem like the 'administrative blueprint of previous – and much smaller and less complex – operations [had] simply [been] dusted off and applied to the Cambodian mission.'[92]

The failure to provide appropriate mandates was also a primary cause of the UN's subsequent troubles. The SRSG in Angola, Margaret Anstee, complained that many of the problems that UNAVEM II had encountered had been 'rooted in the nature of the Peace Accord'. As such, she complained that the UN had been given only a marginal role in the formulation and implementation of the peace plan. Although the reasons for the UN's limited role lay at the doors of the Security Council and the Angolan parties themselves, Anstee had nevertheless found herself in control of institutional structures that relied too heavily on the 'good faith' of the parties concerned and a timetable for demobilization that was hopelessly unrealistic.[93] By providing the UN with a 'by-stander' mandate, the Accords had created institutional arrangements without providing for an arbiter or anyone to ensure the implementation of decisions. No more was this the case than in the CCPM, the chairmanship of which was shared on an alternating basis by the parties themselves. This meant that even when the parties were able to reach a consensus in the CCPM, the resulting decisions often remained only on paper.[94]

UNTAC, on the other hand, had evidently taken on more responsibility than the UN's capabilities could effectively assume. No more was this apparent than in its mandate to create a 'neutral political environment' through the supervision and control of the respective party administrations and their civilian police. Roberts expresses the incredibility of UNTAC's mandate with regard to the supervision of the administrations, when he states quite succinctly that the operation denied:

> ...the inherent possibility of a handful of foreigners, in the space of less than a year, monitoring and imposing neutral behavior upon an authoritarian bureaucracy determined to resist control [when there was] inadequate or inappropriate staffing and a passivity that in some cases [had] bordered on incompetence.[95]

5.3   Disarmament, demobilization, reintegration and the formation of unified armed forces

A lack of planning and sufficient attention to detail was also evident in both countries' disarmament, demobilization and reintegration processes. One of the UN's first and most egregious errors was to rely on the internal parties to establish and supply their respective regroupment/assembly and cantonment areas without even assessing their ability to do so.[96] In Angola the whole process of disarmament was subsequently slowed by the inability of soldiers to reach their assigned areas because both parties had established them in remote areas under their own control. The remoteness of the areas also left the parties unable to supply their encamped troops with sufficient food, medicine and clothing. An inevitable consequence of this was a dramatic increase in crime and insecurity as 'unpaid and underfed troops deserted and roved the countryside in search of sustenance'.[97]

When the UN became party to the CPSC, the likelihood of similar problems was therefore increased when it accepted that the designation of the assembly and cantonment areas would not take place until the operation had already begun. Unfortunately, even after their locations had been designated, the ability and willingness of the parties to maintain the areas was never truly tested.[98] With the PDK's refusal to disarm and the release of the cantoned troops from the other parties on immediate agricultural leave, the issue simply did not arise.

As previously explained, the Angolan Accords also failed to include any direct provision for the future security of demobilizing soldiers. Even when an Interministerial Office to Support the Demobilized Military of Angola was created by the Angolan government in November 1991, a lack of resources and planning meant it could have little effect. For example, the 'resettlement allowance' paid to demobilizing soldiers was as little as $15 and when the CCPM began to seek funding in May 1992 for a number of projects designed to provide them with vocational and other training, none of the international donors approached responded to its requests.[99] The amount requested was only $44.7 million. The sporadic vocational training programs that did take place were therefore hopelessly inadequate for the needs of the situation. The repercussions of this lack of provision were obvious. As SRSG Anstee acknowledged:

> Fear of the unknown must have played a large part in the personal calculations of men who had known no other life than war, and particularly in the case of a guerilla force such as UNITA. As Dr. Savimbi never tired of reminding me, these men had their whole *raison d'etre* in [UNITA's army]. Unlike their opposite numbers in [the Government's armed forces] most of them had no homes to return to, much less jobs, having spent their life on the move, taking their families and goods and chattels with them and setting up self-sufficient villages wherever they went. This was why their assembly areas were so much better organized than those of the Government. It was also why, when demobilized, they stayed where they were, irrespective of the availability of transport, having nowhere else to go.[100]

In Cambodia, the CPSC also contained no direct provision for the reintegration of former soldiers into civilian life. The majority of soldiers were simply expected to return to the agricultural lives they had left behind. This led one senior UNTAC staff officer to express his fears of sending 140,000 'uneducated jobless men on [to] the streets'.[101] And although the international community had committed itself to help with the commencement of economic reconstruction in Cambodia, something it had not done in Angola, international donors remained much more willing to spend money to 'fix' the situation ($2 billion in peacekeeping costs) than they were to help restore the country's economy ($1 billion in pledges). [102]

Finally, both peace processes were to suffer from the lack of a UN role in the creation of professionally trained armies. This was especially the case in Angola where SRSG Anstee believed the UN should have at least been given a verification role in the process and a seat on the CCFA. To be given no role at all in the process was in Anstee's opinion 'absurd'. In practice, UNAVEM II was drawn increasingly into the issue, attempting to provide sufficient accommodation and uniforms to see the new army through its embryonic stages.[103]

5.4 Reform of public security

The Secretary-General expressed the importance of UNTAC's mandate to supervise the civilian police in his report of early 1992, when he stated:

> In the area of public security, the maintenance of law and order is the key not only to the creation of a neutral political environment in which

all Cambodians may exercise their political rights to participate in the electoral process, but also to the effective implementation by UNTAC of all aspects of its mandate. In other words, in order to ensure the success of the transitional arrangements, UNTAC must be able to work as a partner with all the existing administrative structures charged with public security.[104]

To monitor the estimated 50,000 civilian police deployed at some 1,500 police posts, the UN deployed nearly 3,600 UNTAC civilian police monitors (CIVPOLS). This provided a ratio of approximately one CIVPOL to every 15 local policemen, or one CIVPOL to every 3,000 Cambodians. Such ratios, it was hoped, would also allow the CIVPOLS to effectively monitor violations of human rights.[105]

Despite these impressive figures, UNTAC's CIVPOL component was widely perceived as disastrous. Two of its greatest deficiencies were that it was composed of a large number of very small units from a wide range of (mostly developing) countries and that many of its personnel were not even trained police officers. This led to basic communication difficulties, a variation in operating styles and a general problem of poor discipline. There was also little effort made to acquaint CIVPOLS with the history of the Cambodian conflict or to build their sense of cultural awareness.[106]

With such inadequate police supervision there could be no hope that UNTAC might fulfill its requirements under the CPSC to '[foster] an environment in which respect for human rights would be ensured'. UNTAC's human rights component, initially composed of only ten personnel, was to remain significantly understaffed (it reached a peak of 31) and even the revolutionary appointment of a Special Prosecutor's Office in January 1993 could do little to help. Even though the new Special Prosecutor, Mark Plunkett, was able to issue warrants for the arrest of known human rights violators, UNTAC's CIVPOLS, unarmed and already lacking credibility, were in no position to arrest them. Neither was the UN military component, which by its own interpretation lacked the requisite mandate to use force to carry out such duties. And even when human rights violators and criminals were arrested, there existed no impartial judicial system in which to prosecute them.[107]

In Angola there was to be even less emphasis placed on the issue of public security. As in all other spheres of the peace process UNAVEM II's CIVPOLS were forced to work through the joint monitoring mechanisms that, in characteristic fashion, were not fully deployed until June 1992. Only at this stage, after considerable pressure from SRSG Anstee, did the UN finally increase the number of CIVPOLS to 126. The failure of the Accords to address the issue of police training also caused friction in the peace process. The Accords had only stipulated that UNITA's involvement in the national police force should be at the invitation of the Government.

The Government argued, therefore, that it was under no obligation to incorporate the 7,000 to 8,500 personnel UNITA began to insist upon. Only in September, less than a month before the elections, did the Government concede to UNITA's demands. By this time the Government's creation of an anti-riot police squad, into which UNITA claimed military personnel were being transferred, was threatening to derail the whole peace process.[108]

With such a small CIVPOL contingent UNAVEM II could never have hoped to monitor the Angolan police effectively. With such low ratios of police to civilians the ability of its CIVPOLS to monitor violations of human rights was also nominal. In fact human rights *per se* remained outside the mandate of UNAVEM II, which therefore contained no human rights observers. For Anstee the lack of a human rights element to the Angolan mandate was a 'serious omission', which once again stemmed from the fact that the Accords paid 'only cursory attention' to the subject.[109]

5.5   Strategies of conflict resolution

With the end of the Cold War both superpowers had come under domestic pressure to achieve significant peace dividends. The new political climate had also made the financial and military support of clients with dubious human rights records increasingly unsustainable. Nevertheless, a means still had to be found of transforming violent conflicts around the world into peaceful political competition. With the victory of democracy over communism and the continued belief that most of these conflicts were by-products of the Cold War itself, it initially appeared that a little persuasion by the superpowers would be sufficient to convince their former clients to partake of the democratic process. In this fashion one former warring party would win office, whilst the others would be ensured enough votes to make them a significant opposition. Everybody would be satisfied.

However, it was evident in Angola and Cambodia that this was not the case. In both instances the democratic process had failed to provide sufficient security for the parties to either remain in the process itself or to abide by the results once it was over. So, did the problem lie with the parties or with the democratic process? The answer, it seems, is both.

Some scholars have suggested that the foremost problem with liberal democracy is its incompatibility with the cultures into which it is being transplanted. For instance, Gary Klintworth and Michael Leifer have both argued that democracy was an inappropriate conflict resolution mechanism for Cambodia as 'genuine compromise and power-sharing [had] never been part of the political tradition and experience of Indo-China. [Rather, in] that part of the world power has been treated as a possession to be monopolized'.[110]

Building on the work of Abdulgaffar Peang-Meth, Pierre Lizee has also reasoned that the Cambodian parties refused to participate fully in the conflict resolution procedure of the CPSC because their attitudes towards conflict and democracy differed fundamentally from that of the UN. Whilst the key to the transformation of the conflict from a Western perspective was the introduction of liberal democracy, Cambodian society is dominated by Brahmanism and Buddhism, which work to confine social interactions to small groups of personal relations in which 'well defined status and ranks' and predestined 'fatalistic outlooks' preclude its adoption.

When therefore the French introduced legal and administrative structures into the Cambodian state, they did so by superimposing them over the traditional cultural influences of Cambodian society. The Western model of the state and the requisite understanding of democracy had just never properly developed.[111] Indeed, even the words 'society' and 'consensus' are relatively new concepts in the Khmer language.[112] Thus, in Lizee's opinion:

> [The] refusal to move politics beyond factionalism is the common denominator underlying all the actions and the negotiating positions of the Cambodian factions since August 1989. Indeed, the perspective of the factions on the process of national reconciliation during the first Paris Conference, their respective reaction to the Australian plan, their stance on the formation and composition of the SNC, their various attempts to modify the Perm-5 plan, and, lastly their attitude towards the UN presence in Cambodia since the October 1991 agreement, all reveal an understanding of conflict articulated around the 'family-patronage-dynastic-[Buddhist] model'…To put it simply, the UN hoped to impose a liberal democratic political process in a society where this concept remains unclear. It could not work.[113]

A similar situation appeared to exist in Angola. The colonial powers had imposed the Western state system on traditional African cultures with the result that the power of the state had become simply another resource to compete for. In this context democratic elections were perceived as little more than winner-take-all competitions, with the concept of democratic opposition remaining an anathema to so-called political parties mostly formed on ethnic, religious or tribal grounds. This mindset was initially apparent at the negotiations of the Accords. Despite attempts by some of those present to persuade both parties to agree to an accommodation for the eventual losers of the elections, neither party was interested. Indeed, 'each was bent on nothing less than total victory'.[114]

The haste with which UNITA had initially wanted the elections to be held had also indicated that it viewed the electoral process purely as a means to organize a peaceful transference of power. Its confidence in victory must have been boosted greatly by the US, which up to two days before the poll was still openly proclaiming that Savimbi had the 'election in the bag'.[115] All of this was corroborated by UNITA's own electoral office, which acknowledged that it had made mistakes, including taking an undemocratic stance towards the elections based on the certain belief that it would win. UNITA also refused to compete in the second round of presidential elections because it believed it had failed to play an effective role in the election process and in news management in general.[116]

The question is then, should the UN have allowed the elections to continue when it was apparent that the major opposition parties in the Angolan and Cambodian elections were both ill prepared to compete and obviously unwilling to accept defeat? In Somerville's opinion, UNITA's leader was never interested in sharing power in Angola, or in 'playing second fiddle to any other politician or party'.[117] Savimbi did not try to conceal his negative attitude toward elections, stating before the poll that any defeat for UNITA would be evidence of electoral fraud. For Hamill, this was evidence of Savimbi's 'authoritarian mindset that had paved the way for Angola's subsequent tragedy'.[118] The UN's approach of giving its countenance to a peace process in which the parties had obviously not fulfilled their treaty obligations may also have given Savimbi the impression that compliance with the military elements of the Accords was unimportant as he was destined to win power anyway.[119]

However, although the PDK in Cambodia had seemingly exhibited a similar mindset to UNITA, Sorpong Peou argues that there is no evidence that any of the Cambodian parties were bent on destroying the UN's plan from day one. This is especially the case for the Khmer Rouge, who Peou believes not only genuinely intended to implement the CPSC when they signed it, but that they were also serious about competing in the elections.[120] If this is true then their eventual withdrawal from the elections may simply have been induced by their failure to appreciate the organizational requirements of competing in an electoral process. Munck and Kumar note that as in Angola:

> ...important obstacles to the institutionalization of conflict became evident. Right from the very beginning, the Khmer Rouge never really had an agenda upon which to construct a political party...its ability to transform itself from a military to a political force could be doubted from the very outset.[121]

The insecurity of the PDK was also compounded by the failure of UNTAC to properly supervise the SoC administration. Without such supervision there could obviously be no level playing field in the election campaign. The PDK's predicament was acknowledged by Gareth Evans, who believed that UNTAC's failure to deal effectively with the SoC's corruption and intimidation of opposing political figures, gave the PDK at least a 'spurious justification' not to comply with the key provisions of the CPSC'.[122]

Another area of contention was to surround the criteria established to designate eligible voters. As noted earlier, throughout the operation the PDK had refused to accept UN assurances that all 'foreign forces' had left the country. From very early in the negotiations it was evident that the UN and PDK differed fundamentally in their definition of 'foreign forces'. For the UN the term was obviously accepted to mean what it would mean in general international usage – military personnel. The PDK, however, did not make such distinctions. They therefore continued to push for the complete repatriation of all ethnic Vietnamese civilians.

The true effect of glossing over this more than semantic disagreement between the PDK and UN was only realized following the promulgation of UNTAC's first electoral law in April 1992. By allowing 'every Cambodian person...over the age of 18...to be registered as a voter', UNTAC's electoral law not only challenged the Khmer notion that rights of political participation should be based on ethnic criteria but, as far as all the internal parties were concerned (except the CPP), provided for nothing less than 'Vietnamese suffrage'.[123] Later attempts by UNTAC to re-write the law still based enfranchisement on where the person, their parents, or grandparents were born and not on their ethnic grouping. This denied the principle that Cambodian political and civil rights derived from Khmer custom and culture, a notion all parties to the CPSC found unacceptable.[124]

The evidence suggests, therefore, that the PDK's refusal to participate in the electoral campaign was based on a rational calculation that the process could not ensure their post-election survival. As Roberts explains, even UNTAC began to accept that the PDK had genuine security concerns:

> The combination of an insensitive electoral law, the problem of defining the Vietnamese 'foreign forces' and the failure of UNTAC to separate the CPP from the State, as well as questionable responses to these crises, convinced UNTAC's information and education component, tasked with analyzing such issues, that the PDK 'genuinely believed that UNTAC was working in tandem with the [CPP]'; and that the PDK [also] believed that [the information and education component] were links in the alliances inside and outside UNTAC who were colluding with the [Vietnamese].[125]

The PDK was also to see its electoral chances reduced even further with the collapse of the CGDK. Although this was in part due to PDK intransigence, it was also due to the removal of international support for the PDK, which had until then been provided through its share of the seat at the UN. Nevertheless, according to Munck and Kumar, '[with] the breakup of the CGDK coalition...the [PDK] increasingly saw its electoral possibilities diminish. This led it to renege on its promises to participate in the political process and to take steps to undermine a process in which it would inevitably end up a loser'.[126]

For Peou, therefore, the 'socio-insitutionalist' perspective advocated by Klintworth, Leifer, Peang-Meth and Lizee fails to take adequate account of the degree to which democracy had resonated in Cambodian culture despite the relatively short time span of the peace process. The large voter turnout, the participation of 20 political parties in the elections and the knowledge ordinary Cambodians had gained on the democratic process are all cited by Peou in his rejection of the cultural determinism of their thesis. He even cites the power-sharing government formed after the elections as proof that 'after decades of extreme polarization and the practice of exclusionary politics the democratically elected party leaders were learning to share power and made necessary compromises to ensure their effective cooperation in the political process. The elections contributed to the legitimization of power-sharing without any protests over unequal distribution of power an intrinsic and desirable characteristic of democracy'[127] Even more important for Peou, however, was the fact that a civil society had begun to emerge in Cambodia during the transitional period with interest groups powerful and vibrant enough to challenge the policies of government.[128]

6 Conclusion

Perhaps the easiest assessment the UN could have made in 1991 was that the former warring parties in Angola and Cambodia were caught in a shared understanding of aggression. Whilst the parties in Angola had negotiated for little more than a painless means to decide the victor of their civil war, the parties in Cambodia had already described the prospect of complete disarmament as 'an invitation to commit suicide'. Therefore, as the twin-track framework advocated by this text suggests, former warring parties caught in such intense security dilemmas will require Track 1 diplomacy that will provide them with security guarantees for both the disarmament phase and the post-election period. This meant that the UN needed to ensure both the deployment of a sizeable military force and the negotiation of adequate power-sharing arrangements.

However, as this account has illustrated, neither of these elements existed in Angola. Unfortunately, the frugality of the major powers seemed to blind them to the warning signs inherent in UNITA's desire for speedy elections and the MPLA's wish to keep the international presence to a minimum. Thus, as SRSG Anstee explained to the recently appointed Secretary-General in May 1992, the problem they faced was one they had inherited from the past and it 'stemmed from the assignment of an inappropriate role to the UN as a result of compromises hammered out by a group of member states, in negotiations over peace accords in which the [UN] itself had only a tardy and peripheral role'.[129]

At least the UN's integral role in the negotiations for the CPSC meant it was able to secure the deployment of a sizeable military force in Cambodia.

However, the sluggish manner in which it eventually deployed ensured that any confidence the parties might have invested in it had already been significantly drained by the time the rainy season had arrived in April 1992. Notably, the Cambodian parties had managed to negotiate for the retention of up to 30 per cent of their respective forces, thus lessening the intensity of the security dilemma they faced. Though this was a laudable late addition to the CPSC, it was still insufficient to overcome the final security hurdle confronting the parties; the fear of electoral defeat.

Of course, the fear of electoral defeat was present in both countries' peace processes. Neither had attempted to accommodate the potential losers with power-sharing arrangements. In Angola, UNITA had also made no effort to transform itself into a political party and to have expected it to do so in only 12 months was impractical. As it had lost the presidential elections UNITA was therefore faced with accepting a minor role in opposition or of returning to war. Although (as will be discussed in Chapter 7) this might hide the all-important role of Savimbi, in a shared understanding of aggression it was highly unlikely that any party facing such a dilemma would have disarmed.

Similarly, the Khmer Rouge's lack of appreciation for what the democratic process entailed, together with its increasing sense of inevitable defeat, may have been the primary reason it withdrew from the disarmament process. Caught in a shared understanding of aggression and lacking any post-election security guarantees, it probably felt it had no other choice. By mistakenly interpreting these actions as predation, it is also possible that the UN closed off potential avenues for cooperation unnecessarily.

Of course, the UN's task of introducing liberal democracy into societies with no real experience of the concept was always going to be difficult. Therefore, it is testimony to the hard work and perseverance of those UN personnel responsible that the elections eventually involved so many ordinary Angolans and Cambodians. The socio-institutionalist perspective is therefore obviously too static a vision. Cultures can change and second-generation peacekeeping operations like UNAVEM II and UNTAC are one way of inducing it. However, it is also apparent that the UN could have done more to take into account the contextual rationalities at work in Cambodian and Angolan cultures, rationalities that exacerbated the security dilemmas already inherent in the democratic process. These contextual rationalities therefore made the inclusion of internal security guarantees even more essential.

The UN's Track 1 diplomacy at the societal levels of the demobilizing soldiers and general population was to be no more successful. At these levels the UN should have helped provide public security through the creation of credible justice systems, yet in neither country was this accomplished. Whilst in Angola the UN's CIVPOLS were practically non-existent, in Cambodia they were practically useless. Nor could the UN significantly affect the impartiality of either country's judicial systems (this role was not even included in UNAVEM II's mandate). Without the basic security and human rights protection provided by credible justice systems the UN's disarmament processes could never have succeeded.

The UN's Track 2 diplomacy at these levels was also insufficient. Having failed to ensure the provision of adequate demobilization allowances, training programs or employment opportunities to the ex-combatants of both countries, the UN could only hope that most of them would return to the local communities from which they had originally emerged. Of course, as these communities were still suffering from the same problems that had beset them before each peace process had begun, the chances of their successful reintegration was minimal. As neither country had received significant levels of international aid for economic reconstruction, their general populations had also witnessed little Track 2 diplomacy. Therefore, with no credible justice systems, no human rights protection and no disarmament of the party's forces, general disarmament was destined to remain a fleeting hope in both countries.

3
Mozambique 1992–1994

1   Introduction

With the creation of the United Nations Operation in Mozambique (ONUMOZ) in December 1992, the UN had established its thirteenth peacekeeping operation of the post-Cold War era. Thus, in only four years the UN had equaled the number of operations it had conducted during the previous 40. However, the optimism that had been generated in the initial post-Cold War period was now beginning to waver. As described in the previous chapter, democratic elections in Angola had been followed by a return to war and many analysts were blaming the UN's failure to disarm UNITA for the ease with which it had resumed. At the same time, the refusal of the Khmer Rouge to disarm and participate in elections in Cambodia was placing that country's whole peace process in jeopardy. It was to be in this climate of dejection and uncertainty that the peace negotiations for Mozambique were to conclude.

Fortunately for the UN, Mozambique was not to become another Angola or Cambodia. Rather, ONUMOZ's disarmament mandate was to be one of its greatest successes. To explain why, this chapter will utilize the twin-track framework outlined in Chapter 1. As with all the case studies in this text, this chapter will begin with an overview of the events leading up to the signing of the peace agreements. Next, a description of both the UN's mandate and its implementation will be provided. This will be followed by an analysis of ONUMOZ's disarmament process. Finally, the conclusion will assess the utility of the twin-track framework to account for the relative success of disarmament in Mozambique.

2   Background to the conflict

After 11 years of liberation struggle the *Frente da Libertacao de Mocambique* (FRELIMO) finally defeated the country's Portuguese colonialists in 1975. Having inherited the leadership of a country in a state of near collapse, the new government also found itself embroiled in a conflict raging in neighboring Rhodesia (Zimbabwe), until liberation was finally achieved in that country four years later. Following Zimbabwean independence, the Mozambican government was to become involved in yet another neighboring conflict, this time involving the exiled African National Congress (ANC) and the South African Armed Forces. By the mid-1980s, in an effort to destabilize its pro-Marxist neighbor, South Africa had helped transform the Mozambican rebel group, *Resistencia Nacional Mozambicana* (RENAMO), into a formidable military organization.[1]

In the face of such substantial foreign support, FRELIMO had been forced to concede that a military defeat of RENAMO was simply infeasible by the early 1980s.[2] Now more appreciative of the need for a negotiated settlement, FRELIMO had first attempted to strike a peace deal with RENAMO's principle patrons, the South African government. Although this strategy led to the signing of the Nkomati Accords in March 1984, in which both governments agreed to respect each other's sovereignty and independence, South Africa's continued support for RENAMO (in contravention of its Nkomati commitments) meant that the rebel group remained defiant. FRELIMO also tried to sever support for RENAMO coming from Malawian territory. However, when the Malawian government complied with its requests to expel thousands of RENAMO troops, their subsequent movement back into Mozambique threatened even greater disruption.[3]

By the end of the decade the sense of military stalemate had only been reinforced. Although the President of Mozambique, Joaquim Chissano, had offered an amnesty to RENAMO guerillas after his election in 1987, by the end of the following year he could claim only 3,000 beneficiaries of the deal. This number represented approximately 15 per cent of RENAMO's estimated 20,000 troops.[4]

Similarly on the battlefield, although FRELIMO offensives in 1988–89 had managed to dislodge the rebels from territory they had occupied for over four years (including the major transport corridors and communication networks that cut across Mozambique from the Indian Ocean to its landlocked neighbors) it could still not achieve an outright military victory. The success of these offensives had also been dependent on the participation of troops from Tanzania and Zimbabwe, which had been deployed to protect the vital transport corridors that supplied both countries. However, once the offensives had ended, Tanzania withdrew its troops and Zimbabwe, suffering itself from economic hardships and continued RENAMO incursions, began to push FRELIMO to reach a negotiated settlement. The prospects of a FRELIMO (henceforth referred to as the Government) military victory were further weakened by the Soviet Union's decision to reduce its military supplies and withdraw its military advisors from 1989.[5]

In this context the Mozambican Armed Forces (FAM) were put under immense strain. Ever since its inception the FAM had suffered from of a lack of motivation, training and equipment, as well as the absence of any kind of effective command and control system. Nevertheless, though Mozambique was one of the most aid dependent countries in the world, its numbers had still reached as high as 72,000 by 1990. The paramilitaries of the Mozambican militia had fared little better. Short of uniforms, rations and salaries, they were sufficiently supplied only with light weapons. The Government had also distributed somewhere in the region of 1.5 million AK-47s to the civilian population during the civil war.[6]

Just as the Government's external support was declining, so too was RENAMO's. South Africa, its greatest benefactor, had drastically cut its supplies by the end of the 1980s and reports of RENAMO's human rights abuses were making overt support from the US politically unpalatable.[7] US support was also waning due to the Government's increasing embrace of liberal economic reforms.[8] These reforms were also helping to persuade the Portuguese businessmen that had previously bankrolled RENAMO that their future interests lay in economic opportunities in a stabilized Mozambique. Therefore, despite RENAMO's more disciplined forces and sophisticated communications equipment, it could no longer hold out credible hope of defeating its more numerous opponent.

With both parties having therefore abandoned prospects of a military victory, the stage was set for more productive negotiations. One of the earliest attempts to facilitate a resolution of the conflict began in 1987 as the result of a joint Protestant and Catholic Church initiative. In the form of a 'Peace and Reconciliation Commission', both church groups attempted to persuade RENAMO's leaders to partake of the Government's amnesty. However, despite RENAMO's ostensible commitment to end the conflict, the Commission was unable to meet with its leader, Alfonso Dhlakama, until a round of talks was held in Nairobi in August 1989. Led by the Roman Catholic Bishop of Maputo, Cardinal Dos Santos, the Commission presented Dhlakama with the Government's '12 points', which it had offered as a basis for future discussions. The essential *quid pro quo* of the '12 points' was that RENAMO should renounce terrorism, banditry and all other forms of violence, in return for the reintegration of its former insurgents into society.[9] RENAMO replied by presenting its own '16 points' before the meetings ended on 14 August and the Commission returned to Mozambique to brief President Chissano on its efforts.

Although the Government defined most of RENAMO's 'points' as reasonable, it could not consent to its fifth 'point', which demanded that RENAMO be recognized as a political party. The Government was not averse to allowing individual members of RENAMO to compete in democratic elections (through the amnesty or an agreement to end the war), but it could not accept the participation of what it perceived to be a terrorist organization. Chissano's unwillingness to compromise on this issue led him to reject RENAMO's whole package as 'meaningless'.[10] Emboldened by the unfolding events in Angola, which were causing both Mozambican parties to question the utility of further talks, Dhlakama was to be equally as intransigent over the issue. Even the involvement of Presidents Mugabe of Zimbabwe and Moi of Kenya, who Chissano had requested to mediate the conflict earlier that year, could not break the deadlock.

Nevertheless, efforts to maintain a dialogue continued, with the US becoming directly involved in December with the presentation of its own seven-point plan as a basis for talks. Due to the requirement that RENAMO recognize 'the legitimacy of the Republic of Mozambique', Dhlakama initially rejected the US initiative. However, when invited to hold direct talks with the Government by Presidents Moi and Mugabe, he was astute enough to realize that such talks could confer legitimacy, if not parity, to his party. In fact, only strong pressure from the US and South Africa persuaded Dhlakama to drop his insistence that the Government attend the talks as simply another political party, rather than as the legitimate government of Mozambique. Despite both parties' acquiescence to face-to-face talks, only the intervention of *Sant' Egidio* (a Catholic lay organization dedicated to social concerns and based in Rome) led to agreement on an acceptable venue.[11]

All in all, *Sant' Egidio* was to host 12 rounds of talks in Rome between 8 July 1990 and 4 October 1992. Initially, two issues were to leave the talks in deadlock. The first was the issue of third party mediation. Chissano had long hoped to limit the intrusiveness of any third party, as he did not want to see a repeat of the UN and US role in Namibia, which he believed would compromise Mozambican sovereignty. Dhlakama, on the other hand, was well aware of his party's inability to hold the Government to a negotiated agreement and therefore favored a much more proactive role for the mediator, followed by a major role for the UN in the implementation of any agreement.

Therefore, whilst Chissano pushed for the government of Zimbabwe to act as the official mediator of the talks, RENAMO refused to accept the involvement of a state which had not only helped the Government conduct offensives in 1988–89, but which continued to station thousands of its troops on Mozambican soil in order to defend the Beira transport corridor (one of a number of transport corridors guarded by Zimbabwean and Malawian troops). The Government, however, refused to accept Kenya unless Zimbabwe was awarded an equal role. Eventually a compromise was struck to allow four official observers to the talks, all of whom were upgraded to the status of full mediators in September 1991. These were Mario Raffalli, an Italian Socialist parliamentarian, Archbishop Gonclaves, Andre Riccardi and Fr. Matteo Zuppi, the President and a member of *Sant' Egidio* respectively.[12]

The second issue to stall negotiations concerned the sequence of events, both of negotiations and implementation. The Government wanted

RENAMO not only to agree to a cease-fire immediately, but also to accept the country's new constitution and its plans for elections in 1991. RENAMO, on the other hand, wanted an agreement and concrete steps towards reforms to the political system and the constitution before it would adhere to a cease-fire. By the beginning of December only a partial cease-fire operating along the Beira and Limpopo transport corridors had been agreed. Although a Joint Verification Commission (JVC) composed of international observers was formed to monitor adherence to this cease-fire, problems over the demarcation of the corridors left the situation ambiguous. This resulted in RENAMO continuing to violate the cease-fire whilst protesting at the failure of the JVC to fulfill its duties.[13]

With both parties accusing each other of violating the cease-fire, little more was to be agreed before October 1991, except for an agenda for negotiations. Signed on 28 May the agenda outlined six areas requiring eventual agreement, including a future electoral system, military issues, a cease-fire, a law on political parties, a Donors Conference and guarantees for implementation. On the same day the UN Secretary-General, Boutros-Ghali, wrote to Chissano offering his organization's services in helping to implement any future agreement.[14]

The necessary breakthrough in negotiations was only to come in late September, when Dhlakama dropped his insistence on the formation of a transitional government after a cease-fire. He also abandoned his requests for the UN Security Council to take over five key ministries of the Government during a transitional period. Despite a similar arrangement having been agreed for Cambodia, or most probably because of it, the UN rejected such a role.[15]

Dhlakama's greater flexibility was to result in two agreements; Protocol I of 18 October and Protocol II of 13 November. The former agreement settled two issues of contention. The first was the question of the Government's legitimacy, which RENAMO had now accepted. The second was the principle of establishing a commission to oversee and monitor the implementation of the peace process. At this stage the UN was only envisaged as one of a number of members on such a commission.[16] The latter agreement recognized the Government's authority to register political parties, whilst providing for RENAMO to begin activity as a political party once a comprehensive agreement was signed.[17]

The ninth and tenth rounds of negotiations were eventually to result in the signing of Protocol III in March 1992. This agreement called specifically for assistance from the UN and OAU in the electoral process.[18] Discussions then concentrated on military issues, with the eleventh round of negotiations beginning on 10 June. With military issues now part of negotiations, the US, Portugal and Italy, began to adopt greater roles in the peace process. However, whilst the Government also wanted Britain and France to join the negotiations, RENAMO accused both countries of bias. The

Government, still fearful of losing its sovereignty, also rejected RENAMO's request for greater UN involvement. Nevertheless, two UN observers joined the negotiations in June 1992 and by August a UN Senior Political Affairs Officer was also present.[19]

Meanwhile, the parties were able to reach a compromise that allowed the constitution to be reformed before agreement on a cease-fire. This enabled Italian military officials, together with those from other observer delegations, to cooperate in drafting documents covering all military issues and a cease-fire. These drafts were modified to take account of UN procedures and its experiences in Angola.[20]

Chissano and Dhlakama met for the first time in Rome on 7 August, where they signed a joint declaration committing each of them to conclude a comprehensive agreement by 1 October. The joint declaration also committed them to '[accept] the role of the international community and especially that of the United Nations, in monitoring and guaranteeing the implementation of the General Peace Agreement (GPA), in particular the cease-fire and the electoral process.'[21] Boutros-Ghali wrote to Chissano on 19 August detailing the arrangements for a UN operation to help implement the impending GPA. Chissano replied by requesting the Secretary-General to send two technical teams to assess the Organization's requirements for monitoring both a cease-fire and the electoral process. Although Chissano wished the teams to arrive by 26 August, Boutros-Ghali did not dispatch them until the beginning of September.[22]

Though substantial progress had been made, an impasse had been reached on three issues covering the size of the new army, the reform of the police and the future of the State Information and Security Service (SISE). At the beginning of September RENAMO also raised questions over arrangements for territorial control during the transitional period. Dhlakama and Chissano met again on 18 September, this time in Gabarone, where they reached general understandings on the outstanding issues and reiterated their commitment to sign an agreement by 1 October.

Chissano wrote to Boutros-Ghali four days after this meeting to request the UN's financial support in the areas of national reconstruction; the reintegration of refugees; the demobilization of combatants; the formation of a new unified army; and the organization of democratic elections.[23] When the parties met again in Rome on 1 October, negotiations continued in order to reach final agreements on the police, the SISE, the civilian administration and the number and location of assembly areas for the parties' demobilizing troops. Only following these last minute discussions were Protocols IV through VII produced, covering military questions, guarantees, a cease-fire and a Donors Conference respectively. These Protocols were signed as part of the GPA on 4 October at a ceremony in Rome witnessed by several African leaders and the representatives of the observer countries.

3   The UN's disarmament mandate and the nature of the peace agreements

As described in the previous account, the GPA was to eventually consist of seven protocols that covered the agreement's basic principles; the criteria and arrangements for the formation and recognition of political parties; the principles of the Electoral Act; military questions; guarantees; the cease-fire; and Donors Conference respectively.[24]

Protocol I created the central authority with responsibility for overseeing the whole peace process, the Supervisory and Control Commission (CSC). Its role was not only to act as the final arbiter of disputes, but also to coordinate and guide the activities of certain subsidiary commissions. These included the Cease-fire Commission; the Commission for the Reintegration of Demobilized Personnel; the Joint Commission for the Formation of the Mozambican Defense Force; the Police Commission; the National Information Commission; the National Commission on Administration; and the National Election Commission. It was to be composed of equal numbers of representatives from both internal parties, together with representatives from Britain, Italy, Portugal, France and the UN. In recognition of its enhanced role in the peace process the UN was also appointed Chair.

The National Election Commission (CNE) was mandated to oversee the provisions of Protocol III of the Accords, which required it to plan, organize and oversee the electoral process. It was to be composed of individuals whose 'professional and personal qualities [afforded] qualities of balance, objectivity and independence vis-à-vis all political parties', one third of whom were to be nominated by RENAMO.

Elections to the Presidency and Assembly were to be held simultaneously within one year of the GPA's signing (this period could be extended if 'circumstances' arose that might 'preclude its observance'). The presidential elections were to be held on the basis of an absolute majority vote, with the possibility of a second ballot between the two most popular candidates if such a majority had not been achieved.[25] Elections to the Assembly were to be conducted by proportional representation. The UN and Organization of African Unity (OAU) were requested to observe the electoral process and provide technical and material assistance. Funds to help the political parties finance their activities were expected to be provided by a Donors Conference, which the parties called for in Protocol VII and that they hoped would be held within a month of the GPA's signing.

Protocols IV and VI dealt with military questions and the cease-fire. The Cease-Fire Commission (CCF) was given the responsibility for both monitoring the cease-fire and for ensuring the separation, concentration and demobilization of the parties' forces. It was also to ensure the withdrawal of all foreign forces. Implementation was to begin with the cease-fire scheduled for 15 October 1992, a date known euphemistically within the GPA as E-Day.

During the first 30 days of the cease-fire the forces of both parties were to separate and proceed to certain specified assembly areas and billeting points. As the parties were unable to agree on specific locations for these points, the GPA stipulated only that the Government would have 29 of them and RENAMO another 20. Nevertheless, the parties agreed to designate precise locations for them no later than seven days after the signing of the GPA. The UN was to supervise all these specified locations and, in principle, maintain a continuous presence at all of them from E-Day.[26] In order that the UN could conduct its verification duties, the parties' committed themselves to supply it with complete inventories of their respective troop strengths and arms holdings on E-Day-6, E-Day, E-Day+6, E-Day+30 and then every 15 days thereafter.

The CCF was also to ensure the withdrawal of the Zimbabwean and Malawian troops still guarding the transport corridors. Their withdrawal was scheduled to begin at the same time as the concentration of both parties' forces and was to be completed by the end of the concentration process (E-Day+30). UN peacekeepers were to assume responsibility for the inviolability of these corridors until they could be replaced by troops from the new Mozambican armed forces.

Apart from those chosen to join the new armed forces, all assembled ex-combatants were to be immediately demobilized on reaching their specified locations (paramilitary and irregular forces were to be disbanded immediately after E-Day). Demobilization was to take place in five stages, each one lasting 30 days. During each stage 20 per cent of the total number of ex-combatants were to be demobilized, thus allowing the whole process to be complete within six months of E-Day. The UN was to 'assist [the CCF] in the implementation, verification and monitoring of the entire demobilization process'.

The sub-commission responsible for planning, organizing and monitoring the economic and social reintegration of the ex-combatants was the Commission for the Reintegration of Demobilized Personnel (CORE). However, the economic and social reintegration packages that the CORE hoped to provide were to be dependent on 'the resources made available through the framework of the Donors Conference'. The CCF and the CORE were each to be composed of representatives of the Government and RENAMO with the UN presiding as Chair of both.

The UN was not, however, to be given a role in the final three sub-commissions, the Joint Commission for the Formation of the Mozambican Defense Force (CCFADM), the National Police Affairs Commission (COMPOL) and the National Information Commission (COMINFO). The CCFADM was to organize and oversee the formation of the newly unified Mozambican Defense Force (FADM), which was to be 30,000 strong and composed of equal numbers from both parties.[27] Its formation was to take place simultaneously with the concentration, demobilization and reintegration of those troops not selected for it. This was to ensure that by the time the elections were held all former military personnel would have either joined the FADM or have reintegrated into society. The CCFADM was to be composed of former members of the FAM and RENAMO forces, together with representatives of countries selected to advise them in the process.

The COMPOL and COMINFO were expected to monitor the workings of the 18,000 strong Police of the Republic of Mozambique (PRM) and the SISE. Although the UN had offered to supervise the PRM, the Government had refused it on the basis that the role would be too intrusive. Both the COMPOL and the COMINFO were to be composed of 21 members, with the Government and RENAMO contributing six each. The rest were to be chosen in consultation with the country's President.

Despite the lack of a UN role in these latter sub-commissions it was evident that as a whole the GPA had provided the UN with a highly intrusive mandate. And as Boutros-Ghali observed, even though the UN was not required to monitor all proceedings, 'the supervisory role allocated to the Organization carried the implication of responsibility for the entire peace process. The implementation of each part of the process was likely to come under the purview of the CSC and, therefore of the UN.'[28]

4   Implementation

The implementation of the GPA was not to have an auspicious beginning. The UN's only presence in Mozambique during the first five months of the operation was to consist of the newly appointed SRSG, Aldo Ajello, together with 25 military observers and a handful of political and administrative staff. Boutros-Ghali was thus forced to write to both parties stating that the viability of the cease-fire would initially 'depend critically on the political will and strict compliance of the two parties with the agreed modalities'.[29] Unfortunately for the Secretary-General, neither party complied. RENAMO even launched one of its largest military offensives in recent years.

The parties were also unable to agree on the location for their respective troop assembly areas or form any of the commissions designated to oversee the peace process. Whilst the Government blamed the latter problem on the absence of RENAMO's delegations from Maputo, RENAMO blamed it on the Government's failure to provide adequate transport, accommodation and communications for its delegations. Meanwhile, Boutros-Ghali complained that the prevarications of both parties were limiting the capacity of the UN to carry out its own tasks.[30] Only on 4 November, one month after the signing of the GPA, did the CSC hold its first meeting.[31]

Problems were also to arise over the failure of the Zimbabwean and Malawian troops to even begin withdrawing before the date specified for them to have left completely. Although Boutros-Ghali had wanted UN troops to assume responsibility for the Beira and Nacala transport corridors, normal UN procedures meant such a deployment could take up to three or four months to organize. He therefore requested the Italian government to deploy a self-sufficient troop battalion that he hoped would be on the ground within two to three weeks. However, only in early December was President Mugabe successful in persuading Dhlakama to allow an extension of the foreign troops' presence until the Italians could relieve them.[32]

In this context and on the basis of information supplied by the small number of personnel already deployed, Boutros-Ghali concluded his operational plan for ONUMOZ. Instead of the few hundred military observers that had initially been envisaged, he now requested the deployment of an additional 7,500 peacekeepers in order to facilitate the quick withdrawal of the foreign troops. Also, in light of the debacle in Angola, he sought two substantial changes to the UN's original plans. The first was the adoption of a role in ensuring the neutrality of the Mozambican police. Although the Government had previously rejected such a role for the UN, Boutros-Ghali alluded to experience 'elsewhere' that had demonstrated that such a role might be desirable 'in order to inspire confidence that violations of civil liberties, human rights and political freedoms will be avoided'.[33] He therefore authorized SRSG Ajello to re-open discussions on the matter with both parties.[34]

The second proposed change concerned the number of electoral observers. In the aftermath of the Angolan elections, Boutros-Ghali quickly revised the UN's estimate for the number of observers required in Mozambique, deciding to increase their number to 1,200. He also expressed his belief that the elections should not take place 'until the military aspects of the agreement [had] been fully implemented', even if this required an extension of the UN's presence.[35] So, in the midst of a Government counter-offensive designed to recapture territory lost to RENAMO in October, the Secretary-General had proposed a significant expansion of the UN's presence. Accepting his recommendations, the Security Council established ONUMOZ on 16 December 1992 and authorized the dispatch of 7,500 troops with 128 police observers.[36]

As expected, the reaction of the parties to the Secretary-General's report differed fundamentally. Only the Security Council's determination to prevent a recurrence of events in Angola helped the Secretary-General overcome the Government's objections to the size of his proposed force. It had originally expected only 100 to 300 unarmed military observers.[37] On the other hand, RENAMO continued to complain that the failure of the UN to expeditiously deploy its troops was allowing the Government to transform its police into a 'pseudo-military' force and create its own private army of mercenaries. Dhlakama had also begun to insist that he would not demobilize his forces until at least 65 per cent of the UN's troops had deployed.[38]

Although Boutros-Ghali was able to blame the Mozambican parties themselves for much of the delay in deploying UN troops, it was evident that bureaucratic delays in his own organization were also playing a part. Despite valiant attempts to circumvent some of the worst bureaucratic encumbrances, including expediting the deployment of troops before a UN budget had been passed, only by May were the majority of them deployed. This at least allowed the Zimbabwean and Malawian troops guarding the transport corridors to leave. Nevertheless, the UN's slow deployment had simply mirrored the slippage occurring in other areas of the peace process.

The first of these areas was the failure of the parties to form the commissions required to oversee the implementation of the GPA. With most of the commissions either operating sporadically or not at all, important questions relating to the peace process could not even be addressed. The closely related nature of the tasks assigned to each commission also meant that the failure of some of them to function was hampering progress in those already established.[39]

The second area concerned the lack of demobilization. RENAMO's demands for a substantial UN deployment before the start of the demobilization process had resulted in neither party submitting plans for the concentration of their troops before April. The unsuitable conditions existing at most of their designated assembly areas meant the concentration of troops was inadvisable anyway. By the end of June the CCF had approved only 13 assembly areas and only six (three for both parties) were declared by ONUMOZ to have been fully prepared.[40]

With demobilization and the organization of elections falling well behind schedule, the Secretary-General was forced to admit temporary defeat and negotiate a new timetable. The parties now agreed to hold elections one year later than originally planned, in October 1994.[41] The concentration of forces was now to begin in September, with the start of demobilization scheduled for November. At least half of the forces of both parties were to be demobilized by January 1994, with the whole process to be complete by the following May. The FADM was to be formed by September 1994. Even so, Boutros-Ghali still believed the new timetable to be a 'rather tight schedule', during which 'any delays would result in a significant postponement'.[42]

Initially, the peace process was to gather momentum. A series of personal meetings between Dhlakama and Chissano in late August led to a couple of significant agreements, the first of which was to incorporate all RENAMO held areas into the State administration. Dhlakama had made the resolution of this issue yet another prerequisite for RENAMO's demobilization. A second agreement led to a request from both parties for the UN to monitor all police activities, both public and private, as well as to provide support to the COMPOL. The Government had also indicated its intention to seek international help in reorganizing its Quick Reaction Police.[43] By October

Dhlakama had made the deployment of UN police observers another prerequisite for demobilization.[44]

Despite these agreements, the inability of the parties to agree on other fundamental issues led Boutros-Ghali to visit Maputo to meet with both leaders personally. By the time his three-day visit had ended on 20 October he had forged a number of agreements that he believed had created 'a new momentum in the peace process'.[45] These agreements resolved issues relating to the demobilization of the estimated 155,600 paramilitary and other irregular forces present in the country, which were now to be demobilized simultaneously with the regular forces. They also found acceptable chairs for the National Commission on Administration (CNA), COMINFO and COMPOL; settled disagreements over the composition of the CNE and established a timetable for finalizing an electoral law; and lastly, established criteria to enable the CCF to distinguish between troop movements that violated the cease-fire agreement and those that did not. With these obstacles removed a new timetable was approved that allowed an extra two months for the first 50 per cent of their respective forces to be demobilized. Nevertheless, the whole process was still to be complete by May.[46]

Unfortunately, the new momentum produced by the October agreements was to create its own problems. When the assembly process finally began at the end of November, a massive influx of troops to the assembly areas caused severe overcrowding. This was mainly due to the assembly areas having the capacity to accommodate only between 30 and 50 per cent of the total number of troops at any one time. The failure of the soldiers to arrive at the areas incrementally thus led quickly to shortages of food, inadequate lodging, overloaded storage facilities and potential health hazards.[47] These problems were exacerbated by the inability of the parties to find acceptable sites for some of the planned assembly areas. By 20 December only 35 of the 49 assembly areas designated in the GPA were actually operating.

Though initially a much larger proportion of Government than RENAMO troops assembled, this trend was soon reversed. By the end of January 1994 only 22 per cent of Government troops had assembled, whilst 60 per cent of RENAMO's had done the same. The weapons surrendered by both groups were also found to be fewer than expected and in generally poor condition, yet neither party allowed even these to be transferred to regional warehouses. With the storage capacities of the assembly areas already far exceeded, the UN was forced to store the weapons 'at unsafe locations', thereby 'placing at risk not only [Government] and RENAMO soldiers, but also UN personnel.'[48]

With inadequate conditions and over-stretched resources, tensions in the assembly areas were beginning to escalate. ONUMOZ reported 20 violent protests by disgruntled soldiers between January and April alone. And following attacks on UN personnel, the Secretary-General was forced to deploy military contingents around the assembly areas in an attempt to provide greater security. The situation deteriorated even further when the troops of both parties began refusing demobilization due to the Government's failure to administer back-pay and the lower than expected demobilization packages provided to RENAMO's troops.[49]

In a move to try and ease the mounting pressure, both parties agreed to demobilize 17,000 soldiers (including 4,830 disabled combatants) at some 70 locations around the country. They also agreed to send 5,000 troops (2,500 each) to the FADM training centers without first passing them through the assembly areas. Consequently, only 13,000 troops had left the assembly areas by mid-April, a number that included 20 per cent and 3 per cent of Government and RENAMO troops respectively.[50]

The crisis in demobilization was overshadowing greater achievements in other areas. The National Assembly had approved an Electoral Law in December and the CNE had subsequently met for the first time on 15 February 1994. In addition, at least three quarters of the four million internally displaced had resettled in rural areas by April and half of the 1.6 million refuges in neighboring countries had returned home. The transfer of arms from assembly areas to regional depots, which had begun in mid-March, was now being conducted on a regular basis.[51]

Nevertheless, the difficulties facing the demobilization process continued to mount. By early July only 28,000 soldiers had demobilized, leading the Secretary-General to warn that there was 'a danger that three armies [would] be in existence in Mozambique during the election period...[which]...could pose a threat to stability and thus to the holding of free and fair elections...[as well as the]...peaceful formulation of the new government.[52]

By the end of the same month thousands more soldiers had gone on the rampage, seizing hostages, attacking civilians, looting shops and markets and demanding immediate demobilization. UN personnel were threatened and their vehicles highjacked.[53] Realizing that much of the soldiers' protests concerned their desire not to continue in army life, SRSG Ajello warned the parties that forcing their troops to remain in the military was only weakening their credibility. Heeding his warning, both parties agreed to allow individual soldiers to choose whether they wished to join the FADM.[54]

In an effort to 'convey concern at the delays, remind the parties of their obligation' and stress its full support for the peace process, the UN Security Council sent a small mission to visit the country in early August. Although this mission witnessed an acceleration of the demobilization process (it even witnessed the demobilization of President Chissano) its overall assessment was a cautious one. Despite believing that the requisite criteria for the holding of free and fair elections were being achieved, it still warned that:

The country [would] be going into the elections without a fully constituted and properly equipped army. The police are weak, poorly trained and lack the right equipment. On the other had, thousands of soldiers, whose only skill is the use of weapons, have been demobilized and are without alternative employment. Armed banditry is spreading, especially in the countryside and the situation may become critical.[55]

When the Secretary-General produced his report at the end of August his comments reiterated the mission's conclusions. In particular, he noted that during the previous month criminal activity and banditry had increased and rioting among assembled and unassembled soldiers had become 'frequent and violent'.[56]

The good news, however, was that by the end of August the demobilization process had been substantially completed, with 78,000 of the nearly 92,000 registered soldiers having been demobilized. Over 7,000 more had joined the FADM. ONUMOZ had also collected 190,000 weapons from the military and paramilitary forces of both sides (together with some from the general population) and discovered a number of weapons caches, some containing large quantities of arms.[57] Nevertheless, with the continuing refusal of the parties to allow ONUMOZ full access to their storage facilities, it was apparent that huge weapon stocks remained hidden.[58] With the elections just six days away, the Secretary-General expressed his own concerns in his 21 October report, stating that although the electoral process was progressing well, he was:

> ...concerned that there are still so many uncollected weapons and munitions throughout the country, including in undeclared and so far unverified depots. This problem has been exacerbated by the parties' lack of co-operation in the verification of some military bases and certain political installations, including those of the Quick Reaction Police.[59]

The electoral campaign, which had begun in a calm and constructive atmosphere, was itself now degenerating into mutual recriminations and even physical attacks. As the elections approached, RENAMO accused the Government of a number of fraudulent acts that it believed the CNE had failed to investigate.[60] Dhalakama's treatment at a regional summit in Harare also convinced him that he was being pressured into accepting a fixed election.[61] So, despite promising two days before the elections that he would never return to war even if he lost the vote, Dhlakama announced his withdrawal from the ballot the following day.[62] Under pressure from all quarters Dhlakama agreed to rejoin the competition, but to remedy the confusion caused by his actions a third day of voting was added.[63]

Subsequently, the Chair of the CNE announced the election results on 19 November. Between 27–29 October 87.9 per cent of all registered voters had cast their ballots, with 53.3 per cent voting for Chissano and 33.7 per cent voting for Dhlakama.[64] In the legislative elections FRELIMO had won 44.3 per cent of the vote, whilst RENAMO had won a respectable 37.8 per cent.[65] Immediately after the announcement Ajello declared the elections to have been both free and fair. Consequently, the new Assembly of the Republic was installed on 8 December and the inauguration of the newly elected President took place the following day. With these events the ONUMOZ mandate expired and Ajello left the country on 13 December.[66]

5   Analysis of the operation

5.1   Funding, administration and deployment

Although the Cambodian operation had ended during 1993, the UN's increasing commitments in Somalia and Yugoslavia were stretching its resources to breaking point. By the end of January 1994 the UN had accumulated a deficit of more than \$1.4 billion in assessed contributions for its peacekeeping budget alone.[67] At the same time the cost of peacekeeping had risen to around \$3.2 billion a year, compared with a total price tag of just \$9.4 billion for all of the UN's operations since 1948. The number of deployed troops had also reached approximately 70,000.[68]

This emerging crisis in funding had been precipitated by the election of a Republican led US Congress in 1993 and the subsequent fateful experiences of American troops in Somalia. By the end of the year Congress had decided on a number of measures that were to have far-reaching consequences for UN peacekeeping. Firstly, it declared that America's contributions to the UN budget would have to be reduced from 31.7 per cent to 25 per cent. Secondly, it rejected a rather modest proposal from the Pentagon for \$10 million to help strengthen the UN's Situation Center in New York. Thirdly, it decided to withhold 10 per cent of America's regular contributions to the UN until the Secretary-General appointed an Inspector-General to eliminate corruption. And finally, it approved fiscal 1994 spending bills that cut the Administration's peacekeeping request by 32 per cent, 'effectively killing a proposed peacekeeping contingency fund that would have enabled the US to contribute emergency start-up funds to unforeseen peacekeeping operation's the following year'.[69]

The insidious effects of the failure of the US and other states to contribute adequately to the UN budget were already being felt during 1993. For example, in order to facilitate the process of financing the start-up of peacekeeping operations, the UN General Assembly had established a Peacekeeping Reserve Fund in December 1992. Although designed primarily to provide the Secretary-General with sufficient funds to finance the early stages of an operation (whilst the usual cumbersome and timely budgetary processes were pursued), the failure of member states to make systematic payments to the accounts of already existing peacekeeping operations had resulted in the Secretary-General borrowing from the Fund to keep them afloat. This had resulted in the Fund becoming insufficient to provide even the most basic start-up costs for newly established operations.

In this context ONUMOZ was to suffer similar impediments to those that had affected the operations in Angola and Cambodia. As in the case of the latter two, many of the delays in establishing ONUMOZ were to be caused by the absence of an overall budget. The UN's budgetary process, complex and cumbersome enough in any situation, had been exacerbated by the uncertain political situation in Mozambique.[70] Nevertheless, the Security Council made as little as $9.5 million available pending the budget's approval, thereby preventing the purchasing of most of the operation's essential equipment, as well as the long-term leasing of aircraft and office space. The recruitment and deployment of key personnel had also been impeded.[71] Recognizing the effect this was having on the implementation of the GPA, the General Assembly appropriated a lump sum of $140 million to cover the period up to the end of June 1993. The Secretary-General himself acknowledged that only this action allowed the requisitioning for many items of equipment to even begin.[72]

However, the retarded deployment of the military component was not only caused by the lack of an approved budget. Rather, the Secretary-General was to be continually frustrated by the simple reluctance of member states to contribute troops. As he stated as late as April 1993:

> Although I began to approach [troop] contributors...as early as September [1992], the final composition of ONUMOZ military units has not yet been completed. Some countries which several months ago signaled their intention to provide troops to this operation [have] only recently informed the Secretariat of their readiness to dispatch them.[73]

The repercussions of this delay were pervasive. Although necessary to allow the Zimbabwean and Malawian troops to depart, the military component was also expected to play a critical role in the provision of logistical support to the assembly areas and in the collection, storage and destruction of weapons.[74] One year after the Cambodian operation had compelled him to make a similar statement, the Secretary-General reiterated in his April 1993 report that 'the UN clearly needs more rapid and effective means as well as more flexible practices'.[75]

SGSR Ajello, whose own experience of the UN's procurement system had led to him to believe that the administrative units in New York had simply become overwhelmed, shared Boutros-Ghali's exasperation. Although necessary for them to conduct their duties, he could not even supply his military observers with vehicles, because '...to get vehicles I have to go through the Contract Committee in New York...[and]...That takes months!' Although Ajello understood that the UN's budget committees had been designed to protect the interests of the world's taxpayers, he still believed that the kind of mission ONUMOZ was conducting required 'different procedures'.[76] There appeared to be no immediate remedies. By the beginning of March 1994 the progress in the peace process, coupled with the depletion of ONUMOZ's air resources, had begun to aggravate the delivery of basic goods to the assembly areas and had already brought the process of disarming the paramilitaries to a standstill.[77]

5.2   Planning and the nature of the peace agreements

Although ONUMOZ's initial planning was conducted by only the recently appointed SRSG and a small group of UN personnel, it was apparent from the operation's eventual composition and mandate that the UN had learnt many valuable lessons from its experiences in Angola. Firstly, despite the Mozambican government's initial misgivings the UN had insisted on a relatively large military presence. Secondly, the UN had revised the number of electoral observers it required, increasing their number to over 2,100 (these were supplemented by 35,000 observers from the Mozambican parties). And thirdly, the UN had insisted on a much more intrusive role in the commissions designed to oversee the implementation of the peace process.

This latter change owed much to the insistence of the former SRSG in Angola, Margaret Anstee, who had persuaded the Secretary-General to write to the President of the Security Council on the eve of the Rome summit in order to emphasize the importance of entrusting the chair of the supervisory commissions to a third party.[78] By insisting on this provision the Secretary-General provided ONUMOZ with a more effective role in the peace process, allowing it to work as a mediator, to initiate contingency plans and to urge compliance from the parties when necessary.[79]

Unfortunately for ONUMOZ, the pressure that the international community needed to apply on the Mozambican parties to prevent the repetition of previous mistakes was not always forthcoming. In this sense it was obvious that the need for an agreement to be signed seemed once again to outweigh the inherent inadequacies in the agreement itself. As the proceeding accounts will elucidate, this meant that the UN would be compelled to undertake a second negotiating process with the parties in order to enhance its role in the areas of public security and the formation of the unified armed forces.

Perhaps the most ridiculous aspect of the Accords, however, was the initial operational timetable.[80] As Boutros-Ghali realized in December 1992:

> To achieve in one year (of which a month and a half have already passed) the assembly, disarmament and demobilization of the two sides' troops, the formation of new armed forces, the resettlement of 5–6m refugees and displaced persons, the provision of humanitarian relief to all parts of the country and the organization and conduct of elections [would] require a

huge and co-operative effort by the Government and RENAMO and by the international community, with the UN in the lead.[81]

In the environment of deep mistrust that characterized this and other civil conflicts, to expect such a 'huge and co-operative effort' would have been naive in the extreme. To construct a timetable around it, however, was simply ludicrous. SRSG Ajello himself described the timetable as a 'big mistake', as it put a great deal of pressure on ONUMOZ to meet obligations and commitments and gave the parties an opportunity to question the UN's seriousness and capabilities.[82]

5.3   Disarmament, demobilization, reintegration and the formation of unified armed forces

Although ONUMOZ was to eventually achieve great success in its disarmament and demobilization mandates in Mozambique, initially both processes were to suffer from similar problems to those that had beset its previous operations in Angola and Cambodia. These problems were principally caused by two deficiencies. The first was a lack of precision in the Accords, particularly in those areas involving the locations of the assembly areas, the extension of the Government's administration into RENAMO held territory and in the disarmament and demobilization of paramilitary forces. The second was the UN's inability to verify the exact strength of each party's forces due to its lack of independent intelligence gathering capabilities.

The failure to negotiate exact locations for the parties' assembly areas was to cause one of the first delays to the disarmament and demobilization processes. Despite recognition that the size and difficulty of the ONUMOZ operation would be directly related to the number and location of these points, negotiations could only arrive on a consensus to establish a maximum number of 49 before the agreement was signed.[83] The Secretary-General predicted the difficulties that this lack of precision would cause when he informed the Security Council on the eve of the Rome summit that:

> At a similar stage of the peace process in Angola, detailed information was already available about the numbers and locations of the assembly areas agreed by the two sides and a United Nations peacekeeping operation (UNAVEM I) was deployed in that country and, being on the point of completing its mandate was able to devote considerable resources to preparing, on the ground, the new tasks which it would assume under the Peace Agreements of Angola. These conditions do not, unfortunately, exist in the case of Mozambique where the details of the cease-fire agreement are not yet known and the United Nations operation would have to be established from scratch.[84]

When the parties finally did designate their preferred assembly locations the UN found that they had been chosen not for logistical suitability, but simply 'for their importance for control over certain areas'.[85] Inaccessible, lacking essential services and water, and in some cases mined, the geographical location of many of the sites had to be changed at the UN's request. Although this problem had been largely overcome by the end of June 1993, a number of sites that were still awaiting approval by the CCF five months later continued to have their approval delayed on the grounds of 'logistical unsuitability'.[86]

Logistical unsuitability was not, however, the only difficulty facing the assembly process. Just as the GPA had lacked geographical precision in locating the assembly areas, it had also lacked a precise arrangement for the future administrative control of RENAMO held territory. Even before signing the GPA, Dhlakama had made apparent his unwillingness to replace his own representatives with FRELIMO members in areas under his control. Unsurprisingly, Dhlakama believed such a move would be the 'undoing' of his organization.[87]

Under pressure to reach some form of agreement the parties struck a compromise, which although ambiguous enough to enable them to sign, only served to stall the essential practical questions it had failed to address. When the time came for the assembly process to begin, therefore, Dhlakama refused to sanction the necessary orders until these administrative questions had been resolved. And even when an agreement was reached in August 1993 to allow a single administration at the provincial and district levels, the absence of the CNA meant it could not be implemented. The adverse effect of the GPA's ambiguities over administrative issues was manifest in the postponement of the approval of the final 14 assembly areas until January 1994 due to a dispute between the parties over control of two locations at Salamanga and Dunda.[88]

The failure of the GPA to adequately address the existence of paramilitary forces was also to hinder the start of the disarmament and demobilization processes.[89] As in Cambodia the number of irregular forces in Mozambique far exceeded the number of regular troops, yet they were to receive relatively minor attention compared to their more formally organized counterparts. Lacking a precise definition of what constitutes such forces UN verification teams were left reliant on the parties themselves to identify the approximately 156,000 paramilitary troops believed to exist in Mozambique. This allowed bands of militias to continue to exist, some with up to 1,000 members, simply because neither party had presented them for disarmament.[90]

RENAMO was thereby presented with yet another reason to stall its disarmament whilst the parties searched for an agreement on how the disbandment of government irregulars should be conducted. Dhlakama even called for their disbandment before the assembly of regular troops could begin.[91]

Although originally expected to coincide with the disarmament of the regular forces at the beginning of 1993, the lack of an adequate agreement continued to impede the process until January 1994.

The second deficiency to adversely affect the disarmament and demobilization processes was ONUMOZ's inability to independently verify the honesty of the parties' declarations of their military capabilities. As when UNITA in Angola had announced that it had 20,000 fewer troops than it had claimed during negotiations, the vulnerability of the UN to the potential subterfuge of local parties was again made apparent when the Mozambican government announced a revision of its troop strength in April 1994. A full one-and-a-half years after the start of the operation, it now declared it had nearly 15,000 fewer troops than it had originally estimated.[92] Although the parties were able to negotiate a mutually acceptable figure two months later, the ability of the parties to circumvent the UN's verification mechanisms was only fully exposed by post-demobilization verification teams, which found a substantial number of weapons, including tanks, anti-aircraft guns, mines, armored personnel carriers and mortar bombs at 754 locations.[93] Estimations of the number of troops withheld from the disarmament process ranged as high as 2,000 for RENAMO and 4,000 for the Government.[94]

Fortunately, despite the persistence of these problems, the UN's planning for demobilization and reintegration and the resources dedicated to each process had improved exponentially for ONUMOZ. The UN's planning in this regard was initially assisted by work undertaken by the Swiss Agency for Development and Cooperation (SDC), which had been requested by the Mozambican government in the early 1990s to formulate plans for the reduction of the FAM and Ministry of Defense by up to 45,000 and 6,000 personnel respectively.[95] Although the SDC's plans were never implemented as originally intended, they were hurriedly incorporated into the UN's own plans before the Secretary-General presented his operational plan in December 1992.

Included in the Secretary-General's plan was the creation of two bodies that were to play unprecedented roles in the demobilization process. The first was the UN Office for the Coordination of Humanitarian Assistance (UNOHAC), which as part of its coordinating role was to oversee the provision of assistance programs to demobilizing soldiers.[96] This was to be the first time that humanitarian assistance was to be extended to include aspects of a demobilization process.[97] Strengthened by its adoption of the Chair of CORE, UNOHAC designed and coordinated a number of programs for the demobilization and reintegration phases. These included a career counseling and problem-solving service, an occupational skills development program and the creation of a provincial fund to provide small and medium sized grants for the employment of former soldiers.[98]

A fourth component of the reintegration program, entitled the Re-integration Support Scheme (RSS), provided severance pay to demobilizing soldiers. In recognition of the inability of the Mozambican economy to absorb thousands of new job seekers the donor agencies extended the period during which pay would be provided from 6 to 24 months.[99] According to SRSG Ajello this extended RSS achieved two results. The first was that it prevented a great deal of violence and banditry, thus helping to establish an environment more conducive to electoral campaigning. The second was that it limited what he described as the 'Angolan scenario', in which both Angolan parties had held back hidden reserves. 'When we announced that the international community would pay an additional salary of 18 months to all soldiers swiftly demobilized, the first to show up for demobilization were those very reserve troops'.[100]

The second body in the Secretary-General's plan was a Technical Unit, which was to be staffed by civilians and that was to work closely with UNOHAC to provide essential assistance to demobilizing soldiers. This assistance included the distribution of food, medicine and other essential services at the assembly areas; the organization of a database; the supply of civilian clothing; the organization of transport home; and the estab-lishment of a solid-link with the provincial and district authorities responsible for the civilian dimensions of the demobilization process.[101] The Technical Unit, which was subsequently heralded as one of the oper-ation's innovations to peacekeeping, was in fact the embodiment of the SDC's work.[102]

Despite these improvements a lack of finance still threatened the long-term success of reintegration. In late 1993 the Secretary-General reported that the failure of many donors to indicate how they wanted their money spent, together with a shortfall of $70 million in pledges, was causing an 'unnecessary hindrance' to the reintegration programs, including the supply of agricultural seeds and tools.[103] Similar problems were affecting the RSS. Following its initiation in mid-1994 the RSS budget requirement had been estimated to be $31.9 million. However, only $27.6 million had been pledged and by the end of its tenure ONUMOZ had received only $8.9 million.[104] The full extent of the problem was expressed by the Security Council's mission in late 1994, which having witnessed the critical state of Mozambique's social and economic situation, concluded that:

Changes following in the wake of the peace process, including demobi-lization and the return of refugees and displaced persons, are increasing social instability. The humanitarian assistance programs are too limited to address the scope of the problem. In particular, the demobilized could become a source of social unrest for a long time to come. This issue must be carefully reviewed and ways of assisting the present and new Government in addressing the problem beyond the boundaries of the humanitarian assistance component and the ONUMOZ mandate will have to be sought.[105]

Finally, as the GPA had provided no role for the UN in the creation of the FADM it was left with little influence on the parties when the process began to lag behind. For this reason the Secretary-General received permission from the Security Council to allow Ajello to assume the chairmanship of the CCFADM, which held its first meeting on 22 July 1993.[106] ONUMOZ also offered logistical support to the process, but only as far as it did not cause an increase in the mission's overall budget.[107] Although the primary responsibility for the training of the FADM had been entrusted to Britain, France and Portugal, the UN's late and limited support denied the process the essential impetus it required.

Consequently, the FADM's numbers had reached only 10,000 by the time of the elections. However, the reason for its low number of recruits lay more with the combatants themselves than with the parties or the UN. As the operation progressed it became increasingly obvious that the majority of former soldiers simply did not want to continue in army life. This was reflected in a UN poll in late 1994 that showed only 2.1 per cent of assembled soldiers wished to join the new force, whilst 97.7 per cent wanted to be demobilized.[108] Their previous experience of poor conditions and late pay no doubt played a substantial part in their decision.

Nevertheless, the primary reason cited for their preference was the greater assistance awarded to demobilizing soldiers, as well as the latter's option of finding a second income.[109] The failure to recognize this discrepancy in benefits when each party selected the soldiers they wished to join the FADM, led to a number of violent protests in the assembly areas. It was in the hope of avoiding a continuation of these protests that Ajello had persuaded the parties to rely solely on voluntary recruits.

5.4   Reform of public security

Public security was to be another area in which the demand to reach an agreement took precedence over the need to ensure adequate provisions in the GPA. The Agreement itself had provided no role for the UN in ensuring the creation of either a neutral police force or impartial judicial system. Only the Secretary-General's determination to rectify this omission motivated him to include 128 police observers in his operational plan of late 1992. His decision was understandable given that he had already cited the delay in setting up a neutral police force as one of the root causes of the collapse of the Angolan peace process.

Nevertheless, attempting to renegotiate the provisions for police supervision while the operation was progressing made the issue even more difficult to address. Only in late August 1993 was the UN able to illicit a request from the Mozambican parties for ONUMOZ to monitor all police activities, as well as to provide technical support to the COMPOL. Embarrassingly, however, the Secretary-General was forced to inform the parties, during his personal visit to the country two months later, that it was unrealistic to expect even the initial 128 CIVPOLS to be deployed at short notice due to the UN's dearth of finances and other commitments.[110]

When the CIVPOLS eventually were deployed they were to have an immediate effect. Even with fewer than 300 in the country the Secretary-General was still able to declare in April 1994 that the 'beneficial confidence-building effect of an increasing CIVPOL deployment [was] already obvious'.[111] Nevertheless, despite the deployment of 1,059 CIVPOLS by the end of the operation, their introduction had simply come too late in the day.[112] With the PRM still unable to cope with either the rioting of assembled soldiers or the rising tide of banditry, the battle to engender a credible local police force had already been lost. By the end of the operation the PRM had not only failed to establish itself in RENAMO areas, but had also failed to take the disciplinary or preventive measures recommended following CIVPOL investigations into human rights abuses. The Government had also managed to restrict CIVPOL access to both the Quick Reaction Police and a number of police training centers until just two weeks before the elections.[113] As the UN had already discovered that some police were being trained in the use of heavy weapons, the potential repercussions of this were obvious.[114]

5.5 Strategies of conflict resolution

With both parties having retained substantial military capabilities, it was apparent that neither party had complete confidence in their opponent's commitment to the democratic process. However, unlike UNITA in Angola, RENAMO did not return to war even though it lost the elections. As this section will show, the reason for this difference lies with the UN's timely appreciation of the security dilemmas facing the parties as they entered into the democratic process. In this respect the UN had finally learnt the lessons of Angola and Cambodia.

Nevertheless, at least initially, the UN had taken little account of the ability of the parties to compete in the democratic elections it hoped to organize just one year after the signing of the GPA. Although the Government's propaganda apparatus must have provided it with at least a basis for competing in elections, RENAMO had no such facilities. Apart from its call for democratic elections and a market economy, serious questions remained as to whether RENAMO had any independent political platform at all.[115]

For example, when RENAMO's political status was questioned during an insurance claim in 1991, the Commercial Court in London was forced to rule on whether RENAMO held political objectives or was simply the foreign creation of Rhodesia and South Africa. In his decision, Mr. Justice

Saville, explained that the normal criteria used to distinguish political parties would not suffice, because:

> The idea that any genuine political movement would necessarily have to prepare and publish carefully formulated programs or manifestos for future government and seek to disseminate these views in the country is a peculiarly Western concept which to my mind cannot simply be applied to an organization such as RENAMO operating in a country such as Mozambique.[116]

This is reiterated by Young, who suggests that too '[much] has been made...of the absence of a RENAMO political program because in Western conceptions politics is about programs, ideological beliefs, calculations of political support from different kinds of groups and so on'.[117] If these appreciations of RENAMO are correct, they at the very least imply that it was not ready to compete in Western style democratic elections.

The lack of preparation by both parties for their future undertakings first become evident in their inability to form the set of commissions established by the GPA. As one observer of the Rome Summit in 1992 stated, the parties had obviously 'little idea how to set up, let alone operate, the complex set of commissions, committees, and subcommittees they [had] insisted on creating'.[118] Somewhat surprisingly, the GPA had included no provisions to support the parties in setting up these commissions, or for their transformation into political parties in general.[119] The GPA had called only for help from the Donors Conference in funding the activities of the parties.

It was thus at the Donors Conference of December 1992 that the Working Group on the Electoral Process noted that there were no provisions in the UN's budget to support the political parties. Writing to the Secretary-General to convey the results of the Conference, the Italian government stated its agreement with the Working Group's conclusion that 'it was very important that equitable funding be provided for [this purpose] in order to ensure the success of the electoral process'.[120] The Italians reiterated this point in a further letter to the Secretary-General at the end of January, in which their Foreign Minister stated his conviction that there was an urgent need 'to meet the expectations of the Mozambican parties that a trust fund under the United Nations management be created to sustain the political parties at this stage of birth for democracy'.[121] However, only on 10 February, nearly three months after the signing of the GPA, did Boutros-Ghali reply to the Italians to inform them that the UN was now in a position to establish such a fund.[122]

Nevertheless, the actual creation of the 'Trust Fund for the Implementation of the GPA in Mozambique' did not occur until 10 May 1993, following which the Italians made their initial donation. The effect of this delay became immediately apparent when RENAMO refused to negotiate until the money had been paid. Ajello was also forced to provide the parties with a three-month 'safety net' following the rescheduling of the timetable in June 1993 so that they could retire from the process and prepare themselves 'because they [had come] into it with absolutely no cadres and no capacity to organize the complex process of demobilization, forming a new army, and moving to elections, which they had agreed in Rome'.[123] Thus, by both slowing the democratic process and providing sufficient resources to the parties the UN had managed to significantly reduce their security dilemmas.

It was also obvious that in providing greater resources to RENAMO the UN had taken greater account of the contextual rationality at play in Mozambican culture. In November 1993 Boutros-Ghali had called for the establishment of a 'more flexible instrument [than the present Trust Fund] through which to channel about $300,000 per month' to Dhlakama until the elections. In making his plea for additional money for this purpose, Boutros-Ghali explained that if 'the RENAMO leader is not enabled to meet the expectations of his supporters, he will lose the authority and prestige, and the entire peace process will be destabilized'.[124] SRSG Ajello reiterated this assessment, stating that 'Dhlakama is regarded as an African chief... and he needs to be able to act like one. He needs money to pension off his generals, to distribute largesse'. He believed the extra $4 million required to provide Dhlakama with his allowance until the elections was a 'small premium to ensure the future stability of Mozambique'.[125]

The UN had also begun to show greater appreciation for the need for internal security guarantees. This was evident in Ajello's attempts to get the parties to agree to a power-sharing arrangement that would 'make the [future] government comfortable and would prevent the loser feeling not that he has lost an election, but that he has lost the war'.[126] The Government, however, was not prepared to countenance such a settlement. Although President Chissano admitted in the middle of 1994 that he was coming under increasing pressure from foreign governments to form a government of national unity, he refused to accept that those 'who lose the elections should govern alongside those who win'.[127]

Fortunately for Mozambique, Dhlakama, as he so often said himself, was not another Savimbi. However, it was also apparent that Dhlakama's control over his forces was much weaker that his Angolan counterpart's. As ONUMOZ's demobilization process had proven, the vast majority of RENAMO's forces were badly fed and clothed and wanted nothing more than to return to their village homes. By offering Dhlakama and his party over $11 million (part of which bought him a bullet proof Mercedes and a beautiful house overlooking the Indian Ocean) the RENAMO leader was offered a means to save face and a far better alternative than a return to the bush.[128] Ajello expressed the importance of the Trust Fund in this regard, describing it just before the elections as a 'most valuable instrument' with which 'Dhlakama [had] accepted giving up the military option and saw his vital interest in RENAMO's transformation into a political party'.[129] Dhlakama's description of himself after the elections illuminates this delicate balance between democracy and status: 'I am the second most important man in Mozambique and I am leader of the opposition'.[130]

6   Conclusion

As Barbara Walter correctly identifies in her Neo-Realist analysis of the Mozambican peace process, RENAMO's security dilemmas were evident in the fact that it spent most of the negotiations leading to the GPA trying to extract security guarantees for both the implementation phase and the post-election era.[131] As this suggests the parties existed in a shared understanding of aggression during the negotiations, the twin-track framework advocated by this text would also suggest that these guarantees be provided. This would have required both the deployment of a sizeable UN military force and the negotiation of power-sharing arrangements.

However, as this chapter has explained, the Mozambican peace process initially failed to include either element. Only the ultimate failure of the UN's operation in Angola caused it to reassess its commitments in Mozambique, convincing it eventually to deploy a substantial military contingent. As SRSG Ajello noted, once deployed this force acted as 'a strong deterrent against any temptation to violate the cease-fire and...helped reduce the level of localized banditry'. It also played an essential role in the peace process by supplying logistical support and transport facilities to the disarmament of the parties' forces, the formation of the FADM and the electoral process.[132]

Though it had managed to rectify the omission of a sizeable military contingent, the UN could still not convince the Government to accept a power-sharing arrangement. RENAMO obviously possessed no post-election security guarantees without one. It was not surprising to find, therefore, that on top of its already agreed contribution to the FADM, RENAMO also sought to retain forces outside of the UN's disarmament process and to maintain its traditional areas of control.[133] Only through these measures could RENAMO ensure its post-election survival.

However, given that UNITA in Angola and the Khmer Rouge in Cambodia had also retained similar security guarantees, there is evidence to suggest that the shared understanding between the Mozambican parties was already transforming from one of aggression to one of competition by the time of the elections. This sense of transformation was particularly evident in RENAMO's own 'declaration' of the forces it had retained, which SRSG Ajello believed pointed to its good faith.[134] The fact that RENAMO was willing to accept electoral defeat without significant internal security guarantees also points to a transformation in the shared understanding between the parties.[135]

Integral to this transformation, of course, was the UN's sensitivity for RENAMO's initial inability to compete in democratic elections and for the contextual rationality at play in Mozambican culture. Thus, by delaying the elections, by allowing the elections to proceed whilst RENAMO remained armed, and by providing money and resources to RENAMO and Dhlakama, the UN was able to provide them with sufficient security and incentives to stay in the electoral process. Ajello was without doubt alluding to the importance of the all these factors when he attributed the success of ONUMOZ to the fact that it had not applied a fixed model of operations, but had instead taken the 'specific cultural and political environment [of Mozambique] into account'.[136]

Unfortunately, though the UN had also shown a new appreciation for the role of Track 1 diplomacy at the societal levels of ex-combatants and the general population, it was still unable to rectify its failure to initially ensure itself a role in the creation of a credible justice system. When the UN did eventually become involved it was simply too late in the day to have sufficient effect. Thus, by the end of the operation the PRM had still failed to establish itself in large areas of the country and had continued to act primarily as a partisan paramilitary force. Without the requisite security provided by both a neutral police force and an impartial judicial system there could be little hope that demobilized ex-combatants would remain unarmed or that the general population would relinquish its weapons.

Despite this disappointment ONUMOZ did experience impressive results in the disarmament, demobilization and reintegration of the parties' forces. The primary reason for this was obviously the increased resources and planning that had been dedicated to the provision of Track 2 diplomacy at the level of the ex-combatants. The provision and extension of the RSS, together with the improved demobilization and reintegration packages administered by UNOHAC and the Technical Unit, provided them with greater economic security and enticed them away from continued military life.

Unfortunately, the UN could not replicate this success with the creation of the FADM, which had reached only one-third of its intended size and lacked sufficient resources to keep even this number fully operative. The creation of the FADM had in itself taught the UN a number of lessons. Firstly, the Government's failure to provide the logistical and technical support it had promised highlighted the need to limit the ability of internal parties to aggravate such processes in future. Secondly, the tendency of the parties to force unwilling troops to continue in army life had inevitably led to protests in the assembly areas and desertions from the FADM. And thirdly, the discrepancy in benefits between demobilized soldiers and those joining the FADM had practically ensured a lack of interest in recruitment.

As the Secretary-General acknowledged, 'in order to attract soldiers [in the future] provision will have to be made for satisfactory conditions of service, including adequate salary, acceptable quality and quantity of food and decent accommodation.'[137]

Finally, the general population of Mozambique had experienced little Track 2 diplomacy by the end of the peace process. Their general economic situation remained as dire as it had at the beginning of the UN's operation, only now the population had to deal with an influx of former combatants who had increased the level of banditry and who were likely to run out of money in the near future. Once again, therefore, despite the UN's relative success in disarming the parties' forces in Mozambique, general disarmament was to remain a fleeting hope.

4
Somalia 1992–1995

1 Introduction

Unlike its operations in Angola, Cambodia and Mozambique, the UN's disarmament processes in Somalia were not designed as part of a comprehensive peace agreement negotiated between former warring parties. Rather, they were conducted as part of a humanitarian intervention undertaken to prevent the mass starvation of ordinary Somalis who were unable to gain access to food and water due to the extensive devastation wrought by years of drought and civil war. As this chapter will show, disarming the warring parties and controlling the armed bandits that had proliferated in the anarchic conditions of the civil war was perceived by the UN as essential to both the secure delivery of humanitarian aid and the restoration of the Somali state. Despite its recognized importance this disarmament was never achieved.

Though treated by this text as one case study, the international community's intervention in Somalia was actually composed of three operations, two led by the UN and one led by the US. The first of these operations was the United Nations Operation in Somalia (UNOSOM), which was deployed between April 1992 and March 1993. This was a traditional peacekeeping operation established under Chapter VI of the UN Charter and composed of fewer than 3,500 troops. The second UN led operation, UNOSOM II, took over from its predecessor in March 1993 and continued until the end of the intervention in March 1995. This was the first UN peacekeeping operation ever conducted with a Chapter VII mandate and involved the deployment of nearly 30,000 troops from more than 27 countries. Between December 1992 and May 1993 a third operation, the Unified Task Force (UNITAF), was deployed. Led by the US and composed of 38,000 troops from 23 countries, it was also provided with a Chapter VII UN mandate. Together these operations were to witness an expenditure that exceeded $2 billion.

As is apparent from the dates of deployment, the UN and US led operations were technically conducted simultaneously. In effect, however, the

UNITAF operation was a distinct second phase of the intervention, in between those of UNOSOM and UNOSOM II. It is therefore impossible to conduct a thorough analysis of the UN's intervention unless UNITAF is included. This chapter will thus utilize the twin-track framework outlined in Chapter 1 to explain the relative successes and failures witnessed in all three operations. As with all the case studies in this text, this chapter will begin with an overview of the background to the conflict. A description of the mandate assumed by each operation will then be followed by an account of their implementation. An attempt will then be made to analyze the operations as a continuous process of disarmament. Finally, the conclusion will assess the ability of the twin-track framework to explain the failure of the disarmament processes conducted in Somalia.

2   Background to the conflict

On 1 July 1960 the United Nations Trust Territory of Italian Somaliland amalgamated with the northern colony of British Somaliland to form the independent Republic of Somalia. Although its President, Abdirashid Ali Shermarke, tried to build an enduring post-colonial nationalism based on allegiance to the new State, continuing power struggles amongst Somalia's political elites and the persistence of clan loyalties hindered its achievement. Even Shermarke's attempts to unify the country through irredentist claims against Somalia's neighbors achieved little but the indignation of Western governments. His regime's increasing dependence on Soviet arms also annoyed the West, as it provided the USSR with a foothold in the Horn of Africa.

Shermarke's rule was to end in a *coup d'etat* in October 1969 led by the then Commander of the National Armed Forces, Siad Barre. Once he had assumed absolute power Barre attempted to replicate the Soviet model of government, notwithstanding Somalia's own idiosyncratic cultural influences. This meant that whilst the Soviets tried to build allegiance to their regime through a 'nomenclatura', Barre's regime tried to do it through a 'clankatura'. This ensured that only 'clan relatives and other political loyalists' were appointed to important positions. By the mid-1970s Barre had also greatly expanded the Somali armed forces, increasing its number from 12,000 to 37,000.[1]

Just like his predecessor, Barre endeavored to build a Somali pan-nationalism through the pursuit of a 'Greater Somalia'. And just as clan loyalties had frustrated Shermarke's desires, so too were they for Barre. This was especially so following Somalia's defeat at the hands of Ethiopia in the Ogaden War of 1977. With opposition growing within the country, only Barre's skillful political maneuverings allowed his regime to survive. With the top echelons of his government consisting mostly of members of his own sub-clan, these actions often took the form of repression.[2] This included several state orchestrated mass murders of elites belonging to opposing clans.[3]

The first serious crisis for the Barre regime was to occur in mid-1988 with an uprising in northern Somalia, led by the Somali National Movement (SNM). Drawn mainly from the Isaaq clan, the SNM's insurrection began in response to its perception that the leadership of the southern clans (especially the Marehan to which Barre belonged) had monopolized power and abused it to raid their economic wealth. In retaliation the Barre regime launched a genocidal campaign that left Somalia's second largest city, Hargeisa, reduced to rubble. An estimated 5,000 Issaqs were killed and another 400,000 became refugees during the month of May alone.[4]

Under pressure from international human rights organizations, a number of governments imposed modest sanctions on Somalia as a result. Perhaps the most damaging of these was the freezing of US economic support from June 1989 and the suspension of its military assistance the following month.[5] By the middle of 1990 Barre's regime was beginning to disintegrate, as the SNM in the north and the United Somali Congress (USC) in the south began to make ever-greater advances against government forces. However, even the regime's ultimate collapse in January 1991 failed to herald a more peaceful age for Somalia. Rather, after taking control of the capital, Mogadishu, the USC became embroiled in an internal power struggle that was to turn the city into a bloodbath.

The USC internal conflict arose from the self-appointment of its leader, Ali Mahdi Mohammed, as Interim President of Somalia on the group's arrival in the capital. Convinced that he had played a greater role in the military defeat of Barre than his political superiors, the USC Military Commander, General Mohammed Farah Aideed, refused to accept Ali Mahdi's accession and so began the battle for the city. Even in this conflict clan politics were to play a part. Although both men were members of the Hawiye clan, they were each drawn from different sub-clans; Ali Mahdi from the Abgal and Aideed from the Habar Gidir. Having now lost control of the capital, Barre's troops retreated south, inflicting a scorched earth policy throughout the farming belt of the Juba Valley on their way. So, whilst Mogadishu was caught in the midst of its own bloody conflict, devastation and starvation were spreading throughout southern Somalia.[6] In these anarchic conditions looting and banditry also increased, mainly due to the existence of gangs of Qat-chewing teenagers with guns, known as *mooryaan*.

Exacerbated by the drought of 1991, the fighting had thus left Somalia in the grip of one of the greatest humanitarian disasters since the Ethiopian famine of the mid-1980s. By 1992 the UN had estimated a death toll of 300,000, with more than 700,000 refugees in neighboring Kenya and Ethiopia.[7] Only the presence of a number of international non-governmental organizations provided any succor to the population. The UN, which had previously maintained a presence in the country, began to evacuate its personnel as early as 1988 and by 1991 was completely absent. As the future Secretary-General's Special Representative (SGSR), Mohammed Sahnoun, commented of the failure of the international community at that time: 'neither the UN nor the regional organizations were providing any leadership for serious mediation efforts and the fragile and isolated endeavors of a few governments could have no impact'.[8] When the UN did eventually return to Somalia, opening offices in the capital, Mogadishu, and northwest of the country, it was forced to close its offices three months later due to rising levels of insecurity.[9]

The first substantial UN involvement in the Somali tragedy, therefore, was to come only a full year after the fall of the Barre regime. On 23 January 1992, the Security Council adopted Resolution 733, in which it invited the Secretary-General to mediate the conflict and imposed an arms embargo on Somalia.[10] As in previous operations, this was also to be the UN's first involvement in disarmament. Subsequently, Under-Secretary-General, James Jonah, visited Mogadishu the same month to try and persuade the rival factions to sign and implement an immediate cease-fire.

3 Disarmament mandates

3.1 UNOSOM

Established pursuant to Security Council Resolution 751 of 24 April 1992, UNOSOM was given no explicit role in the disarmament of the civil warring factions or of the Somali population. Composed initially of only 50 UN observers, its role was simply to monitor the cease-fire that had recently been reached between the factions in Mogadishu. Through Resolution 751 the Security Council also agreed with the Secretary-General's recommendation to deploy a further 500 UN peacekeepers to provide protection for humanitarian relief convoys, UN personnel, equipment and supplies. Still, no explicit mention was made of their potential role in any disarmament process.[11]

Despite this omission it was evident that the Secretary-General perceived disarmament to be essential to both the creation of a stable security situation and the safe delivery of humanitarian aid. As early as his April 1992 report to the Security Council, Boutros-Ghali stated that there was a 'pressing need to recover [an] enormous number of small and medium sized arms which are already in the hands of the civilian population throughout Somalia and particularly Mogadishu'. He also noted that his representatives had twice raised the issue of a possible 'food-for-arms' exchange program with the Interim President, Ali Mahdi, a program the Secretary-General thought would be 'an imaginative way of tackling the two most acute problems facing the people of Somalia...namely the threat of famine and an almost total breakdown of law and order.'[12]

Boutros-Ghali was also encouraged to become involved in disarmament by the Somali leaders themselves. In March 1992 the Secretary-General noted that Ali Mahdi had requested a UN peacekeeping force not only to ensure a lasting cease-fire and protect the stockpiling and distribution of humanitarian aid, but also to help disarm civilians.[13] And in July he reported that 'all [the] political leaders and Elders in Somalia [had] requested UN assistance in disarming the population and demobilizing the irregular forces'.[14]

It was in this context that the Secretary-General announced the implementation of a 'Consolidated Inter-Agency 90-day Plan of Action' in April. This plan was designed to provide sufficient quantities of relief food to reduce the risk of any further deterioration in security conditions 'as well as promote the demobilization of large numbers of military personnel'. In July he also proposed the decentralization of UN activities through the creation of four operational zones in the northwest (Berbera), northeast (Bassasso), Central Rangelands and Mogadishu and the south (Kismayo). In each of these zones a consolidated UN operation was to carry out a number of primary activities envisaged in Resolution 751, including the provision of security and assistance in disarmament and demobilization.[15] Boutros-Ghali also sent a technical team to Somalia between 6 and 15 August to examine, amongst other things, the feasibility of a 'food-for-arms' exchange program.

3.2 UNITAF

As had been the case with UNOSOM, UNITAF was not provided with an explicit role in disarmament when it was established by Security Council Resolution 794 of 3 December 1992. Rather, a more ambiguous mandate was provided, one that requested UNITAF 'to use all necessary means to establish as soon as possible a secure environment for humanitarian relief operations in Somalia'.[16] Nevertheless, the Secretary-General continued to perceive disarmament as essential to the production of such a secure environment and therefore interpreted the resolution to have implied such a role. The US, which had first offered to lead a multi-national humanitarian intervention at a meeting between Boutros-Ghali and US Acting Secretary of State, Lawrence Eagleburger, on 25 November, did not. Disarmament was therefore to become the first and greatest point of contention between the UN Secretariat and the US administration and was to remain so throughout UNITAF's tenure.

The US could not have been surprised at the Secretary-General's expectations. Even before the adoption of Resolution 794 his wishes for the potential role of the operation had been made clear. On 29 November he had already outlined five alternatives for the international community, given that in his opinion the security conditions in Somalia had deteriorated to such an extent that the conflict was no longer susceptible to the treatment of traditional peacekeeping. Three of the options involved the use of force, including an enforcement operation under the command and control of member states, as UNITAF was to be. As he stated of these options:

> The purpose of each of the three options involving the possible use of force would be to ensure, on a lasting basis, that the current violence against the international relief effort was brought to an end. To achieve this, it would be necessary for at least the heavy weapons of the organized factions to be neutralized and brought under international control and for the irregular forces and gangs to be disarmed. It is to be noted that this action would help *de facto* to bring about a cease-fire between the warring factions and this would be a positive factor in the context of national reconciliation.[17]

However, despite his recommendation that the enabling resolution should state that the subsequent operation 'would be replaced by a UN peacekeeping operation, organized on conventional lines, as soon as the irregular groups had been disarmed and the heavy weapons of the organized factions brought under international control', no such specifics were included in Resolution 794.

Boutros-Ghali again reiterated his concern about the importance of including disarmament in UNITAF's mandate in a letter to US President Bush on 8 December. Having already raised his concerns with representatives of the US Government earlier that month, the Secretary-General warned President Bush that without the disarmament he desired the secure environment envisaged in Resolution 794 could not be achieved. He even went as far as to caution the President that in 'such circumstances [he] would not be in a position to recommend to the Council that it decide to make the transition to continued peacekeeping operations'.[18]

Despite the Secretary-General's insistence the US administration remained adamantly opposed to adopting a general disarmament mandate. As Robert Patman explains, there were four principle reasons for this. The first was that the administration felt that disarmament would only embroil it further in Somali politics and thus require it to lengthen its stay. Secondly, the expected need to forcibly disarm the Somali factions risked large numbers of American casualties. Thirdly, the cost of the intervention would increase substantially. And finally, the administration questioned whether general disarmament was even feasible in a society lacking basic law and order and in which gun-ownership was so widespread.[19] Thus, the day after the adoption of Resolution 794 President Bush wrote to Boutros-Ghali emphasizing that the coalition's mission would be 'limited and specific: to create security conditions which will permit the feeding of the starving Somali people and allow the transfer of this security function to the UN peacekeeping force'.[20] And in meetings with Boutros-Ghali in late

November and early December Eagleburger reiterated this position, stating that US forces would only engage in limited disarmament when it was felt necessary for self-protection and the protection of humanitarian relief.[21]

Nevertheless, Boutros-Ghali's hopes for a change of mind must have been encouraged by the subsequent statements of President Bush, who announced later in December that the US mission was 'humanitarian, but [would] not tolerate armed gangs ripping off their own people, condemning them to death by starvation'. He went even further by stating that 'General [William] Hoar and his troops [had] the authority to take whatever military action [was] necessary to safeguard the lives of our troops and the lives of Somalia's people...the outlaw elements in Somalia must understand this is a serious business'.[22] As will be seen, the actual implementation of disarmament by UNITAF was to fall somewhere in between the respective interpretations of the UN Secretariat and the US administration.

3.3   UNOSOM II

Of the five options that the Secretary-General had presented to the Security Council in his letter of 29 November 1992, the final option was for a nation-wide enforcement action under the command and control of the UN. As at that time he believed the UN was incapable of mounting an operation of the size and complexity as that required by Somalia he discounted it as a viable option, despite it being his first preference. Instead, he hoped that a traditional UN peacekeeping operation could be mounted once a multi-national coalition had created the requisite conditions.[23] However, the US continued to insist that it was not going to disarm the warring factions, the most important prerequisite for the establishment of a traditional operation in the mind of the Secretary-General. In his report of 19 December the Secretary-General noted that the US representatives he had met did not believe general disarmament was part of their mandate, but rather:

> envisaged UNITAF [being] replaced by a new UNOSOM operation which would be under United Nations command and control but whose mandate, concept of operations, level of armament and rule of engagement would be little different from those of UNITAF. [They] argued that a force mandated and organized on normal peacekeeping lines would not be capable of protecting humanitarian activities from factional forces or gangs which would not have been neutralized or disarmed during the UNITAF presence.[24]

The Secretary-General did not initially give up hope that the US administration might change its mind, entitling his 19 December report, 'A proposal that UNITAF extend its operations to the whole of Somalia and disarm the factions before handing over operational responsibility to a new

United Nations peacekeeping operation'. Nevertheless, in the same report he acknowledged that in the absence of a secure environment necessary for a traditional peacekeeping operation, the situation 'would require a further decision by the Security Council' to create an operation that 'would be analogous to the fifth option for which [he had previously] expressed a preference'.[25]

Disappointed at the failure of UNITAF to assume the role he believed essential to the creation of a secure environment, the Secretary-General began to prepare for a UN operation that would. Integral to his plans, therefore, was a mandate to enforce the disarmament of the warring factions and the general population. Boutros-Ghali explained his rationale in March 1993, when he argued that to be 'effective' the disarmament agreement that had been concluded between the Somali factions in Addis Ababa three months earlier 'should be enforceable'. If this were the case then '[t]hose factions or personnel who [failed] to comply with timetables or other modalities of the process would have their weapons and equipment confiscated and/or destroyed'. Under these conditions 'the disarmament process would be continuous and irreversible'; a faction that had relinquished its weapons 'would not be entitled to reclaim those weapons'. The Secretary-General also wanted the new operation to have the power to seize the small arms of all unauthorized elements.[26]

On 26 March the Security Council adopted Resolution 814 creating UNOSOM II and acknowledging the fundamental importance of a comprehensive and effective disarmament program. So, despite only encouraging the Secretary-General to 'assist' the people of Somalia in the rehabilitation of their political institutions and economy, the Security Council 'demanded' that all the parties (including movements and factions) comply fully with the agreements they had concluded in Addis Ababa, in particular those relating to the cease-fire and disarmament.[27] As a report into the subsequent actions of UNOSOM II later clarified:

> In this context the UN Security Council adopted Resolution 814... expanding the size and mandate of UNOSOM to include not only the protection of humanitarian relief supplies and personnel, but also to compel the Somali militias to disarm...This unlike UNITAF...[meant that] UNOSOM II was mandated to disarm Somali militias under Chapter VII of the United Nations Charter.[28]

4 Implementation

4.1 UNOSOM

When the recently appointed SGSR, Mohammed Sahnoun, arrived in Mogadishu in May 1992 he was faced with a city in chaos. Nevertheless, he quickly realized that the dynamics of insecurity in the capital were chang-ing. Rather than fighting each other for control of the capital, the warring militias were now principally targeting humanitarian relief workers and their storage depots.[29] So too were a large number of armed gangs, none of which were controlled by either of the two main factions. This changing dynamic in the conflict had already forced the relief organizations in the city to employ armed guards to protect their personnel and supplies.[30]

The Somali leaders themselves shared Sahnoun's concern for security. As he noted, 'all of the Somali leaders...insisted on the need to launch an urgent and large humanitarian operation as well as a recovery program. They were concerned that they would lose control of some of the young militia, who might join other unruly youths already engaged in looting'.[31] Sahnoun knew that despite the request by many of the Somali leaders for UN assistance in demobilizing their forces, the militias themselves would not disarm unless offered an incentive to do so. He believed this incentive would have to be in the form of a food basket or temporary employment. However, as of mid-1992, neither of these incentives was available.[32]

In this context Sahoun continued to negotiate with the Somali leaders whilst attempting to increase the quantity of food being delivered by the UN and relief agencies. He believed that the lack of food in Somalia was breeding insecurity, which in turn was causing the instability that led to further starvation, suffering and disease. 'Breaking this diabolical and vicious cycle', Sahnoun proposed, '[might] be the key to resolving the intri-cate social and political problems in Somalia'.[33] He therefore recommended that at least 50,000 metric tons of food be delivered every month through-out the Secretary-General's 90-day plan of action. However, unable to repli-cate the international relief efforts that had occurred in Biafra and Ethiopia in the 1960s and 1980s respectively, the UN and relief agencies only managed to deliver fewer than 10,000 metric tons per month until August 1992. Even in the following months this number only reached 20,000 metric tons.[34]

A similar lack of support was to have equally detrimental effects on Sahnoun's negotiating strategy. Although Sahnoun had continued to nego-tiate with both faction leaders in Mogadishu, in order to gain their acquies-cence to the deployment of UN personnel, Aideed's continual suspicions that the UN wanted to marginalize his position made these negotiations particularly arduous. It took Sahnoun two months just to persuade him to allow the deployment of 50 unarmed observers.[35] Negotiations for the deployment of a further 500 UN troops were even more difficult, despite the help of local elders. A significant reason for this was Aideed's increased suspicions following an incident on 25 June when a Russian Antonov aircraft under charter to the World Food Program, and still bearing UN markings, undertook an illegal flight into Ali Mahdi controlled northern Mogadishu. Allegedly carrying Somali currency and military equipment,

Aideed's supporters interpreted the flight as yet another example of UN bias and tensions rose accordingly.[36] Under the circumstances, Sahnoun believed these reactions were 'understandable' and criticized his own organization's 'lack of vigilance'.[37]

Despite this setback Sahnoun was ultimately successful in persuading Aideed of the need for a further UN deployment and on 12 August he and his allies in the Somali National Alliance (SNA) signed an agreement allowing for the deployment of another 500 UN peacekeepers. However, as part of that agreement Sahnoun promised Aideed that any further deployments would require the consent of his SNA leadership.[38] Sahnoun was therefore as surprised as Aideed when the Secretary-General announced in his 24 August report that he wanted to increase the size of UNOSOM to 3,500 and deploy the extra troops in four operational zones across the country. The Security Council approved this recommendation four days later, together with the proposed creation of a police force and a food-for-arms program, neither of which Aideed had agreed to.[39] Knowing that this announcement threatened to undo all his long worked for local support, because it had been made 'without consulting the Somali leaders and community elders', Sahnoun attempted to have the deployments postponed until he could negotiate with Aideed.[40] UN Headquarters was unsympathetic to his requests.

Also in his report of 24 August the Secretary-General noted the conclusions of the technical team he had sent to Somalia in order to assess, amongst other things, the feasibility of a food-for-arms program. Having visited Mogadishu between 6 and 15 August, the team advised the Secretary-General that as of that time 'the general effectiveness of such a program in isolation [would be] doubtful. This was mainly because 'Somali's [saw] arms as a means not only of personal security but also of survival'. Although the Secretary-General continued to view a food-for-arms initiative as an important component of an effort to improve security conditions, he acknowledged that any program for disarmament and demobilization would also have to include educational and vocational programs that offered alternative employment opportunities so that the international community could 'provide [Somali's] with real alternatives for survival other than the possession of arms'.[41]

Unfortunately for the Secretary-General, the deteriorating security conditions in Mogadishu were making the implementation of any such disarmament program increasingly unlikely. His unilateral decision to increase the size of UNOSOM had angered Aideed so greatly that the SNA leader was now refusing to accept the deployment of the 500 troops he had agreed to in August. These troops, the first of which had arrived in mid-September, were unable to secure either the seaport or the airport due to a lack of weapons and the increased animosity of the SNA. Both ports were essential to the delivery of humanitarian supplies.

In the face of growing criticism from UN headquarters Sahnoun offered his resignation on 26 October. His replacement, Ismat Kittani, was appointed to face an even more belligerent Aideed, who had already announced that he would no longer tolerate patrols by the UN Pakistani battalion in Mogadishu; that the UNOSOM Coordinator for Humanitarian Assistance be expelled within 48 hours; and that any forcible deployment of UNOSOM troops would be met by force. The Secretary-General could only employ one of his spokespersons to reiterate that the 'purposes and methods of the UN under Mr. Kittani's leadership [would] remain unchanged' and that 'the UN [could] only succeed with the consent and support of the Somali people'. This statement, he hoped, would allay the fears of the worried populace of Mogadishu, whom he felt were suffering from a bout of 'invasion syndrome'.[42]

4.2   UNITAF

Despite the US refusal to write a disarmament process into UNITAF's mandate, the Bush administration was still prepared to allow it to conduct disarmament to protect both its personnel and humanitarian deliveries. In essence, therefore, disarmament was to be an operational decision to be made by the Field Commander as and when the need arose. Consequently, in planning for the operation, US Central Command in Florida ensured that adequate allowances were made for the possibility that UNITAF might take on the task of disarmament as a secondary mission objective.[43]

With this policy in mind the US facilitated negotiations between Aideed and Ali Mahdi to try and secure the capital. Their first success was to come on 11 December 1992 when both leaders signed a 'Seven Point Agreement' committing each of them to a cease-fire, the removal of barriers dividing the city and the cantonment of their heavy weapons. Although the cease-fire took hold immediately, neither side began to canton their heavy weapons until 26 December.[44] Their initial hesitancy was probably due to the fact that the first comprehensive all party talks on disarmament were due to take place in Addis Ababa the following month.

At these talks a dozen Somali factions committed themselves to construct a national charter and discuss the formation of a new interim government at a reconciliation conference to be held on 15 March. By this date they were also to have cantoned all their heavy weapons and placed their militia members in transition sites so that they could be disarmed and demobilized or transferred to a new Somali army. Though it was agreed that UNITAF and UNOSOM I would immediately establish a cease-fire monitoring group comprised of representatives of the Somali factions to oversee this agreement, no detailed plans or cost analyses were made as to how the disarmament process was to proceed.[45]

UNITAF did not seek to oversee the implementation of the Addis Ababa agreement itself, both for logistical reasons and because it was not seen to be part of its mandate. Nevertheless, the US commander of UNITAF, Lt. General Robert Johnston, did announce a step up in UNITAF operations in Mogadishu in early January 1993, with the main objectives being to destroy the infamous 'technicals' (road-trucks with mounted machine-guns) and to confiscate weapons in certain areas from certain groups.[46] The official UNITAF rules of engagement authorized troops to 'use all necessary force' to confiscate weapons and technicals, 'whether or not the [individual or crew] demonstrated hostile intent'. However, this was only to be applied in areas under UNITAF control.[47] The application of this policy led to a number of raids on weapon storage sites, including two raids on 7 and 8 January, the first on a 'gun-market' in northeastern Mogadishu and the second on a couple of military compounds owned by Aideed. It is speculated that this latter event may have encouraged Aideed to sign up to the Addis Ababa agreement.[48]

UNITAF disarmament initiatives at this time were not confined to forceful acts. Whilst maintaining that disarmament was not integral to UNITAF's mandate, Lt. General Johnston did allow his senior policy staff to experiment with more consensually based disarmament programs. The first of these was a food-for-arms program of the same type the UN technical team of August 1992 had dismissed as unworkable. Starting in the penultimate week of January, US Marines began issuing special receipts for every weapon turned in, as well as for information on locations leading to the seizure of weapons and ammunition. These receipts could be exchanged for bags of food from the relief agencies.[49] Unfortunately, due to the limited amount of food available, the aid agencies could not cope with the program and the initiative was dropped following heightened tensions between the agencies and UNITAF command. The emphasis of UNITAF disarmament therefore returned to confiscation.[50]

This renewed emphasis on confiscation served only to increase tensions between UNITAF and the relief agencies. As previously mentioned, due to the high level of insecurity throughout the country all the aid agencies had within their employ a number of Somali guards. These guards were present at every humanitarian agency residence, warehouse or facility. Indeed, an agency could not rent either a building or vehicle without the landlord providing guards as part of the rental package or at least insisting that the agency supply them to protect their investment.[51] The amount of money appropriated by these guards was estimated to be hundreds of thousands of dollars each month in Mogadishu alone. Whilst a house could cost up to $12,000 a month, the armed guards required to protect it could cost an extra $2,000 a month per man. Technicals fetched as much as $300 a day.[52] Ironically, with large agencies such as the International Committee of the Red Cross (ICRC) reportedly employing as many as 20,000 guards on their own, this type of employment for local Somalis was increasing the demand for weapons in itself. As Natsios explains:

> It is indeed ironic that the very humanitarian organizations most vocally demanding that the US and later the UN peacekeeping forces disarm Somalia, inadvertently fuelled a good deal of the Somali appetite for weapons both by their hiring of guards and by agreeing to the diversion of food resources by the warlords in order to gain their protection, who then used the food to purchase more weapons.[53]

By creating this demand the existence of these private armies was also driving the prices of weapons and ammunition up higher than they would have been if only the civil conflict were affecting prices. These higher prices, in turn, attracted more weapons from across the Ethiopian border.[54]

UNITAF was caught in a quandary about these guards. As it was not really willing to provide emergency assistance to agencies under attack, UNITAF acknowledged the security they provided. However, the US command did not believe it could continue to allow them to carry their weapons in public, especially as most of them were members of one militia faction or other and a number were known to moonlight as bandits when they finished duty.[55] UNITAF therefore adopted the policy of confiscating all openly brandished weapons, whether or not the owner showed hostile intent. This policy was applied to both individual light weapons and the crew-served technicals.

Unfortunately, this policy was to have two detrimental effects. Firstly, rather than have them confiscated or destroyed, the factions simply moved their weapons to districts outside of UNITAF control. Although this served UNITAF objectives, the areas absorbing the weapons began to suffer from greater insecurity.[56] Secondly, by failing to standardize the confiscation policy throughout the UNITAF area of control, the various commanders exercised different levels of toleration. Whilst some commanders ordered the confiscation of all weapons, even those owned by agency guards, others were more lenient and confiscated only those carried by unofficial Somalis. This, of course, created a security nightmare for those agencies traversing the many sectors that existed under UNITAF control.[57]

So, despite having initially welcomed the more aggressive disarmament policy and having accepted the generally benign effect it was having on security conditions in Mogadishu, the agencies felt bound to petition UNITAF for the return of their weapons. This unfortunate situation 'often resulted in the ironic and almost comic result of meetings to arrange support to humanitarian programs being dominated by discussions focused on the nuances of UNITAF weapons policies with relief workers departing burdened with recovered AK-47s and M-16s'. With UNITAF returning weapons pending a standardization of policy within its areas of operation, such a u-turn in the middle of implementation essentially resulted in an 'asphyxiation of the disarmament process'.[58] UNITAF's subsequent attempts to standardize policy, including the issuing of standard weapons policy cards to its troops in April, never really dealt adequately with the problem.

There also existed a lack of standardization in the interpretation of disarmament policy amongst the contingents making up UNITAF. Just as the lack of a strategic policy allowed various interpretations to exist within the US force sectors, it also allowed them to exist in areas in which contingents from other nations were deployed. The Canadians and Australians conducted quite stringent disarmament policies in their sectors, as did the French. In applying what they thought to be UNITAF's policy of confiscating weapons found in vehicles, the latter were nevertheless rebuked by the Americans for exceeding their operational mandate.[59]

Therefore, whilst the Secretary-General continued to press the UNITAF command to widen its mandate to include a complete disarmament process on a countrywide basis, UNITAF remained limited to approximately 40 per cent of Somalia attempting to implement a fractured and failing disarmament policy. And whilst the Secretary-General also continued to believe that the disarmament of the regular and irregular forces should be enforced, US political and military personnel continued to protest at the incredibility of such an endeavor.[60]

Despite these disagreements UNITAF and UNOSOM personnel continued to cooperate in order to develop a disarmament concept and plan for the UN's follow-on mission. This was initially done through the 'Future Operations Office', which was composed of senior officers drawn from UNITAF and the Operations Branch of UNOSOM. On the basis of the Addis Ababa agreement of January, this group developed a plan that was subsequently presented to the Security Council by the Secretary-General in his 3 March 1993 report. The proposed process was to be continuous and irreversible, involving a standardized and simple process that would be used to disarm all the factions and that would place their weapons and personnel in cantonment and transition sites respectively.[61] The UN, which was to maintain these sites, would also have unlimited access to them.

Although the Secretary-General insisted that to be effective this disarmament plan would have to be enforced, he also considered alternative methods, such as material or financial incentives. These he believed were an option 'to be kept under review in the light of the experience that [would] be gathered in [the] process'. By the end of April UNITAF and the UN had completed an operational plan for disarmament, with UNITAF creating a Cease-fire and Disarmament Division within its Force Command. This reflected a new appreciation of the importance of disarmament by UNITAF, even if it was not explicit in its mandate. However, the Force Command refused to begin its implementation in areas in which it did not have superiority in firepower and manpower and so the disarmament process remained stalled until the transition to UNOSOM II.[62]

4.3 UNOSOM II

Despite the Secretary-General's recognition that the UN was incapable of implementing a peace-enforcement operation in November 1992, it was obvious he was losing patience with the ostensible commitments of the internal factions to voluntary disarmament. The factions had already committed themselves to voluntary disarmament in Addis Ababa in January 1993 and they had reiterated their commitments at a National Reconciliation Conference held once again in Addis Ababa in March. At this conference 15 of the factions agreed to a comprehensive, impartial and transparent disarmament process and had even urged the UN to 'apply strong and effective sanctions against those responsible for any violation of the Cease-Fire Agreement of January 1993'.[63] The factions undertook to complete the disarmament process by June of the same year, a hopelessly unrealistic expectation under the circumstances. UNITAF was not a nation-wide operation, so it could not monitor or enforce the agreement; the UN had neither deployed or planned in preparation for such a rapid disarmament process; and the non-governmental organizations present on the ground were neither sufficiently integrated or resourced to deal with the humanitarian needs of thousands of demobilizing troops and their families.[64]

With security conditions in the capital deteriorating through the middle of 1993, the conditions necessary for voluntary disarmament were becoming increasingly difficult to establish. This was especially the case after Belgian forces prevented an ally of Aideed, General Hersi Morgan, from recapturing the city of Kismayo in early May. Whilst Aideed cited the incident as yet another example of UN bias, the UN blamed Aideed's growing animosity on the threat he was feeling from UNOSOM's strategy of helping non-factional representatives to assume greater power and its creation of independent police and judicial systems.[65]

Either way, security conditions throughout the country were worsening, which caused UNOSOM II to change the disarmament policy it had adopted after planning with UNITAF in two fundamental ways. Firstly, it decided to extend its disarmament operations into areas it had not yet secured and where, therefore, the risks of confrontation would be higher. Secondly, it abandoned the idea of providing inducements for voluntary disarmament.[66] As Clement Adibe notes, this latter change was important because it reflected a move away from complete disarmament towards limiting the threat of organized violence perpetrated by the armed factions. It also held the added advantage of ameliorating the relief community's criticism that cash-for-weapons and similar programs simply rewarded those violent criminals that had caused the greatest harm. Instead, UNOSOM II was now determined to actively re-establish the basic institutions of law and order, especially those of the civilian police and judicial systems.[67]

UNOSOM II subsequently adopted a new four-stage concept for disarmament. The first stage foresaw UNOSOM II's preparation for disarmament, including an increase in civil-military relations, the identification of cantonment and transition sites and the selection of appropriate developmental projects for the various regions. The second stage expected an increased role for the military, so as to appropriately convey UNOSOM II's commitment to implement the process. The third-stage was to be the threshold of final disarmament, a period during which the factions would be disarmed, their heavy weapons would be cantoned and the UN would conduct large-scale disarmament verification missions. The fourth and final stage envisaged the consolidation of post-disarmament peace through the reintegration of demobilized personnel into civilian life, the creation of a functioning justice system, the restoration of the Somali social infrastructure and the generation of a civil society.[68]

The greatest changes to UNOSOM II's disarmament plans, however, were to come as a result of events on 5 June 1993. When UNOSOM II took over from UNITAF at the end of May there were seven Authorized Weapons Storage Sites (AWSS) where the two rival factions in Mogadishu had complied with the Addis Ababa agreements and cantoned their heavy weapons. Five of these AWSS were attributed to Aideed and two to Ali Mahdi. When UNOSOM II received reports that heavy weapons had been removed from one of Aideed's AWSS, a decision was taken to inspect them in order to take an inventory. On 4 June UNOSOM II officially informed one of Aideed's closest associates, Mohammed Hassan Awale Qaibdid, that it intended to inspect the AWSS the following day. His response was to warn that if the inspections went ahead they would lead to 'war'.[69]

The SNA's fear of inspections was not due simply to the potential detection of its deception. Rather the main threat was the possible confiscation of its radio station, Radio Mogadishu, which it had captured during the civil war and that had subsequently become the main source of Aideed's propaganda. Located at one of the AWSS to be inspected, Radio Mogadishu had intensified its criticisms of UNOSOM II since the events of early May, even accusing the UN and US of being 'aggressors trying to colonize Somalia and to establish a trusteeship'.[70] The SGSR, Admiral Howe, had attempted to negotiate an end to the propaganda with Aideed, but the onslaught continued as UNOSOM II debated whether the station should be forcibly shut down. Eleven of the factions even wrote to the Secretary-General on 31 May urging him 'to take over the radio station'.[71]

The SNA's fears were not completely unfounded. UNOSOM II's Pakistani brigade had actually been requested in mid-May to draw up contingency plans for shutting the radio station down. However, the Pakistanis had informed UNOSOM II Command that they did not possess the technical expertise to handle such an operation. Thus, US Special Forces technicians accompanied UNOSOM II inspection teams to the Radio Mogadishu AWSS in order to survey the installation. It was not surprising, therefore, that knowing the SNA were aware of the UNOSOM II discussions surrounding the future of the station and the generally poor relations between Aideed and the UN, that rumors circulated within the SNA that the UN intended to seize the facility.

When the Pakistani brigade carried out their inspections on 5 June, they were ambushed at Radio Mogadishu, at a UN feeding center and on their return to barracks from other AWSS when they traversed 21 October Road. In the gun battles that ensued 24 Pakistani soldiers were killed and 56 wounded, 11 of whom were crippled for life.[72] On 6 June the Security Council adopted Resolution 837 expressing its outrage at the loss of life and reaffirmed the Secretary-General's authority to 'take all measures necessary against all those responsible for the armed attacks…including to secure the investigation of their actions and their arrest and detention for prosecution, trial and punishment'.[73] On 17 June Admiral Howe called publicly for the arrest of Aideed and offered a $25,000 reward for his capture.

Over the next two months UNOSOM II, together with help from US Special Forces, conducted a number of raids on SNA installations to 'restore security and law and order in Mogadishu by implementing a comprehensive program for disarmament in the capital, neutralizing broadcasting systems and other propaganda mechanisms used to incite violence and preventing further violations of the cease-fire'.[74] At the culmination of these actions the Secretary-General stated that '[although] still a threat to stability, it [was] expected that the SNA militia in Mogadishu [would] now be less of an impediment to disarmament, political reconciliation and rehabilitation'. He expected UNOSOM II to be able to continue to disarm the SNA until all their weapons had been captured or destroyed and then conduct 'an orderly sector-by-sector disarmament of the city'. He also hoped that disarmament could once again become voluntary as soon as possible.[75] Unfortunately, he could not have been more wrong.

The fighting in the capital was to have detrimental effects on disarmament throughout the country. As the Secretary-General admitted, 'since voluntary disarmament can succeed only if it proceeds simultaneously in a fair and balanced manner, it was not surprising that factions became fearful of giving up their weapons after the fighting erupted in Mogadishu'.[76] And even the Cease-fire and Disarmament Committee, established in Addis Ababa in January 1993 to develop procedures for handling cease-fire violations and guidelines for voluntary disarmament, stopped functioning after the fighting erupted on 5 June.[77] Regardless of the effects of the fighting the Secretary-General, Security Council and regional organizations, continued to insist as late as August that while voluntary disarmament remained the basic assumption underlying the disarmament program, 'if certain factions refuse to disarm voluntarily, UNOSOM [was] left with no choice but to disarm them through compulsion'.[78]

However, the final blow to the UN's strategy was to come on 3 October, following the attempted arrest of Aideed and his 'war cabinet' at the Olympic Hotel in Mogadishu. The US Special Forces dispatched to conduct the arrests found themselves ensnared in a battle that left 18 of them dead and 75 wounded. Several score Somali were also killed and wounded. Compounding unrest in the US over the high number killed, 'televised images of chanting Somalis dragging a US soldier's body through the streets and pictures of a distressed helicopter pilot held hostage' resulted in the immediate collapse of US domestic support for the Somali operation. On 7 October President Clinton made a televised announcement of a complete withdrawal of US forces by March 1994.[79]

With general support for the operation collapsing Boutros-Ghali visited Mogadishu personally in October. In his report to the Security Council the following month he proposed four options for UNOSOM II's disarmament strategy in light of recent events. The first envisioned a continuation of the present mandate, an unlikely scenario given the experience of the contributing states. The second option involved only voluntary disarmament, in line with the traditional principles of peacekeeping. The objective of this mission would be to keep the main humanitarian supply routes open, help with the building and repair of the country's infrastructure and facilitate political reconciliation. The third option was to be based on similar principles, but was designed only to secure the main points of entry for humanitarian aid, such as the seaports and airports. It would therefore require only 5,000 troops, rather than the 16,000 required for the second option. The final option was a complete withdrawal. Given the state of Somalia and the overwhelming number of Somalis who wanted UN help, the Secretary-General believed this option was unacceptable.[80]

Rather than make an immediate decision the Security Council waited until the Secretary-General had resubmitted his proposals in January 1994. Although Boutros-Ghali would have preferred to continue the disarmament policy UNOSOM II had been implementing, he realized that the withdrawal of a number of the contributing states and the unwillingness of those remaining to become involved in coercive disarmament made it impossible. He therefore recommended the second option. On 4 February the Security Council adopted his recommendation, pursuant to Resolution 897, and provided for 8,000 more troops than he had requested. The Security Council also reaffirmed the objective that UNOSOM complete its mission by March 1995, through 'encouraging and assisting the Somali parties in implementing the Addis Ababa Agreements, in particular in their cooperative efforts to achieve disarmament and to respect the cease-fire.'[81] As peace-enforcement was no longer part of UNOSOM II's mandate it could no longer engage in coercive disarmament, nor was it allowed to use force in response to cease-fire violations by the Somali factions. This had actually been UNOSOM II's *de facto* policy since October 1993.

5   Analysis of the operations

5.1   Planning, administration and deployment

Just as they had hampered the operations in Angola, Cambodia and Mozambique, the institutional inadequacies of the UN Secretariat were also to cause problems for UNOSOM and UNOSOM II. Indeed, with UNOSOM II's foray into peace-enforcement the inadequacies of the Secretariat were to become even more apparent. As Thomas Weiss observed in 1995, the UN's 'capacity to plan, support and command peacekeeping, let alone enforcement, is scarcely greater than during the Cold War – it is barely functional'.[82] And as Chester Crocker commented in the final months of the Somalia operation, the UN's attempt at a peace-enforcement operation, 'shows that it cannot manage complex political-military operations when its own structure is an undisciplined and often chaotic set of rival fiefdoms that resist unified command and control in the field at both the civilian and military levels'.[83] It was therefore not surprising to find that the Secretariat's inadequacies began to show from the very beginning of the operation.

UNOSOM's first delays were to occur in staff appointments. In principle UNOSOM began operations in April 1992 as a one-man operation, with the SGSR Sahnoun relying on a small staff placed at his disposal by UNICEF and which he was to share with the coordinator for humanitarian assistance. This shortage of personnel was exacerbated by the fact that it 'took several weeks before the Headquarters in New York finally designated Livio Bota from the UN Office in Geneva and Leonard Kapungo from the Political Department to be [his] assistants, and some more weeks before a support staff could join [them]'.[84] Sahnoun asserts that UNOSOM was only really taking shape by the time he was leaving Somalia, a full six months after his initial appointment.[85]

Sahnoun also blames the UN's organizational and decision-making structures for a number of other mistakes made by the Secretariat and its agencies in the field. Though it would have been inappropriate to give Aideed a veto on the deployment of UN peacekeepers, it nevertheless made Sahnoun's life much more difficult when the decision was taken to enlarge UNOSOM by 3,000 troops before the UN had deployed the 500 troops he had already negotiated for. The delay in deploying this initial contingent had negative effects in itself. As Sahnoun explains, 'there is no doubt, [that] had these 500 troops been fully deployed as late as a month after the agreement, that is, at the beginning of September, it would have made an appreciable difference in the environment'.[86] These delays in deployment and the subsequent decision to enlarge the force without his prior agreement,

Sahnoun blamed on 'bureaucratic delays and the skirmishes at Head-quarters between different departments [which] led to [a] total confusion of priorities.'[87]

The UN's slow deployments were also to have adverse effects on the strategies of UNOSOM II. Though it eventually reached a peak of 29,284 troops, the pressures of a worldwide expansion in peacekeeping forced UNOSOM II to operate well below this level for most of its tenure. The greatest effect this had on the UN's plans was to force it to completely abandon the thought of deploying outside of south and central Somalia, the repercussions of which will be discussed below. It is interesting at this point, however, to compare the UN's lethargic deployments to that of the American dominated UNITAF, which managed to deploy 38,000 combat-ready forces from 23 nations and have them operating within six weeks of the adoption of Resolution 794.[88]

Though UNOSOM II's ambitions were naturally affected by its lack of manpower, the American decision to limit UNITAF's deployment to only 40 per cent of Somalia was made for different reasons. As noted earlier, this limited deployment had led to increased insecurity in areas outside of UNITAF's control when weapons were removed and hidden from its forces. The main problem with such limited deployment, however, was that more stable areas like the northeast and northwest received little if any help at all. Sahnoun had recognized the potential of these areas before his departure, noting that during his tenure:

> The leadership in the North-East and the elders of the area had, probably more than any others, committed themselves to cooperate fully with the UN...Our hope was to establish the North-East as a model for the other regions of Somalia. Consensus prevailed in the region among the different clans and subclans, and UNOSOM's suggestions for organizing local and regional administrations were being actively discussed and gradually implemented. But everything was missing. No infrastructure whatsoever was available. Despite our pressing appeals to UN agencies to have some presence in Bossasso and Garoe and to provide some assistance, at least to the displaced people in the area, we received only pledges and promises. It became difficult for me, as head of UNOSOM, to revisit the people there because we were not able to deliver the UNOSOM part of the agreement entered into with the local communities.[89]

In fact Sahoun even went as far as to state that he thought the northeast, because of its relative stability and cooperation, 'might be [the] key to an overall solution of the Somali problem'.[90]

The failure to deploy in these areas had detrimental effects all round. As the Secretary-General argued in his report of 23 January 1993, the lack of

UNOSOM or UNITAF deployments in the north meant there existed no 'ready capability to assist in [a] disarming exercise in that region, even if a decision to do so were taken'. He also accepted that factions in central and southern Somalia were unlikely to disarm if there was no monitoring force present in the north.[91] Ironically, the UNITAF decision not to deploy in the north was taken on the basis that the region was in much better shape than the rest of the country and therefore did not take precedence.[92] Instead, UNITAF and later UNOSOM II concentrated on Mogadishu, thereby allowing the situation in the capital to dictate the direction of each operation. Even when the four operational zones were created to try and prevent this, as described earlier, a dispersion of operations was not conducted properly.

UNOSOM II's ability to conduct a nationwide disarmament process was also hindered by the Secretary-General's decision to prevent it from planning adequately for such a role. Together with other senior Secretariat staff he was believed to be reticent about allowing planning for the transfer to UNOSOM II to proceed whilst UNITAF had not accepted the larger mandate he had advocated. The Secretariat was also seemingly under the impression that the US would refuse to accept any role in disarmament once UNOSOM II was created. As Robert Oakley and John Hirsch assert, this particular misapprehension seems to have been an important factor behind the delay in [UN] planning. Altogether these approaches prevented the UN from drawing up a plan for disarmament, demobilization and reintegration, despite all its previous experience. Only at the Fourth Humanitarian Conference in Addis Ababa at the end of November 1993 did the UN put forward preliminary ideas for a disarmament plan covering all of Somalia.[93]

5.2   Peace-enforcement and coercive disarmament

With the end of the Cold War and the successful execution of the first ever Chapter VII enforcement action in the Persian Gulf it seemed little could stand in the way of a united Security Council. This belief was given added potency by President George H.W. Bush's heralding of a 'new world order' in 1991. At the same time many analysts of civil conflicts began to question whether the principles of traditional peacekeeping were appropriate in the emerging post-Cold War era, including the UN Secretary-General himself. Thus, when in January 1992 the Security Council requested that he report on ways that UN peacekeeping might be strengthened in the future, his replying document, *Agenda for Peace,* included a suggestion for 'peace-enforcement units'. These, he envisaged, might be used to enforce a cease-fire where one was not already present.[94]

Despite the Secretary-General's adherence to the theoretical possibilities of peace-enforcement, his pragmatism had obviously prevented him from allowing the UN to assume such a role before mid-1993. However, despite his best efforts, UNITAF had refused to assume the mandate he had proposed for it and the secure environment necessary for traditional peacekeeping had not therefore been established. Without this secure environment he was left with the difficult choice of trying to use UN forces to implement the mandate he had wanted UNITAF to adopt, or of deploying a traditional peacekeeping operation in conditions he thought ill suited to the concept. As he had already expressed his belief that the threat of enforcement was an essential element to any disarmament agreement between the Somali factions, his choice was rather predictable.

Significantly, the UNITAF operation had already provided evidence of the beneficial effects of peace-enforcement. For example, Robert Patman cites the willingness of UNITAF's Australian contingent to undertake peace-enforcement as the primary reason it has been widely accepted as the intervention's greatest success story.[95] Beginning in January 1993, in an operation that lasted just 17 weeks, the Australians managed to transform the Baidoa Humanitarian Relief Sector (HRS) in Central Somalia into a stable environment in which relief agencies could operate freely and major elements of traditional Somali civil society had begun to reassert themselves.

The reason for this success, Patman suggests, was the 'multi-faceted' nature of the Australian's peace-enforcement operation. Firstly, by donning the mantle of 'military governor' the Australians placed themselves above the military factions and immediately began a counter-insurgency style operation. A central element of this was the provision of security to the local population and NGOs through the maintenance of a constant and visible presence in the Baidoa HRS. This 'community policing' style of operation was perceived by the Australians to be the 'bread and butter' of their mission, as 'it kept the [the] armed factions and bandits off-balance and facilitated the enforcement of weapons reduction whether through house to house searches, counter-ambush actions, pursuit after contact, and cordon and search activities'. By the end of their stay the Australians had confiscated nearly half of the 2,250 small arms and heavy weapons that UNITAF had seized as a whole by that time.[96]

The second facet of the Australian strategy was the creation of a local justice system. The Australians 'went further than any other UNITAF partner in restoring a fully functioning legal system based on the 1962 Somali penal code' and were quick to react to the US initiative of establishing an auxiliary police force composed of local Somalis.[97] The improved security and stability provided by these institutions even generated greater intelligence for the Australians, as the local population began to inform on the most notorious criminals in their midst. Following the arrest and prosecution of a number of these criminals the sense of security in the region increased substantially.[98]

Patman also accounts for the significant effect the creation of public security institutions had on disarmament in Baidoa.

> By responding energetically to the [clan] elders' requests to reestablish a police force and judicial system the Australians not only provided a model for the rest of the UN operation, but also consolidated local support for disarmament in the Baidoa HRS. In this connection, Colonel David Hurley [Commander of 1st Battalion of the Royal Australian Regiment] said 'elders would sometimes walk as far as 90 kilometers to report weapons [dumps] which they felt the Aussies would have to deal with'.[99]

Colonel Hurley's anecdote highlights the third important facet of the Australian strategy: a 'bottom-up' approach to political reconstruction. Frequent meetings with clan elders not only helped the Australians to enforce disarmament and reconstruct a public security system, but also enabled them to 'get their message out' to the local population.[100] Equally as effective was their refusal to allow the warlords and military factions to dominate political negotiations. Together with active support for what the Australians deemed were more legitimate political representatives, their strategy allowed a truly 'grass-roots' political movement to assert itself in the Baidoa HRS.[101]

The success of the Australians can be compared with the much less successful experience of the US controlled UNITAF operation in Mogadishu. Here, instead of actively seeking to limit the power of the major factions, the US sought to ensure their consent at every juncture. As the following sections will reiterate, negotiating with only the warlords may have provided the US with quicker responses than the 'bottom-up' approach applied by the Australians, but it also provided the warlords with unwarranted legitimacy and undermined already existing traditional institutions.

The American determination to keep their stay as brief and as uncomplicated as possible also led them to interpret their mandate in the most restrictive terms. Thus, they repudiated any role in 'nation-building' and conducted only limited and sporadic disarmament operations. They also refused to conduct the type of community policing that had fostered such good relations between the Australians and the local population and NGOs (and subsequent intelligence) in Baidoa. The result was a general sense of disillusionment in the capital, a feeling compounded by the inadequate attempts made to reestablish a justice system in the city. In comparison to the Australians, therefore, 'the US approach was short-term, reactive, crisis-orientated and compartmentalized'.[102]

Given its smaller size and much more limited capabilities, the chances of UNOSOM II succeeding where UNITAF had failed were always going to be slim. Nevertheless, the decision to avenge the deaths of the 24 Pakistani peacekeepers killed in the ambush of 5 June seemed a logical decision from both a political and military standpoint. If Aideed had been allowed to kill UN peacekeepers without prosecution, then the lives of peacekeepers all over the world might have been placed in jeopardy.

The response of the Security Council was swift and decisive. Through the adoption of Resolution 837 on 6 June the Council condemned the killings and authorized the 'arrest, prosecution and trial' of those responsible and called for a 'comprehensive program for disarmament'.[103] These two elements of the resolution were obviously designed to ensure an eradication of Aideed's SNA, a policy the UN and US applied with vigor in the initial months after its adoption. The decision to seek retribution also enjoyed general support amongst the military. Major General Lewis MacKensie argued that unlike Bosnia, 'Somalia was a relatively easy military problem. The point about the credibility of the UN in the merging new world disorder had to be made somewhere, and Somalia was the right place to make it'.[104] Major General Thomas Montgomery, the UNOSOM II Deputy Commander, also supported the manhunt, calling it a 'logical decision from a military standpoint' and even commended Admiral Howe's decision to offer the $25,000 reward for his capture.[105]

Nevertheless, having failed to create a Somali police and judiciary and lacking the kind of local support the Australians had eventually received in Baidoa, the UN and US were compelled to conduct the manhunt with their own forces and in a completely unfavorable environment. This led the Americans to continuously ratchet up the level of violence, thereby further alienating the local population. For example, during mid-1993 US Special Forces conducted a number of unsuccessful raids, perhaps the most disastrous of which occurred on 12 July, when an attack on a suspected SNA headquarters ended with the deaths of more than 50 Somalis, including key religious leaders and clan elders.[106] These traditional elders, belonging to the Habir Gedir, Ogadeni, Dir, Majerteen, Murosade, Sheikhal and other tribes, were believed to be meeting to develop a negotiating strategy with UNOSOM II. Mark Bradbury has speculated that the 'killing of these people prevented an early resolution of the conflict'.[107]

Similarly, American attacks on SNA arms dumps led to further Somali fatalities, thereby increasing Aideed's credibility within the local population and his own organization. As Patman points out, it was ironic that UN reprisals melted internal opposition to Aideed within his own Habir Gedir sub-clan, resulting in his chairmanship of the USC being extended for six months whilst he evaded arrest.[108] And as Oakley and Hirsch observed, following the attacks, the SNA became more militant, more disciplined and better organized from necessity; almost all the important Habir Gedir, including tribal elders rallied around it. Also, with the Habir Gedir and other subclans fearing elimination, sympathizers from the Ogadeni moved from central Somalia to reinforce the SNA militia, a significant factor that Oakley and Hirsch believe was underestimated by the UN and US.[109]

Local cultural factors also reinforced the need for less reactionary and more indigenous responses to the threat from Aideed and the SNA. For instance, it seems that even the decision to capture and try Aideed as an individual was fundamentally flawed because it misunderstood Somali culture. As Gary Anderson explains, the Somalis never understood the personalization of the conflict because the traditional clan structure of Somali society dictates that an attack on one member is an attack on all. If one member of a clan is guilty of a crime, the whole clan assumes responsibility. Therefore, when the UN attacked Aideed, it automatically attacked all the members of his Habir-Gedir subclan.[110]

In such an environment peace-enforcement conducted by foreign forces presents its own problems. One of these is the difficulty of using force in urban areas. As a commander of one of the American 10th Divisions' battalions explained, it 'is the worst kind of warfare because it is insidious. You are surrounded by the enemy. You are surrounded by the friendlies. You are surrounded by the innocent and the guilty'.[111] This dilemma was exacerbated by the tendency of militia members to shield themselves with women and children as they attacked UN peacekeepers. Unwilling to fire into a crowd, UN troops found themselves defenseless against rifle and grenade attack, often resulting in large numbers of casualties. When the peacekeepers did fire back, as occurred hours after a raid on an Aideed arms dump in June, the peacekeepers were portrayed by the SNA as killers of women and children and therefore out of control.

Finally, there are scholars like Kenneth Menkhaus and Ramesh Thakur who believe that by conducting peace-enforcement the UN lost its credibility as an impartial mediator between the Somali factions. As Menkhaus explains, 'for peace-enforcement, the UN had to be impartial...But having once embarked on enforcement measures against a serious violation, the UN could not simultaneously play the role of a neutral mediator in national reconciliation.'[112] However, it is hard to see how the UN could have maintained its neutrality in any constructive role, as even its attempts to rebuild local public security and promote political reconciliation through traditional Somali institutions would have been enough to convince the warlords that the their power base was being threatened.

Still, for military and political reasons, it is obviously better for UN mandated coalitions like UNITAF to conduct peace-enforcement and coercive disarmament operations than it is for UN peacekeepers to do so. Nevertheless, whichever type of forces are called upon, it is evident that their success in peace-enforcement and disarmament will depend to a great extent on how well they can conduct the type of 'multi-faceted' peacekeeping that the Australians exemplified. In essence, by acting as a local leviathan, by acting quickly to create a Somali justice system and by working to promote political reconciliation from the 'bottom-up', the Australians (and their French successors) implemented the 'twin-track' approach advocated by this text.

Unfortunately, by failing to deploy forces that could conduct this type of operation in the areas that were most stable, such as the North-East of Somalia, the UN and US missed an excellent opportunity to conduct disarmament and consolidate peace in the country's outlying regions, whilst they worked simultaneously to do the same in Mogadishu. Given the lack of a conception of the centralized State within Somali society, this strategy would have also been more culturally apt. However, both UNITAF and UNOSOM II concentrated too much on the capital, allowing the situation there to dictate the direction of each operation.

5.3   Reform of public security

As the previous section has made evident, the creation of a functioning justice system was essential to the achievement of any level of disarmament in Somalia. The Secretary-General acknowledged this in his report of 17 August 1993 when he stated that 'a well organized and effective police force would be able to limit the spread of light weapons'. Four months later he added that a Somali police force might be one of the 'key instruments' in creating the perception that disarmament was a 'Somali program'.[113] This indigenous police force was also expected to assume some of the security roles that UN troops were currently conducting. Unfortunately, through a combination of strategic mistakes and lack of resources, neither the UN nor the US were able to create a credible justice system in time to compliment their operations.

The first mistake made by the UN was the failure to realize that the core of a Somali police force already existed when UNOSOM first deployed. The outbreak of civil war had caused the already existing 15,000 strong Somali police force to disperse, mostly to their home clan regions. This had the unintended result of creating regional police forces, particularly in the northeast of the country, where they continued to conduct routine police duties. A similar scenario had occurred for judges. However, in October 1992 SGSR Sahnoun had decided that the creation of a national police force, although an option to be explored, would present serious problems in the absence of national reconciliation. He therefore decided to create a small security force of Somalis to assist UN personnel at major ports and distribution centers. This he hoped might eventually form the nucleus of a Somali police countrywide.[114] For Martin Ganzglass the decision to dismiss the existence of the regional forces and the credibility of the former police meant that 'Sahnoun failed to capitalize on what every subsequent report on the police noted, that the Somali police were well trained, disciplined and generally non-tribal. The nucleus for a Somali police, already existed, acceptable to Somalis in the regions where they were stationed.'[115]

The second mistake was the failure of UNITAF to maximize the effect of its civil affairs expertise in restoring a Somali criminal justice system. The original US plan for UNITAF had involved the deployment of ten Army

Reserve Civil Affairs units, which were to have assisted in the restoration of government functions, particularly the police and judicial systems. However, the US Joint Chiefs of Staff subsequently decided that as UNITAF was only expected to last for six weeks such involvement would constitute 'mission creep'.[116] Thus, despite the fact that increasing attacks on US forces had compelled UNITAF to create a 4,000 strong Auxiliary Police Force by March 1993 (composed almost completely of former Somali police) the 'failure to implement a full scale civil affairs program... ultimately led to the insertion of US combat forces in the hunt for Aideed...[when a] retrained Somali Police Force would have been much better suited for what was essentially a police function in the back streets of Mogadishu'.[117]

Decisions by the UN Secretariat also led to the wasting of UNOSOM II's initial planning. UNOSOM II's Justice division had drawn up ambitious plans for the restoration and expansion of the police and judicial systems, the budget for which was approved in principle by the Under-Secretary-General for Peacekeeping, Kofi Annan. Nevertheless, without informing Admiral Howe, who presumed that the DPKO was in the process of implementing the staffing and funding for the program, Annan decided to postpone requesting donor countries to contribute police instructors, equipment and funding until local, district and regional councils were established to assume supervisory authority over the forces.[118]

This was a fatal decision, not only because the UN CIVPOLS could have supervised the forces in the interim, but also because the formation of the councils were subject to the usual political stumbling blocks. As Kenneth Menkhaus asserts, in this case the political 'bottom-up' approach was as fundamentally flawed as the 'top-down approach' for which the UN was so heavily criticized. Through its insistence on the creation of local district councils the UN actually impeded peace-building efforts by 'forcing the militias into structures with fixed numbers of seats, therefore like conferences forcing them into assessing and agreeing on their relative size and importance'.[119] By making their formation a prerequisite for the creation of a Somali police force Annan imposed a serious delay on UNOSOM's whole justice program.

Therefore, despite the Secretary-General's realization of the importance of a Somali justice system, both to the reestablishment of law and order and to disarmament, it was apparent that a less than concerted approach had been taken in its creation. In the opinion of Oakley and Hirsch, when UNOSOM took over from UNITAF on 4 May it provided only 'limited resources to the fledgling police and judiciary'. Whilst awaiting an experts' report on the establishment of a national justice system the UN allowed the existing police to dwindle 'because of sporadic salary payments, an end to military liaison and assistance previously provided by UNITAF, and a drop in morale, as well as the confrontations with the SNA before the report was finally published in late August'.[120] When the US finally realized the full importance of a Somali police force, following the US Rangers' battle on 3 October, it responded by donating $6 million to the funding of the justice program, as well as $25 million worth of equipment. However, it was simply too late in the day.[121]

5.4   Strategies of conflict resolution

As the Somalian intervention lacked a comprehensive agreement, there was obviously no established framework for dealing with the warring parties when UNOSOM began. The first SRSG, Mohamed Sahnoun, was therefore forced to draw principally on his previous experience as a former Algerian diplomat in his dealings with the Somali factions and community leaders. Showing an impressive appreciation of Somali culture Sahnoun negotiated with the faction leaders yet placed his greatest emphasis on trying to increase the political influence of traditional and intellectual members of Somali society. For this he is credited as being the first diplomat to initiate a truly second track diplomacy of 'building peace...from below [by] involving all strata of the shattered Somali communities'.[122]

Unfortunately, despite its growing success, UN impatience was to end Sahnoun's strategy and replace it with one designed to achieve quicker results. This led to the faction leaders being awarded too much importance, a mistake repeated by the US negotiators. The UN's first blunder was to implicitly accept Ali Mahdi as Interim President of Somalia during James Jonah's official visit in January 1992. This not only elevated him to an unwarranted position, but also initiated Aideed's suspicions of UN bias.

Similarly inappropriate concentration on the Somali warlords was exhibited when only they were invited to the Addis Ababa disarmament talks in December 1992. And even when pressure from NGOs and others ensured greater participation for community and clan elders in the Addis Ababa talks of March 1993, only the 15 faction leaders were required to sign the final agreement. Though disappointed with the ability of the clan leaders to affect the crisis, the UN and US continued to sponsor a number of local level, community based, reconciliation conferences in order to broaden Somali participation in peacemaking efforts. However, by vacillating between including and excluding the clan elders in negotiations with the faction leaders, the UN and US succeeded only in upsetting both constituencies.[123]

Elevating the importance of faction leaders was inappropriate not only because they had the least incentives to seek a peaceful solution, but also because the inherent weaknesses of their position often left them unable to deliver on their promises. As Sahnoun has admitted, even he was not always certain that the warlords he was negotiating with were in control of the militias they led. Despite being considered one of the strongest faction leaders even Aideed was known to have trouble controlling his fighters and ensuring public safety in the areas he controlled. Andrew Natsios describes the predicament of faction leaders well: 'the tenuousness of warlord grasp on power put a premium on providing their militias with booty to keep their loyalty. Feeding the militias was not enough, the warlords were pressed to maintain their militias in the lifestyle to which they were accustomed'.[124]

The faction leaders obviously had the power to mobilize their men. The most pertinent question, however, was whether they had the power to demobilize them. Therefore, rather than simply negotiating with the faction leaders to sign grandiose disarmament agreements, the UN should have focused its greatest energies on creating viable public security institutions and an economy with sufficient financial incentives and employment opportunities to entice faction members into more constructive lifestyles. Ken Menkhaus highlights the UN's weaknesses in this regard:

> The international community thus had an unpalatable choice – either it could work to marginalize the conflict constituency, with the very real risk of protracted armed conflict, or it could attempt to transform the interests of these communities, to give them a stake in peaceful reconciliation. The latter option would have required a great deal of economic development funding, which UNOSOM did not have, to provide market incentives to lure merchants into a peace constituency and job training to give young militiamen alternatives to banditry and war.[125]

This need for a concerted developmental approach was reiterated by John Prendergast, who recommended that to dilute the attractiveness of militia membership and looting as permanent professions the UN needed to create employment, education and micro-credit programs which specifically targeted the young, urban males, whose numbers had increased dramatically. Proposals to address the needs of future generations also included primary and secondary education facilities, together with Koranic schools.[126]

6 Conclusion

Of all the cases included in this text it is Somalia that had come closest to a manifestation of the Hobbesian 'state of nature' when the UN first deployed. With the fall of Siad Barre's regime in 1991 the capital had descended into chaos and a humanitarian catastrophe looked certain. That Somalia required some kind of international intervention is therefore an axiom.

However, the type of intervention Somalia required is still contested. For example, Richard Betts argues that if the UN or US was unable to deploy a 'Leviathan' in the form of a nation-wide peace-enforcement operation, then they should have continued to weaken Aideed whilst '[championing] one of his contenders'. This would, he suggests, have tipped the balance of power comprehensively in favor of at least one of the warlords and stability might thus have been achieved.[127]

Given that the factions fighting for power in Mogadishu existed in an intersubjective understanding of aggression composed by a relationship of predation, the twin-track framework advocated by this text also suggests that a nation-wide peace-enforcement operation would have been appropriate. If such a force had been able to conduct on a nation-wide basis the kind of 'multi-faceted' peace-enforcement operation that the Australian contingent of UNITAF had found so successful, then maybe general disarmament could have been achieved.

Indeed, rather than concentrating only on Mogadishu, as UNITAF and UNOSOM II were inclined to do, such a force could have provided security to regions that were already more stable and where the intersubjective understanding between local factions and clans was more cooperative. For instance, Ian Spears provides a prime example of constructivist logic at work when he describes how a major clan faction in Northern Somaliland, disappointed with the progress being made on disarmament (following the establishment of a new constitutional structure for the region in 1993), entered the city of Hargeisa and unilaterally surrendered its heavy weapons.

> [This] action was regarded as enormously symbolic and shamed the remaining armed factions into following suit. The fact that so many heavy weapons were turned in had the effect of launching a much more widespread disarmament process. While the act involved obvious risks insofar as it momentarily left the clan faction exposed, the dramatic nature of the event unequivocally conveyed an intention to pursue peace and its trust in its adversaries – confidence which was almost immediately reciprocated by the remaining clans.[128]

Thus, by first signaling their desire for peace to the other factions and then following through with the act of disarming, the first faction initiated a transformation in the intersubjective understanding between the clans and factions present in the region. Significantly, this all occurred without the benefit of third party security guarantees.

Without a nation-wide operation the international community still had the option of tipping the balance in favor of one of the warlords, as Betts also suggests. However, the evidence of Somali history suggests that such action would not have brought lasting peace. Rather, the key to sustainable peace in Somalia lay in the continuation of SRSG Sahnoun's political 'bottom-up' strategy that had achieved so much in a relatively short time period. This strategy was equally successful when applied by the Australians in the Baidoa HRS. Unfortunately, by the time the UN and US realized its utility it was simply too late to turn back the tide.

So, it is evident that even with a limited intervention the UN and US could have achieved a great deal more than they actually did. Nevertheless, though both actors made mistakes, peace-enforcement *per se* was not one of them. Mats Berdal argues rightfully that:

> The debate on doctrine and the use of force in peace operations was not helped by the introduction of the notion of a so-called 'Mogasdishu line'. The idea of such a 'line' gave the misleading impression, easily shot down by critics, that consent was somehow an absolute quality; either you possessed it or you did not. Quite clearly consent is not an absolute quality, and the aforementioned experience of Australian troops in Somalia shows that the margin of consent that does exist in 'messy' or 'grey' operational environments can be enlarged and built upon by an enterprising outside force.[129]

However, it is somewhat misleading to argue, as Robert Patman does, that peace-enforcement 'can enhance rather than diminish the impartiality of the UN in a lawless environment'.[130] Even if the peace-enforcement operation declares itself impartial at its outset, it is by its very nature opposed to those who see their self-interest in a continuation of the lawless state. As Berdal again identifies, 'it is more likely that a warring faction which is militarily and politically disadvantaged by the actions of a 'peace restoration' or a supposedly impartial peace enforcement mission, will take little comfort from not having been formally designated an *enemy*'.[131] Indeed, Patman's own account shows that the Australian success lay not in their impartiality, but in their willingness to actively support those factions and community members that truly wished to see peace established and to ostracize from the political process those that did not.

The UN and US also failed to apply adequate Track 1 diplomacy at the levels of ex-combatants and the general population. Without the creation of a credible Somali police force and justice system there could be no hope of generating the safe 'political space' within which a robust civil society could reemerge without fear of intimidation or retaliation.[132] At the same time they also failed to apply sufficient Track 2 diplomacy through the provision of economic incentives to attract faction members away from their predatory lifestyles.

In fact it was apparent from the UN's experience in Somalia that large-scale interventions could actually undermine Track 2 diplomacy by unintentionally transforming local economies. These effects could also hinder the achievement of disarmament. For example, Andrew Natsios argues that the influx of hard currency that accompanied the intervention and relief effort in Somalia unbalanced the local economy and diminished the incentives for traditional trading. Thus:

> [the] chaos and relief effort conspired unknowingly to create a set of pernicious incentives which simultaneously corrupted the natural instinct of the merchant class for some modicum of law and order, increased the demand for weapons and caused an increase in supply as their price rose, and reinforced the power of the most irresponsible elements of Somali society, the warlords, by providing them with more wealth, taken by extortion, protection rackets, and looting, for them to prosecute their clan wars and maintain their tenuous hold on power.[133]

The answer to this conundrum is not, of course, to argue against intervention, but to try to make interventions more sensitive to local conditions. One way is to introduce projects such as monetization, which puts the traditional structures of society to work for relief and development. Monetization was accepted as a project worth supporting in Somalia as merchants seldom had their food looted. This was because they could seek retribution through the traditional legal systems of Somali society, which generally involved clan elders paying compensation and disciplining the thieves concerned. However, when SRSG Sahnoun tried to introduce monetization he was never able to procure the support it required, despite his many pleas.[134]

The need to encourage the creation of a civil society that could contribute to the generation of sustainable peace also highlighted the importance of understanding the contextual rationality at work in Somali culture. As the above discussion has reiterated, the most obvious mistake was to elevate the faction leaders to unwarranted positions of authority by ignoring those members of Somali society that could have had a restraining effect on their behavior.

However, just as the UN must take account of local culture in its strategies for conflict resolution, it must not expect traditional methods to be immediately successful. This is especially the case when, as in Somalia, the collapse of the state has been accompanied by the breakdown of the traditional structures of society. During the intervention there were many recorded instances in which Somali elders had refrained from engaging in the condemnation or censorship of unruly youths, simply because the traditional respect accorded to them had disappeared in the years of anarchy and fighting. Equally, when traditional methods were used to negotiate disarmament agreements, faction leaders like Aideed continued to show their willingness to circumvent them in order to maintain their positions.[135] So, although there can be little hope of a successful outcome if the traditional methods of agreement are ignored, cultural sensitivity by the UN cannot in itself be viewed as a panacea for the ailments of any conflict ridden society.

5
Yugoslavia 1991–1995

1   Introduction

As in the case of Somalia, the UN's role in disarmament in the former
Yugoslavia was not to arise as part of an overall political settlement.
Rather, it was to emanate both from interim arrangements and from the
need to protect civilian populations under attack from besieging forces.
Established in February 1992, the United Nations Protection Force
(UNPROFOR) was initially mandated to protect and disarm three so-called
United Nations Protected Areas (UNPAs) in the country's second largest
constituent republic, Croatia. By June of the same year the UN had extended its mandate to include operations in the neighboring republic of
Bosnia and Herzegovina (from herein referred to as Bosnia), in order to
ensure the safe delivery of humanitarian aid. As the international community continued its search for a solution to the escalating conflict, the UN
forces on the ground became ever more involved in disarmament operations designed to protect civilian populations from the fighting. This was
manifest in the creation of six United Nations Safe Areas (UNSAs) in the
Bosnian republic in May 1993.[1]

At its peak the UNPROFOR operation was to involve nearly 40,000 UN
personnel. Despite this extensive commitment the UN was unable to
secure the disarmament of any of the warring parties. Rather, throughout
UNPROFOR's tenure, all the main belligerents remained heavily armed
and persisted in their attempts to qualitatively and quantitatively improve
their arsenals. To explain why, this chapter will utilize the twin-track
framework outlined in Chapter 1. It will begin with the customary
account of the origins of the conflict, which will be followed in turn by a
description of the UN's disarmament mandate. The third and fourth sections will provide an account and assessment of its implementation.
Finally, the conclusion will assess the utility of the 'twin-track' framework
advocated by this text to explain the failure of disarmament in the former
Yugoslavia.

2   Background to the conflict

As one scholar has expressed it, the Yugoslav tragedy frames the 20th Century like bookends.[2] Born from the ashes of the collapsed Austro-Hungarian empire, the Kingdom of the Serbs, Croats and Slovenes was renamed Yugoslavia in 1929 by King Alexander, whose inability to resolve the rivalries between the republic's three constituent nationalities led to his own assassination just five years later. In 1941 Yugoslav history took another turn when the Germans routed its national army in under a week. During the subsequent period of foreign occupation three resistance groups emerged, all of which fought each other with the same ferocity with which they fought the Nazis. Two of the groups, the 'Ustashes' and 'Chetniks', were Croatian and Serb nationalists respectively, and each of them became infamous for the atrocities they committed against other ethnic groups. The third resistance movement, the Communist 'Partisans', was Yugoslavia's only supranational party and though they concentrated primarily on defeating the Germans they also killed political opponents at home. Led by Josip Broz, a half-Slovene, half-Croat, who went by the name of Tito, the Partisans offered the dual benefit of emancipation from the Germans and freedom from Serb domination. This was enough to win them multi-ethnic support and subsequent post-war power.

Tito's control over Yugoslavia depended on both his cult of personality and his deft manipulation of the numerous ethnic groups that existed within his country's population of 23.5 million. This manipulation was manifest in his 1974 Constitution, which created a federation of six equal republics and two autonomous provinces. These latter provinces lay within Serbia, the largest and most eastern of the six republics. Although Serbia was populated predominately by Eastern Orthodox Slavs, its southern province of Kosovo and its northern province of Vojvodina had strong Albanian-Muslim and Hungarian minorities respectively. Croatia, the country's second largest republic, lay to the West and had a majority Catholic Slav population. So too did Slovenia, which bordered Croatia to the northwest. In between Croatia and Serbia lay the republic of Bosnia, which had a multi-ethnic composition with a Muslim plurality. Along with the greater autonomy provided to Kosovo and Vojvodina, the 1974 Constitution's other important provision was its recognition of Muslims as a constituent nation. This, Tito hoped, might help dissipate the popular belief that Muslims were either Catholics or Orthodox Slavs whose conversion had simply been an historical mistake.[3]

Recognizing that Yugoslavia could only exist if Serbia's bureaucracy was kept on a relatively short leash, Tito's Constitution devolved most powers to the republics, except those over economic policy, defense and international affairs. Nevertheless, he also knew he could not afford for the Serbs to feel excluded and so he ensured the relative strength of Serb politicians in Croatia, Bosnia, Vojvodina and Kosovo, as well as at the federal level. Tito's strategy, as Glenny describes it, was a highly sophisticated game of divide and rule.[4] Unfortunately, even this sophisticated strategy could not provide the security guarantees that the ethnic minorities craved, nor eradicate completely the sense of loss the Serbians felt Tito's decentralizing constitution had inflicted upon them. This cauldron of discontent was to boil over as soon as Tito died in 1980.

The location for the first serious protests was to be the autonomous province of Kosovo, where Muslim students had initiated demonstrations in March 1981 to demand a greater political role for their compatriots. These anti-Serb demonstrations were to reach such a scale that the Yugoslav army eventually intervened.[5] The same ethno-nationalist sentiments were apparent in the rest of Serbia. The most infamous example of this was the Memorandum of the Serbian Academy of Sciences and Arts of 1986, which claimed that the Serbs had been forced into an unjust position by Tito's arrangements and that political and economic discrimination was threatening the Serbian nation's very existence. Their plight was greatest, the document alleged, in the province of Kosovo, where they faced total genocide.[6] At the same time, the Serbian media began retelling stories of the Second World War, thus reviving the emotional memories and folklore of Ustasha atrocities, Chetnik responses and Partisan revenge.[7]

Likened to a great oak tree under whose shade nothing else could grow, Tito could leave no heir apparent. Rather, his legacy was a hopelessly inefficient eight-member collective presidency, comprised of one member from each of the six republics and Serbia's two autonomous provinces. As the legitimacy of the federal institutions had already begun to deteriorate along with Tito's health, this new unwieldy institution was to inherit a country that consisted of little more than eight regionally based Communist parties, the secret police and the army.[8] When, by 1987, Serbian protests in Kosovo had reached a scale that demanded a personal response from then President, Ivan Stambolic, he elected not to travel to the region himself. Rather, he sent his friend and protégé of 25 years, Slobodan Milosevic, a decision that was to begin his own downfall and hurtle Milosevic on his destiny to infamy. Although Milosevic had shown little interest in the plight of the Kosovar Serbs prior to his visit, he nevertheless recognized the potential of the situation. By stoking the fires of Serbian nationalism in Kosovo and then actively spreading them throughout Serbia, he had managed to ensure Stambolic's dismissal as president by the end of 1987.

Within another 12 months Milosevic had utilized the same tactics to force the resignations of the governments of both Serbia's autonomous area of Vojvadina and Yugoslavia's smallest republic, Montenegro. The significance of these developments was not lost on the nation's other republics. With Milosevic's eventual revocation of autonomy for Kosovo and Vojvadina in March 1989, Serbia had taken possession of three of the eight votes in the Yugoslav Presidency. And with Montenegro now under his effective control, Milosevic held four votes, half of those available and enough to block any federal action he objected to. Exacerbated by his calls for the unification of the Serbian nation, the fears of the other republics were simply becoming too great to keep the country together.

The first republic to strain at the federal reigns was Slovenia. Arguing that Serbia's decision to reform its constitution without consulting the other republics meant that they therefore had the right to do the same, the Slovene's proposed a number of amendments to their own constitution. To the chagrin of the Serbians these amendments included the right to decide for themselves when the army could take action in their republic; when to declare a state-of-emergency; what Slovenia's relationship should be with the other republics; and which parts of federal law they wished to implement. Claiming the amendments would violate the 1974 Constitution the Serbians initially hoped the army would intervene to prevent the Slovenes from adopting them. Until this time, Milosevic had successfully convinced the Yugoslav People's Army (JNA), the fifth largest army in Europe, that he alone was the last politician striving to keep the federation intact. For this reason the JNA had colluded in his exploits to centralize Serbian power. However, on this occasion the head of the JNA, General Kadijevic, decided against intervention (despite having previously agreed it) fearing that such action might be unconstitutional.[9]

Despite applying all the political pressure he could muster Milosevic failed to persuade the Slovenes to back down. And so, determined to continue on their path towards independence, the Slovenes held democratic elections in April 1990 in which (following a second round of polling) the former head of the Slovene Communist party, Milan Kucan, was elected President. However, without informing the new government the JNA moved in to disarm the Slovene Territorial Defense forces (TO) two days after it had assumed office. Although the 1974 Constitution ensured that the TOs were officially part of the Yugoslav armed forces, Tito's desire to decentralize the country's defenses ensured that they were organized and prepared by 'the responsible authorities of the republics and autonomous provinces'.[10] However, to the JNA (which had its own supreme command) and Serbian authorities they represented little more than potential armies for Yugoslav republics desiring independence.[11]

By the time President Kucan became aware of the JNA's actions and was able to send out an order to try and stop it, the Slovene TO had already lost over two-thirds of its weapons. Left with only 10,000 weapons for a force of around 70,000, the new government's defense minister instigated a clandestine weapons program designed to convert the TO into a credible national army. When the JNA intensified its campaign to disarm the TO in September, taking control of its headquarters in Lubjana on

4 October, Kucan was made aware of the program and gave his consent to it.[12]

The Croatians were to suffer a similar fate after they too held elections in April in which a former JNA general and historian, Franjo Tudjman, was elected President. The JNA had moved in to disarm the Croatian TO at the same time as its Slovenian counterpart, but in this case had achieved even greater success. Left with little more that 15,000 weapons and one armored personnel carrier, the Croatian government was also compelled to begin a clandestine weapons program, but with the intention of building a national force from its police force rather than its TO.[13]

Significantly, although both states desired greater independence, Slovenia and Croatia differed fundamentally in their ethnic composition. Whilst Slovenia was essentially ethnically homogenous, Croatia contained around 600,000 ethnic Serbs, the most radical of whom were concentrated in the Krajina region adjacent to the Bosnian border.[14] When the new Tudjman government produced a constitution that defined the Croatian state as the sovereign state of the Croatian nation, making no mention of the ethnic Serbs living within its borders, its inevitable effect was to embolden the position of the Krajina Serbs who had already begun to demand independence and secession.[15] Relations were to deteriorate even further when an unsuccessful attempt by the Croatian police to prevent a referendum on independence being held in the Krajina during August only intensified the Serbs' siege mentality.

Without a Serbian diaspora to manipulate, Milosevic had been forced to accept the inevitability of Slovenian independence. However, this was not the case with Croatia, where the increasingly militant Krajina Serbs continued to arm themselves in preparation for war. Though Milosevic had managed to persuade the Federal Presidency to issue an order demanding that the Croatian paramilitaries disarm by 20 January, he was unable to muster enough votes within the Presidency to mandate the JNA to do it by force. Milosevic's actual intent was not to use the JNA to keep the Croats in the federation (although as they were still committed to Tito's ideals the leaders of the JNA were disposed to this idea), but rather to deploy it in Serb dominated areas in order to allow them to secede.[16] When the Krajina Serbs eventually declared their independence on 16 March, the Serbian government immediately recognized them as the 'Serb Autonomous Province of Krajina'.[17] This was followed by Croatia's own referendum on 19 May, in which over 90 per cent voted for independence, though most of the republic's ethnic Serb population boycotted it.[18]

With Yugoslavia hurtling towards disintegration, the first outside organization to become involved was the European Community (EC – later to become the European Union (EU) in November 1992).[19] Though both the EC and US wanted the constituent republics to negotiate an internal arrangement that would maintain the integrity of the Yugoslav state, neither entity took an active role in encouraging a specific alternative. Thus, throughout the summer the republics continued to argue over whether they should continue as a federation, as the Serbs proposed, or as a loose association of sovereign states (modeled on the EU itself) as the Croats and Slovenes preferred. Bosnia and Macedonia also favored a confederal model, although the former wanted to retain closer links between the republics than the latter.[20] In this cauldron of intensifying nationalism their respective positions remained irreconcilable and the Serbian decision in May to prevent the rotation of the Presidency to the Croatian, Stipe Mesic, so it could precipitate a state of emergency and declare martial law, only persuaded Croatia and Slovenia that no accommodation would ever be found.[21] Once they were sure America would not intervene to stop them, both republics declared their independence on 25 June 1991. The EC and US were therefore left supporting something that no longer existed.[22]

Within hours of Slovenia's declaration a small force of 400 federal police, 270 federal customs officers and nearly 2,000 JNA troops were ordered to secure the republic's borders and airport. The JNA had not expected resistance and were therefore caught off-guard when the Slovene TO surrounded their barracks (cutting off electricity and water) and forcibly prevented their deployment. The JNA was thus left with the option of either withdrawing completely or of seeking to capture the whole republic. Unlike the JNA, however, the Serbian leadership had already forsaken the idea of using force to maintain the integrity of Yugoslavia and therefore pressed it to withdraw. Nevertheless, Milosevic knew that to ensure the army's withdrawal the Presidency would have to be reconstituted.[23]

The EC's first major response to the JNA's actions in Slovenia was to send a 'Troika' of past, present and future presidents of the European Council to negotiate a cease-fire. Acting as though he was making a concession, Milosevic gave the Troika his acquiescence to the succession of Mesic, thereby reactivating the Presidency as he himself desired. With the EC having already imposed a nation-wide arms embargo the parties met again on the island of Brioni on 7 July. Here the Troika helped negotiate a three-month 'cooling off period' during which Slovenia and Croatia agreed not to implement their claims to independence. The parties also negotiated a cease-fire and an agreement to begin negotiations on all aspects of Yugoslavia's future by 1 August. Finally, they also agreed to allow the deployment of a European Community Monitoring Mission, which was to operate within the framework of the Conference on Security and Co-operation in Europe and was to be a semi-military, yet open and flexible monitoring operation.[24] Though the EC had declared its refusal to accept the redrawing of borders by force, the Yugoslav Presidency's decision on 18 July to withdraw the JNA from Slovenia within three months meant the small western republic had effectively achieved just that. The whole incident had also inflicted a massive humiliation upon the JNA, which could no longer claim it was acting to protect the integrity of the Yugoslav state. Instead, it was rapidly transforming into the army of Greater Serbia, the consequences of which were to become immediately apparent in Croatia.

By the time the three-month moratorium on independence was due to expire on 8 October the EC baton had passed to Lord Carrington, a former NATO Secretary-General and British Foreign Secretary, who first attempted to negotiate a constitutional compromise with the parties on 7 September. Although he understood that Slovenia's independence was now a *fait acompli*, he also recognized the dangers of its immediate recognition and therefore insisted that it not be awarded it until such a constitutional compromise had been found.[25] His first major breakthrough was to come on 4 October, when all the parties agreed that their negotiations should proceed on the basis of three principles. Firstly, that they should form a loose association or alliance of sovereign or independent republics. Secondly, that adequate arrangements should be made for the protection of communities. And thirdly, that there would be no unilateral border changes. This last commitment was obviously a major concession from Milosevic.[26]

With the war in Croatia escalating, Carrington presented the parties with a proposal on 16 October that offered to rearrange the Yugoslav republics along the lines of the EC itself. In this respect it mirrored the proposals that Slovenia, Croatia, Bosnia and Macedonia had made during the previous summer.[27] Unfortunately for Milosevic, though Carrington's plan awarded extensive individual, cultural and political rights to ethnic Serbs living outside Serbia, it naturally did the same for ethnic Albanians living in Kosovo. This, of course, was unacceptable to a man who had built his political career on the removal of those very same rights. He therefore dismissed Carrington's plan for meddling in Serbia's internal affairs. Though the Montenegrin leader, President Momir Bulatovic, had initially surprised the other five republican leaders by supporting the Carrington plan, intense Serbian pressure forced him to call a referendum on the issue for the end of October. It was also sufficient to persuade him to support a joint amendment to Carrington's plan, along with the Serbians, calling for a clause declaring that the federal republic of Yugoslavia should continue to exist for those who did not wish to secede. Conscious of Milosevic's desire to use the amendment to carve a rump Yugoslavia out of the Serb dominated areas of Bosnia and Croatia, Carrington found it 'totally unacceptable'. Montenegro's referendum, not unexpectedly, resulted in an overwhelming vote for the republic to stay in Yugoslavia.[28]

Whist Milosevic continued to stonewall in The Hague, the JNA increased its bombardments of the historic Croatian cities of Vukovar and Dubrovnik. Though the destruction of Vukovar appeared to have no military rationale, the international community refused to intervene in order to stop what Silber and Little describe as an 'orgy of vengeance'.[29] The EC's only response was to threaten Milosevic with economic sanctions if he had not accepted

Carrington's plan by 3 November. When this failed to elicit the desired response, the EC recommended trade sanctions against Yugoslavia, including an oil embargo, on 8 November. Although they were initially applied to the whole country, they were soon lifted for all the republics except Serbia and Montenegro.[30] With Carrington's initiative effectively stalled and international pressure mounting for something to be done, the EC began to look to the UN to assume control of the on-going discussions for a cease-fire and peacekeeping operation. By mid-November, therefore, a multi-track peace process had developed, with the UN Secretary-General's Special Envoy to Yugoslavia, Cyrus Vance, taking the diplomatic lead.

3   The UN's disarmament mandate

The original request for a UN peacekeeping operation in the former Yugoslavia was made by the Yugoslav State Secretary for National Defense, together with the Presidents of Croatia and Serbia, at a meeting with Cyrus Vance on 23 November 1991. On the basis of this request the Secretary-General prepared a report, subsequently to be known as the 'Vance Plan', which created the framework for a UN peacekeeping operation in the constituent republic of Croatia. Although fearful of deploying troops in a non-consensual environment, his concern that not to do so might cause the latest cease-fire to collapse convinced him to recommend its establishment in early February 1992.[31] Thus, on 21 February, the Security Council established UNPROFOR for an initial period of 12 months.[32]

UNPROFOR's *raison d'etre* was essentially to help create the conditions of peace and security required for the negotiation of an overall settlement for the former Yugoslavia.[33] To these ends the force was to deploy in three so-called United Nations Protected Areas (UNPAs) within Croatia. The UNPAs, covering Eastern Slavonia, Western Slavonia and Krajina, were chosen on the basis that Serbians constituted a majority, or significant minority, within them. Once deployed, the UN was to ensure that the UNPAs were de-militarized and that all persons residing in them were protected from the fear of armed attack.

Demilitarization under the Vance Plan required that all JNA and Croatian National Guard units be withdrawn from the UNPAs. TO units, together with any paramilitary units, irregular or volunteer forces were also to be withdrawn, but any that remained were to be disbanded and demobilized.[34] Their command structures were to suffer the same fate. Weapons belonging to these forces were to be handed over to the JNA before its withdrawal or placed in the hands of the UN for safekeeping during the 'interim period' of the operation.

To protect the residents of the UNPAs, UNPROFOR was to control access to them, as well as monitor their local police forces. Each UNPA's police force was to be formed from its own residents, who were to be chosen in proportions reflecting the ethnic composition of the population that resided there before the outbreak of hostilities.[35] The Vance Plan also excluded the restoration of Croatian laws and institutions in the UNPAs until an overall settlement had been achieved.[36] Lastly, UNPROFOR was to supervise the withdrawal of the JNA from the whole of Croatia and support humanitarian agencies in the return of displaced persons.[37] There was no timetable established for the completion of any of these tasks, the Vance Plan requiring only that they be achieved as soon as possible.[38]

As the proceeding sections will explain, UNPROFOR's disarmament mandate was to undergo a number of enlargements before the operation's conclusion in late 1995. The most significant of these followed the extension of its operations into the republic of Bosnia in June 1992. Thus, by the end of its mandate UNPROFOR was to become involved in protecting both humanitarian aid deliveries and besieged populations and, to a certain degree, was also to become involved in coercive disarmament.

4 Implementation

From the very beginning of its tenure in Croatia UNPROFOR lacked the requisite cooperation from either party to fully implement its disarmament mandate. Whilst the Croatians, unhappy at the UN's failure to disarm the Serbs, continued to seize strategic sites within the UNPAs, the Serbs themselves refused to disarm citing the need to defend themselves against the Croatian army's revanchivist actions. And whilst the Croatian government continued to insist that the UNPAs be formally reincorporated into Croatia, the Serbs refused even to discuss their status until the Croatian authorities had recognized the UNPAs as the State of the Republic of Serbian Krajina (RSK).[39]

Three developments were to further complicate the UN's predicament during 1992. The first of these was the slow deployment of UNPROFOR's 13,000 troops and 530 civilian police (CIVPOL). According to one human rights group UNPROFOR's lethargic deployment allowed ethnic cleansing in the UNPAs to proceed virtually unchecked. Thus, by the time it had fully deployed in June 1992 most of the UNPAs' non-Serbian populations had already been expelled.[40]

The second development came with the UN's realization that it had inherited a much more militarized situation than it had initially expected. This had been principally caused by JNA units withdrawing from the UNPAs and leaving behind copious amounts of arms and equipment for local Serb militias. The withdrawal of the JNA from Yugoslavia's other republics, following the formation of the Federal Republic of Yugoslavia by Serbia and Montenegro on 27 April, also had the effect of leaving behind large numbers of well-armed troops in Croatia and Bosnia, many of whom were keen to join local militias.[41] UNPROFOR's difficulties were only compounded when, in a third development, its mandate was extended in June to cover the so-called 'pink zones'. These were areas outside the UNPAs that had previously been controlled by the JNA and which contained significant numbers of Serbs. UNPROFOR was now mandated to demilitarize them in the same manner as the UNPAs.

Despite these difficulties UNPROFOR had achieved some notable successes by the beginning of July. Not only had it ensured the withdrawal of the JNA, but having divided the UNPAs into four sectors (Sector East covered eastern Slavonia; Sector West covered western Slavonia; Sector North covered the northern part of the Krajina; Sector South covered the southern part of the Krajina) it had actually succeeded in demilitarizing one of them – Sector West. However, unable to do the same in the other three, UNPROFOR resigned itself to organizing the withdrawal of heavy weapons to a distance of 30 kilometers from the present lines of confrontation. This resulted in a considerable lessening of tensions in all the UNPAs.[42]

Meanwhile, peace negotiations remained fruitless. Though Carrington's peace proposal of late 1991 had initially floundered on Milosevic's refusal to reinstate the political and cultural rights he had removed from the Kosovan Albanians in 1989, the fatal blow was actually to be inflicted by Germany's unilateral recognition of Croatia and Slovenia on 19 December. Though member states like France and Britain remained fundamentally opposed to early recognition, their desire to maintain European solidarity before the impending Maastricht summit led them to support the EC's recognition of both republics on 15 January 1992. Even the pleas of Carrington, Cyrus Vance, Bosnian President Izetbegovic and the UN Secretary-General were insufficient to dissuade them.[43]

Izetbegovic was therefore left with three choices for the future of his republic. The first was to stay in a rump Yugoslavia dominated by the Serbians, an obviously unpalatable scenario. The second was to accept the territorial division of his republic along ethnic lines. And the third was to follow the lead of Slovenia and Croatia and apply for EC recognition. He knew, of course, that the Bosnian Serbs would never accept independence for Bosnia in its present form and that war would therefore be an inevitable consequence. Nevertheless, with EC recognition for Croatia and Slovenia only weeks away, he officially requested recognition on 20 December 1991.

In the knowledge that Bosnian independence was virtually assured, Carrington and the Portuguese Ambassador to Yugoslavia, Jose Cuitilero (Portugal was holding the EU Presidency at the time), began to mediate talks between the three Bosnian parties. A major breakthrough appeared to have been achieved on 18 March when the parties not only agreed to recognize the existing borders of their republic, but also endorsed the formation of national territorial units within it.[44] Whilst the former represented a major compromise for the Serbs and Croats, the latter was a fundamental shift for Izetbegovic. However, almost immediately Izetbegovic began to recoil from his commitments, thereby drawing heavy criticism from many quarters for ditching Bosnia's last chance to avert war. In the wake of the Bosnian referendum held at the end of February, in which the vast majority voted for independence, Izetbegovic continued to press for recognition. By the time the EC and US recognized Bosnia on 6 and 7 April respectively, the republic was already in the midst of civil war.[45]

With the war escalating the Security Council reacted by imposing an economic embargo on Serbia and Montenegro at the end of May. It also called on all parties to help 'create immediately the necessary conditions for the unimpeded delivery of humanitarian supplies to Sarajevo and other destinations in [Bosnia], including the establishment of a security zone encompassing Sarajevo airport'.[46] When the Bosnian parties signed the Sarajevo Airport Agreement (SAA) on 5 June the Council therefore extended UNPROFOR's operations into Bosnia to help implement it three days later.

As it was designed to open up the airport for the delivery of humanitarian aid the SAA required the parties to place all their heavy weapons within range of the airport under UNPROFOR supervision. UNPROFOR was also to establish and control a number of security corridors between the airport and the city. However, despite having deployed 1,100 military observers at the start of the month, Boutros-Ghali was forced to acknowledge in July that neither a cease-fire nor the concentration of weapons under UNPRO-FOR observation had been fully achieved.[47]

Later the same month all three Bosnian parties signed a further agreement, again brokered by Carrington, that required each of them to place their heavy weapons around Sarajevo under international control. However, Boutros-Ghali complained that this new mandate was not only impossible to execute, but that the Security Council had 'thrust' it upon UNPROFOR without adequate consultation and without the necessary financial or material commitments. As none of the parties had declared either the locations or the quantities of weapons to be supervised, Boutros-Ghali believed the new mandate would require at least an additional 1,000 observers. The UN believed this break in communication had been caused by its lack of representation at the discussions leading to the Security Council request and argued that 'such difficulties could [have] been avoided if the whole peace negotiations were handled by the world organization.'[48]

In response to the Secretary-General's criticisms Britain proposed the International Conference on the Former Yugoslavia (ICFY), convened by the EC in late August. By this time around 50,000 (mostly civilians) had been killed and more than 2 million made homeless in Bosnia and Croatia, mostly by Serbian aggression.[49] Although the London Conference, as it was subsequently known, was designed to pressure the Bosnian parties into negotiating a comprehensive political settlement, it nevertheless also recognized the need to achieve 'the grouping of heavy weaponry under international control' and the 'demilitarization of major towns and the monitoring of them by international observers'. Furthermore, the Conference suggested that an international peacekeeping force under UN auspices might be created to maintain the cease-fire, control military movements and undertake other confidence-building measures.[50] Though the Bosnian Serbs agreed to place all their heavy weapons around the towns of Sarajevo, Bihac, Gorazde and Jajce under UN supervision within seven days, they made no attempt to do so. One of the first tasks of the ICFY negotiators (Carrington had now been replaced by Lord David Owen), therefore, was to ask them to fulfill their pledge by 12 September. Even this request was only partially honored.[51]

With little evidence of improvement in the condition of the Muslim population, the UN was being forced by public opinion to take a more concerted approach. This led to the adoption of a number of resolutions by the Security Council, including Resolution 770 of 13 August 1992, which under Chapter VII of the UN Charter called 'upon all states to take nationally or through regional agencies or arrangements all measures necessary to facilitate in co-ordination with the UN' the delivery of humanitarian aid to Sarajevo and wherever needed in other parts of Bosnia.[52] The Security Council also adopted Resolution 776 on 14 September, formally extending UNPROFOR's operations into Bosnia. Under this latter resolution UNPRO-FOR was mandated to provide protection to humanitarian relief deliveries and convoys of released detainees at the request, or approval, of the UNHCR and ICRC respectively.[53]

UNPROFOR was subsequently strengthened by nearly 8,000 troops to implement this new mandate. However, although Resolution 776 was also adopted under Chapter VII, thereby legally providing it with the option of using force to ensure its implementation, UNPROFOR was advised to use force only in the event that an aid convoy was attacked.[54] The Security Council also established a 'no-fly zone' over Bosnian airspace and called upon UNPROFOR to deploy observers on Bosnia's borders before the end of the year.

Having already expanded UNPROFOR's mandate in Croatia to include the 'pink zones', the Security Council was to expand it two more times before the end of the year. In early August the Security Council requested UNPROFOR to perform immigration and customs duties on UNPA boundaries coinciding with international borders. And in October it was requested to ensure the withdrawal of the JNA from the region of Dubrovnik and the adjacent Prevlaka peninsula.[55] Nevertheless, as the end of the year approached UNPROFOR was still confined to a *'de facto* minimalist position' in Croatia, with one UN report explaining that 'the role of UNPROFOR in present circumstances is thus to prevent the resumption or escalation of conflict; to provide a breathing space for the continued efforts of peacemakers; and to support the provision of essential humanitarian assistance'.[56] Reporting on developments, the Secretary-General stated that the attitude of the parties and the dangers to which the force had been exposed had left him 'sorely tempted' to recommend the withdrawal of UNPROFOR from Croatia altogether. Only the potential repercussions of such action prevented him from doing so.[57]

The situation was to deteriorate even further with the Croatian offensive against the Krajina UNPA and its adjacent 'pink zone' on 22 January 1993. The Croatian government cited the slow progress of negotiations over the various economic facilities in and adjacent to the UNPAs and 'pink zones' as the reason for its attack. The Serbs responded by breaking into a number of UN weapon storage areas and removing arms and heavy weapons.[58] After three days of fighting the Security Council adopted Resolution 802 demanding that the Croatian army withdraw from designated Serbian territory and that the Serbian forces return their heavy weapons. With security worsening the Security Council invited the Secretary-General to take all appropriate measures to strengthen the security of UNPROFOR and recommended he study the possibility of carrying out such local redeployments of the force as might be required to ensure its protection. Unfortunately, the two agreements reached between the parties to rectify the Croatian assault, the first on 6 April and the second on 15–16 July, were never implemented. In the case of the first, the 2,000 UN troops that were supposed to ensure the withdrawal of Croatian troops behind the pre-January cease-fire lines were never deployed. In the case of the second, 2,000 UN troops were actually moved into areas adjacent to strategic sites that the Croatians had captured and from which they were to withdraw, but the Croatian authorities never allowed them to deploy.[59]

Unable to get the Bosnian parties to agree to a comprehensive settlement, the co-chairs of the ICFY eventually proposed an initial settlement of their own in January 1993. Subsequently labeled the Vance-Owen Peace Plan (VOPP), it proposed the cantonization (or 'reconstitution' as Owen called it) of Bosnia into ten provinces.[60] Although the VOPP recognized Bosnia's existing borders it also granted substantial autonomy to the provinces, which were distributed primarily on ethnic grounds. Three of the provinces were to have a Serb majority, three Muslim majorities and two Croat majorities. One province was to have a mixed Croat-Muslim population and the tenth, Sarajevo, was to be controlled by a power-sharing arrangement involving all three ethnic groups. Distributed like a patchwork quilt, the provinces of similar ethnicity did not have contiguous borders, but were to be connected through five major corridors designed to allow the safe passage of civilians and humanitarian aid. Although the republic was to retain a central government, its powers were to be minimal.[61]

The VOPP also contained a number of disarmament provisions. These included an unconditional cessation of hostilities throughout Bosnia, the withdrawal of heavy weapons, the separation of forces in contact and the monitoring of the demilitarized zone in-between. The corridors between the provinces were to be controlled by UNPROFOR and any 'war-related material, weapons and ammunition [were] forbidden. If found, the items [were to] be confiscated and subsequently destroyed under the control of UNPROFOR and the parties'.[62] Sarajevo was also to be demilitarized and UNPROFOR and EC military observers were to monitor the borders of Bosnia in order to prevent the transfer of irregular forces, weapons and ammunition.[63]

As it fulfilled all their strategic objectives, the Croats accepted the VOPP immediately. Their provinces formed large blocks of territory, joined to Croatia proper, stretching into the very heart of central Bosnia. The Bosnian Government, on the other hand, initially rejected it, arguing that the provinces had been given too much autonomy, essentially setting the path towards an ethnic partition of the country. However, under intense pressure from Western governments, President Izetbegovic eventually accepted it in March 1993.[64] As the VOPP required the Bosnian Serb leadership to legally recognize the Bosnian Government, as well as hand back a third of the territory they now controlled, they also initially rejected it. They refused to accept it until they relented under heavy international pressure at a conference in Athens on 2 May. However, having itself rejected it, the Serbian parliament decided to put the plan to a referendum of the Bosnian Serbs, who on 15 and 16 May voted almost unanimously for RSK independence.

In the meantime the Muslim enclaves in eastern Bosnia had come under increasing pressure. At the beginning of March 1993 reports indicated that Serbian forces had overrun the town of Cerska and its surrounding villages and were threatening the region of Srebrenica.[65] Unable to defend itself any longer, Srebrenica surrendered on 14 April, with the Muslim forces agreeing to disarm within 72 hours. In return, the Bosnian Serb military leader, General Ratko Mladic, allowed 170 Canadian peacekeepers that he had been preventing from entering the town since early April to do so. These UN forces were to disarm all Bosnian Government forces within the stated time limit, with the whole process to be overseen by Bosnian Serb liaison officers.[66]

Somewhat ironically, given the events of the previous days and weeks, the Security Council adopted Resolution 819 on 16 April declaring Srebrenica and its surrounding areas a 'safe area' and demanded an end to Serbian attacks on the city. With the adoption of Resolution 824 on 6 May, the same status was awarded to the towns of Tuzla, Zepa, Gorazde, Bihac and Sarajevo. This accreditation, however, failed to prevent further attacks. Gorazde alone was 'bombarded by Bosnian Serb militia for 18 consecutive days in June' leaving 'half its houses destroyed'.[67] This occurred despite the Security Council's adoption of Resolution 836 on 4 June authorizing

UNPROFOR to act in 'self defense [and] to take the necessary measures, including the use of force, in reply to bombardments of the safe areas by any of the parties, or to armed incursion into them or in the event of any deliberate obstruction in or around those areas to the freedom of movement of UNPROFOR or of protected humanitarian convoys'.[68] Although Boutros-Ghali had informed the Security Council that a force of 34,000 would be required to 'obtain deterrence through strength', the Council authorized the enlargement of UNPROFOR in the 'safe areas' by only 7,500. This number represented the minimum 'light option' the Secretary-General believed was necessary to begin the implementation of its mandate and as such would be 'dependent on the consent and cooperation of all the parties.'[69]

Even before the Bosnian Serb parliament had rejected the VOPP in May 1993, the Americans had already begun to distance themselves from it. Instead, they proposed to lift the arms embargo on the Bosnian Government and use air power to protect its forces whilst they were being trained and equipped. The Europeans rejected this 'lift and strike' policy outright, arguing that it would only expose their troops to retaliation and threaten a general widening of the war. Without a clear political objective to accomplish, many on both sides of the Atlantic also believed air strikes would prove ineffective.[70]

With the policy of 'lift and strike' still-born the US, Russia, France, UK and Spain proposed the 'Joint Action Plan (JAP)' on 22 May, which called for the sealing of Bosnia's borders (to prevent incursions and military support from Croatia and Serbia) and support for the creation of the six Muslim 'safe-areas'. Although there was technically little 'action' in the JAP, it nevertheless still represented the end of negotiations based on the VOPP.[71]

By June developments on the ground had led to an effective anti-Muslim coalition between the Croats and Serbs. Unable to persuade the veto wielding states on the Security Council to lift the arms embargo, the Bosnian Army, with an estimated 120,000 soldiers and 80,000 reserves, had managed to defend only 10 per cent of Bosnia's territory.[72] The Bosnian Serbs, on the other hand, had managed to defend 70 per cent of Bosnia's territory with only 60,000 troops (albeit much better armed) and 20,000 JNA troops.[73]

With the VOPP abandoned, the co-chairs of the ICFY, Lord Owen and Thorwald Stoltenberg (who had replaced Cyrus Vance as UN envoy in May) began work on what the former called a 'painful compromise'. At a meeting held on board HMS Invincible in August 1993 they submitted a final plan that proposed the effective partition of the country into three ethnically defined republics. In its final version the plan gave 52 per cent of contiguous Bosnian territory to the Serbs, 17 per cent to the Croats (divided into two parts) and the remaining 30 per cent to the Muslims. Sarajevo and

Mostar were to be given a special status and administered under a UN and EC mandate for two years. [74] The plan also called for the demilitarization of the three republics. Implementation of the 'Invincible Package' was to be the responsibility of 50,000 NATO troops, half of which were to be provided by the Americans. Britain and France were to provide 8,000 each. [75]

Although Izetbegovic initially accepted the new plan, he later retracted his decision. The Bosnian Parliament also rejected it on 29 September. By the end of the year the Bosnian Army had gained substantial territorial victories leading to the displacement of almost half the 90,000 strong Bosnian Croat population. [76] However, these victories were tempered by the decision of Fikret Abdic, the Muslim leader controlling the northwestern enclave of Bihac, to break with the Izetbegovic government in October. The Bosnian government was therefore forced to open up a second front against Abdic's forces, which were now receiving supplies from Serbian Krajina and the Bosnian Serbs.

The first half of 1994 was to see a reduction in the overall intensity of the conflict in Bosnia and a corresponding improvement in the delivery of humanitarian aid. This was mainly the result of two developments. The first was the establishment of a heavy weapons exclusion zone around Sarajevo and the second was a general cease-fire reached between the Croatian and Muslim forces. The heavy weapons exclusion zone was the result of the UN's reaction to a mortar attack on a Sarajevan market place on 5 February that killed 68 civilians and wounded nearly 200. Although the source of the mortar was never conclusively proven, the credibility of the UNPROFOR operation began to rest on the ability of the UN to end the siege of Bosnia's historic capital. On 9 February NATO issued a ten-day ultimatum for all heavy weapons within a 20 km radius of the city to be withdrawn or placed under UN control. Any heavy weapons not in compliance were to be subject to NATO air strikes.

Nevertheless, UNPROFOR's Force Commander in Bosnia, Lt. General Sir Michael Rose, did everything in his power to prevent NATO action, even relaxing the definition of 'control' to ensure Serb compliance. This led to a bitter public dispute between NATO and the UN, as the latter insisted that it did not require physical possession of the weapons in order to exercise effective control over them. [77] Just as it looked like the Serbs might push the UN and NATO to the wire, the Russians announced on 17 February that separate talks in Pale had resulted in an agreement to replace Serbs in the exclusion zone with some 800 Russian peacekeepers.

On 1 March the Croatian and Bosnian governments signed the Washington Agreements, which consisted of the 'Framework Agreement establishing a Federation in the Area of the Republic of Bosnia-Herzegovina with a Majority Bosniac and Croat Population' and the 'Outline of a Preliminary Agreement for a Confederation between the Republic of Croatia and the Federation'. The 'Federation Agreement' incorporated a number of disarmament measures, including the immediate disengagement of both parties' forces and their withdrawal to a safe distance to be specified in the military agreement. It also called for the withdrawal of all foreign forces from the territory of the Federation, except those present by the agreement of the Republic of Bosnia or the authorization of the UN Security Council. As a result of these agreements UNPROFOR was to become involved in monitoring the cease-fire of February 1994, overseeing the separation of forces and controlling heavy weapons through the creation of weapons collection points and active sites.[78]

The creation of the Federation also led to UN mandates for the demilitarization of Mostar and Stari Vitez (neither of which were safe areas), in the case of the former as a precondition for the establishment of an EU administration there on 23 July 1994. With their new alliance and easier access to resources, the Bosnian Muslims began to turn the tide, symbolized by their refusal to accept a cessation of hostilities agreement in June.[79] In the meantime the Bosnian Serb parliament rejected the possibility of joining the new Croat-Muslim Federation in March, despite support for the proposal coming from the Bosnian Serb leader, Radovan Karadzic.

Following the signing of the Washington Agreements the Croatian Government signed another cease-fire agreement on 29 March 1994, this time with the leadership of the RSK. Relations between them had improved following the election in January of the more moderate RSK president, Milan Martic. The agreement called for an immediate end to hostilities and for a cease-fire from 4 April. Both parties were to withdraw their forces behind a line of separation, which was to be no less than one kilometer in width. UNPROFOR was to assume exclusive control over the zone of separation, which in the end covered over 1,300 kilometers of land.[80]

Though the Serbs were slower to implement the agreement than the Croatians, the UN was still able to report virtual compliance by the end of May.[81] However, though hostilities decreased, the agreement in no way impaired either party's capabilities. As it was unable to maintain a permanent presence at the weapons storage sites, UNPROFOR was forced to inspect them on a routine basis. Besides which, weapons were regularly removed from the sites for training and maintenance.[82] Thus, when later that year the Croatian Government threatened to use force to take back the UNPAs, the Serbs simply took back their heavy weapons.[83]

Although the threat of air strikes had been sufficient to end the siege of Sarajevo, this was not to be the case for the more eastern enclave of Gorazde. When Serb forces stepped up their bombardment of the city through March and early April, threatening the safety of UN observers as well as civilians, Lt. General Rose called for NATO air strikes on 10 and 11 April. Despite the execution of these air strikes (the first of their kind in UN history), the Serbs continued their offensive, albeit at a slightly lower intensity. They also took 150 UN personnel hostage and downed a British

Harrier aircraft providing close air support to UN observers on 16 April. Anxious to prevent any further escalation the Russians brokered a deal with the Serbs in which they agreed to a cease-fire and the release of the UN hostages in return for a halt to combat air patrols over the city. Despite these commitments the Serbs continued their preparations for a final assault on the city, angering the Russians to such a degree that their Foreign Minister, Andrei Kozyrev, publicly backed NATO's threats to bomb the Serbs if they did not withdraw.[84]

With no relaxation in the Serb bombardment Boutros-Ghali requested NATO on 19 April to authorize strikes against artillery, mortar positions or tanks attacking Gorazde, Tuzla, Zepa, Bihac and Srebrenica.[85] Three days later NATO authorized air strikes against Serb forces that had not withdrawn at least 3 kilometers from the center of Gorazde by noon on 24 April. In a separate decision it also established a 'military exclusion zone' of 20 km around the city and ordered the removal of Serb heavy weapons from the area by noon on 27 April. Although continued shelling by the Serbs caused NATO to request authorization for air strikes, they were denied by SRSG Yasushi Akashi on the basis that the Serbs had at least begun to withdraw their heavy weapons.[86] At the same time UN representatives meeting with Bosnian Serb leaders in Belgrade reached an agreement for a cease-fire and the deployment of an UNPROFOR battalion to monitor the withdrawal of the Bosnian Serbs from the 3-kilometer exclusion zone. In addition, it was agreed that their heavy weapons would be withdrawn to areas outside the 20 km exclusion zone by 2200 hours GMT on 26 April.[87]

Although the UN later reported 'substantial compliance' with NATO's demands, thereby removing the need for air strikes, the maintenance of around 300 Serb soldiers in the 3-kilometer exclusion zone continued to cause problems as the summer approached. In his May report, Boutros-Ghali noted that the continued harassment and obstruction of UNPROFOR convoys, the denial of movement for UNCIVPOL and the non-granting of clearances for medical evacuations from Gorazde, made it 'appear [that there was] a pattern of defiance, which could endanger all the efforts made by [his] Special Representative and UNPROFOR to diffuse the crisis at Gorazde.'[88]

On the diplomatic level a 'Contact Group' was established on 26 April in an attempt to inject new momentum into the stalled negotiations. Composed of the US, Russia, France, Germany and the UK, the Group proposed a 51–49 per cent split of Bosnian territory between the Croat-Muslim Federation and the Bosnian Serbs respectively. Although the Contact Group plan offered the Bosnian Government a more extensive and viable portion of land than any previous proposal, they nevertheless rejected it as 'seriously flawed' for rewarding the Serbs with land they had ethnically cleansed. The Serbs also rejected the distribution of territory and demanded that they be given the enclaves of Gorazde, Zepa and Srebrenica, as well as half of Sarajevo. Lt. General Rose sympathized with the Serb position, calling the plan 'unrealistic, ill-conceived and unfair' for offering them only 49 per cent of Bosnia when they already occupied 70 per cent.[89]

Under international pressure the Bosnian Government eventually accepted the plan on 17 July. However, despite facing the threat of diplomatic isolation and increased sanctions if they did not do the same, the Bosnian Serbs rejected it two days later. Conscious of the further sanctions that would be applied to Serbia proper if they did not change their position, Slobodan Milosevic called their rejection of the plan 'senseless and absurd' and accused Karadzic of being driven by 'mad political ambitions and greed'.[90] He also allowed the deployment of 135 UN observers on Serbia's borders in return for the lifting of international embargoes on civilian air traffic and cultural and sporting links.[91] These developments significantly affected the Bosnian Serbs' war-fighting capability. In an attempt to ratchet up pressure on the Bosnian Serbs even further, President Clinton threatened in early August to lift the arms embargo on the Bosnian Muslims if they did not accept the Contact Group's plan by 15 October. Only the fear expressed by the other Contact Group members that to do so would escalate the fighting persuaded him not to.[92]

Also in August, Bosnian Government forces defeated those of Fikret Abdic, thereby destroying his self-proclaimed 'Autonomous Province of Western Bosnia'. Now able to concentrate fully on the Bosnian Serbs, the Bosnian Army went on to achieve their largest territorial victory to date. However, in a counter-attack the Serbs not only quickly recaptured their lost territory, but also closed in even further to the town. Though the US tried to convince France and Britain to establish and enforce a weapons exclusion zone around the city, neither country was willing to do so because the Muslims had started the fighting themselves and air strikes might have endangered their peacekeepers on the ground.[93]

Nevertheless, when two Serbian planes from the Ubdina airbase in Krajina attacked Bihac in mid-November, the Security Council responded by extending the mandate of Resolution 836 to include attacks launched from Croatia. This allowed NATO to launch air strikes against the Ubdina airfield on 22 November. In the following days NATO planes also attacked two Serb SAM sites in response to Bosnian Serb attempts to shoot them down. The Serbs responded by taking 400 UN personnel hostage, whilst another 1,000 remained trapped in Bihac itself. Despite UNPROFOR's efforts to negotiate a cease-fire, the Serbs continued to advance towards the town, although they stopped short of entering it.[94] NATO eventually ended its attempts to destroy the heavy weapons pounding the city, as air strikes were deemed too dangerous for the safety of civilians and UN personnel.[95]

The US strained its relationship with the Europeans even further when, in addition to its threat to lift the arms embargo, it also threatened to stop sharing intelligence on arms shipments with its allies from mid-November.

Only a relaxation of its demands for air strikes, together with a commitment to deploy troops in a potential UNPROFOR rescue operation, helped mollify the seething Europeans.[96] Returning to a less aggressive posture the US supported a visit to Bosnia by its former president, Jimmy Carter, whose diplomatic endeavors helped the Bosnian Serbs and Bosnian Government reach an 'Agreement on the Complete Cessation of Hostilities' on 31 December. Due to last for four months, this agreement called for a separation of forces and for a prohibition on the use of all explosive munitions. UNPROFOR was requested to monitor the cease-fire and to deploy as a buffer between the forces where appropriate.[97]

By the middle of January 1995 President Tudjman had begun to insist that the 12,000 UN troops stationed in Croatia be provided with a new mandate or be withdrawn at the end of their present mandate on 31 March.[98] Following this demand, the US and Russian ambassadors to Croatia, along with Ambassadors Ahrens and Eide from the ICFY (who were together known as the 'Zagreb Four') presented a 'Draft agreement on the Krajina, Salvonia, Southern Baranja and Western Sirmium' to both sides on 30 January. While the Croatian Government at least accepted the plan as a basis for negotiations, the Serbs refused to do so until the future presence of UNPROFOR had been assured.

Thus began a series of tactical deployments that both sides hoped would allow them to seize strategic ground in the zone of separation once UNPROFOR had ceased to function. Though they had already formed their own alliance with the Bosnian Serbs in February, the Krajina Serbs reacted to the news of a new alliance between the Croatian Government and the Federation of Bosnia-Herzegovina with an 'immediate war alert' in March.[99] Having concluded that the 'failure of the parties to commence serious political negotiations had brought them to the brink of a major war', Boutros-Ghali argued that only a reduced UN force in Croatia under a new mandate could prevent its occurrence.[100]

Consequently, the Security Council restructured UNPROFOR into three separate but interlinked operations on 31 March. The first of these was the UN Confidence Restoration Operation (UNCRO), which it hoped might help create conditions conducive to the achievement of a political settlement between the parties.[101] UNCRO's mandate was essentially to help implement the cease-fire and economic agreements of 29 March and 2 December 1994 respectively. It was therefore to monitor the zone of separation and verify that all weapons systems specified in the cease-fire agreement were deployed in accordance with its provisions.[102]

Despite the restructuring of the UN force, approximately 2,500 Croatian troops attacked Western Slavonia on 1 May 1995.[103] Though the Krajina Serbs responded by firing missiles into nearby towns, the Croatians rejected a cease-fire proposal from the Secretary-General, in his mind revealing that their true intention was to establish complete control over Sector West.[104]

On 3 August the Croatian army launched another major offensive, this time into the Krajina UNPA. The Croatian Foreign Minister, Pavel Granic, blamed this latest attack on the 'failure to implement the mandate of UNCRO which [had] been proven totally ineffective' and the 'policy of appeasement of the international community towards the Belgrade government, the sponsor of the occupation of the parts of Croatia and Bosnia.'[105]

Only after the Croatians had captured all of the UN Sectors, except Sector East, was a basic agreement on the region of Eastern Salvonia, Baranja and Western Sirmium signed on 12 November. This agreement provided for the creation of a regional transitional administration for 12 months (and maybe a further 12 months), as well as the region's demilitarization within 30 days of the agreement's initiation. In addition, it envisaged the creation and training of a temporary local police force, as well as the deployment of international monitors along the Sector's international borders. Although President Tudjman wanted the demilitarization process to begin on 1 December, it had not yet been determined which States, international organizations or institutions, would perform these tasks. UNCRO's mandate was scheduled to end on 30 November and, according to the Secretary-General, was not in a position 'as presently mandated and constituted, to facilitate the demilitarization envisaged in the basic agreement'.[106]

Meanwhile, except in the area of Bihac, the Bosnian cease-fire agreement of December 1994 had been generally respected. However, in the latter half of March 1995 the Bosnian Army's continuing offensive in the Tuzla area incited retaliatory shelling of Sarajevo by the Bosnian Serbs. Although NATO subsequently threatened air strikes, they were not carried out. NATO also rejected requests from the Bosnian Government for air strikes, blaming the Muslims themselves for starting the fighting.

With the expiration of the cessation of hostilities agreement on 1 May the fighting around Sarajevo intensified. When a Serbian mortar attack on the city killed ten people on 7 May the UN military commander in Bosnia, Lt. General Smith, requested NATO air strikes on Serb positions. This request was vetoed by SRSG Akashi, a decision criticized by a number of states, including the US and Britain. When Serb shelling of the city escalated following the removal of their heavy weapons from collection points around the city, the decision was taken to use all available means to restore compliance with the heavy weapons agreement of February 1994. Consequently, on 24 May, Akashi warned the Serbs to stop using their heavy weapons and to return them to their collection points by noon the following day. When the Serbs failed to meet the deadline NATO planes attacked a number of ammunition dumps near Pale on 25 and 26 May. In response, the Serbs shelled all the UNSAs except Zepa, surrounded their heavy weapons collection points and took 199 UN hostages.[107]

In a move to quell international outrage at this provocation the UN announced its intention to deploy a 10,000 strong Rapid Reaction Force

(RRF) in Bosnia in mid-June. Its role in the UNPROFOR operation, however, had not been fully clarified. Therefore, rather than releasing all their hostages, the Serbs simply kept a number of them as blackmail against a strengthening of the UN's mandate and particularly against the future role of the RRF. This forced the UN to capitulate to Serb demands by releasing four Serbian detainees in Sarajevo and by abandoning the last weapons collection points around the city in return for the release of the final 26 hostages on 18 June.[108]

Sensing the UN's weakness in the face of their continued onslaught, the Serbs launched a major offensive against the Srebrenica UNSA on 6 July. Despite NATO air strikes on 11 July, the city fell the same day. Whilst they continued to ethnically cleanse Srebrenica, the Bosnian Serbs also launched an assault against the Zepa UNSA, which took less than two weeks to fall. Emboldened by their successes in the east, they then cooperated with the forces of Fikret Abdic to launch an attack on the western UNSA of Bihac. Determined to prevent the Serbs from capturing Bihac and thereby forming a contiguous Serbian territory from Croatia to Serbia proper, the governments of Croatia and Bosnia signed the Split Declaration, which committed each of them to a joint defense against Serb aggression. Only the fall of the Krajina to Croatian forces following their early August offensive and the subsequent surrender of Abdic's forces finally released the pressure on Bihac.

Although Bihac had been secured, the fall of Srebrenica and Zepa meant that Gorazde stood on its own as the last enclave in eastern Bosnia. To many, including at least one UN commander, it was simply indefensible.[109] It also represented a stumbling block against Bosnian Serb acceptance of the Contact Group peace plan. Therefore, when a third of the UN contingent began to withdraw on 23 August, the UN was criticized for abandoning the enclave to the same fate as its predecessors.[110] However, when a mortar attack killed 37 civilians in a market place in Sarajevo on 28 August, NATO responded with air strikes against targets near Tuzla, Gorazde, Zepa and the hills overlooking Mostar. The new RRF was also called into action.

Following the shuttle diplomacy of the US Assistant Secretary of State, Richard Holbrooke, an announcement of talks in Geneva was made as NATO's air strikes came to an end on 1 September. However, when the Serbs still refused to comply with the UNSA conditions, NATO resumed its air strikes four days later and continued them for another nine days. Thus, in a two-week period NATO had flown 3,400 sorties, including 750 attack missions against 56 ground targets.[111]

Taking advantage of the damage these strikes had inflicted upon the Serbs, the Muslims and Croatians launched a joint offensive in north-western Bosnia. Although this was politically embarrassing for the UN and NATO, the resulting defeat of the Bosnian Serbs was the greatest they had suffered since the beginning of the war.[112] By mid-September the amount of Bosnia occupied by the Serbs had dropped from 70 per cent to only 50 per cent, much nearer the amount offered to them by the Contact Group proposal. By October the Muslims and Croatians were within days, possibly hours, of overrunning the last significant Bosnian city under Serb control, Banja Luka. Then, on 12 October, without warning, the US demanded an immediate cease-fire.[113] Except for the Bosnian Serbs, who were represented by the Serbian Government, the parties subsequently met in Dayton, Ohio, where they negotiated a comprehensive peace settlement in November. They signed it in Paris the following month.

5   Assessment of the operations

5.1   Planning, administration and deployment

Given its multi-faceted nature and complex operational environment, UNPROFOR's planning and deployment were always going to difficult. However, matters were not to be helped by the UN's serious institutional and organizational inadequacies, both in New York and in the field. As Berdal notes, the fragmented structure at UN Headquarters and the diffusion of responsibilities among Departments, Divisions and Offices made it very difficult to provide unified direction and effective support to UNPROFOR on the ground.[114] The failure of Headquarters to properly delegate financial authority to its operatives in the field also affected UNPROFOR's effectiveness, as did the restraints placed upon its medium and long-term budget planning by the allocation of short mandate periods.[115] And although the UN had introduced a number of initiatives and reforms in an attempt to enhance its planning and support capabilities in New York, few of them had significantly impacted upon UNPROFOR's field activities.[116] There was to be no better testimony of the UN's planning inadequacies than that provided by UNPROFOR's first commanding officer, General Satish Nambiar, who believed the 'very short preparation time' of only four days provided to him in New York had a 'severely limiting effect on the implementation of the mission'.[117]

In the field itself, UNPROFOR's most serious deficiencies were to be found in its logistics and procurement systems, as well as in its command, control and communications. As with the UN's other peacekeeping operations, the lack of an appropriately integrated and coordinated logistics system and the absence of an adequate capability to direct its flow into the mission area delayed the force's deployment. Yet even when deployed, UNPROFOR continued to suffer from an acute lack of spare parts, maintenance facilities and stocks of peacekeeping equipment. These problems were exacerbated by the difficulties experienced in obtaining logistic and engineering units from member states.

In the area of command, control and communications UNPROFOR was also to be affected by both its multi-component nature and its general shortage of even the most basic equipment. Whilst the nature of the mission required numerous civilian agencies to work alongside the military, a relationship that sometimes worked to undermine the unity and integrity of the force's command structure, the contributing nations themselves persisted in their tendency not to cede full command authority over their troops to the UNPROFOR force commander. Theses difficulties were exacerbated by the shortages of equipment available to UNPROFOR and the incompatibility of equipment brought to the field by various contingents.[118]

Succinct testimony to the overall difficulties faced by UNPROFOR commanders in-theatre was provided by Brigadier John Wilson, who having served as chief military observer for UNPROFOR in 1992, exclaimed that 'inadequate communications equipment, complex and often fragmented command structures, slow force build-up, an unresponsive logistics system, unacceptable conduct by members of some national contingents [and] inefficient Headquarters' made life extremely difficult on the ground.[119] In Berdal's opinion UNPROFOR had 'exposed the obsolescence of [the UN's] traditional methods of organization and management, many of which [were] now clearly undermining the effectiveness of troops and civilians deployed in the field'.[120]

5.2   Disarmament, demobilization and reintegration

As the preceding sections have elucidated, UNPROFOR's role in disarmament in the former Yugoslavia was not to emanate from a comprehensive peace settlement, but rather from temporary demilitarization agreements and from the need to protect besieged civilian populations. In the case of the former, it was mandated to protect and demilitarize three Croatian UNPAs, as well as their adjacent 'pink zones'. It was also mandated to ensure compliance with disarmament agreements brokered between the parties in both Croatia and Bosnia. In the case of the latter, UNPROFOR was mandated to protect six Bosnian UNSAs and was later required to monitor compliance with military exclusion zones created in their surrounding areas.

Although destined for ultimate failure, UNPROFOR's attempts to demilitarize the Croatian UNPAs and 'pink zones' were initially successful. By July 1992 it had not only collected all the heavy weapons belonging to TO units in all four Sectors, but had also begun to disarm paramilitary groups present within them.[121] However, only in Sector West could it complete the demilitarization process, doing so by 7 July.[122]

As Raevsky notes, despite this quick success the sector received relatively little media attention, primarily because it was believed to be calmer and therefore easier to control than the others. Significantly, this superficial analysis underestimated the complexity of the sector. For instance, it was the only sector in which Serbs and Croats were still living when UNPRO-

FOR deployed. Its terrain was mostly flat, which facilitated offensive military actions and it was isolated from the other three sectors. It also suffered from strong Bosnian Serb influence.[123]

The explanation for UNPROFOR's success in Sector West therefore seems to lie in a mixture of fortune and fortitude. To begin with, most inhabitants of the sector were not even aware of the demilitarization requirements of the Vance Plan when UNPROFOR first deployed and were reportedly in a state of 'disbelief' when informed. This ignorance appears to have created a more receptive environment for UNPROFOR's conviction to ensure demilitarization and, if necessary, to use force to achieve it.[124]

However, in Raevsky's opinion the real key to UNPROFOR's success was its determination to fully involve the local authorities of both communities in its disarmament operations. By 'skillfully manipulating the situation', UNPROFOR was able to elevate the civil authorities to a higher position relative to their military counterparts, thereby 're-establishing [them] as a relevant social and political component' of the sector. This was done by firstly offering to provide a number of services in their respective zones of control in return for their assistance and full cooperation. And secondly, by insisting that the civil authorities be present during all meetings and negotiations and by providing them with goods and services that they could deliver to their respective populations.[125] Interestingly, therefore, UNPROFOR had utilized a similar strategy to the Australian contingent of UNITAF in Somalia and had achieved comparable success.

Nevertheless, demilitarizing the other sectors was always going to be more difficult. As highlighted by Ekwall-Uebelhart's study, the cultural background, as well as the political and strategic situation, differed considerably from sector to sector. Consequently, so did the problems associated with the implementation of the disarmament components of the Vance Plan.[126] Most difficult of all were the Krajina Serbs who, according to Glenny, had developed an 'extraordinary affinity with weaponry'. Indeed, 'a person's standing [in this culture is] enhanced and confirmed by his or her ability to wield a gun'.[127] During his travels in the region all the people Glenny spoke to exclaimed the idea of disarming them as a dishonor in itself. Leaders like Milan Babic, who rejected the Vance Plan on the basis that nobody could be allowed to disarm the Krajina Serbs, manipulated this reaction. Though simply furthering his own political aims, Babic knew his call would command almost unanimous support amongst the people he represented.[128]

The Serbs in the Krajina and UNPA East had also been the least co-operative with UNPROFOR and this had manifest itself in the tendency to simply convert their soldiers into police forces in an attempt to circumvent their Vance Plan commitments. The Serb militia in UNPA East numbered 16,000 and included former JNA members, yet it was allowed to operate as a Serbian 'police force'.[129] And in many areas of Sectors North and South,

Serb forces had simply exchanged their military uniforms for crisp new 'police' uniforms and had their military vehicles (now painted blue instead of green) reassigned to them as police vehicles.

Disarming the Krajina Serbs was therefore only ever going to be possible with a large-scale enforcement operation, something UNPROFOR was neither mandated nor capable of conducting.[130] Of course, whatever hope did exist of consolidating UNPROFOR's success in Sector West and of repeating it in the other three sectors ended abruptly with the Croatian offensives in January 1993. Between then and May and August 1995, when the UNPAs were attacked again, the only disarmament that was to take place was to occur in close proximity to the lines of confrontation. In fact, the UNPAs in general were to witness the augmentation of Serb military capabilities due to porous borders and the futile efforts of UNPROFOR to control traffic across them. For their part, the Croatians had spent an estimated $5.5 billion on military supplies since late 1991 and though details of these arms shipments had been provided to the Security Council it had done nothing to halt them. As this was also happening in full view of the Serbs, their refusal to disarm and demobilize was even more understandable.[131]

The failure to acknowledge the large-scale smuggling being conducted by the Croatians was just one aspect of perhaps the most divisive issue in the debate over how to deal with the former Yugoslavia: whether or not to lift the arms embargo in order to help the Bosnian Muslims. On one side of the argument lay those who believed the embargo to be simply immoral. To this group the embargo was preventing the Muslims from defending themselves against the true aggressors of the Yugoslav wars, the Serbs. Particularly vocal in this regard was the Clinton administration (although for the sake of NATO integrity it eventually opposed lifting the embargo unilaterally when the US Senate voted to do so on 12 May 1995). The moral force of their argument was implicit in NATO Secretary-General Manfred Woerner's retort to British Prime Minister John Major's opposition to lifting the embargo. Had the US not supplied arms to Britain during World War Two, Woerner surmised, they might not have defeated Hitler.[132]

On the other side of the argument were those who believed, like Major, that lifting the arms embargo would simply increase the level of violence (not particularly in favor of the Muslims) and threaten the UN's attempts to ameliorate and resolve the conflict. One such individual was ICFY Co-Chairman, David Owen, who did not believe the question to be the clear-cut moral issue the embargo's opponents suggested it to be. Rather, Owen argued that lifting the embargo would have been a 'profound mistake' as it was more likely to lead to an influx of 1990s weapons from the former Soviet Union to the JNA, thereby tilting the balance even further towards the Serbs.[133] The Serbs were also likely to use as much force as possible before the Muslims could be armed, including their military aircraft, thus resulting in large numbers of fatalities.[134]

Owen also recognized, along with the UN Secretary-General and most contributing countries, that UNPROFOR would be unable to continue its humanitarian presence under these conditions. Failing to persevere with the embargo, therefore, risked condemning the hundreds of thousands of lives they believed UNPROFOR had saved in its first few years alone.[135] Other risks were also apparent. The mediation role of the ICFY would have all but ended. Restricting the influence of more fundamentalist elements from outside Yugoslavia would have become more difficult. And there seemed little chance of preventing the spread of the conflict to the Croatian UNPAs and even Kosovo and Macedonia.[136]

As it happened, the West had preferred not to apply a truly effective embargo regime anyway.[137] Rather a 'pragmatic relaxation' of the embargo had developed as the Muslims were allowed to smuggle ever-increasing amounts of weaponry, mostly through Croatia. At one point President Izetbegovic openly admitted having smuggled 30,000 rifles, 20 million bullets, 37,000 mines, 46,000 anti-armor rockets and 20,000 hand grenades.[138] The Muslims also had their own indigenous source of arms. The largest and most important cities and economic centers in Bosnia remained in Muslim hands throughout the war. These included cities such as Sarajevo, Tuzla, Zenica and Konjic, which were able to produce large supplies of ammunition for infantry weapons along with artillery, multiple rocket launchers and even a few tanks.[139] Nevertheless, it was obvious that the embargo was having a significant affect on their ability to acquire heavy weapons, which the Croatians refused to supply or allow passage in case the Muslim forces became too strong.[140]

The embargo was also leaving the Muslims vulnerable to air attacks and it was for this reason that the no-fly zone was proposed in 1992. As Owen reasoned, '[there] was an obligation on us to compensate for the Bosnian Serb supremacy in arms by neutralizing wherever possible certain categories of weapons...we had to redress the total imbalance in air power or face renewed and more credible demands for lifting the arms embargo.'[141] Unfortunately, the failure of the UN and NATO to neutralize the Serbs heavy weapons meant the asymmetrical effects of the embargo continued.

However, despite the inability of the West to manipulate the balance of power in the Muslims' favor, there existed no support for either a peace-enforcement operation or for lifting the embargo. When Boutros-Ghali suggested in 1994 that UNPROFOR hand things over to a multinational force run by the Contact Group members, he received no support from Western governments.[142] The British, French and Spanish preferred instead to continue with air strikes and the embargo. So too did the Americans, as lifting the embargo might have forced them to deploy troops to help withdraw UN personnel or defend Muslim communities. Even the Bosnian

Government opposed lifting the embargo for fear that to do so might not ensure their victory.[143]

The eventual decision to use overwhelming force against the Bosnian Serbs was to come only after the use of limited air strikes had been proven ineffectual in either deterring attacks on the UNSAs or in enforcing the weapons exclusion zones around them. In Owen's opinion the decision to establish the UNSAs was the 'most irresponsible' one taken by the Security Council during his whole tenure as ICFY Co-chairman. This was because the UN had taken its first serious step towards an enforcement operation without any intention of following through with the necessary resources.[144] There was to be no better example of this than the Security Council's decision to deploy a 'light option' of only 7,600 troops to protect the UNSAs, despite the Secretary-General's warning that such a limited presence would require the consent and cooperation of the warring parties to be successful.[145] Even then it was to take a year for these troops to arrive.[146]

Short of the necessary manpower UNPROFOR was forced to rely on NATO airpower to help defend and deter attacks against the UNSAs.[147] However, as the UN and NATO were to find out to their detriment, a number of 'technical constraints' worked to limit the effectiveness of airpower. These included the difficulty in identifying suitable targets, especially when much of the fighting consisted of close combat in civilian areas; the need to conduct repeated air engagements at considerable distances from the Safe Areas in order to blunt a determined attack, coupled with the increased presence of Serb SAM sites; and the 'unavoidable vulnerability' of UNPROFOR troops who could neither be tactically deployed nor secure their lines of communication and were therefore highly susceptible to being taken hostage. Venting his frustration at the shortcomings of the UNSA concept, the Secretary-General acknowledged at the end of 1994 that the combination of UNPROFOR's limited deployment and NATO airpower could not protect their civilian populations. These shortcomings had been demonstrated 'once again, and even more strikingly' by the recent attacks on Bihac, where the civilian population had 'found themselves in a pitiable plight.'[148]

UNPROFOR experienced similar problems during its attempts to enforce the weapon exclusion zones. Widely dispersed at weapons collection points UN troops were vulnerable to being taken hostage and could not prevent a determined effort to remove weapons from them. The parties were also able to retain undetected weapons. As with air strikes designed to deter attacks on the UNSAs, the supervision and enforcement of the weapon exclusion zones also threatened UNPROFOR's impartiality. For these reasons UNPROFOR often went to extensive lengths to avoid enforcement action. For example, Silber and Little pour opprobrium on the actions of Lt. General Rose, who negotiated with the Serbs besieging Sarajevo during the ten-day ultimatum imposed by NATO in February 1994. Rose was so determined to avert NATO strikes that he eventually allowed the Serbs to choose eight locations in which to concentrate their heavy weapons under UN control. This infuriated the Bosnian Muslims, who claimed they were the very same strategic locations from which they had attacked the city for the past 22 months.[149] Even then, Rose did not expect to take physical control of the Serb weapons, but rather monitor them through electronic surveillance. Only the insistence of US officials on a stricter interpretation prevented this effective relaxation of NATO's ultimatum.[150]

If failing to deploy sufficient UN troops was the greatest flaw in the UNSA regime, the failure to insist on their demilitarization was to run a close second. Protected by the UN presence and therefore relatively safe from Serb attacks, the designated towns inevitably became Muslim garrisons. Whilst Sarajevo housed the General Command of the Government Army, Tuzla and Bihac harbored the headquarters of its Second and Fifth Corps respectively. Srebrenica, Gorazde and Zepa also maintained a substantial number of troops. Factories capable of producing ammunition, chemicals and other products for military use were also located within the UNSAs.[151] Allowing this military presence to continue not only provoked Serb attacks (the Serbs argued that the 1949 Geneva Conventions required such areas to be demilitarized before they could receive protection, a point acknowledged by the Secretary-General), but also allowed the Muslims to exploit the UN's protection by launching offensives from them.[152] When UNPROFOR's mandate required it to defend the UNSAs against Serb counter-attacks, it was inevitably construed as having taken sides. For these reasons the Secretary-General believed that the primary objective of the UNSAs could not be achieved without their complete demilitarization.[153]

Despite its legal importance and the Secretary-General's insistence, there existed strong opposition to demilitarization. Firstly, none of the major Security Council members were prepared to deploy the troops its implementation would have necessitated. And secondly, Muslim political leaders recognized that assuaging the plight of towns like Sarajevo and Srebrenica would inadvertently remove the most effective argument in their appeal for American intervention. For this reason the Vice-President of Bosnia, Ejup Ganic, appeared to block a settlement designed to end the siege of Sarajevo in late 1992.[154] Political leaders in Sarajevo also pressured the local Muslim commander in Srebrenica not to comply with the demilitarization agreement negotiated as a condition of that town's surrender in March 1993.[155] Consequently, fewer than half the weapons in the enclave had been surrendered before even more weapons began to flow into it, together with other armed parties.[156] Thus, the failure to demilitarize them, their strategic importance to the Serbs and the Security Council's lack of determination to protect them, all combined to ensure that the three most eastern UNSAs would be subjected to the worst atrocities witnessed in Europe since the end of World War II.[157]

5.3   Reform of public security

All the countries studied in this text had utilized their public security apparatus as a means of state control before the UN's intervention, and the former Yugoslavia was to be no exception. The rise in ethnic tensions that accompanied the collapse of the Yugoslav state only helped consolidate this role, as local police forces were converted into agents of intimidation and brutality against those of a different ethnic origin.[158] This evolution was to be exemplified in Croatia, where Tudjman lost no time in converting the local police into an armed force capable of confronting the might of the JNA.

As the JNA had already disarmed the republic's Territorial Defense forces the police remained the only Croatian armed force still capable of acting independently of the Yugoslav authorities. The new government therefore sought to arm them with sufficient quantities of weapons and purge them of their ethnic Serb members. At the same time, a recruitment drive to attract new Croatian members led to an influx of militant nationalists who were hurriedly trained and in many cases promoted to positions unwarranted for their age and experience.[159] These policies inevitably led to heightened Serb insecurity as they not only promoted an atmosphere of national exclusivity and intolerance, but also 'involved depriving Serbs of their most important possession, the gun.'[160]

In these conditions there was no hope that UNPROFOR might fulfill its original mandate to help create police forces of mixed ethnic origin within the UNPAs. Nor could it establish an environment conducive to the return of displaced persons. With both sides intentionally blurring the distinction between their police and regular armies, CIVPOL was unable even to stymie the deterioration of the existing local police forces, resulting in the UNPAs having no real system of law and order by September 1992.[161] Though it had relatively greater success in patrolling the zone of separation, operating in the midst of such well-armed local military and paramilitary organizations left UNPROFOR's CIVPOL contingent essentially powerless throughout its three-and-a-half-year tenure in Croatia.[162]

A similar scenario existed in Bosnia, where the expansion of police cadre in all three communities had produced a ratio of police to civilians several times higher than that in the rest of Europe. As in Croatia, each community swelled their ranks with zealot nationalists who possessed little or no training and experience. With many recruits having a paramilitary background, movement between the police and military also remained fluid, helped no doubt by the fact that the standard police uniform was the same fatigues worn by their military counterparts and that both forces used the AK-47 as their basic weapon. Police units required for combat also came under the command of their respective armed forces when the need arose.[163] However, UNPROFOR's CIVPOL component in Bosnia did not have a uniform mandate for the whole mission area as it did in Croatia.

Rather it had a limited mandate to operate in Srebrenica, Tuzla and Mostar and unofficial agreements to do so in Sarajevo and Gorazde. Hope that a similar uniform mandate might help consolidate the establishment of the Muslim-Croat Federation and protect human rights led the Secretary-General to ask the Security Council to consider providing one in late 1994.[164]

Though the uncooperative nature of CIVPOL's operating environment made its task practically impossible, it was nevertheless apparent that it still suffered from the typical selection of organizational and institutional inadequacies that affected other components of UNPROFOR. Primary among these was its lack of planning and institutional memory; deficiencies compounded by the inexperience and incompetence of many of its personnel.[165] Though matters improved with the creation of a quality selection unit at CIVPOL headquarters in June 1992, the CIVPOLs themselves did not receive manuals or guidelines outlining appropriate methods and procedures until December 1993. This meant the success of the mission depended heavily on the skills, initiative and background of each CIVPOL; a factor Holm found had a generally negative effect on the component's effectiveness in his study of Eastern Slavonia. Despite these problems Holm does emphasize that the CIVPOL component provided significant humanitarian assistance to the local population, even if this role had developed out of its inability to occupy itself with its principal duties.[166]

5.4 Strategies of conflict resolution

As the preceding accounts have made explicit, until late 1995 the international community's approach to dealing with the Yugoslav crisis was detrimentally affected by the fact that at any one time it lacked either a common strategy or the will to implement it when one existed. Without a concurrent combination of these elements the UN could never have hoped to provide the requisite security to ensure the disarmament of the warring parties or the civilian population.

This was no more evident than in the initial months of the crisis when a common policy did exist; that of trying to keep the Yugoslav federation intact. Of course, the international community's first mistake was to delay its involvement until after the JNA had used force in Slovenia and Croatia, a development that made its task practically impossible. This delay also left the international community reacting to events rather than anticipating them.[167] However, what little hope that remained was to die with the political misdiagnosis of the two main international actors, the US and EC.

The failure of the US to properly diagnose the crisis was evident as early as June 1991 with the visit to Yugoslavia of Secretary of State James Baker. Lacking detailed knowledge of the country's politics Baker failed to convey sufficient American concern to the respective republican leaders, thereby precipitating declarations of independence from Slovenia and Croatia only four days after he had left Belgrade. Baker's apathy was essentially a reflection of the ambivalence that existed within the US administration, in which those who possessed the least knowledge on the subject wielded the greatest power.[168] The EC's misdiagnosis, on the other hand, is captured best by Silber and Little, who contend that the Troika sent in mid-1991 continued to act as if there was no rational motivation behind the violence of the seceding republics, the JNA or the Serbian authorities. Rather, they 'behaved as though the conflict was caused by no more than some ill-defined but frequently alluded to Balkan temperament, a south Slavic pre-disposition – either cultural or genetic – toward fratricide. They behaved as though all they had to do was persuade the belligerents of the folly of war'. In their opinion this approach was to characterize the EC's efforts, with few exceptions, for many months.[169]

As the EC had asked for and been awarded (only too happily by the Americans) the preeminent role in dealing with the crisis at this stage, its failure to act in a determined fashion was particularly ruinous. The EC needed to threaten diplomatic isolation and the possible use of force if it ever hoped to persuade the republics to negotiate a new (con)federal arrangement, or to prevent the country's disintegration before the rights of ethnic minorities in all the republics had been assured. Instead, under German pressure the EC backed away, eventually acquiescing to Slovene and Croatian independence before any such agreements had been reached.

Therefore, as Gow describes, 'in the space of half a year the EC had moved from a unified position on the maintenance of the Yugoslav state, through growing internal dispute and disarray on how to handle the war, to a common but hastily discordant policy on inviting those republics seeking independence to submit applications'.[170] The EC's political discord was matched only by its military dissonance. With Germany constrained by its pacifist constitution, Greece attempting to prevent itself from becom-ing embroiled (not least because Turkey was doing the same) and France and Britain arguing that the conflict was far too complex to be dealt with militarily, there was no conviction for a forceful response.[171] As Warren Zimmerman has asserted, if the US (or EC) had at least used airpower against the JNA forces attacking Dubrovnik and Vukovar in late 1991, the Serbs would have been taught a lesson about Western resolve. As it was they were taught a different lesson, 'that there was no Western resolve and that they could push as far as their power could take them.'[172]

Just as the international community's political disunity and lack of mili-tary resolve were to condemn the Yugoslav federation to an ignominious end, they were to do the same for the principal peace proposals in the ensuing months. Whether or not the Lisbon Agreement of mid-1992 could have prevented the war spreading to Bosnia is still hotly debated. Without doubt there were major impediments to its implementation, even if Izetbegovic had not renounced his previous acceptance of it. For one, the agreement did not include a precise division of territory and given the ethnic diversity of Bosnia it is hard to imagine that one could have been agreed without significant population transfers. The international community was not yet ready to be complicit in such a cynical and despairing operation.

Secondly, the republic's ethnic diversity would have resulted in many towns still being contested, regardless of what the parties might have agreed, making violence almost unavoidable.[173] And finally, the question still persists of whether the Serbs would have actually implemented such a settlement in 1992. It was obvious that they had been preparing for war together with the JNA for several months and their military superiority soon rewarded them with 70 per cent of Bosnia's territory. Is it really feasible that they would have settled for less than that without a credible commitment from the international community to prevent their impending offensive?[174] With Western resolve as it was, no such commitment was forthcoming.[175]

Just as the Lisbon Agreement elicits accusations of missed opportunities, so too does the VOPP. For example, in his condemnatory text, *Triumph of the Lack of Will*, James Gow insists that the VOPP could have ended the war 'two-and-a-half years [earlier than the Dayton Accords] and on better terms'.[176] And for its architect Lord Owen, it was difficult to contradict Slobodan Milosevic's appraisal in August 1995 that had the agreement been accepted two years earlier '[hundreds] of thousands of people would have avoided the horrors of war'.[177] Though both Gow and Owen place the principle blame for the failure of the VOPP on the Serbs, a great deal of their disapprobation is poured upon the Americans and Europeans for their failure to provide sufficient support to ensure its implementation.

Though the VOPP left many important issues to be resolved by the parties after their signatures and was not without significant flaws, its basic principles and modalities were admired by many.[178] For Silber and Little 'there was never a more comprehensive plan' than the VOPP, an agreement that at least preserved a multi-ethnic Bosnia within its internationally recognized borders.[179] And amongst all the plans preceding the Dayton Accords, Burg and Shoup believe the VOPP '[stood] out as the most fully articulated…the one that made the fewest concessions to partition, and the one that included the most specific provisions for international supervision of the outcome'. Indeed, in their opinion, the VOPP 'appeared to amount to the establishment of an international trusteeship over the country'.[180] The VOPP also prevented Serb territorial contiguity and offered them only 43 per cent of Bosnian territory, 7 per cent less than they were eventually given at Dayton.[181]

Thus, to most observers the Clinton administration was being more than a little disingenuous when it criticized the VOPP for rewarding ethnic cleansing. The true source of American antipathy, it was believed, was the fear of having to deploy half of the 50,000 troops enforcement of the agreement would have required.[182] Ironically, the lack of American resolve to enforce a plan had itself contributed to the very weaknesses they complained about. Having acknowledged the remote likelihood of international enforcement the co-chairmen had been forced to make concessions to the Bosnian parties throughout the early part of the year before presenting their final proposal in May 1993. These included draft provisions for the withdrawal of forces that were devoid of specific deadlines and for which no enforcement mechanism was specified.[183]

Nevertheless, Owen himself recognized that if the plan were to have any credibility its implementation required at least an element of imposition, otherwise the Serbs would never withdraw from the sensitive territory they occupied. What exasperated the co-chairmen most, however, was that the US was obviously willing to abandon the VOPP without replacing it with a credible alternative. Without one the co-chairmen were resigned to making even greater concessions to the Serbs, eventually negotiating what was essentially a disguised partition plan in the form of the 'Invincible package' in August.

For a number of analysts the move away from the VOPP and towards some form of physical separation of the ethnic groups was a necessary development. As Weslcy has correctly identified, without sufficient leverage to compel the uncooperative Bosnian Serbs to comply with their mediation designs the co-chairmen could never have succeeded with an agreement that clashed so significantly with their interests. The unfortunate reality is that the 'acceptability of a UN mediation mission…is determined by the accuracy of the UN's reading of the conflict dynamic and its military balance, and its ability to use this understanding to dictate a feasible response.'[184]

The only feasible response in these circumstances was partition, a remedy that for Glitman and Chaim Kaufman was the only one that acknowledged the futility of trying to maintain a unified Bosnia when the intensity of the security dilemma for each ethnic group had simply become too great.[185] Full partition, however, was still considered a political and moral anathema by the Western powers and so negotiations continued in order to achieve at least a legally unified Bosnia.[186] All that remained for the Americans was a desire to improve the amount of territory provided to the Muslims, who in the Invincible Package and EU plan of early 1994 had been awarded only 30 and 33.5 per cent of the country respectively.[187]

With its organization of the Muslim/Croat Federation in March of the same year the US had managed to avoid the politically noxious prospect of a Muslim enclave in the Balkans. Yet, even at this stage the Americans were unwilling to commit themselves militarily and so the Bosnian Serbs continued to reject the Contact Group's proposals without fear of stiff punishment for doing so.[188] Only after Clinton had accepted the inevitability of

US involvement did the necessary resolve to enforce a settlement material-ize the following year.[189]

6 Conclusion

Whether or not the Yugoslav civil wars were caused by a security dilemma or by the predatory intentions of the Serbian leadership is still hotly contested. For example Paul Roe argues that because Milosevic and the Bosnian Serbs intentionally sought a Greater Serbia and were prepared to kill anyone who stood in their way, a security dilemma was simply not present.[190] This argument is succinctly expressed by Cigar, who argues that the 'war was not caused by understandable Bosnian Serb desires for self-determination or by the international recognition of Bosnia...[Their] envi-sioned territorial expansion meant that the Serbs would unavoidably become a minority unless non-Serbs were killed, expelled, or assimilated on a large scale'.[191]

Susan Woodward, on the other hand, posits that there is little evidence to prove the predatory actor hypothesis. Instead, she argues that those who believe there was no security dilemma in the run up to war in Croatia and Bosnia, because it is a 'structural argument that ignores agency and thus denies leaders' culpability for manufacturing fears and defensiveness miss the point of the security dilemma: that it is perceptions that matter, and that it is a relational dynamic between two or more actors that leads to violence'.[192]

To understand the fears and defensive positioning that led the Bosnian Serb leaders to abandon political negotiations and shift to war in April 1992 does not, for Woodward, excuse them from the consequences of their decision. However, it is also still important, she argues, to recognize that their decision was essentially 'a preemptive strike in a context that includ-ed warnings and fears fully broadcast in advance by the Muslim leadership and the international community.' These included Izetbegovic's defection the previous October and December from the constitutional obligation that all three nations reach consensus; the decision of the US to reenter the conflict in support of Izetbegovic's request for immediate recognition and the EU's decision to ignore both Bosnian constitutionality and the explicit warnings of its own Arbitration Commission when most Serbs boycotted the referendum; and the March exodus of the JNA from Croatia, where they had been protecting Serbs in border areas (and by implication in Bosnia), to be replaced by UN peacekeepers monitoring a cease-fire agreement.[193]

As this disagreement suggests, making an accurate determination of the extent to which Serb actions were driven by security fears or predatory behavior is difficult even after a decade of reflection. Nevertheless, what was obvious from the beginning of the UN's intervention in 1991 was that the parties existed in a shared understanding of aggression. Thus, only with the application of Track 1 diplomacy that provided the parties with security guarantees for both the intervention and post-intervention phases might the UN ever have hoped to achieve disarmament. This meant it needed to ensure the deployment of a significant military force and the negotiation of internal security guarantees.

Of course, in the environment presented by Yugoslavia a 'significant' military force required at least the potential to enforce a peace upon relatively well-trained, organized and funded militaries. Instead, the international community chose to deploy a lightly armed UN peacekeeping force in a situation in which there existed no peace to keep. Even when NATO eventually became involved, it did so incrementally and in a less than determined fashion. This was not surprising given that the involvement of the Alliance was being directed by the same states that had attempted to use the UN as a means of avoiding a forceful response earlier in the intervention.

Political will is therefore an essential ingredient of any third party action. As the UN found in Sector West in Croatia, even a false perception of political will can be a powerful force multiplier in disarmament operations. However, the determination of the third party will inevitably be tested by local actors and it cannot, therefore, be found wanting as it was in January 1993 with the Croatian offensives against the UNPAs.

Lastly, with ineffective Track 1 diplomacy at the level of the parties, there could be little hope for successful Track 1 or Track 2 diplomacy at the societal levels of combatants and the general population. The longer the civil wars continued the more inseparable the existing justice systems became from the militaries of each party. And without the international community's determination to impose a settlement it was impossible to create sufficient political space for a civil society to grow strong enough to challenge the leadership of the parties. Unfortunately, this was not to change until the US finally found the political will to impose itself on the conflict in 1995.

6
El Salvador 1991–1997

1 Introduction

This chapter is concerned with the United Nations Operation in El Salvador (ONUSAL), which was officially launched in May 1991 to verify compliance with the San Jose Agreement of July 1990. To ensure the implementation of outstanding commitments the UN continued its presence in the country through two consecutive, though smaller, missions. Launched in May 1995 and May 1996 respectively, these were the United Nations Mission in El Salvador (MINUSAL) and the United Nations Office of Verification in El Salvador (ONUV). Only in July 1997, a full six years after its initial deployment, did the UN feel sufficiently satisfied to end its peacekeeping presence.

By the end of its tenure ONUSAL's disarmament mandate was deemed to be one of its greatest successes. The purpose of this chapter, therefore, is to ascertain the reasons for this success. To do so this chapter will utilize the twin-track framework outlined in Chapter 1. Maintaining the format of previous case studies, this chapter will begin with an overview of the events leading up to the signing of the country's peace agreements. Accounts of both the UN's mandate and its implementation will then be followed by an analysis of the disarmament process itself. The conclusion will then assess the utility of the twin-track framework in explaining the success of the UN's disarmament process in El Salvador.

2 Background to the conflict

The modern political system in El Salvador emerged after the suppression of a peasant revolt in 1932, inspired by the Communist party under the leadership of Farabundo Marti. Although the socio-economic causes of the Salvadoran crisis can be traced back to the last century, this event solidified the symbiotic relationship of the country's armed forces and landed oligarchy. Whilst the former became the guardians of the political order, the latter continued to direct events through the ownership of capital.[1] Over the following 47 years this corporate arrangement worked to maintain the socio-economic *status quo*, so that by 1980 the poorest fifth of the population still earned only 2 per cent of national income, whilst the richest fifth earned 66 per cent.[2]

With social unrest increasingly evident, an American supported military coup ousted the government of General Romero in October 1979.[3] Recognizing that Romero's brutal repression had generated increasing popular support for left-wing revolutionaries, the new junta hoped to appease the deepest unrest in Salvadoran society through the formation of a centrist, reformist government. However, unwilling to see its power weakened, the landed oligarchy, together with rich ex-patriots in Miami, developed a military plan involving the creation of 'death squads' and a political party, both subsequently led by Roberto D'Aubuisson. Although the new junta had initially hoped to break the traditional relationship between the military and the oligarchy, it actively cooperated with the 'death squads' to repress those suspected of left-wing sentiments. Meanwhile, the US, fearful that repression alone might engender a Nicaraguan style revolution, began to encourage the Salvadoran government to apply a dual policy of 'low-intensity conflict' together with socio-economic reforms and a transition to democracy.[4]

In an attempt to increase its credibility as a reformist government, the military junta formed a coalition with the Christian Democratic Party (PDC), led by Jose Napoleon Duarte. Although Duarte subsequently became President of El Savador in December 1980, the army still held the reigns of power. It was therefore able to suspend indefinitely the agrarian reform program the junta had announced after seizing power. It was also able to continue its repression of the civilian population. With an estimated 15,000 lives lost in 1980 alone, the UN recorded its dismay at the 'murders, disappearances and other violations of human rights that had been reported.[5]

In October 1980 the five main Salvadoran revolutionary groups amalgamated to form the *Frente Farabundo Marti para la Liberacion Nacional* (FMLN).[6] Hoping to seize power before Ronald Reagan assumed office as US President, the FMLN launched a 'final offensive' in January 1981. Conducted in combination with a general strike and a popular insurrection, the attempt was ultimately unsuccessful. Nonetheless, it did pressure the government to announce its intention to hold elections for the Constituent Assembly in 1982 and for the Presidency and Legislative Assembly in 1983. The party of the oligarchy, the *Aliaza Republican Nationalista* (ARENA) was founded in May 1981 to contest these elections.

Just as the FMLN had feared, the transfer of power to the Reagan administration was to have dire effects on the prospects for peace in El Salvador. Viewing the conflict as a microcosm of the global battle against communism, the new administration began to supply increasing amounts of financial aid and training support to the Salvadoran military. However, because of incompetence and mismanagement the military was unable to capitalize on its newfound wealth and advice, leading the Pentagon to admit by 1983 that the insurgents were in fact winning the war. Reagan's response was to pour even more money in, with the result that between 1983 and 1986 the size of the Salvadoran military grew from 11,000 to 56,000 troops as US aid almost doubled.[7]

The FMLN, and the insurgent group with which it was aligned, the *Frente Democratico Revolucionario* (FDR), had both made offers to the Salvadoran government and the US to conduct negotiations in 1981 and 1982.[8] Unwilling to talk to the rebels the US, as noted above, had continued to seek a military victory. The FMLN, however, had received its own increase in supplies from Nicaragua, Cuba and the USSR. Together with the adoption of counter-tactics (which involved downsizing the size of its forces from approximately 10,000–12,000 troops to between 5,000–8,000 and conducting hit-and-run missions on military and economic targets), this increased aid ensured that the conflict had by the mid-1980's reached a 'dynamic equilibrium' rather than the often-cited stalemate.[9]

In an attempt to break the political impasse the governments of Colombia, Mexico, Panama and Venezuela formed the 'Contadora Group' in January 1983. Although all the countries of the region ostensibly supported the group, including the US, it truly received very little support.[10] A similar fate was to befall the early initiatives of the newly elected President Duarte who, once inaugurated President on 1 June 1984, broke with US policy and invited the FMLN to talks in October.[11] Unfortunately for Duarte both sides to the conflict remained intransigent. Whilst the Salvadoran oligarchy and US continued to believe in the possibility of military victory, the FMLN, bolstered by its battlefield successes, also persevered in its hopes of forcing Duarte into a power-sharing arrangement 'that would arrange new elections, reorganize the military, abolish the 1983 Constitution and establish new political rules of the game'.[12]

In this uncompromising context (and despite the creation of a 'Contadora Support Group' by the countries of Argentina, Brazil, Peru and Uruguay in 1985) the first real breakthrough in negotiations did not occur until February 1987. This breakthrough came in the form of a peace plan presented by Costa Rican President, Oscar Arias, which in itself was an 'attempt to bring peace and stability to the region by taking the initiative away from the external actors, the US, USSR, Cuba and the Contadora and Contadora Support Group countries'.[13] Arias' plan committed each of the five Central American countries to launch democratic processes at home and to terminate support for irregular forces or insurrectionist movements in others. It also committed them to establish cease-fires, provide amnesties to insurgents and prevent their territories from being used to destabilize other countries in the region. Signed by the five Central American presidents on 7 August 1987, the agreement became known informally as 'Esquipulas II'.

Although the agreement did not satisfy all the demands of the insurgents, it did contribute to the increasingly favorable political climate evident since the 1984 elections. It therefore helped lead the FMLN and FDR into a reassessment of their strategies. This process culminated in an offer by the FMLN to compete in the 1989 presidential elections on the condition that the Government postpone them from March until September. The significance of this offer lay in the FMLN's acceptance of the electoral outcome, which meant that it was now willing to drop its power-sharing demands and recognize the 1983 Constitution.[14] However, the FMLN was not prepared to call a permanent cease-fire (it had only proposed a suspension of activities in the days surrounding the elections) and so, under pressure from those who believed the FMLN to be in a no-lose situation, Duarte refused to postpone the elections.[15]

Nevertheless, changes were also apparent in ARENA's strategy. In June 1988 it had elected a new leader, Alfredo Cristiani, a US-educated 'young oligarch'. The party's new approach to the conflict was evident in Cristiani's inauguration speech following his victory in the 1989 presidential elections. For the first time Cristiani referred to the civil war as his country's main problem, acknowledged that the insurgents were more than mere terrorists and unveiled a five-point plan for talks with the FMLN.[16]

Two months later the five Central American Presidents met in Tela, Honduras, to discuss an offer made by the Nicaraguan government to hold democratic elections in return for the disarmament of the Nicaraguan resistance. Although the possibility of linking the disarmament of the insurgents in Nicaragua to those in El Salvador was discussed at the meeting, the Nicaraguan government opposed the linkage. The meeting therefore ended with a simple call for the Salvadoran government and the FMLN to hold meaningful negotiations leading to a cease-fire and the rebel group's reintegration into society. The need for independent verification of the commitments contained within the Tela Declaration, signed by the five presidents on 7 August, led to the creation of the United Nations Observer Mission in Central America (ONUCA) on 7 November 1989.[17]

When the Government and the FMLN finally did sit down to talks in mid-October, negotiations were to fail for two reasons. The first was the intransigence of the political Right and the military. With both of these groups under the mistaken impression that the FMLN was on the verge of surrender, the military refused to even consider reform and instead declared its 'organic structure' to be non-negotiable. The second reason was the continued assassinations of individuals on both sides of the political divide, which eventually culminated in the military's bombing of the National Federation of Salvadoran Workers Union (FENESTRAS) Headquarters on 31 October.[18]

The FMLN's response to this collapse in negotiations was to conduct its most successful offensive to date in November.[19] With fighting having engulfed the capital for the first time, the FMLN's unexpected success was to fundamentally change the direction of negotiations. This was because the offensive had taught three fundamental lessons. Firstly, it had highlighted the utter failure of Salvadoran and US intelligence, which both believed the FMLN incapable of such major offensive actions. Secondly, the failure to defeat the insurgents had exposed the impotency of the Salvadoran armed forces. And thirdly, it had exposed the commensurate failure of nine years of US foreign policy towards the country.[20]

Symbolized by the deaths of six Jesuit priests along with their housemaid and her daughter at the hands of the military on 16 November, it was evident that US foreign policy had not achieved either the establishment of democracy or the subordination of the military to civilian control. Neither had it achieved the containment of the insurgents. Having donated over $4 billion in military and economic aid since 1984 and having witnessed the deaths of an estimated 60,000 Salvadorans, the US Congress began to reassess its approach to the conflict.[21] Consequently, so too did the new Bush administration. Expressing this reappraisal, Secretary of State James Baker stated in February 1990 that the US believed that year to be the 'year to end the war through a negotiated settlement which [would guarantee] safe political space for all Salvadorans'.[22] The reduction in support for the FMLN at the end of the Cold War, together with the surprise defeat of the Sandanista government in the February 1990 Nicaraguan elections, served to strengthen the new American policy.

The foundation for the UN's subsequent role in the Salvadoran peace process was to be laid at a meeting in April 1990 at which UN Secretary-General Perez de Cuellar announced his willingness to oversee a political solution to the crisis.[23] This led to a further meeting on 21 May in Caracas, where an agreement was signed establishing a two-phase process to negotiations. The first phase was designed to reach political agreements on such issues as human rights, the armed forces, the judiciary and electoral reform, in order that a cease-fire could be negotiated. The second phase was to address the same issues, but this time with the purpose of enabling the FMLN to reintegrate into society.[24] In agreeing to this process the Government departed from its long-standing insistence that a cease-fire precede any substantial political and legal reforms. The parties also agreed to establish a 'Group of Friends', to be composed of the governments of Mexico, Colombia, Venezuela and Spain, to assist them in negotiations.[25]

The first phase of negotiations continued to be blocked by disagreements over the extent of military reform. In Montgomery's opinion 'the fundamental problem was that the Government viewed the problem within the military as a matter of criminal and corrupt individuals; the FMLN defined the problem as systemic'.[26] With the issue threatening to derail the whole peace process, only the intervention of the Special Representative of the Secretary-General (SRSG), Alvaro de Soto, was to enable further progress. In an ingenious move De Soto persuaded the parties to reach agreements on other issues, thereby circumventing the question of military reform. The result was to be the first substantial agreement between the Salvadoran parties: the San Jose Agreement on Human Rights of 26 July 1990.

The San Jose Agreement provided for the establishment of a UN verification mission to monitor nationwide respect for, and guarantee of, human rights and fundamental freedoms. Although it was initially envisaged that the mission would begin at the cessation of the armed conflict, the Secretary-General was requested by both parties to send a preliminary mission to assess the feasibility of deploying monitors before the fighting had actually stopped. This mission was sent in March 1991, thus allowing ONUSAL to be officially launched on 20 May 1991. ONUSAL's initial mandate was, therefore, simply to verify the compliance of the parties with the commitments they had made at San Jose nearly a year before.[27]

Nevertheless, substantial progress was to be made on the issue of military reform in the months between the San Jose Agreement and the establishment of ONUSAL. Initially two factors were to encourage the parties to compromise. The first was the decision of the US Congress in mid-October to cut American aid to the Salvadoran government by 50 per cent, with its restoration to be dependent on progress in the peace negotiations and on investigations into the murders of the Jesuit priests in 1989. The second was the decision of both Salvadoran parties to enhance De Soto's role to that of a full-blown mediator at a meeting in Mexico City in late October. This change enabled the UN to present proposals in an attempt to break the deadlock.[28]

Unfortunately, after the UN presented both parties with reform proposals on 1 January 1991 two subsequent decisions were to hinder real progress on the issue. The first was the decision of the US Congress to restore aid to El Salvador following the downing of an American helicopter in mid-January. This gave added confidence to the Salvadoran government (henceforth referred to as the Government) and military, neither of which had met the original criteria set for the restoration of aid. The second was the decision of the FMLN to hold out on any commitments so as to prevent the Government from claiming credit for a peace settlement before the legislative elections in March. However, following the success of the Democratic Convergence (the political party created by the FDR) in these elections, the FMLN was given added confidence to accelerate negotiations.[29]

With both sides more appreciative of the need for compromise, a further three weeks of intensive discussions eventually led to the signing of the Mexico Agreement on 27 April 1991. This agreement included a formula of constitutional reforms covering the areas of the armed forces, the electoral system and the judiciary. For the military these reforms included its clearer subordination to civilian authority and the creation and separation from military command of a new National Civil Police and State Intelligence Agency. Improvements to the justicial system included new rules for the election of Supreme Court Justices, the creation of a National Counsel of the Judiciary and the establishment of a Judicial Training School. The electoral system was to be enhanced by the creation of a politically independent Supreme Electoral Tribunal (TSE), which was to become the highest authority in electoral matters. Finally, the agreement also called for the creation of a Commission on the Truth that could investigate human rights violations committed since 1980.

Fearful of the consequences of unilateral disarmament, the FMLN had previously called for the complete abolition of the country's armed forces. Recognizing the futility of this demand the FMLN had instead begun to push more heavily for the integration of some of its members into the force. However, at the Iberoamerican Summit in Guadalajara, Mexico, on 18–19 July, the FMLN was informed that its demands for integration had no international support.[30] This was mostly because of the military's vehement reaction to the Mexico Agreement. With increasing threats from death squads and constant rumors of a potential military coup, army negotiators had already been forced to hold meetings with lower-rank officers to quell their discontent. Cristiani had also reassured the army that its dissolution was not on the table and that the US had announced a multimillion dollar assistance program to help demobilized soldiers reintegrate into society.[31] There were obvious fears that the imposition of FMLN integration might be the straw to break the camel's back.

Another contentious issue at this juncture was the timing of a cease-fire. Whilst the Government was refusing to negotiate further reforms to the military until a cease-fire was established, the FMLN was refusing to enter into a cease-fire until the negotiations on the reform of the military were concluded. To try and overcome this gridlock the Secretary-General invited both parties to a series of meetings in New York in September.[32] Here the parties were presented with a package of proposals, including the creation of an Ad Hoc Commission to purify the military of human rights abusers; the integration of the FMLN into the new police force; the establishment of a National Commission for the Consolidation of Peace, a multi-party body charged with supervision of the peace agreements; and a reduction in the size of the military. Agrarian reform was also included. By discussing all these issues at once the UN had effectively abandoned the two-phase process of negotiations adopted after Caracas in favor of a 'compressed agenda'. This was deemed necessary to overcome the parties' inability to agree on mutually acceptable cease-fire terms.[33]

The New York Agreement of 25 September 1991 thus formed the second major breakthrough in negotiations after the San Jose Agreement.

Significantly, in exchange for dropping its insistence on integration with the military the FMLN had received a commitment that 20 per cent of the new police force would be composed of its former combatants. Although it could not convince the Government to allow it to police its areas of major influence, this agreement nevertheless still assured the FMLN a significant sector of the only body responsible for civil security in the post-conflict era.[34] Political pressure from all parties, together with the threat of the full cessation of US aid, had also persuaded the military to accept a 50 per cent cut in its numbers.[35] With the conclusion of this last agreement, the parties signed the Act of New York at Mexico City's Chapultepec Castle on 16 January 1992, henceforth known as the Chapultepec Agreements.

3   The UN's disarmament mandate and the nature of the peace agreements

As explained in the preceding section, the negotiations leading to the resolution of the Salvadoran conflict were a piecemeal affair. Significantly, it was precisely because of the difficulties experienced in reaching a comprehensive agreement that the Salvadoran parties eventually requested the UN to begin verifying the San Jose Agreement before their conflict had actually ended. This was to make ONUSAL 'without precedent in the history of UN peacekeeping and peacemaking missions, the first mission to accomplish its tasks of verification and observation of respect for human rights and international law *during* an internal conflict.'[36]

The completion of negotiations on military and police reform thus required an enlargement of both ONUSAL's size and mandate. This occurred on 14 January 1992 with the creation of ONUSAL's Military and Police Divisions, which were initially composed of 380 and 631 monitors respectively.[37] These were to join the 57 monitors already deployed in ONUSAL's Human Rights Division.[38]

To oversee the implementation of the whole peace process the New York Agreement had established a National Commission for the Consolidation of Peace (COPAZ), which was to function as a 'mechanism for the monitoring of and the participation of civilian society in the process of changes resulting from the negotiations'. It was to be composed of two representatives of the Government (including one from the FAES), two from the FMLN and one each from the parties represented in the country's Legislative Assembly. The Archbishop of San Salvador and a delegate of ONUSAL could be present as observers.

Although it did not possess legislative or executive powers, the COPAZ could still make binding recommendations relating to the Agreements, as well as draft legislation for adoption by the Legislative Assembly. In addition, all parties were obliged to consult it before adopting decisions or measures relating to relevant aspects of the Agreements. The UN's role was thus to verify implementation of the Agreements in parallel with the COPAZ.

The period known as the 'Cessation of the Armed Conflict (CAC)' was to begin on 1 February (known within the Agreements as D-Day) and end on 31 October 1992. It was to consist of three elements: a cease-fire; the separation of forces; and the dismantling of the 'military structure of [the] FMLN and the reintegration of its members, within a framework of full legality, into the civil, political and institutional life of the country'. In order that ONUSAL could verify all three of these elements, the parties agreed to provide it with detailed information regarding their respective military strengths as soon as possible after the signing of the Agreements, but no later than two weeks before D-Day.

The first element of the CAC, the informal cease-fire, was to begin on D-Day. This was to be followed by the separation of forces, which itself was to take place in two stages. The first stage required each force to concentrate in areas that generally reflected their present deployments and was to be complete by D-Day+5. Whilst this meant the FAES was to regroup at 100 locations, the FMLN was to do so at 50. Stage two of their separation, which was to be complete by D-Day+30, required the FAES to concentrate at 62 locations and the FMLN at 15. The precise designation of the locations for both of these stages were to be determined through consultation between ONUSAL and the parties during the informal cease-fire period.

As already mentioned, the third element of the CAC was to consist of the reintegration of former FMLN combatants. This was to take place in five stages, with 20 per cent of the ex-combatants to be reintegrated at each stage. These stages were set for D-Day+90, D-Day+120, D-Day+180 and D-Day+240, thus allowing the whole process to be complete by the end of the CAC period.

The main social and economic mechanism included in the Agreements to help the ex-combatants of both parties reintegrate was the 'land-transfer program'. Through this program the Government committed itself to redistribute State-owned farmland to those who needed it, in particular those 'former combatants of both Parties who…are of peasant origin and familiar with farming, and possess no land of any kind'. In addition to agricultural land, ex-combatants were also to be given access to credit and technical assistance. Other mechanisms, such as employment training and access to credit to establish small businesses, were to be provided to those wishing to reintegrate into urban areas. The Government also agreed to respect the 'land-tenure situation in conflict zones' until a 'satisfactory legal solution' could be arrived at.

The Agreements also called upon the Government to submit a National Reconstruction Plan (NRP) within 30 days of signing the Agreements. The main objectives of the NRP were to integrate the former conflict zones, reconstruct infrastructure damaged by the war and to satisfy 'the most immediate needs of the population hardest hit by the conflict and of former combatants of both Parties'. In particular the NRP was to facilitate the reintegration of the FMLN into the country's civil, institutional and political life, including fellowship, employment and pension programs, housing programs and programs for starting up new businesses'. It was also to pay special attention to the promotion of job creation on 'a massive scale' and include programs for the war-disabled and relatives of victims among the civilian population.

Obviously, the credibility of the peace process also depended heavily on its success in reforming the Salvadoran Armed Forces (FAES), the main objectives of which were to ensure its subordination to civilian authority and end its involvement in the provision of public security. The Agreements therefore limited its future role to that of national defense and abolished the former military controlled National Guard (GN) and Treasury Police (PT). The personnel of these two bodies were to be transferred into the FAES by D-Day+30.[39] For the same reason a new civilian State Intelligence Agency was to replace the National Intelligence Department.

The FAES was also to be reduced in size. Following its prior agreement with the FMLN the Government submitted a plan to reduce its numbers by 50 per cent to approximately 30,000 troops. This reduction was to be achieved primarily through the demobilization of five rapid deployment infantry battalions (BIRIs), which were now deemed inappropriate for the new 'doctrine and functions' of the FAES. Starting in the sixth month of the peace process, one of these BIRIs was to be demobilized every 30 days. In an effort to end the role of paramilitary forces, the old Civil Defense forces and armed forces reserves were to be replaced with a new system in which volunteers could only undertake missions if assigned to active duty in the FAES.

In an attempt to change the public perception of the FAES the Agreements also required that it be purged of officers found to have committed human rights abuses. For this purpose an Ad Hoc Commission was to be formed from 'three Salvadorans of recognized independence of judgment and unimpeachable democratic credentials' together with 'two officers of the armed forces with impeccable professional records'.[40] The Commission was to evaluate all officers within the FAES and recommend the removal of any found guilty of such crimes. It was to be established by D-Day+105 and its recommendations were to be implemented by the end of the CAC. Obviously, whilst a purge of the military's worst officers was a welcome first step, the improvement of its remaining personnel was essential to its long-term credibility. Thus, the education traditionally provided to FAES members was to be broadened to include a particular emphasis on human rights.

Nevertheless, in terms of human rights abuses the body ostensibly responsible for public security throughout the conflict, the National Police

(PN), had fared little better than the FAES. The Agreements therefore sought to replace it with a new National Civil Police (PNC) that was to have 'new organization, new officers, new education and training mechanisms and a new doctrine.' In an effort to ensure a more professional force, all PNC officers were required to graduate from the yet to be established National Public Security Academy (PNSA). Also, to ensure its independence from the FAES, the PNC was to be placed under civilian control and was to remain under the direct authority of the President of El Salvador until the transitional period (24 months after the first contingent of recruits entered the PNSA) had ended.

To take over those duties that the military had previously performed, new units needed to be established in the PNC. These included a Criminal Investigation Division (CID) and Frontiers Division (DF), which were to assume the former duties of the GN and PT respectively. In consideration of the particular concerns of those living in areas that had traditionally been 'conflict zones during the armed conflict' the Director-General of the PNC was to create a 'special regime' to police them until the PNC could be fully deployed.

By the end of the transitional period the PNSA was expected to have graduated at least 5,700 new officers (it hoped to have 10,000 graduates within five years). Candidates for these positions were to be selected 'in such a way as to ensure that most recruits [had] not [participated] directly in the armed conflict and that the proportion of former FMLN combatants [was] no greater than that of the former members of the PN, and vice versa'. This meant that former members of the FLMN and PN were to each make up 20 per cent of the new force.

Recognizing that the transition from the old PN to the new PNC was likely to be difficult, the Secretary-General believed the UN's role in the sphere of public security would have to entail more than mere verification. Instead, to be effective, ONUSAL needed to monitor the PN during the transitional period. This could only be achieved, he argued, if ONUSAL observers were deployed at all levels of the PN.[41]

To ensure the impartiality of the Salvadoran judicial system the Agreements also called for the creation of a National Council of the Judiciary and a new Judicial Training School. Together, they were to 'ensure a steady improvement in the professional training of judges and other judicial officials' and foster 'a coherent overall vision of the function of the judiciary in a democratic State'. Their tasks were to be aided by the creation of an Office of the National Counsel for the Defense of Human Rights.

In order to help COPAZ fulfill its functions two sub-commissions were formed at the beginning of the operation. The first of these was designated to deal with the land transfer program and the second was to assist in the formation of the PNC. A joint working group, consisting of ONUSAL's

Chief Military Observer and one representative from each of the parties, was also formed to help implement the three elements of the CAC.

4   Implementation

4.1   ONUSAL

Though much had been achieved in the implementation of the Agreements by the end of 1992, still more remained to be done. Citing the Government's failure to fulfill its commitments in reforming public security and providing reintegration support, the FMLN had already suspended the demobilization of its combatants on three occasions. The Government had retaliated each time by suspending the downsizing of the FAES. The delays caused by these suspensions had also forced the Secretary-General to renegotiate the implementation timetable three times. Nevertheless, by the end of the year 11,000 former combatants of the FMLN had demobilized, thus enabling it to register as a political party on 15 December. With this historic event the armed conflict was officially declared over. It was, in the words of the Secretary-General, a 'defining moment in the history of El Salvador.'[42]

However, an extensive list of outstanding commitments remained. The Government had shown extreme reluctance to disband the FAES, PT, GN or PN. It had even begun to transfer personnel from the first three organizations into the PN, citing the need to combat the country's rising tide of crime. ONUSAL continued to protest that these actions were irreconcilable with the aim of the Agreements to replace the existing security bodies with the PNC.[43] The PNC's deployment was also lagging behind schedule, not least because its first Director had only been appointed in July and the PNSA had only begun training recruits in September (four months after the date expected). As FMLN combatants had subsequently begun to fill the public security vacuum that had formed in the former zones of conflict, the Government began to deploy the 'special regime' it had promised for these areas in October. Named the Auxiliary Transitory Police (PAT), it was composed of cadets from the PNSA who were commanded by ONUSAL.[44]

One of the most contentious issues of the first year was to be the land-transfer program. The sluggishness of the transfer process had caused a number of peasant groups to seize land in former zones of conflict, only for them to be evicted later by Government forces. To try and avert further clashes Under-Secretary-General for Peacekeeping, Marrack Goulding, visited the country personally in March. Despite his success in negotiating a temporary cessation of the evictions, the land-transfer program remained static. To prevent the issue from derailing the whole peace process the Secretary-General therefore presented a proposal to both parties in October that envisaged a transfer of land in three phases over the following year.[45]

Although the Secretary-General's proposal may have dampened tensions over the land-transfer program, the reports of the Ad Hoc Commission and the Commission on the Truth only served to raise them again. Released on 24 September 1992, the report of the Ad Hoc Commission had gone even further than expected by recommending the dismissal of 76 military officers and the transfer to other functions of another 26. Afraid that pushing Cristiani to implement these recommendations too quickly might stir up a political backlash, the FMLN and ONUSAL agreed to a one-month post-ponement.[46] In return, ONUSAL was to retain a small number of 'sophisti-cated weapons' belonging to the FMLN, which it was to destroy after the Government had complied with the Commission's recommendations. This arrangement was 'understood and accepted' by the Government.[47]

However, ONUSAL was to be left as the last defender of the Ad Hoc Commission's recommendations when the Government negotiated directly with the FMLN to allow a delay in the resignation of certain top-level army officers and the transfer into the PNC of two law enforcement organiza-tions, the Special Investigative Unit (SIU) and the Executive Anti-Narcotics Unit (UEA). The FMLN had compromised its position in return for a package of training, stipends and credits for 600 of its mid-level comman-ders and the transfer of certain desirable plots of land to its former combat-ants.[48] Only the refusal of ONUSAL to accept this arrangement and its continued insistence that the Commission's recommendations be imple-mented in full ensured the Government's compliance by July 1993.[49]

Before issuing its report on 15 March 1993 the Commission on the Truth had received 22,000 complaints of serious acts of violence committed between January 1980 and July 1991. Having found that 95 per cent of these acts had been perpetrated by the State, with the FMLN responsible for only the remain-ing 5 per cent, the Commission made a number of recommendations. These included the resignation of the majority of officers already named by the Ad Hoc Commission, the resignation of the Supreme Court and the com-mencement of an investigation into the actions of 'private armed groups', a euphemism for the notorious death squads. The Secretary-General described the reaction to these recommendations in his May 1993 report.

> Extreme positions were adopted and tension mounted as the High Command of the Armed Forces, the President of the Supreme Court, highly placed government officials and some political leaders, as well as segments of the media, vehemently and publicly rejected the findings and recommendations of the Commission on the Truth. There was stri-dent criticism of the UN and renewed publication of anonymous threats against ONUSAL.[50]

The Government's response was to push a general amnesty through the Legislative Assembly in the week following the report's release, thereby exonerating all those named. This was done despite the Commission's recommendation against prosecutions, a decision it had made in the belief that the likely failure of the country's corrupt legal system to properly prosecute the accused would only exacerbate the tenuous feeling of national reconciliation that then existed. Although the Secretary-General was not averse to an amnesty law, he nevertheless believed that 'it would have been preferable if the amnesty had been enacted after creating a broad degree of national consensus in its favor.'[51]

A decision by the Government in December to accelerate the demobilization of the FAES had allowed the process to be completed by the end of March 1993. However, the credibility of the whole disarmament process was to be severely challenged when an accidental explosion occurred in an automobile shop in Minagua, Nicaragua, on 23 May. This explosion led to the discovery of an FMLN weapons cache that included, amongst other things, large quantities of ammunition, military weapons, explosives and a number of surface-to-air missiles. Although ONUSAL had questioned the credibility of its weapons inventories throughout the disarmament process, the FMLN had continued to insist that all its weapons had been surrendered. The Secretary-General expressed the seriousness of this deception when he argued that 'such a deliberate attempt to mislead [him] placed [his] credibility in doubt and raised very serious questions of confidence and trust.'[52]

The severity of the FMLN's deception was only to become apparent over the subsequent months. With the cooperation of all five FMLN constituent groups ONUSAL uncovered a total of 114 arms caches located in Nicaragua, Honduras and El Salvador. Altogether the arms found and surrendered corresponded to approximately 30 per cent of the FMLN's original inventory.[53] All these arms were destroyed by 18 August, thus allowing the Secretary-General to inform the Security Council 12 days later that the military structure of the FMLN had finally been dismantled and its personnel demobilized and reintegrated.[54] The explosion in Minagua did not prevent the Security Council voting on 27 May to create an electoral division within ONUSAL, following an official request for it to do so by the Salvadoran government in January.[55]

With the start of the electoral campaign on 20 November the Secretary-General was compelled to express his 'considerable concern' that such a significant phase of the peace process should have begun when 'some very important elements in the [Agreements] remain only partially implemented'.[56] The failure of the Government to properly comply with any of the public security provisions of the Agreements had led the Secretary-General to send a UN mission to the country on 16 November to assess the problem. Rather than disbanding the PN, the Government's plans to demobilize the force (which were submitted to the UN eight months late in October) had actually shown an increase in its numbers since the

Agreements were signed. The detrimental effects of its prolonged existence were made apparent in the fact that its members had perpetrated over one-third of all the human rights abuses reported to ONUSAL by the end of 1993. These crimes included summary executions and torture.[57]

The land transfer program was also in crisis. By the end of 1993 little more than 10 per cent of the 47,500 potential beneficiaries of the program had received land titles.[58] Demonstrations by ex-combatants had already occurred in San Salvador and had sometimes been put down violently by the PN and PNC. The Secretary-General also expressed his fears over the slow pace of the other reintegration programs, even to the extent of questioning their viability.[59]

The credibility of the PNC was also being questioned. The Government and the PNC's newly appointed Deputy Director of Operations, Oscar Pena Duran, were doing everything in their power to circumvent ONUSAL's verification and undermine the new force. This included transferring former military personnel into the PNC, denying it the requisite funding and creating unaccountable intelligence bodies to monitor members that were former FMLN combatants. Although the PNC had deployed just under 2,000 officers by the end of 1993, it possessed only 67 vehicles, 31 motor-cycles and 134 portable radios. Whilst calling for the speedy appointment of an Inspector-General to help monitor the PNC's activities and respect for human rights, the Secretary-General noted that the reports he was receiv-ing were creating 'the impression that at some levels in the Government there may be a lack of commitment to the objective enshrined in the [Agreements]'.[60]

The elections in March 1994 were not, therefore, to represent the culmi-nation of the peace process as the Secretary-General had hoped. Rather, they were to occur during a period in which significant elements of the Agreements remained outstanding. Even the elections themselves were to be surrounded in controversy. On 20 March elections were held simultane-ously for the Presidency, the Legislative Assembly, Municipalities and Central American Parliament. The UN's observation was beyond reproach, with the deployment of 900 international observers in all of El Salvador's 262 municipalities. However, on election day many of those who had made it through the complex and time-consuming registration process found that a lack of public transport, or the inability to find the correct voting tables at polling stations, had made voting impossible. Still more found their names simply omitted from the voting rolls. Reasonable estimates have placed the number of people who wished to vote, but were unable to do so, at approximately 300,000. This figure represents 20 per cent of the total number that actually voted.[61]

As the first round of voting failed to produce an outright victor, a second round was conducted. The ARENA candidate, Calderon Sol, emerged the eventual winner with 68 per cent of the vote. His opposition, the FMLN candidate, Ruben Zamora, polled only 32 per cent. Disappointment was expressed at the low voter turnout, with only 55 per cent of the electorate voting in the first round of elections and 46 per cent in the second. Though the reasons for this apparent apathy remained unclear, the Secretary-General did note that the 'drawbacks of an electoral system that [had been] inaugurated in the early 1980s [had] still not [been] corrected in time for the elections'. With this in mind he tentatively declared on 21 March that 'despite the serious flaws regarding organization and transparency...the elections [could] be considered acceptable.'[62]

At the request of the Secretary-General the parties agreed to establish a new timetable for the pending aspects of the Agreements on 19 May. Problems had continued to beset the areas of public security and reintegration and it was hoped the new timetable would address them. The Government had requested an extension of the deadline for the demobilization of the PN and this had been accepted by the FMLN. Although the Secretary-General was pushing the Government to complete the process by 31 January, it had until March 1995 if required.

ONUSAL also sought to ensure the civilian character of the PNC. The continued militarization of the PNC had prompted Human Rights Watch to warn in March 1994 that the 'contamination of the new police force with existing police units notorious for abuse [posed] a serious and potentially permanent problem'.[63] Nowhere was this more evident that in the PNC's command structure, in which there existed a heavy concentration of former members of the PN, SIU and UEA.[64] With former FMLN personnel making up only 13 per cent of new PNSA recruits, there seemed little hope of future voluntary change. ONUSAL therefore negotiated a 'work program' with the Government that required it to verify the 'assignment of duties' and monitor 'the necessary balance between the personnel of different origins' in the PNC. It also required ONUSAL to verify the workings of the PNSA and restore the technical assistance the PNC had rejected since October.[65]

Although one of the primary recommendations of the Commission on the Truth, the investigation into the workings of 'private armed groups' was not to begin until nine months after its report was released. It was only after the deaths in October of a number of top FMLN officials in a 'style reminiscent of the death squads' and a visit from Marrack Goulding in November that the Government was persuaded to create the Joint Group for the Investigation of Politically Motivated Armed Groups. Created on 8 December, it was mandated to investigate the actions of such groups between 16 January 1992 and the present. It was to be composed of two independent nominees of President Cristiani, the Human Rights Ombudsman and the Director of ONUSAL's Human Rights Division.

Following a two-month extension to its investigations, the Joint Group finally submitted its report on 28 July 1994. To the Government's embarrassment the report showed the continuing involvement of members of the FAES and PN in the country's organized crime networks. It also found evidence that the FAES was still conducting intelligence work in clear violation of its new constitutional role.[66] The Joint Group's chief recommendations were to strengthen the mechanisms of police investigation and for the State Intelligence Agency to assume its constitutional function; for the Supreme Court to purify the legal system of corrupt and inept judges; and for the National Council for the Defense of Human Rights to create a technical verification mechanism to monitor such crimes.

Although the May timetable had envisaged the completion of the majority of reintegration programs for the FMLN and FAES by mid-1996, their slow implementation had caused tensions among ex-combatants to rise to explosive levels.[67] This unrest was to culminate in the takeover of the Legislative Assembly on 26–28 September 1994 by a group of disgruntled former FAES soldiers. Whilst holding 27 hostages, they negotiated an agreement with the Government to accelerate the completion of compensation payments, the implementation of established programs and the incorporation of former members of the paramilitary bodies into the regular social programs.[68] Following further demonstrations in January 1995 the Secretary-General expressed his belief that these demonstrations were 'symptom[s] of lingering discontent at the failure to implement some parts' of the Agreements, particularly those concerning land tenure, the judiciary, electoral reform, the Commission on the Truth and reintegration programs in general.[69]

Although the Secretary-General recognized that the failure to implement these outstanding commitments might 'call into question the irreversibility of the peace process as a whole', the impending expiration of ONUSAL's mandate was forcing him to scale down the UN's deployment.[70] Initially he recommended a smaller verification mechanism to replace ONUSAL after 30 April, one that would consist of around eight professionals with the necessary support staff. The Security Council accepted this proposal on 17 February 1995.[71] However, a lack of progress in implementing the Agreements had caused the Secretary-General to revise his estimates by March. Although he wanted to continue ONUSAL's presence, he had received clear indications from members of the Security Council that they wanted the operation brought to an end. Extension was not, therefore, a viable option. Nevertheless, he still believed a 'somewhat larger team' than that previously proposed might now be required.[72]

The Secretary-General had reason to be cautious. The PN had finally been declared demobilized in December 1994 and ONUSAL's tenacity had ensured that those members of the SIU and UEA transferred *en bloc* into the PNC were required to attend the PNSA (leading to the dismissal and resignation of nearly 400 such personnel). Nevertheless, there were ominous signs for the new police force. These included a Government decision to allow joint FAES-PNC rural patrols (a decision that had itself not been taken in accordance with the proper constitutional procedures) and the general failure of the campaign to promote civilian admissions to the PNSA. And whilst the PNC's Inspector-General and disciplinary investigative units remained ineffective, the policemen themselves continued to be housed in barracks.[73]

Serious problems also continued to plague the reintegration programs. By the end of ONUSAL's tenure fewer than half the potential beneficiaries had received land titles. And of those that had, fewer than 3,000 had received the agricultural credit and technical assistance necessary to allow them to prepare for the April/May planting season. A lack of money in The Fund for the Protection of the Wounded and War Disabled as a Consequence of the Armed Conflict had also left 12,000 war-disabled and 18,000 war victims in critical need of financial help.[74]

4.2   MINUSAL

On 27 April, three days before the end of ONUSAL's mandate, the parties negotiated a work program that envisaged the implementation of the remaining aspects of the Agreements by the following October. The UN Mission in El Salvador (MINUSAL) began operations on 1 May 1995 with a mandate to verify its implementation.

Initially, events threatened to reverse the progress that had already been made. Although the number of PNSA graduates had already exceeded the number expected by the Agreements by 2,500, the PNC was still believed by many to be too small to cope with the explosion in organized crime, drug trafficking and street gangs that had since occurred. This encouraged the Government to continue joint FAES-PNC patrols in rural areas and even consider extending them into urban areas.[75] ONUSAL, recognizing the potential danger this represented thus began to call for legislation to ensure that the FAES could only be used in exceptional circumstances and when adequate information had been provided to the Legislative Assembly.

The credibility of the PNC also remained suspect. Problems posed by the creation of unaccountable police units, together with illegal acts committed by PNC members, had been exacerbated by a five-month delay in the appointment of a new Inspector-General (after the former incumbent had been dismissed in April). Awareness of the deteriorating situation led the Government and the FMLN to request MINUSAL to conduct an evaluation of the public security sector.

Delays had also continued to beset the land-transfer program. Although 74 per cent of potential beneficiaries had received land titles by September, only 25 per cent of these had had their land titles registered with the land registry, an essential requirement before the process could be legally deemed complete. Nevertheless, the Secretary-General was sufficiently satisfied with the progress made to recommend a reduction in the size of

MINUSAL from 11 international staff and 8 civilian police consultants, to 10 and 4 respectively. Recognizing that implementation was still incomplete, he also recommended an extension of MINUSAL's mandate for a further six months until 30 April 1996.

By the time these extra six months had passed there had been a number of significant steps taken in implementing the Agreements, although overall progress remained precarious. The PNC now had a new Inspector-General, but the ineffectiveness of its internal control mechanisms meant that 'neither uniform criteria nor rigor [were] evident in the resolution of the most serious breaches of professional and ethical conduct'.[76] The implementation of the land-transfer program had improved substantially, with 92.6 per cent of former combatants having received titles by March 1996. However, only 49.6 per cent of these were actually registered. A lack of credit, harsh loan terms and a scarcity of technical assistance had also left many beneficiaries of land without the agricultural products they required. Together with owners of small businesses, many were also left unable to meet debt repayments.

Nevertheless, on 23 April the Government and FMLN wrote a joint letter to the Secretary-General in which they expressed their opinion that only a small team composed of the 'minimum essential personnel (three or four officials)', would now be required to verify the implementation of remaining aspects of the Agreements.

4.3 ONUV

In line with the wishes of both parties, the UN Office of Verification in El Salvador (ONUV) began operations on 1 May 1996. Composed of the SRSG and a small support staff, ONUV's mandate lasted for 12 months. Although by the end of this time all the individual commitments in the Agreements concerning public security had been implemented, the new regime remained fragile. This was recognized by the Secretary-General in his final report of July 1997, in which he noted that criminal investigations by groups on the fringe of the PNC's institutional structure, the deployment of the FAES and the creation of vigilante-like 'neighborhood groups' had all 'come perilously close to practices of the past'. He also expressed concern at the recent creation of a 'rural police force' without adequate clarification from the Government as to whether it would form part of the PNC or constitute a separate force in violation of the Agreements.[77]

Other similarities to the past were evident in the growing number of human rights abuses. The National Council for the Defense of Human Rights was receiving more accusations of human rights abuses than ONUSAL had ever done, including threats to the lives of its own members. Some of the executions reported were being carried out in the name of 'social cleansing' by death squads of the type investigated by the Joint Group. Despite this, the Government still refused to heed the Joint Group's recommendation to establish a specialized unit within the PNC to deal with this type of crime.

Although the land-transfer program was near completion, attempts by the Government to accelerate the transfer of land had caused confusion and uncertainty over the security of land tenures. Much of the improvement in the land-transfer program since the end of ONUSAL's mandate had been achieved by the distribution of land *pro-indivisio*. This consisted of transferring properties *en bloc* to a number of beneficiaries in equal shares, but without specifying an exact plot for each individual. With the low incentives for production and investment inherent in such insecure circumstances, debts among ex-combatants had increased and loan repayments had fallen. Although matters improved when the Government forgave 70 per cent of these debts in May 1996, the success of the land-transfer program still depended on legally dividing these properties between beneficiaries.

Finally, following the problems experienced in the 1994 elections, the Government had established an Inter-Party Commission to make recommendations on possible improvements to the electoral system. However, by the time elections were held for the Legislative Assembly and municipalities in March 1997, none of the reforms the Commission had subsequently recommended had been adopted. The elections were therefore to be conducted with the same inadequacies that had beset those of three years earlier. In this situation the best the Secretary-General could hope for was that the new political conditions established in the wake of these elections might provide some impetus to the adoption of the reforms before the Presidential elections due for 1999.[78]

5   Analysis of the operations

5.1   Disarmament, demobilization, reintegration and the reform of the armed forces

The UN's successes in disarmament and demobilization in El Salvador were substantial. By the end of 1993, 11,000 FMLN ex-combatants had surrendered 10,000 automatic weapons, rifles and handguns, 74 missiles and over 9,000 grenades.[79] The number of troops in the FAES had also been reduced by over 33,000, an even deeper cut than that envisaged in the Agreements.[80] Nevertheless, the danger remained that these impressive figures might serve only to mask persistent problems in the UN's planning for, and verification of, its disarmament and demobilization mandates. They also threatened to obscure areas of the peace process in which much less success had been achieved, including the reform of the FAES and the reintegration of ex-combatants.

The UN's planning problems had once again become manifest in its failure to ensure adequate conditions at the regroupment areas. One of the principal reasons cited by the FMLN for suspending the demobilization of its first contingent in late 1992 was the lack of infrastructure, including water, food, shelter and road networks, health and education at the regroupment areas.[81] To cope with this emergency the UN had been forced to call on a number of organizations, including the WHO and WFP, to help improve conditions for assembling troops. UNICEF had also become involved, focusing its main effort on helping the 186,000 family members (most of whom were women and children) that had clustered around the areas.

The problems inherent in the UN's role as a verifier of disarmament and demobilization lay principally with its own lack of independent verification techniques. Without such capabilities the UN remained reliant on the good faith of the parties and therefore vulnerable to their inevitable deception. For instance, despite ONUSAL's complaints from early 1992 that the FMLN's weapons inventories were incomplete, the group continued to insist that they were accurate. As ONUSAL was incapable of locating and verifying undeclared weapons it could do little more than apply diplomatic pressure until the explosion in Minagua literally unearthed the FMLN's deceit. Although the FMLN apologized and moved quickly to declare its hidden arms, this event seriously undermined the UN's global credibility as an independent verifier of disarmament agreements.[82]

Similarly, both the Government and FAES were unwilling to provide credible information to ONUSAL. This was evident at the very beginning of the operation when the FAES estimated its troop strength at 63,000, whilst ONUSAL and the FMLN agreed on a number nearer 40,000.[83] The Government also failed to provide ONUSAL with important information on the territorial service and FAES controlled public security bodies. And the collection of military style weapons distributed by the FAES during the civil war to members of the general public was made practically impossible by the 'likelihood that the FAES inventory [did] not include all the weapons [it had] distributed'.[84]

Though, as already mentioned, the reduction of the FAES was ultimately more successful than even the Agreements had expected, its reform remained in the words of SRSG Alvaro de Soto, the 'most difficult item on the agenda'.[85] Only the threat of the cessation of US military aid and the promise of thousands of dollars in reintegration assistance helped convince the FAES to accept reform. However, the international community recognized that the FAES could still derail the whole peace process and so refrained from pressuring it to accept the integration of former FMLN members. Nevertheless, without such integration, ensuring the FAES was subjected to civilian authority and purged of its human rights abusers gained added importance. Despite its valiant efforts ONUSAL could ensure neither.

The subjugation of the FAES to civilian control was undermined for a number of reasons. Firstly, the type of reduction that took place reduced the number of troops, but allowed the brunt of the cuts to affect the lower-ranked officers and poor conscripts. This left the higher-ranked officer corps virtually untouched. As the figures for demobilization concurred, whilst the ordinary troop numbers had been reduced by 33,314, representing a cut of 56 per cent, the number of officers was reduced by 1,104, a cut of only 33.2 per cent.[86] Running on essentially the same budget as before, the process had left the FAES with its institutional core intact, its troops better trained and equipped and its officer corps wealthier. It had also retained a force of 31,000 in a country without any known external threats.[87]

The failure of the Agreements to deal with the military's control of key state institutions also undermined the establishment of civilian authority. These institutions included the National Administration of Telecommunications (ANTEL) the National Administration of Water and Sewers (ANDA) and the Postal Service. The military's intention to keep control of these institutions was made apparent when the departing Defense Minister, General Rene Ponce, was subsequently appointed head of ANTEL. His new post gave him potential control of lucrative contracts and intelligence sources.[88] Ponce's appointment was even more shocking given that his name had appeared in both reports of the Ad Hoc Commission and the Commission on the Truth.

The treatment Ponce received was not extraordinary for those named by the commissions. All the military officers named were allowed to retire with full honors and pensions, leading many to question the real extent of civilian control of the military. The extent of the purges did little to reassure these doubters. Although the Agreements stipulated that the Ad Hoc Commission was to purify the armed forces 'based on an evaluation of all [its] members', attention was obviously directed at the officer corps. In fact the Agreements included the criteria through which the 'past performance of each officer' would be evaluated.[89] Nevertheless, with only three months to conduct its investigations even the evaluation of the 2,293 active duty officers was deemed impracticable. Therefore, only the 232 most senior officers were reviewed, a far from comprehensive purge.[90]

Evidence that the reform of the military was less than complete was present in its extreme reluctance to transfer resources to the PNC. By the end of ONUSAL's mandate the Secretary-General could only conclude that resistance from certain sectors of the military had 'adversely affected the training, organization and deployment of the new police force'.[91] As Gino Costa points out, it was therefore paradoxical that the continued role of the FAES in public security was justified on the basis that it had retained the resources and experience necessary to combat crime, which the PNC lacked.[92] The dangers of the continued role of military intelligence in internal security and of joint FAES-PNC patrols was highlighted by the report of the Joint Group, which found evidence of collusion between the military and organized crime. This collusion extended to the conduct of politically motivated murders.[93]

Somewhat surprisingly, the Government was not to be the only supporter of an expansion in the FAES' constitutional role. The US Army, believing that the FAES should help reconstruct the infrastructure of the country, also supported efforts to involve it in reconstruction 'civic actions' programs. However, though wanting to involve the FAES in such work was an understandable sentiment, it nevertheless exhibited a monumental lack of insight into both the nature of Salvadoran society and the character of its military. As in practice the FAES often found itself competing with civil organizations conducting the same programs, it was obvious that 'any US policy which [enhanced] the capacity of the [FAES] to carry out [such work] clearly [contradicted] the spirit and purpose of the agreements which ended the war'.[94]

According to SRSG De Soto, the reintegration of former combatants, refugees, displaced persons, war-disabled and other marginalized groups, was one of the most difficult and challenging tasks of the UN's peace-building role in El Salvador.[95] The need for success in this area had been made ever more palpable by the disastrous consequences of its neglect in neighboring Nicaragua, where efforts at reconciliation had been stunted and former combatants had rearmed. The inclusion of reintegration programs in the Agreements was, therefore, a conscious effort to avert a repeat of the Nicaraguan failure.[96]

Nevertheless, as previously discussed, the UN was to witness less success in this area than it had in either disarmament or demobilization. In the case of former FAES soldiers the UN was forced to deal with the tendency of the Government and FAES to obstruct its efforts to verify and improve the provision of reintegration programs. Most of ONUSAL's criticisms were directed at the military's high command, headed by the ubiquitous General Ponce, which it claimed was particularly disinclined to provide such benefits.[97]

The desperation of former soldiers eventually expressed itself in a number of violent demonstrations, including the forceful takeover of the Legislative Assembly and Lands Bank. Only following these incidents did the Government agree to pay compensation to 6,000 former soldiers, a disturbing development in the mind of the Secretary-General because it risked giving 'the impression that benefits could be obtained by resorting to force'.[98] These demonstrations were not, however, concerned only with the failure of the Government to provide reintegration support to its regular soldiers. They were also designed to protest the abandonment of the former members of the armed forces reserves, all of which had previously received payments from the Government. By failing to ensure the provision of adequate demobilization and reintegration assistance to the estimated 50,000 to 250,000 paramilitaries involved meant the

Agreements had essentially ignored the needs of a sizeable portion of the military establishment.[99]

The fundamental problem facing former Government soldiers was that their bargaining powers were even weaker than their former FMLN counterparts. As Yvon Grenier and Jean Daudelin noticed, these soldiers 'clearly had fewer resources to exchange in the first place: they had no autonomous organizational resources, no sympathy from abroad, no political or social clout, and their guns were formally owned by the army'.[100] The lack of international sympathy for FAES soldiers was reflected in the overwhelming tendency of NGOs to operate in former zones of conflict, where they had managed to build strong relationships and develop a significant organizational base. These areas were thus able to attract external funding and forge ahead with a variety of developmental projects from the beginning of the peace process. Unfortunately, although former FAES soldiers eventually formed an Association of Former Members of the Armed Forces (ADEFAES) to represent their interests, it was not the type of organization required to plan and conduct developmental programs. Neither did it have the support of influential politicians. Years after their demobilization, therefore, former FAES soldiers remained poorly organized and scarcely represented in the corridors of power.[101]

The reintegration programs themselves were intended to help ex-combatants of both parties settle in either rural or urban areas. The cornerstone of the rural reintegration effort was to be the land-transfer program. Through this program ex-combatants were to receive titles to land, together with access to agricultural credit and technical assistance. Alternatively, ex-combatants wishing to reintegrate into urban areas were to be provided with training in the industrial and service sectors of the economy. Access to credit and technical assistance was also to be made available to those wishing to establish small businesses.[102]

Despite its recognized importance, Fen Osler Hampson believes the land-transfer program was perhaps the central weakness of the Agreements.[103] The initial difficulties it encountered stemmed from a lack of preparation and planning. Although the Government had begun to study reconstruction needs from the spring of 1991, the land issue was to gain scant attention before the Agreements were actually signed. Only in the final month of negotiations were broad understandings reached on the issue, leaving the finer details to be worked out during implementation.[104]

The damaging effects of this lack of preparation were immediate. In the initial months of the operation, tensions rose to critical levels as the agreement to respect the land tenure situation in former zones of conflict was ignored and property seizures by various peasant groups, evictions by public security bodies and lawsuits by landowners brought the whole process close to collapse.[105] Only the submission of a proposal by the UN in October 1992 allowed the process to proceed, although as previously noted this did not signify an end to the problems affecting the land-transfer program.

Other reintegration programs suffered from a similar lack of preparation. For example, the emergency programs created by the Government to provide immediate help to ex-combatants were soon affected by a series of technical difficulties that significantly reduced their effectiveness.[106] The Secretary-General also pointed to a lack of preparation when he outlined the three main problems that had beset the short-term reintegration programs. The first of these was the absence of a global strategy in their formulation. The second was the failure to synchronize the programs with the dates of demobilization (this had resulted in some beneficiaries registering on programs for economic need rather than as a preference or vocation to learn). And finally, a lack of overall planning had allowed the same mistakes to be repeated in the different programs.[107]

The second factor to adversely affect both the rural and urban reintegration programs was a general lack of finance. Essentially the problems with finance lay in two areas. The first was the restrictions placed on public spending by IMF and World Bank (WB) structural adjustment programs. In March 1992 the Government had initiated a National Reconstruction Plan (NRP) with the objective of alleviating poverty, improving social services and rebuilding the economic infrastructure of the former zones of conflict. However, the Government was unable to properly fund the NRP due to limitations imposed on its spending by the IMF and World Bank. As the Secretary-General observed in late 1995, 'the discipline required by the adjustment and stabilization process (although creating conditions for a favorable rate of growth) entailed a social cost...seen in the restrictions imposed on the development of anti-poverty programs, particularly in rural areas and in those directly affected by the conflict'. In his opinion this situation underscored the need for changes in the developmental model.[108]

The second area was the extent and direction of international donor funding. Although international donors initially pledged more money than was actually requested by the Government, very little of it was made available for reintegration efforts. This was because the donors preferred to direct their funding towards infrastructure and environmental projects. A general decline in donations after 1994 only served to exacerbate this problem. According to the Secretary-General the decline in resources explained, in part, the difficulties that had arisen in implementing the various reintegration programs and had to some extent influenced the rescheduling of the commitments established in the Agreements.[109]

Nevertheless, a lack of finance and planning could not explain all the delays suffered by the reintegration programs. It was obvious that political factors were also playing a part. Although both parties were guilty of this at some stage in the process, ONUSAL's greatest criticisms were leveled at the Government and mid-level administrators at the Lands Bank, whose actions had 'suggested' that political factors had contributed to the delays.[110]

Thus, a dearth of planning and finance, compounded by a lack of political will, had conspired to leave thousands of ex-combatants without the reintegration support they had expected or required. With many beneficiaries in *pro-indivisio* plots still awaiting legal clarification of their positions and still more waiting to have their land registered, insecurity amongst ex-combatants had become rife. Therefore, whilst those without registered land could not receive agricultural credit, those that already had could not invest it productively. In his final report on ONUSAL, the Secretary-General warned that there was a 'danger that frustrated efforts at rural reintegration [might] be condemned to reproduce the marginality that was one of the origins of the conflict'.[111]

The successes of urban reintegration efforts were also precarious. When the Secretary-General reported in March 1995 that the majority of small business credit had been disbursed, he also noted that it had been estimated that only 26 per cent of FMLN and 51 per cent of former FAES recipients had invested their credit productively. Commensurately, only 16 per cent of FMLN and 30 per cent of former FAES beneficiaries were making timely repayments on the interest due. This was compared to the program for former FMLN commanders, which had provided relatively more training, orientation and technical assistance and had subsequently shown better results.[112]

5.2   Reform of public security

The aspects of the Agreements dealing with public security were perhaps the most ambitious of the whole peace process. Whilst the judiciary was to be reformed, the former police force was to be completely dismantled and replaced. The importance of success in this endeavor was not only based on the need for a more credible justice system, but also on the need to reintegrate thousands of former combatants and police personnel. By allocating each party a 20 per cent quota of recruits, the PNC was to provide both communities with the security they required and at the same time produce a tangible symbol of national reconciliation. However, as the Secretary-General noted in July 1997, the model established by the Agreements was not to be consolidated without distortions.[113]

The greatest impediment to the successful creation of the PNC was without doubt the intransigence of the Government and FAES. Having failed to take any preparatory measures to establish the new force, both parties subsequently obstructed the PNC's construction by denying it resources, delaying appointments and refusing to allocate sites for the PNSA.[114] In order to obstruct ONUSAL's verification of applicants to the PNSA they had also refused to supply it with the lists of demobilized personnel from the FAES and former security bodies. The incorporation of these people into the PNC meant that it continued to operate without the proper internal security mechanisms and the specialized unit to investigate politically motivated murders recommended by the Joint Group.[115]

The insidious effects of the circumvention of the Agreements by the Government and FAES had become increasingly apparent. The Director of the PNC had been forced to suspend 25 officers in late 1995 following the suspicious death of a medical student, whilst another had been charged with the murder of an FMLN leader before the 1994 elections. Its brutal handling of public demonstrations, increasing allegations of human rights abuses and its involvement with death squads and corruption, had all contributed to the mounting pressure for a purge of the PNC by the end of ONUSAL's tenure.[116] There can be little surprise then, that compounded by the Government's less than enthusiastic campaign, the PNC was unable to attract sufficient applications from civilians and former FMLN combatants to fill their assigned quotas.

Matters would have been much worse had ONUSAL not persisted in pressuring the Government to ensure all PNC recruits attended the requisite courses at the PNSA. As noted earlier, most of the UEA and SIU personnel that had been improperly transferred resigned rather than attend the courses. Whilst demonstrating the essential role of ONUSAL, this process also highlighted its weaknesses, given that it took almost two years of constant harassment before the situation came to a head. Matters could have been different. Coordinating financial pressure from the international donors with ONUSAL's objectives had succeeded in eliciting greater information on the public security bodies and had encouraged the Government to request evaluations of the PNC on two occasions. If a comparable level of coordination had existed earlier in the operation then even more success could have been achieved.[117] As it was, by the time ONUSAL received a request for it to restore its technical assistance and conduct its first evaluation, its CIVPOL component had already begun to downsize (it had only ever reached a peak of 314 personnel, due primarily to a limited number of donor countries) and was therefore unable to provide the significant hands-on assistance required by the rapidly growing PNC.[118]

The reform of the justicial system was to be an equally slow and arduous process. This was reflected in the Government's refusal to compel the Supreme Court to resign, despite a specific recommendation of the Commission on the Truth that it do so. It was therefore able to continue operating until its tenure expired in June 1994, which was three months after the elections. Even then it was to take months of political wrangling before the Government finally compromised and allowed the election of a new Supreme Court.[119] In this environment it was hardly surprising to find that the protection of human rights remained weak. However, matters were not to be helped by the tendency of ONUSAL to water down its own reports on human rights abuses in order to present a more favorable impression of the conditions in which the elections were to take place.[120]

The final area of public security that was to receive belated support from the Government was the recovery of military style weapons in the hands of the general public. With an estimated 200,000 to 300,000 such weapons in civilian hands, the collection and seizure of these weapons obviously required a comprehensive effort on the part of the civil authorities. However, it was only in the post-election period, when these weapons served no other purpose than to heighten insecurity and supply illegal elements that the Government began to demonstrate a willingness to act effectively. This included cooperating with ONUSAL and the UN Center for Disarmament (UNCDA) for the introduction of 'buy-back' programs.[121]

5.3   Strategies of conflict resolution

As in its operations in Angola, Cambodia and Mozambique, the UN's main conflict resolution mechanism in El Salvador was to be the introduction of liberal democracy. However, as the previous sections have explained, in this case democratic elections were neither new nor perceived as winner-take-all competitions. Thus, as the parties had already internalized the norms and values of the democratic process by the time the UN's operation began, their fears for post-election survival had already been greatly overcome.

The move towards democracy in El Salvador was itself a reaction to the political revolutions taking place across the globe during the 1980s. Marc Chernik notes the importance of these developments for El Salvador when he argues that the 'importance of the transformation of ideology and politics…[could not] be underestimated: the embrace of democracy contributed greatly to the move toward peace. The idea of democracy finally seemed to resonate in Latin America'.[122] The acceptance of democracy as the key to peace in Central America had manifest itself as early as the 1987 Esquipulas II Accords in which all the signatories had agreed to launch democratic processes.

The collapse of communism and the subsequent transition to democracy in the Soviet Union and Eastern Europe also profoundly affected the political outlook of the Left in Central America. This was particularly apparent in the willingness of the Nicaraguan Sandanista government to peacefully cede power after unexpectedly losing internationally supervised elections in February 1990. By 1989 the FMLN had also dropped its insistence on power sharing and would probably have competed in the elections of that year had it also been willing to call a permanent cease-fire.

The post-election security fears of the Salvadoran parties had also been allayed by the success that both ends of the political spectrum had experienced in the elections of the late 1980s and early 1990s. Gerardo Munck and Chetan Kumar describe the growing confidence with which democratic competition and the peace process were accepted:

> [T]he decisions of the leaders that were part of the FDR-FMLN to move into the electoral arena that continued to operate with restrictions during the civil war had an important effect. Thus, when the Democratic Convergence participated in the electoral process in March 1991, before the signing of the peace accords, and was able to gain significant representation in the unicameral National Legislature, the move toward electoral competition was given great momentum. With their former allies already participating in elections, the FMLN's decision to face the ballot boxes would not be a jump into a vacuum. With polls taken throughout 1992 showing the FMLN emerging as the second most popular political force, the perceived ability of the former guerillas to transform themselves from a military to a political force increased. On the other side, the good electoral performance of the government party, ARENA, in the 1988, 1989 and 1991 elections, gave the Right a greater confidence in their ability to operate successfully in a future democratic system. On both sides, then, the main actor's perceptions of their electoral chances reinforced their determination to see the peace accords successfully implemented.[123]

In El Salvador, therefore, the UN was not faced with military organizations with little or no experience of democracy. Nor was it faced with a situation in which one of the parties felt democracy would be the end of its existence. Rather, over a period of many years the parties had become increasingly committed to liberal democracy and through the implementation of the Agreements had signaled that commitment to each other. With the country's business elite also aware that their future prosperity lay in the maintenance of political stability, the commitment to democracy by all sectors of Salvadoran society was further reinforced.[124]

6   Conclusion

The extent of ONUSAL's success in El Salvador is perhaps captured most eloquently by the Secretary-General himself, when he observed in his final report of July 1997 that:

> Five years after the conclusion of the negotiations in far-ranging and ambitious peace agreements, an extraordinary transformation has taken place in El Salvador. The peace process has generated, in a slow but steady manner, conditions that provide the basis for the gradual consolidation of democracy within the country...El Salvador has largely been demilitarized: the armed structure of FMLN has disappeared and its

combatants reintegrated into civilian life; and the armed forces have been reduced and have respected the profound changes in their nature and role called for by the Peace Agreements...A climate of tolerance prevails today, unlike any the country has known before.[125]

The explanation for this success can be found in both the environment in which the UN deployed and its ability to apply the twin-track approach outlined in Chapter 1.

At the level of the internal parties it is evident from the account of their growing embrace of liberal democracy that a transformation in their shared understanding had already begun before the UN had deployed. International and regional pressures, together with their own realization of the futility of continued conflict, had convinced both parties that their futures lay in democratic competition by the end of the 1980s. However, whilst still fearful of one another, it was impossible for each of them to fully convey to the other their changed identity without the mediation of the UN. Nevertheless, as the parties now existed in a shared understanding of competition, they did not require the third party security guarantees during the implementation phase that the other cases in this text required. Nor did the FMLN require the security of a power-sharing arrangement. Rather, as Mark Peceny and William Stanley argue:

> The intensive UN-mediated peace negotiations helped the combatants to recognize that their adversaries had changed and could be trusted to honor their agreements. Then, during a five-year peace-building mission, the UN pushed for the social reconstruction of El Salvador, strengthening liberal political institutions and promoting dialogue, compromise and nonviolent conflict resolution, successfully diffusing liberal practices to state bureaucracies and a society that had not lived by such norms in the past.[126]

Thus, through a mutually constitutive process of identity formation and shared understanding, aided and abetted by the UN, the parties had come closer than ever to a culture of cooperation. For this reason the FMLN was willing to unilaterally disarm without the protection of a major UN military presence and before the majority of commitments in the Agreements had been implemented. It also lacked any credible institutional guarantees for the future.[127]

Obviously, given the FMLN's lack of both internal and external security guarantees, its initial retention of arms outside of the UN's verification process was understandable. However, once this deception had been uncovered, the FMLN's fears that further revelations would seriously hurt its chances in the 1994 elections led it to even greater openness with the UN and thus to a more thorough disarmament of the group than might otherwise have occurred.[128] This suggests that by 1993 the FMLN's concerns about its electoral success were greater than its fears about security.[129]

Once the FMLN had unilaterally disarmed it was naturally in a weaker position in regard to ensuring the full implementation of the Agreements. In the words of the FMLN itself, it had lost its 'last negotiating card'.[130] Thus, once the FMLN had been disarmed, the only entity capable of pressuring the Government to fulfill its commitments was the UN. Yet as one FMLN letter to the Secretary-General contended, the effectiveness of the UN 'does not depend only on the sincerity, dedication and commitment of the Secretary-General and his colleagues'.[131]

The question therefore remains of whether the FMLN's disarmament and demobilization should have been synchronized with the Government's implementation of its commitments. This theory was actually applied at the beginning of the operation when the FMLN's demobilization was suspended on more than one occasion to encourage the Government to provide adequate reintegration assistance. It was also applied when ONUSAL retained a number of FMLN missiles until the Government had complied with the recommendations of the Ad Hoc Commission (a policy agreed to by the Government itself).

So, it would appear that when the Secretary-General suggested in May 1992 that 'suspicions that FMLN [was] retaining clandestine caches of arms and ammunition [were having] a destabilizing effect on the whole implementation process', it was the clandestine nature of these weapons that was causing the insecurity and not the retention of them *per se*.[132] Thus, by allowing the FMLN to openly retain its weapons ONUSAL would have both reduced the group's security dilemmas and strengthened its own ability to ensure the implementation of the Agreements. As William Stanley and David Holiday observed, UN mediation suddenly became less salient once the Government had achieved its primary aim of disarming the FMLN.[133] Though the discovery of clandestine weapons in May 1993 temporarily enhanced ONUSAL's powers, the knowledge that the FMLN's military structure had already been dismantled meant they could have only a limited effect.

In the case of Track 1 diplomacy at the level of ex-combatants and the general population the UN had, by the end of its tenure, helped to create a police force that was better educated, better trained, more transparent and more respectful of human rights than its predecessor.[134] However, questions still remained over the Government's commitment to maintain the PNC's credibility as an independent force free of human rights abusers. Similarly, despite the improved sense of human rights protection provided by unprecedented reforms to the country's justice system, suspicions persisted that the Government lacked the commitment to consolidate the process.

The UN was also able to ensure a significant degree of Track 2 diplomacy at the level of the ex-combatants. The Agreements had ensured the provision of reintegration assistance to ex-combatants through a number of rural and urban reintegration programs. They were also provided with quotas in the PNC. However, as the previous accounts have illustrated, there are a number of lessons that can be learnt from the UN's experiences in demobilization and reintegration in El Salvador.

Firstly, the question remains of whether a unified army should have been created. The inclusion of even a limited number of former FMLN commanders may have said more about the transformation of the FAES and its new relationship with society than any new constitution or doctrine. The military backed down over the issue of its reduction and reform when the US threatened to cut off all its financial and material aid. It did the same over the Ad Hoc Commission when the US withheld $11 million dollars.[135] Maybe the Achilles heal of the military was not sufficiently tested on the issue of integration.

Nevertheless, it was evident that if integration was not on the agenda then an extra effort had to be made to ensure the proper reform of the military. As this analysis has shown ONUSAL's powers in this regard were far too limited. When it was able to make a difference it did so valiantly, the most prominent example being its determination to see the implementation of the Ad Hoc Commission's recommendations. However, both the purge itself and ONUSAL's access to information were insufficient. Whilst the vast majority of officers were not even evaluated, all ONUSAL could do as its mandate expired was request information on the military's budget and the strength of its officer corps.[136] A similar situation existed over information regarding the reintegration programs for former soldiers.

The reintegration of former FMLN combatants also points to the dangers inherent on relying on one of the parties to fund and administer demobilization programs. Although removing the parties from the process completely is impracticable, many of the delays in El Salvador could have been averted if greater amounts of funding had been funneled through the UN and NGOs. Hampson, for one, criticizes the fact that ONUSAL's budget did not finance activities such as reintegration and the promotion of democratic institutions, beyond electoral monitoring and assistance. If only the short and medium term programs had been funded and administered through the UN, then maybe fewer former combatants would have resorted to criminal activities to survive. More funding and administration could also have been channeled through NGOs, which would have attacked the problem at a grass-roots level through organizations with proven expertise, knowledge of prevailing conditions and long-standing community relationships.[137]

Unfortunately, the degree of Track 2 diplomacy at the level of the general population had not substantially improved. The effect of the NRP on the poorest elements of the population had been stunted by the restrictions imposed by international financial institutions and the country's unemployment rate remained around 50 per cent at the end of the operation. Thus, coupled with the potential danger of thousands of ex-combatants unable to adapt to their new society (due to the failure of reintegration programs), there can be little surprise that the general public retained so many military style weapons. The public's confidence in the Government cannot have been enhanced by the latter's record of implementation and its fateful decision to allow the military to accompany the PNC on its rural patrols. The Government had also done little to encourage general disarmament until after the 1994 elections. So, despite the UN's success in ensuring the disarmament and demobilization of the parties' forces, general disarmament was to remain incomplete.

7
Angola 1993–1999

1   Introduction

As explained in Chapter 2, much of the blame for the collapse of the first Angolan peace process in late 1992 was leveled at the UN. The greatest criticisms were that it tried to implement an inappropriate mandate in too short a time period with too few personnel and insufficient finances. Finally, it was also criticized for agreeing to winner-takes-all democratic elections in a culture ill suited to its inevitable consequences.

It came as little surprise, therefore, that when the UN established its third Angolan Verification Mission (UNAVEM III) in early 1995 it exhibited a determination to avoid a repeat of its past mistakes. This time it would thwart accusations of frugality by deploying 7,000 military troops, 350 military observers and 260 police observers. The Angolan parties were also persuaded to form a power-sharing government, thus ensuring a stake for each of them in the post-conflict era. The UN even stipulated that elections would not be held until all the requisite conditions had been established. This commitment resulted in the need to create a follow-on mission, the UN Observer Mission in Angola (MONUA) in June 1997. And by the time the mandates of both UN missions had expired in February 1999 their combined operational budgets had exceeded $1.5 billion.

Unfortunately, despite these dramatic changes UNAVEM III and MONUA were to be no more successful than their predecessor in resolving the Angolan civil war. Nor were they to be any more successful in ensuring the disarmament of the former warring parties. To understand why, this chapter will undertake an analysis of UNAVEM III's disarmament process. As in preceding chapters this analysis will begin with an account of the events leading up to the signing of the latest peace agreements. Overviews of both the UN's mandate and its implementation will then be followed by an analysis of the disarmament process. Finally, the conclusion will assess the utility of the twin-track framework to explain the UN's continued inability to ensure disarmament in Angola.

2   Background to the operation

Reporting to the Security Council in January 1993 Secretary-General Boutros Boutros-Ghali acknowledged that 'to all intents and purposes Angola [had] returned to civil war and [was] probably in an even worse situation than before the peace agreements were signed in May 1991'.[1] With the outbreak of hostilities and the subsequent breakdown of the joint monitoring mechanisms the original mandate of the UN operation, he believed, had become 'less and less relevant'. Consequently, he recommended that UNAVEM II confine itself to the country's capital, Luanda, yet retain one or two outposts and the capability to deploy to six provincial sites if required. In this way the UN could continue to support the Special Representative of the Secretary-General (SRSG), Margaret Anstee, in her peacemaking efforts. Acquiescing to Boutros-Ghali's request, the Security Council voted to extend the mandate of UNAVEM II by two months on 29 January.[2]

Attempts to end the war had seemingly reached a diplomatic stalemate. Although UNITA's leader, Jonas Savimbi, had officially accepted the election results in a letter he had sent to Anstee in November, he had still refused to become involved in the transitional government established by the Angolan President, Jose Eduardo dos Santos, in early December.[3] Instead, Savimbi had begun to call for a cease-fire and the deployment of a substantial number of UN troops. However, suspicious that Savimbi's requests were nothing but a ruse through which he could consolidate his military gains, the Government refused to accept a cease-fire until UNITA had withdrawn from the cities it had captured after the elections.

It was in this context that the UN managed to persuade both parties to meet in Addis Ababa, Ethiopia, in late January. With Anstee presiding, the parties agreed to a four item agenda for talks, including the reestablishment of the cease-fire, the implementation of the remaining aspects of the Accords, the release of prisoners and the role of the UN as a monitor, guarantor and electoral organizer. Despite reaching agreement on a number of issues at the meeting, a cease-fire remained elusive. Even so, the parties agreed to meet again on 10 February to discuss any outstanding matters. Before this meeting could be held, however, UNITA requested a postponement, citing logistical difficulties and security problems for its inability to attend. Unable to elicit an alternative date from UNITA, despite offering UN aircraft and security guarantees, Anstee decided UNITA's decision was inappropriate and cancelled the meeting completely. Savimbi responded by demanding that she be replaced with an African mediator and UNITA's radio station even went as far as to imply a threat to her life.[4]

Only following bilateral talks with the US did UNITA finally agree to meet the Government on 12 April in Abidjan, Cote D'Ivoire. At this stage the parties could hardly have been further apart. UNITA was now in control of up to two-thirds of Angolan territory, including many of its major cities. In fact many observers expressed resignation that Savimbi had achieved more in the previous two months than in the previous two decades.[5] On the other hand, the Government had begun a major offensive to recapture its lost territory and was beginning to make inroads into stretched UNITA defenses. Thus, whilst UNITA called for a new settlement that would take account of the 'new [military] reality in Angola', including a transitional power-sharing government and decentralization, the Government continued to demand that UNITA accept the election results and disarm.[6]

With the talks now floundering, the observer countries (Portugal, Russia and the US) introduced their own 'Memorandum of Understanding of the Abidjan Protocol' in order to revive them. Despite this intervention the talks were suspended on 21 May with the parties having reached agreement on only two of UNITA's three principle demands. These were that a UN force of up to 12,000 troops be deployed before UNITA would be required to withdraw from its areas of control and that the extension of the State administration would be directly linked to the introduction of UNITA members into all levels of government. UNITA's third demand, calling for the simultaneous movement and quartering of Government and UNITA troops rather than just UNITA troops as required by the Memorandum, was denied.[7]

Whilst the parties remained at loggerheads the humanitarian situation was deteriorating rapidly. Estimates suggested that the war was generating up to 1,000 casualties per day and that another two million Angolans were facing hunger, drought and disease. UNAVEM II had also been forced to evacuate all but four of its remaining locations and was therefore unable to gain access to the majority of the affected population. In this context the Secretary-General accepted SRSG Anstee's request to be replaced, but stressed that 'it would be unthinkable for the UN to abandon Angola [at such a] critical juncture.'[8]

Anstee's replacement, Alioune Blondin Beye, was to take over during a period of increasingly vocal UN criticism of UNITA. On 1 June the Security Council passed Resolution 834, which not only issued the UN's sternest rebuke of UNITA's actions to date, but also threatened the imposition of sanctions if significant progress had not been achieved by 15 September. With little progress evident by this date, the Security Council imposed an arms and petroleum embargo on UNITA from the 26 September. Although this meant that Savimbi had failed in his attempts to avert the imposition of sanctions, he had still been free to replenish his forces relatively unhindered for 12 months after returning to war.

In a further attempt to increase its pressure on UNITA the Security Council threatened the imposition of additional sanctions if it had not committed itself to a cease-fire and the implementation of the Bicesse Accords by the beginning of November. In response, UNITA informed Beye that it was not only willing to accept the 'validity' of the Accords, but also the election results, the Abidjan Protocol and even the principle of withdrawal from urban areas captured since September 1992.[9] However, by the time exploratory talks began in late October, UNITA had not even ceased its military offensives. Although the Secretary-General therefore recommended the imposition of additional sanctions, as the parties were still negotiating he also requested that they be postponed until 1 December.[10]

With the threat of greater sanctions ever present, the negotiations initially gained momentum. By early December the parties had managed to reach agreement on all the military issues on the agenda, including the reestablishment of a cease-fire; the withdrawal, quartering and demobilization of UNITA forces; the disarming of the civilian population; and the completion of the formation of the Angolan Armed Forces (FAA). Both parties insisted that the UN be given an increased mandate in all these areas.[11] Although this was enough to once again postpone the Security Council's threat, UNITA walked out of the talks on 11 December after accusing the Government of trying to assassinate its leader.

Only on 5 January did UNITA return to the talks, thus enabling an agreement on the restructuring of the police to be struck by the end of the month. Another agreement, this time on the general principles relating to national reconciliation, followed on 17 February. At this stage, therefore, the only significant outstanding issue concerned the posts UNITA would assume in the power-sharing government. Though UNITA had been offered a number of ministerial posts, these had not included its most prized departments of Defense, Finance and Foreign Affairs. And despite having managed to persuade the Government to accept most of its demands for provincial governorships, it had not been successful in the cases of Benguela and Huambo.[12]

Though Benguela's importance lay in the railroad and diamond track that ran through it, the significance of Huambo was much more symbolic.[13] As the country's second largest city, it was also the main urban center of the Ovimbundu ethnic group from which most of UNITA's leaders and supporters were drawn. It had been captured by UNITA in March 1993, following a 55-day siege that had left 12,000 dead, 15,000 wounded and 100,000 refugees. Once in control of the city UNITA had immediately begun to treat it as its own capital, establishing the semblance of a government, placing police on its streets and even issuing visas to visitors arriving at its airport.[14] The Government therefore deemed Huambo's recapture as imperative.

Although the parties managed to reach agreement on the presidential run-off elections in May, differences over power-sharing still threatened to stall the negotiations indefinitely. This led Beye and the observer states to submit their own proposals, which apart from UNITA's refusal to secede control of Huambo were accepted by both parties in June. With UNITA's subsequent willingness to consider a deputy-governorship of Huambo, Beye felt confident enough to announce that 95 per cent of the agenda had been completed.[15] However, this did not include the question of Savimbi, who was now declaring his wish to remain as UNITA's leader, rather than accept a position in the new government. Unsurprisingly, suspicions persisted that this was designed to leave him free to return to war if the elections once again did not go his way.[16]

UNITA's more amiable disposition at this time may have been due greatly to the severe blow to its support base inflicted by the election of Nelson Mandela as President of South Africa in April 1994. Although Mandela wished to end his country's support for UNITA, he was also aware that any future peace agreement would have to include Savimbi. He therefore met with Dos Santos and other regional leaders on 7 July and invited Savimbi to meet with him in South Africa. It was only the prospect of this latter meeting that persuaded the UN to postpone further sanctions.[17] However, although he initially accepted Mandela's invitation, Savimbi never actually made the trip. Nevertheless, Mandela continued to try and persuade him to accept the power-sharing proposals then being offered.

In a significant show of displeasure at UNITA's prevarications, the Security Council released a statement on 12 August threatening to review the UN's whole involvement in Angola if the parties had not concluded their negotiations on national reconciliation by the end of September. Three days later the negotiations turned to a compromise document submitted by Beye and the observer states concerning the mechanisms for the implementation of the peace process. These mechanisms included the complete UN mandate relating to military issues, the police, national reconciliation and the electoral process. Though the parties were able to reach agreement on the majority of the document within two weeks, UNITA requested another suspension of the talks on 31 August due to a Government offensive on Huambo.[18]

When the talks resumed on 5 September the Secretary-General received a letter from UNITA conveying its formal acceptance of the complete set of proposals on national reconciliation. Although this change of heart was not sufficient to convince the Government to end its attacks on Huambo, it did alleviate the threat of further Security Council sanctions.[19] With the national reconciliation package now accepted, the talks moved back to the mechanisms for implementation, with all the articles relating to the UN's mandate and the role of the observer states agreed by 16 and 17 September respectively.

Discussions on the new body to replace the old Joint Political and Military Commission (CCPM), which had overseen the implementation of the Bicesse Accords, began on 19 September. Although the composition and functions of the new body were agreed within two days, it was only given the title of 'The Joint Commission' in mid-October. The negotiations on national reconciliation were finally concluded on 14 October, when agreement was reached on the remaining localities to be administered by UNITA.[20] After a further two weeks of intensive negotiations the parties initialed a comprehensive peace agreement on 31 October.

With meetings between high-ranking military representatives due to take place beforehand, a formal signing ceremony was initially scheduled for 15 November.[21] However, bolstered by its recent victories, the Government was determined to recapture as much territory as possible before the new UN operation could begin and so continued its military offensives. In particular, the Government wanted to recapture Huambo, which eventually fell to its forces on 10 November. Having now lost his headquarters Savimbi refused to sign the peace agreement until the Government's forces had withdrawn. The formal signing ceremony was therefore suspended whilst the UN tried to persuade the Government to end its attacks and accept a cease-fire.[22]

Under increasing international pressure, both parties eventually agreed to a truce beginning on the evening of 16 November. This achievement compelled Beye to declare, rather optimistically, that 'there [was] going to be no more killing in Angola'.[23] Less than 24 hours later Government forces attacked Uige, the last provincial capital under UNITA control. Although the Government denied the attack, UNITA pulled out of negotiations in protest. Nevertheless, whilst continuing to accuse each other of truce violations until the day before, both parties signed the Lusaka Protocol on 20 November. However, Savimbi did not appear to sign the Protocol himself, ostensibly due to Government attacks on his new headquarters. Instead he sent UNITA's Secretary-General, Eugenio Manuvakola, to sign it. In response, the Government's Foreign Minister, Venancio de Moura, was delegated to sign for President Dos Santos, who refused to put his signature alongside that of a UNITA deputy.[24]

3   The UN's disarmament mandate and the nature of the peace agreements

At the request of both Angolan parties the UN was to play 'an enlarged and reinforced role in the implementation of the Bicesse Accords and the Lusaka Protocol'. Consisting of eight annexes, the Protocol covered all the legal, military and political agreements reached by the parties since their return to war in late 1992. The main military issues included the re-establishment of the cease-fire, the withdrawal, quartering and demilitarization of UNITA forces, the disarming of the civilian population and the completion of the formation of the FAA. The main political issues concerned the UN's mandate, the creation of a new police force, the role of the observer states, the completion of the electoral process and the question of national reconciliation.[25]

The body created to replace the old CCPM was the Joint Commission (JC). Its mandate was to 'watch over the implementation of all the political, administrative and military provisions not yet implemented in the [Bicesse Accords] and all the provisions of the Lusaka Protocol'.[26] It was therefore endowed with the authority to make all final decisions on matters relating to violations of the agreements. Whilst the Angolan parties were to attend the JC as full members, the states of Portugal, Russia and the US were to do so as observers, just as they had in the CCPM. However, this time the UN was to assume the role of Chair, a significant development from the days of the CCPM when it could only attend meetings at the invitation of the Angolan parties.

The military aspects of the Protocol were to take place in three phases. The first phase was to begin 17 days after D-Day, the euphemism used in the Protocol to designate the day on which the parties initialed their agreements. Over the next 28 days the UN was to supervise the end of offensive movements and the withdrawal of the parties' forces to specified locations. The parties promised to provide the UN with full details on the forces and locations involved.[27]

The second phase was to begin with the identification of UNITA's quartering areas. As well as monitoring the movement of UNITA's troops to these areas, the UN also agreed to monitor the territory they would be vacating in order to prevent it from being captured by the Government before the FAA was formed. Once they had reached their quartering areas the UN was to collect their weapons and store them in separate locations. This phase was to be completed within six months of D-Day.

Once the quartering process was concluded, phase three was to begin with the selection and incorporation of UNITA personnel into the FAA. This included the UNITA generals that had fled after the 1992 elections. All of the ex-combatants not chosen for the FAA were to be demobilized, as too were all Government troops not retained for the same purpose. Preparation for the formation of the FAA was to be conducted by a 'working group' composed of representatives of the Angolan parties and the UN, which was to be established as soon as possible after D-Day. This group was to decide on issues ranging from the size of the new force and the selection criteria for new recruits, to the logistical and administrative resources that would be required to complete the process. The UN was to verify the completion of the FAA and the demobilization of any excess personnel from D-Day+455. Along with helping establish an indigenous capacity for demining operations, the UN also promised to provide support to the Government's national program of social reintegration for ex-soldiers.

Although the FAA and Angolan National Police Force (ANP) were to be 'organically and functionally independent', they were both expected to act as instruments to reinforce national reconciliation through the inclusion of former UNITA personnel.[28] UNITA was therefore to supply 5,500 personnel to the ANP, with 1,200 of these designated for the specialized Rapid Reaction Police (RRP). The selection and incorporation of police personnel was to begin after the quartering of UNITA's troops and was to conclude before D-Day+455.

To guarantee the neutrality of the ANP and RRP the UN was to monitor their activities and verify the RRP's quartering and adaptation into a force more suitable to the nature of its future mission. It was also to monitor the regular security operations of the ANP and its protection of UNITA leaders, Polling Station Officers and candidate agents during the elections. Finally, once UNITA's forces had been quartered, the UN was to monitor and verify the ANP's collection and storage of civilian-owned weapons.

The implementation of the national reconciliation agreements was scheduled to begin six months after D-Day. These commitments included the installation into the National Assembly of the first 70 deputies elected on the lists of UNITA candidates in the 1992 elections and the incorporation of UNITA personnel into the Government of National Unity (GURN), State administration and diplomatic missions abroad.[29] The normalization of the State administration was also to begin during this period and UNITA was to be given adequate facilities to act as a political party.

Once these commitments had been fulfilled the UN and JC were then to verify that the requisite conditions had been created for holding the second round of Presidential elections. However, the Protocol insisted that the elections not take place before D-Day+455. Although the Angolan Electoral Council (AEC) was to organize the elections, the UN was expected to play an extensive role in verifying, monitoring and supporting its actions.[30]

4 Implementation

4.1 UNAVEM III

The implementation of the Protocol was not to have an auspicious beginning. Though both parties announced the start of the official cease-fire in their radio bulletins of 22 November, neither of them appealed to their troops to hold fire. In fact, having made its announcement, UNITA's radio station then accused the Government of continuing to attack Uige, when the Government itself was claiming to have already captured it the week before.[31] SRSG Beye and the observer states were also to be frustrated in their attempts to get Dos Santos and Savimbi to meet. Beye had not seen Savimibi since the previous October and his lack of public appearances was fuelling speculation that he had been seriously injured during a Government offensive.[32]

By mid-1995 conflicting interpretations of the state of the peace process were evident. The Security Council had voted on 8 February to deploy 7,000 troops, 350 military observers and 260 police observers in the third United Nations Angolan Verification Mission (UNAVEM III), but the parties were also reported to be massively replenishing their armies. Nevertheless, citing reports that the number of cease-fire violations had decreased, Beye insisted that implementation was going well and that the peace process was now irreversible. However, UNAVEM III's Force Commander, Major-General Christopher Garuba, did not share Beye's equanimity.[33]

Following intense international pressure both Angolan leaders finally met on 6 May and agreed to consolidate the cease-fire, speed up implementation of the agreements and form the GURN. Imitating the political model established in South Africa the Government eventually offered Savimbi one of two vice-presidential positions in June. This offer was conditioned on the demobilization of UNITA's forces and on the parties reaching a political consensus.

With most of the locations for the assembly of their respective troops already determined, both leaders met again in Franceville on 10 August. Here they confirmed an agreement, initially reached in April, to bring all their troops together in a single unified force before a gradual process of demobilization left a 90,000 strong FAA.[34] Savimbi also accepted the offer of a vice-presidential position for his party, but insisted that UNITA itself should retain the right to decide who should serve in the post. Both leaders also agreed that the legislative elections should be held before the proposed four-year period.[35]

Despite their apparent reconciliation, the commitment of the parties to the peace process remained suspect. Although both parties' forces had remained *in situ,* as demanded by the Protocol, they had continued to enlarge and consolidate the areas they controlled. They had also failed to provide the UN with the information they had promised on their respective troop strengths. Nor had they supplied it with detailed information on the arrangements for the quartering of UNITA's forces, the FAA's return to barracks, or the proposed incorporation and demobilization processes. And whilst the Government declined to provide the UN with information on the strength and assembly locations for the RRP, the ANP continued to deny the UN access to RRP units.[36]

Events were to take a decided turn for the worse before the year's end. Though UNITA's troops had begun to arrive at the first of its 15 official quartering areas, it had suspended the process only a few weeks later due to the Government's capture of several locations in the oil-producing region of Zaire. As well as imposing restrictions on UNAVEM III's movements, UNITA had also withdrawn its liaison officers from UN team sites and threatened to shoot down UN aircraft flying without its prior clearance. Though the parties subsequently managed to negotiate a resumption of the peace process, UNITA had done little to fulfil its promises by the beginning of 1996, blaming military threats towards its forces in several parts of the country.[37]

Following a two-month absence, UNITA's delegation eventually returned to Luanda on 11 January where it negotiated a new implementation timetable with the Government. It also agreed to supply the FAA with 26,000 troops in addition to the 2,500 that had already been incorporated during the Bicesse process.[38] However, despite also promising to quarter at least 16,500 of the 62,500 troops it had officially declared by 8 February, fewer than a thousand had done so by this time and even these were mostly underage soldiers who had arrived with old, substandard weapons and without uniforms.[39]

In an attempt to inject greater momentum into the process, Beye presented another revised timetable to the parties, which was adopted by the JC at the end of February. On 1 March Dos Santos and Savimbi met again and committed themselves to complete the quartering process and the formation of the FAA by June. Savimbi also provided a list of UNITA officials for the GURN, which both leaders promised to form by July. Eight days later the parties reached agreement on the posts to be filled by UNITA within the FAA. These included 18 Generals, the Vice-Minister of Defense, the Deputy-Chief of the General Staff and Commander of one of the military regions. Also included was the position of Commander of the proposed Fourth Branch of the FAA, which was expected to perform tasks associated with national reconciliation.[40]

Hopes that a UNITA Congress held in late August might expedite the peace process were to be short-lived. Although it managed to adopt resolutions reaffirming its transformation into a political party, it declined to tackle the main outstanding issues, such as the completion of the FAA or the extension of the State administration. It even rejected the Government's offer of a vice-presidential position for Savimbi, claiming his guidance during the transitional period was indispensable.[41]

By the time UNITA's quartering areas were officially closed to new intakes on 9 September, the number of registered troops had reached 63,000. This was in fact 500 more than it had originally declared. However, 25,000 of them had arrived without weapons and 11,000 had deserted the areas before being demobilized. Aid workers and UN officials also believed that at least half of those remaining were not even real soldiers.[42] Particularly worrying was the congregation around the camps of 120,000 family dependents, whose needs were draining essential resources required for the social reintegration of the troops themselves. And despite Beye's presentation of a 'Mediation Document' that envisaged the completion of the majority of the remaining military and political tasks by 20 September, the Secretary-General could only report at the beginning of October that 'marginal progress [had] been achieved'. This included the selection of 10,000 UNITA soldiers for the FAA and the incorporation of five of its ten generals.[43] With the rainy season imminent, the Secretary-General also warned that any further delays in demobilization could threaten the whole peace process.[44]

Reflecting the Secretary-General's concern, the Security Council passed Resolution 1075 on 11 October in which it threatened UNITA with additional sanctions if it continued to delay the demobilization of its troops. It also accepted the Secretary-General's recommendation to extend UNAVEM III's mandate by only two months.[45] Under this not inconsiderable pressure, the parties agreed yet another implementation timetable, this time adopted by the JC on 31 October. UNITA also managed to provide a list of its nominated officials for the GURN and an updated list of deputies for the National Assembly.

Initially, events were not to bode well for the new agreement. UNAVEM III continued to receive reports that UNITA was distributing weapons to so-called local 'self-defense' groups. It was also discovering UNITA 'police' in areas from which the group's military forces had already withdrawn. Numbering around 5,500, these police personnel had never been declared by UNITA and were not, therefore, included in the Protocol. And despite UNAVEM III's discovery on 26 October of a company's worth of weapons in a warehouse in Negage, UNITA still refused to surrender them until 18 November.[46]

Despite UNITA's prevarications Beye was still able to announce on 22 November that over 75 per cent of the outstanding tasks in the 31 October timetable had now been fulfilled. This included UNITA's complete withdrawal from Cabinda province, the quartering of 75 per cent of UNITA's 'police' and the removal of 80 per cent of its illegal checkpoints.[47] Feeling that conditions now permitted a reduction of UNAVEM III forces, the Secretary-General also announced his intention to withdraw around 700 infantry personnel by the end of the year.[48]

Nevertheless, more than two years after the signing of the Protocol the demobilization of UNITA's troops had yet to begin. Though the quartering process had been declared complete on 14 December, with nearly 70,000 having registered, only underage soldiers had actually been demobilized by this time. UNAVEM III was also receiving reports that even these had been forced by UNITA commanders to re-deploy in military camps outside urban areas. Similarly, the formation of the FAA and the normalization of the State administration had yet to begin in earnest. The JC's final act before the end of the year was thus to adopt yet another implementation timetable on 19 December. This time the incorporation of UNITA personnel into the FAA was scheduled to begin on 20 December and any deputies that had not yet taken their seats in the National Assembly were to do so by 17 January. This would allow the GURN to be inaugurated by 25 January.[49]

UNITA's New Year resolutions were not to include greater compliance with agreed timetables. The first issue to obstruct progress was Savimbi's special status. Having already rejected the Government's offer of a vice-presidential position, UNITA now refused to implement the remaining political aspects of the Protocol until an agreement on his status had been reached. Savimbi himself was now proposing that he be granted the status of principal advisor to the President, a post he expected would include supervisory powers over several government ministries and a substantive coordinating role in the spheres of rural development and national reconciliation. Compounded by the failure of its officials to assume their duties in the capital, the delay caused by UNITA's obstructionism forced the JC in late January to postpone the formation of the GURN until after 12 February. By this time UNITA promised to have all its GURN officials present in Luanda.[50]

With such uncertainty still affecting the peace process the Secretary-General was forced to reassess his plans for the withdrawal of UNAVEM III. Although he had originally foreseen a quicker process, he now intended to reduce it by one battalion per month between March and August. Recognizing that a UN presence would still be required until the end of the year, he also recommended a follow-on mission whose emphasis would be 'on peace consolidation, confidence-building and national reconciliation, with a view to creating an environment conducive to long-term stability'.[51] In order to maintain sufficient pressure on UNITA he also advised the Security Council to extend UNAVEM III's mandate by only one month if its officials had not arrived in Luanda by 12 February. On 27 February, exasperated at the failure of UNITA to meet another agreed timetable, the Security Council complied.[52]

Whilst the UN continued to pressure UNITA to comply with its commitments, its forces were deserting their quartering areas in droves. Of the 70,904 troops that were now registered in the areas, 27,000 had already deserted. Only 2,028 (underage) soldiers had actually been demobilized. The selection process for the FAA had also been terminated on 12 March with only 17,209 soldiers chosen. And with just 450 UNITA personnel meeting the criteria for incorporation into the ANP, the JC was forced to adopt yet another revised timetable.

Desiring a first-hand assessment, the UN's new Secretary-General, Kofi Annan, visited Angola personally in late March. Following what he described as a 'frank tête à tête' with Savimbi, the latter promised to have all UNITA's officials present in Luanda within 24 hours.[53] Consequently, the day after Savimbi's special status was enacted into law on 8 April, 67 of UNITA's 70 deputies were sworn into the National Assembly. A second Vice-President and a second Secretary of the Assembly were then elected from amongst the new UNITA members. Two days later, on 11 April, the GURN was inaugurated at a ceremony attended by the dignitaries of several countries and the OAU. For the Secretary-General the formation of the GURN represented a 'milestone in the Angolan peace process'.[54]

With the GURN's first meeting on the 18 April and another timetable adopted by the JC five days later, the peace process initially gained momentum. Assisted by the adoption in April of a rapid demobilization plan, 23,000 UNITA ex-combatants had been demobilized (now called Selection and Demobilization Centers (SDC)) and transported to places of their choice by the beginning of June. However, UNITA's half-hearted approach to the peace process remained evident. Although it had declared its command posts closed and had provided UNAVEM III with lists of its communications equipment, it had refused to hand any of it over as the Protocol demanded. And with the number of UNITA deserters and absentees from SDC's now exceeding 35 per cent of those registered, the Government continued to accuse it of hiding forces in different parts of the country.[55]

Thus, despite having adjusted the withdrawal of UNAVEM III several times already, the Secretary-General was compelled to do so again. With demobilization expected to continue until August he decided to retain two infantry battalions until September, so as to provide security for the final SDCs. At the same time he also acknowledged that the proposed follow-on mission would have to assume greater responsibilities than had originally been envisaged. These included monitoring the normalization of the State administration, verifying the neutrality of the new police force and monitoring the collection of civilian weapons. Both Angolan parties also continued to call for an enhanced UN human rights component.

4.2   MONUA

Pursuant to Resolution 1118 the Security Council created the UN Observer Mission in Angola (MONUA) on 30 June 1997. On the same day the parties closed yet another disheartening chapter of the peace process by terminating UNITA's incorporation into the ANP with only 524 of its personnel selected.[56] In fact, the overall state of the peace process was to deteriorate over the next few months with the first issue of contention being MONUA's attempts to demobilize the troops UNITA had retained to protect Savimbi (the Presidential Guard) and its mining interests (mining police). Despite numerous attempts to persuade it to provide accurate assessments of these forces, by mid-August UNITA had owned up to only 6,000, a number Beye believed to be incomplete.[57]

The second issue affecting the peace process was the Government's desire to ensure the normalization of the State administration. Having spurned a UNITA offer to normalize 41 new locations (arguing that the designated areas were totally isolated from each other behind UNITA lines) the Government had begun to threaten a unilateral normalization of outstanding areas from the end of July. Although MONUA acknowledged that UNITA's offer was unsatisfactory, it nonetheless tried to persuade the Government to resist from following through with its threat.[58]

The persistence of UNITA's subterfuge was most evident in its military preparations. MONUA had recorded 120 flights into UNITA controlled areas during July alone and had continued to monitor last minute changes to the destinations of its demobilized troops. MONUA's movements were also being restricted and several of UNITA's local commanders at SDCs were exhibiting an increasing hostility to the whole demobilization process.[59] To try and reverse these deteriorating conditions the Security Council voted on 28 August to place UNITA in diplomatic isolation. However, this action was suspended until 30 September, by which time the Secretary-General was to have reported on whether it had made 'concrete and irreversible steps' to comply with the Protocol.[60]

Although the Security Council voted once more to suspend UNITA's diplomatic isolation, the pressure of further sanctions was insufficient to elicit the required response and so they came into effect on 30 October. UNITA reacted angrily by severing all contact with the Government and MONUA, except at the level of the JC, for three weeks. This stalled the demobilization of UNITA's 'residual' forces and the extension of the State administration until both processes were able to resume in late November.

Discussions between Beye, Dos Santos and Savimbi continued, however, eventually leading the Government to propose a new timetable on 17 December that envisaged the completion of all pending tasks by mid-January. Following counter-proposals by UNITA, a final agreement was reached on 9 January 1998, in which the remaining elements of the Protocol were to be implemented by the end of February. Significantly, before the end of 1997, all of UNITA's 15 SDCs were officially closed with nearly 42,000 ex-combatants demobilized and 10,880 incorporated into the FAA. Approximately 25,000 soldiers had deserted the SDCs before being demobilized and discussions were continuing to enable them to complete the process before June 1998.[61]

Once again an agreed timetable was to fall by the wayside as tensions increased during late January and February. With Beye absent from the country for medical treatment, the parties became increasingly intransigent. Whilst the Government argued that UNITA was reneging on its commitments, UNITA cited recorded abuses by the ANP against its supporters in areas recently incorporated into the State administration. This, UNITA argued, was evidence that the Government's real intention was to dismantle its political base throughout the country. Still, when UNITA declared its demilitarization complete on 6 March (following the demobilization of nearly 8,000 of its 'residual forces' in February) the JC responded by approving a 12-point revised timetable that postponed the implementation of the remaining elements of the Protocol until the end of March. The Government responded by appointing the three governors and seven vice-governors nominated by UNITA to the GURN.[62]

By the time the latest timetable had expired, little had been achieved beyond the promulgation on 31 March of a law providing a special status for Savimbi as leader of the largest opposition party. In fact, the security situation had deteriorated, as MONUA continued to report heavy fighting and renewed mine laying by both sides. The number of refugees had also risen to approximately 1.3 million, more than ten per cent of the country's population. In an attempt to put the peace process back on track Beye presented the parties with a 'crisis resolution plan' on 15 May that provided for the full normalization of the State administration by the end of the month. It also sought to end the Government's increasingly hostile rhetoric and the ANP's harassment of UNITA members. Though neither side complied with the timetable, UNITA did request more time so that it could organize the handover of its four remaining strongholds of Andulo, Bailundo, Mungo and N'Harea in June.[63] It was while this extension was pending that Beye lost his life in an air-crash in Cote D'Ivoire on 27 June. The objective of his trip had been to try and persuade governments in the region to terminate their support for UNITA.

Having passed further sanctions on 12 June and having failed to witness any change in UNITA's behavior, the Security Council allowed them to come into effect on 1 July. These sanctions froze UNITA's foreign financial assets and prohibited contact with areas of Angola not yet incorporated into the State administration.[64] In anticipation of their adoption UNITA's senior members in Luanda pulled out of the JC, though they returned on 6 August. In the meantime UNITA accused the Government of systematically eliminating its party structures in localities where the State administration had already been extended. Similarly, the Government accused UNITA of attempting to make the country ungovernable by reoccupying 70 localities and by killing hundreds of government functionaries and civilians.[65]

On their return to the JC in early August the UNITA delegation presented a proposal to extend the State administration to its remaining four strongholds by 15 October. Although MONUA proposed a compromise date of 15 September, the Government remained adamant that the extension had to be complete by 31 August. When its own deadline passed, the Government suspended UNITA's representatives in the GURN and National Assembly. Two days later one of the suspended officials, Jorge Valentim, announced that a number of UNITA's senior members had decided to form a group with the objective of 'democratizing' UNITA and implementing the remaining elements of the Protocol. The Government immediately recognized this breakaway group, which called itself the Renovation Committee of UNITA, as the sole representative of UNITA on the JC. The Government also called on MONUA to severe its contacts with Savimbi.[66]

Having now taken control of UNITA's headquarters in Luanda and further emboldened by the support of the South African Defense Community (which had branded Savimbi a 'war criminal' and called on the UN to recognize the Renovation Committee at a summit in mid-September) the Government threatened to cease all contacts with Beye's successor as SGSR, Issa Diallo, if he attempted even to meet with Savimbi. Though the Government eventually lifted the suspension of UNITA's representatives in

Luanda on 23 September, it dismissed one UNITA minister and one vice-minister the same day. Two days later the Permanent Commission of the National Assembly requested the Renovation Committee to replace 15 of UNITA's 70 deputies by 15 October and openly questioned the continuation of Savimbi's special status. Despite the Renovation Committee's reversal of the decision to suspend the 15 deputies at a party conference in mid-October, the National Assembly still abrogated Savimbi's special status on 27 October. The Secretary-General warned that this latter act 'might prevent all possibility of political accommodation'.[67]

The Secretary-General's warning was to fall on deaf ears. With the JC paralyzed and the peace process effectively stalled, both sides had begun to prepare for war. Recent fighting had been particularly heavy in the north and northeast of the country, but it was to become more widespread when the Government launched an offensive in the central highlands in early December. In his opening address to an MPLA Conference only a few days after this attack, Dos Santos expressed his belief that the only path to lasting peace was the total isolation of Savimbi and his group. He also called for the termination of MONUA's mandate. In these deteriorating conditions MONUA was forced to withdraw from UNITA controlled areas on 6 December. Horrifically, when two UN aircraft were shot down near Huambo on 26 December and 2 January, with the loss of 15 people, neither party showed any willingness to cease military operations and cooperate in finding the wreckages.[68]

In his January 1999 report Secretary-General Annan acknowledged that the events of the previous months had clearly demonstrated that for 'all intents and purposes the Angolan peace process [had] collapsed and the country [was] now in a state of war'. On 27 January the National Assembly adopted several resolutions that branded Savimbi a 'war criminal' and called for the 'total annihilation of the subversion' he commanded. The Assembly also accused the international community of complacency and bias for allowing UNITA to rearm and called for the end to MONUA's mandate. Two days later Dos Santos appointed a new cabinet and temporarily assumed the functions of both Prime Minister and Commander in Chief of the FAA. On 18 February the Secretary-General received a letter from Savimbi that characteristically cited the Government as the sole and exclusive party responsible for the renewed war. Although Savimbi wanted MONUA to continue as a useful witness and facilitator of a future UNITA-Government rapprochement, a lack of safety for UN personnel led to its complete withdrawal to Luanda by 23 February. Refusing to give up completely on Angola the Secretary-General promised to appoint a Special Envoy who would be based in New York, but who could redeploy to Angola if matters improved. With over half the country now cut off from humanitarian aid, MONUA's mandate expired on 26 February 1999.[69]

5   Analysis of the operations

5.1   Funding, administration and deployment

The insidious effects of the American reaction to the catastrophe in Somalia were to be continually felt throughout UNAVEM III's tenure. Within 12 months of assuming office the new Clinton Administration's attitude towards the role of the UN in its foreign policy had changed dramatically. In what it described as a more 'balanced view', the Administration began to look upon the UN as more of a 'contributor to' than the 'centerpiece of' its national security policy. Essentially, the US no longer 'intended to expand UN peacekeeping, but to help fix it'.[70]

The cornerstone of this new policy was to be Presidential Decision Directive 25 (PDD25- Reforming Multilateral Peace Operations) released in May 1994. PDD25 involved a complete reassessment of US support for new and continuing UN operations and was to have major repercussions for the UN's peacekeeping capabilities. Before the US would participate in any new UN operation it was now to ask a number of questions. These included whether participation would advance US national interests; whether there existed a threat to international peace and security; if the operation had clear objectives and whether its scope was clearly defined; whether an end-point to participation could be identified; and whether a cease-fire existed or if peace-enforcement might be required. PDD25 also sought to reduce the American share of the UN peacekeeping budget to 25 per cent and emphasized that the President would decide only on a case-by-case basis whether US forces could be placed under the operational control of a competent UN commander.[71] The new US position was clarified in July 1995 by its Ambassador to the UN, Madelaine Albright, when she stated that:

> [in the] current budgetary climate, neither [the US] nor the UN can continue to pour resources into operations for which we can see no end...Each time we vote to create or extend a peacekeeping operation, we must consider whether that use of resources is justified or whether the limited funds available should be spent elsewhere.[72]

This new frugality was also beginning to pervade the corridors of the UN itself. Noting that the number of UN peacekeeping operations being conducted had risen from 5 in 1988 to 16 in 1995 Boutros-Ghali had stated that 'the number of UN operations, the scale of the operations [and] the money spent on operations, [could not] keep growing indefinitely. The limits [were] being reached.[73] With the cost of peacekeeping in 1995 estimated to be approximately $3.1 billion, he had already begun to take a number of steps in order to reduce expenditure, including streamlining and restructuring the UN departments dealing with peacekeeping and reducing or ending operations that were no longer cost effective.

Nevertheless, by September 1995 outstanding payments to the UN's regular and peacekeeping budgets had reached $3.7 billion. And with the optimism of previous years eroding member states were finding even less reason to be prompt and up to date with their contributions. Despite being required to pay their installments within 30 days of receiving an assessment, the UN was now recouping only 45 per cent of contributions in the first three months and only 68 per cent after 180 days.[74] Little was to change over the proceeding years. When the MONUA operation came to an end in February 1999 the United Nations was still owed $1.6 billion for its peacekeeping budget. MONUA itself was short by over $100 million.[75]

In these circumstances a slow deployment of UNAVEM III might have been expected. However, the fact that the majority of UNAVEM III did not deploy until late 1995 was in large part due to the deliberate policies of the US and UN. In line with its new policy on peacekeeping, and to placate its Republican led Congress, the Clinton Administration requested that the deployment of around 60 per cent of UNAVEM III's military component be delayed until an advance team had provided an inventory of UNITA forces already assembled at their specified locations. Supported in this hesitant approach by a UN fearful of a repetition of its experiences in Bosnia and Somalia, UNAVEM III thus conducted a phased deployment.[76]

Matters were not to be helped by Angola's lack of mine-free roads for travel and transport. One reason for this was that the UN had received only $1.28 million of the $12 million the international community had pledged for mine-clearance.[77] Together with the usual problems of persuading contributing states to deploy their troops as scheduled, this policy meant UNAVEM III's military component was not fully deployed until April 1996.[78] Once again, therefore, the UN's slow deployments were to facilitate an abuse of the peace accords by both Angolan parties.[79]

5.2   Planning and the nature of the peace accords

As the account of the Mozambican operation in Chapter 3 testifies, the UN had learnt many valuable lessons from the collapse of the first Angolan peace process. Almost immediately the UN had incorporated those lessons into its mandate in Mozambique, insisting on a substantial military presence, a greater number of electoral observers and a more intrusive role in the bodies created to verify the implementation of the agreements. Unfortunately, as it was forced to renegotiate more appropriate roles in monitoring the Mozambican police and in the formation of the unified army whilst the peace process was proceeding, the UN was unable to have sufficient effect on either process.

Nevertheless, the UN obviously hoped to replicate the general success of the Mozambican operation when it agreed to try again in Angola and so incorporated the same lessons into its mandate for UNAVEM III. The UN therefore deployed a substantial military contingent and insisted on the chairmanship of the verification bodies created to oversee the peace process. And although the majority of the peace process was designed to be complete within 15 months, the second round of Presidential elections could not be conducted until the UN had verified that the parties had created the requisite conditions. UNITA had also been guaranteed a role in government through the creation of the GURN. However, it was noticeable that UNAVEM III's CIVPOL component still consisted of only 260 police observers (far fewer than the 3,600 deployed in Cambodia and even fewer than the number deployed in Mozambique) and that the UN had not adopted a particularly prominent role in helping establish a more professional FAA.

The familiarity of the UN with Angola was an obvious bonus for its pre-operational planning. In essence there had been a continuous UN peace-keeping presence in the country since it had first begun to verify the withdrawal of Cuban troops back in 1988. Although UNAVEM II had suffered from obvious planning inadequacies there were fewer reasons for the same mistakes to be repeated in 1995. The peace negotiations leading to the Lusaka Protocol had begun virtually immediately after the return to war in late 1992, providing over two years of preparation time. As one article in *The Economist* noted in the same month UNAVEM III was established, '[for] once, the UN has had time to plan the whole business well in advance'.[80] As the next section will show, however, a mixture of inadequate detail in the agreements, together with a dearth of finance, was to cause problems for even the UN's best-laid plans.

5.3 Disarmament, demobilization, reintegration and the formation of unified armed forces

Just as it had hampered the disarmament and demobilization processes in previous operations, the failure to ensure sufficient detail in the peace agreements was to do the same for UNAVEM III. As one UN study into the provision of humanitarian assistance in Angola commented in 1998, the military provisions of the Protocol were 'especially vague'. There was not even agreement on the ultimate size of the FAA.[81] Most of the military aspects of the peace process were to be discussed by the working group that was to be established after the Protocol had been signed. Understandably, this strategy may have been chosen to ensure the quickest possible cease-fire, as attempting to achieve greater detail might have prolonged the war at an even greater cost to human life.[82] However, as the report also noted, this strategy was to have unintended consequences.

The first of these consequences was that the UN was left to oversee a second post-agreement negotiating process in order to actually implement the peace agreements. The second was that the UN's planning was forced to occur in a vacuum until key details such as the number of soldiers to be demobilized and the timeframe within which they were to be released into civilian society could be ascertained. And a third was that under such uncertain conditions it became equally difficult to recruit and retain staff and raise the necessary funds. In a conclusion that would have been appropriate for any of the operations included in this text, the report urged future negotiators to endeavor to include as much detail as possible on key provisions in peace agreements to reduce the delays that will inevitably be incurred later.[83]

As already noted, the delay in deploying UNAVEM III was to facilitate both parties in their prevarications. Although the Protocol timetable envisioned that the quartering process would be complete within five months, the absence of UN troops on the ground to help construct the quartering sites made that deadline impossible.[84] Fortunately for the UN the first UNITA troops did not arrive at quartering areas until late November 1995, a full year after the Protocol had been signed, thereby providing extra preparation time. However, with the slow deployment of its peacekeepers the UN was still forced to employ a commercial contractor to help with 10 of the 15 UNITA quartering sites. As previous disarmament operations had taught, relying on the internal parties to construct their own quartering sites is a precarious business and UNITA's behavior was consistent with the worst expectations. Having a commercial contractor on hand at the beginning of operations to ensure speedy construction of quartering areas would seem to be money well spent.[85]

Established within the UN Humanitarian Assistance Coordination Unit (UCAH) in February 1995, the body responsible for planning and coordinating the demobilization and reintegration of former combatants was the Demobilization and Reintegration Office (DRO). The location of the DRO within UCAH was a deliberate attempt to ensure that a civilian body was in charge of the demobilization and reintegration phases, rather than the military through UNAVEM III and the DPKO. This was important not only for symbolic reasons, but also to make cooperation with NGOs and the attraction of voluntary funding easier.[86] With knowledge of its impending role UCAH had been able to begin laying a framework for demobilization and reintegration as early as 1994. Whilst the DRO was charged with developing a strategy for both demobilization and reintegration, the UNDP was given the primary responsibility for assisting the Government in developing and implementing its reintegration support programs.[87]

Although the Protocol had envisioned some form of vocational training for those combatants not chosen for the FAA or ANP, details of how these provisions were to be provided were also left to post-agreement discussions. Realizing that disagreements in the JC on issues not related to quartering and demobilization were hindering both processes through 1995 and early 1996, SRSG Beye helped create a Technical Working Group for Demobilization and Reintegration (TWGDR) as a sub-committee of the JC. Although the composition of the TWGDR on the whole mirrored that of its parent commission, it also involved other organizations including UCAH, IOM, government agencies, FAA and NGOs. Regularly chaired by the UN Humanitarian Coordinator, the TWGDR not only helped limit purely political and opportunistic considerations in the peace process from affecting the demobilization and reintegration phases, but also helped the Government design a comprehensive national demobilization and reintegration plan adopted by the Council of Ministers on 15 August 1996.[88]

This national plan was developed in response to a major change in strategy. The original intention of the parties had been to incorporate all the combatants into one 190,000-strong unified force before slowly demobilizing all but 90,000 of them over a period of two years. The FAA had even prepared a plan to incorporate the excess 100,000 into a Fourth Branch of the FAA, where they were to be organized into brigades and used to reconstruct the country's infrastructure. Whilst helping the country rehabilitate, these soldiers were also to learn a new skill, be provided with land on which to build a house and be guaranteed that the military would buy their first year's harvest.[89] Those with previous experience of demobilization processes also supported this original strategy, fearing the likely consequences of releasing ill-prepared former soldiers into the unwelcoming hands of a war-destroyed economy.[90] Angolan Chief of Staff, General Joao de Matos, explained the strategy's rationale:

> Personally I think a soldier after 12–15 years in the army is not a farm worker – the only thing he knows is war. He'll immediately sell [any farming kit and spend the money given to him], waste it…he has no experience of economy or organization and in two weeks he's a potential bandit. In contrast our program would mean that for four years he'll obey military orders, get paid, get fed, have health and education support, with a guarantee of a house and land which will belong to him. We have a chance with our program of transforming soldiers into civilians and of guaranteeing the stability of Angola. Without it the FAA will have a lot of work to do to maintain military stability.[91]

However, this 'global incorporation plan', as it was called, was rejected for two reasons. The first was that the international community was unwilling to pay the $800 million required to see the plan through, especially when it was recognized that immediate demobilization would cost around a tenth of that amount. The second reason was the Government's fears that such a large force might give the military too much power in the post-conflict state. As Brittain notes, the Government's position ignored its own lack of capacity.[92] Nevertheless, together these two factors were to kill the global incorporation plan by mid-1996.

Preempting the actual collapse of the global incorporation plan UCAH had already begun in early 1996 to urge donors to contribute to a quick response fund in order to enable it to deal with the now impending demobilization of 100,000 UNITA and FAA soldiers. It also began to encourage the UNDP to begin planning for concrete reintegration activities. In May 1996 the UN submitted a program of support for demobilization and reintegration to the Government that involved four main components. These were a community counseling and referral service; quick impact projects to increase the absorption capacity of the receiving communities and to facilitate reintegration; a professional training program to meet training demands and requirements; and a physical rehabilitation program targeting the war disabled.[93]

As previously mentioned, the UN and TWGDR's preparation was to culminate in the adoption of a national demobilization and reintegration plan in August 1996. This plan established the institutional and programmatic framework for the implementation of the demobilization and reintegration processes, including the legal and *ad hoc* benefits to be provided by the Government and international community to the former soldiers and their dependents.[94] Along with the components mentioned above, each soldier was to be supplied with six months severance pay and a 12-month food ration by the Government and international community respectively. Each demobilized soldier was also to be supplied with a demobilization kit, which included clothing, household items, personal hygiene items, seeds, agricultural tools and basic tools with which to construct housing. Their families were also to receive a three-month food ration. The IOM, which was in charge of distributing the demobilization kits, was also to transport each family to the destination of their choice.[95]

Fortunately for the UN no significant demobilization was to take place before mid-1997, giving it the extra time it needed to plan and prepare these programs.[96] Nevertheless, this also meant that the quartering process, originally expected to last between three and five months, had lasted three times longer than planned. This extension obviously placed great strain upon already limited resources and fostered discontent amongst UNITA soldiers, some of whom had been encamped since late 1995. Complaints by UNITA that poor conditions in the quartering areas were responsible for the failure of its troops to arrive and for the high number of subsequent desertions led the JC to investigate during March and April 1996. The JC found conditions in the first few operative quartering areas to be 'generally acceptable', a position supported by the Secretary-General, who argued that the UN, its agencies and the NGOs involved were providing the quartered troops with adequate supplies and services, including food, health facilities and civic education.[97] This appreciation of conditions in the quartering areas is contradicted somewhat by Victoria Brittain, a long-time reporter and writer on Angola, who described them as 'bleak and frightening places [where] discipline [by UNITA] was harsh, with casual brutality, corporal punishment and summary executions reported by UN personnel working with them'.[98]

The failure to anticipate the needs of demobilizing soldiers' families was also to cause problems for the quartering process. Although similar phenomena had occurred in Nicaragua and El Salvador, the UN had not planned for the large numbers of family members who began to congregate around the quartering areas. Unprepared and lacking the necessary resources, UNAVEM III initially argued that the UNITA family areas were not an integral part of the quartering process. The Protocol had not included provision for dependents and so senior UNAVEM III staff were able to argue that the maintenance of the family areas should not be charged to the UN's assessed budget and that they should not be involved in establishing or maintaining the areas or even in ensuring mine clearance and water supplies.[99] This was obviously an untenable position given the fact that over 120,000 dependents had congregated in the family areas and that UNITA soldiers would not remain encamped whilst their families suffered outside. Although UNAVEM III personnel became more flexible as the operation progressed, their resistance on this issue threatened to undermine the demobilization process and contributed to a significant degree of tension between themselves and other humanitarian personnel in the field.[100]

The central role adopted by NGOs in the delivery of services to UNITA's quartering areas was itself a significant development on previous demobilization processes. This time a number of NGOs undertook the distribution of food, the provision of health care and the organization of civic education programs in the areas. This increased role for NGOs was a deliberate policy by UCAH, drawing on lessons learnt in Mozambique and El Salvador. As well as helping deliver essential services, NGOs also alleviated some of the pressure on the UN to recruit appropriate staff. It also reduced UCAH's funding responsibilities as, in principle, the NGOs were responsible for attracting the voluntary donations they required to fund their own activities during the quartering process. However, their role was not without controversy. As most of the NGOs experienced in demobilization processes declined to become involved in Angola, UCAH was forced to accept those with little or no corporate experience in war-torn countries. This led to losses and mismanagement of WFP food in quartering areas because some NGOs had inadequate experience in the storage, management and distribution of food.[101]

One of the principal reasons for the refusal of experienced NGOs to become involved in Angola was their previous experience of arbitrary demobilization timetables. All the peace processes included in this text had adopted timetables for disarmament and demobilization that were hopelessly unrealistic. The quartering and demobilization processes in Mozambique took nine months rather than the scheduled six weeks. In El Salvador the equivalent processes lasted 11 months instead of the planned six. It came as little surprise, therefore, when the original timetable to quarter

UNITA's forces within three to five months was exceeded. Not wishing to make themselves hostage to another delayed demobilization program, some NGOs therefore declined to participate. At least one relatively experienced NGO actually decided to withdraw from its quartering area in January 1997 because it felt that with no clear end to quartering in sight its work there was diverting it from its core activities.[102]

In order to release the quartered troops as quickly as possible, reduce the amount of resources required and prevent the complications of passing over control of the areas to the Government, a Rapid Demobilization Plan (RDP) was adopted in March 1997. Although it was hoped that the RDP could be complete within six months, the worsening political and security conditions in Angola meant that it lasted until January 1998. Unfortunately, UNITA's systematic attempts to prevent its demobilized troops from returning to civilian life had already effectively undermined the whole process.[103]

Nevertheless, UNITA's duplicity was not the only problem the disarmament process in Angola was facing. From the very beginning of the operation the failure of the international community to fulfill its funding commitments had jeopardized the success of the quartering, demobilization and reintegration processes. No more was this the case than with the $993 million committed by the international community to help with rehabilitation, reconstruction and national reconciliation at a Donors Conference held in Brussels in September 1995. Almost two years later, in August 1997, the Secretary-General was forced to report that only $6.8 million of that money had been donated. By the same time only $16.4 million of the $56.6 million required for demobilization had been received and the IOM had acquired only $5.5 million of the $26 million it needed to continue operations.[104] The response to the 1998 inter-agency appeal was so low that the Secretary-General was compelled to warn that without additional funds the UNHCR, IOM and UNICEF would have to 'reduce their activities in the country drastically', even if the worsening security situation did not force them to.[105]

Once again, therefore, the inadequate manner in which demobilization and reintegration processes are funded during UN operations was exposed. Forced to rely on voluntary funds for essential projects in both processes, the UN could do little more than protest when states that had previously volunteered contributions refused to donate them until either the Government had implemented economic reforms or the parties had demonstrated a greater commitment to peace. Having learnt from their previous experiences in places like El Salvador, the coordination of the UN, IMF and WB was to be much greater in Angola, with both the latter organizations designing their reform and adjustment programs to create a 'synergy' with the relief and rehabilitation activities of the UN system as a whole. However, the Angolan government was to be caught between adopting economic reforms to place more investment in production, reconstruction and welfare or continuing its preparations for a return to war. Although the IMF continued its negotiations with the Government throughout UNAVEM III's tenure, by mid-1998 inflation had reached approximately 5 per cent per month, unemployment had reached 45 per cent and at least 67 per cent of Angolans were living below the poverty line. In these conditions the Government was constantly falling behind in paying its subsidies to demobilizing soldiers and in paying for national reconstruction projects designed to help communities rehabilitate.[106]

Leaving the discussions over how the new FAA would be formed until after the Protocol was signed also resulted in negative repercussions for the whole peace process. Highly suspicious of each other and unwilling to make concessions, the parties could not even agree on the number of UNITA troops to be incorporated until January 1996. Together with disagreements over issues such as the type of posts to be filled by UNITA generals, these delays impacted significantly on an already sluggish demobilization process. And by the time nearly 11,000 UNITA troops had been incorporated into the FAA in early 1998 the confidence-building effects that a unified army could have provided had already been lost amidst the continued fighting and constant rearming of both parties.

Nevertheless, with estimates of the number of quartered UNITA personnel who were not actually soldiers ranging form anywhere between 40 and 80 per cent, it was obvious that UNITA had never really committed itself to a unified army anyway. At every opportunity UNITA had prevaricated over sending its troops to the quartering areas with the appropriate quantity and quality of weapons. The fact that UNITA was withholding troops from the disarmament process was so widely recognized that UCAH had actually engaged in contingency planning for the future demobilization of thousands of elite soldiers that UNITA had refused to acknowledge even existed.[107] And despite retaining these forces UNITA still ensured that its demobilized troops were quickly redeployed in readiness for renewed warfare.

For its part, the Government was left with a 110,000 strong FAA (the largest standing army in Africa) and a military budget that was spiraling out of control.[108] The FAA itself remained underfed and badly equipped and many of its soldiers seldom received their meager $17 per month salary. Morale was thus extremely low.[109] And whether or not the lack of international assistance in providing the FAA with professional training would have affected its overall success obviously became an irrelevant question with the end of the peace process itself.[110]

5.4   Reform of public security

In the context of such deep mistrust the reform of public security in Angola was always going to be difficult. The key to the transformation of the existing public security bodies was to be the incorporation of up to 5,500 UNITA personnel into the ANP. However, by the time MONUA's mandate expired in February 1999 only 525 UNITA personnel had been selected for the new force. By the same time ANP officers were actively fighting alongside the FAA and were known to have committed gross human rights violations against civilians. In these conditions there could be no real disarmament of the general population as the Protocol had prescribed. The failure of the peace process to improve public security was not, however, only caused by a lack of political will on behalf of the internal parties. The UN was also to play a role through its tendency to ignore human rights violations, whilst the international community continued to provide insufficient funds for the reform of Angola's criminal justice system.

The first problem to beset the reform process was a lack of cooperation from both parties. Whilst UNITA prevaricated over supplying the UN with any information concerning its military capabilities, the Government was to be equally reticent in providing information on the ANP and RRP. Though an agreement on the incorporation of UNITA members into the ANP was reached on 26 October 1996, neither party was committed to its implementation. Whilst UNITA eventually quartered only 4,900 members of its police force, which was known to be much larger, the Government continued to insist on educational requirements for ANP recruits that UNITA's police personnel were simply unable to meet. Despite succumbing to pressure from the UN to loosen its selection criteria, only 524 had been chosen by June 1997. With this sad fact the process was concluded. The Government's lack of commitment to reform was also apparent in its tendency to obstruct UN verification of the 5,450 RRP personnel that had been quartered at 13 different locations. In three of them UNAVEM III had even been allowed take head counts. The Government's intentions became most apparent when UNAVEM III observed the RRP conducting military training during 1997.[111]

One of the first casualties of the failure to create a neutral police force was the UN's mandate to ensure the disarmament of the general population. Although the Government had initially wanted to stick to the letter of the Protocol and begin collecting civilian held weapons only after UNITA's forces had been quartered, a widespread deterioration in law and order forced it to start the process earlier. Consequently, the Government launched a program for disarming the civilian population ahead of schedule on 1 July 1996.

The ANP's plan of action for disarming civilians consisted of three phases. The first involved a public awareness campaign, whilst the second requested a voluntary hand-over of weapons. The third and final phase was designed to enforce the collection of any remaining illegal weapons. By early 1997 the ANP had already begun to implement the second phase of its plan in Government controlled areas, but had still collected fewer than

3,000 weapons. Describing these results as 'far from satisfactory' Secretary-General Annan urged the Government to introduce an incentive-based scheme in order to encourage civilians to hand over their weapons. He also requested the Government to begin collecting the weapons of the Civil Defense Corp, whose members were spread throughout all of Angola's provinces.[112]

When the ANP resumed the collection of civilian weapons following a temporary suspension in the process during mid-1997, it did so predominantly in areas recently incorporated into the State administration. Consequently UNITA began to accuse the Government and ANP of dismantling its political structures and of disarming only one section of the population. After receiving increasing reports of ANP human rights violations committed in former UNITA controlled areas, the JC called upon the Government to suspend the disarmament of civilians until the normalization process had been concluded throughout the country. In the meantime the Secretary-General tried to convince the Government to allow MONUA to provide the ANP and RRP with additional training in internationally accepted police procedures. However, only in late 1998 was the human rights component of MONUA requested to provide training at the provincial level of the ANP in the application of human rights principles in law enforcement.[113]

Angola's judicial system was also unable to provide sufficient security to the country's beleaguered population. In June 1998 the Secretary-General reported that the judicial system continued to suffer from an acute lack of human and physical resources, which had resulted in gross violations of detainees rights.[114] Until the same time an understaffed UNAVEM III human rights component had also resisted from reporting human rights abuses that continued to be perpetrated by both sides, seemingly under direction from SGSR Beye not to upset the delicate political situation. As Alex Vines notes, 'the UN approach to human rights issues in the period November 1994 to May 1998 did little to create awareness of human rights issues or accountability for even the gravest abuses. It achieved even less in advancing a culture of respect for human rights in Angolan society'. When Beye finally approved a change in strategy in late May 1998, calling on MONUA to carry out its investigations more expeditiously, the newly revamped human rights component had only six months to achieve its goals in a rapidly deteriorating political context.[115]

5.5   Strategies of conflict resolution

It was evident from the provisions of the Lusaka Protocol that the UN had learnt many lessons from its previous operations. This time the UN had ensured that the agreements had included an impressive array of security guarantees to encourage both parties to implement the peace process. Firstly, each party was ensured post-election security through the creation of the GURN. Similarly, the creation of unified police and armed forces would provide added security in the post-conflict era. UNITA's leader, Savimbi, was also provided with a 'special status' that eventually accorded him the recognition of being the President of the Main Opposition Party. It also gave him various protocol privileges and a 'dignified salary including subsidies, advances and allowances'.[116]

However, as former SRSG Anstee notes in her post-operation analysis, it is difficult to avoid concluding that given his actions during the 1990s nothing less than the Presidency of Angola would have satisfied Savimbi.[117] Suspicions that he was not completely committed to implementing the Protocol were initially heightened when he failed to arrive to sign it. By February 1995 he had publicly described the agreement as a 'collection of lies' and a 'meaningless piece of paper' and had relieved Manuvakola (UNITA's Secretary-General and signatory of the Protocol) of his position. Nevertheless, as was characteristic of Savimbi, he still retained the capacity to be reverent when the need arose. So by the following May he had publicly embraced Dos Santos in Lusaka and declared that 'he is my President and I will serve him'.[118]

Nevertheless, if Savimbi had indeed been nothing more than duplicitous throughout the many years of the peace process, then it must call into question the impartial nature of the UN's operations during that time. Victoria Brittain is particularly vocal on this point, criticizing not only the US for its failure to reconstruct its approach to Savimbi, but also the UN for treating the Angolan leaders as equals after the war had resumed in 1992. Thus, whilst the US remained tied to the myth of Savimbi's democratic credentials, the latter 'illustrated [its] grotesque position...on the new war: that both sides were to blame and had the same legitimate concerns.'[119]

One can only speculate on whether an alternative approach by the UN may have prevented subsequent tragedies. UNITA had gained much from the return to war, controlling up to 70 per cent of Angolan territory by early 1993. It had also been free to replenish and augment its forces for a full year before the UN imposed an arms and petroleum embargo upon it. Once the Government had reacted to the initial UNITA blitzkrieg and had begun to recapture the territory it had lost, UNITA subsequently assumed a greater urgency in finding a peace settlement. Anstee herself acknowledges that the breakthrough in Lusaka was only made possible because of the change in the military balance caused by UNITA's serious losses over the previous year and a half.[120] The FAA had even recaptured Huambo in November 1994 and was anxious to continue its rout of UNITA by attacking its new headquarters in Bailundo. However, with the imminent signing of the Protocol the US and UN pressured the Government to rein in its military so as to leave Savimbi an outcome short of complete defeat.[121]

The consequences of this strategy were apparent. The FAA had stopped short of total victory and through the terms of the Protocol was forced to dispense with the services of Executive Outcomes, the military company whose involvement had played an instrumental role in turning the tide of the war before the Protocol was signed.[122] For its part UNITA began to consolidate the territory it still controlled and continued to seek an effective partition of the country. In the meantime it was earning at least $1 million per day from diamond sales that it continued to fly out of Andulo, Bailundo and Negage, despite a UN presence in all three areas.[123]

Despite UNITA's obvious lack of political will to see the Protocol implemented, the UN and international community persisted in their commitment to a negotiated settlement throughout UNAVEM III's tenure. As late as 24 September 1998 the three observer countries issued a statement 'stressing that there could be no military solution to the conflict in Angola and underlying the validity of the Lusaka Protocol'.[124] This position was reiterated by the Secretary-General in his report of November 1998 when he stated that he 'remained convinced that there [could] be no lasting military solution to the conflict in Angola and that only a political settlement on the basis of the Lusaka Protocol [could] help avoid further suffering for the Angolan people.'[125] Although the rejection of a military solution in the hope that both parties would not return to outright war was an understandable reaction from a humanitarian point of view, it still leaves open the question of whether the impartial nature of the operation was appropriate to begin with.

There were, of course, major factors militating against a military solution to the conflict. For one there was a definite ethnic dimension to it. Driven by personal ambition Savimbi had broken from the revolutionary group for which he had been 'foreign minister' in exile to establish UNITA on the power base of the Ovimbundu people, to which he [belonged].[126] Through a blend of pre-colonial African traditions and more enlightened Western values Savimbi continued his political manipulation of the Ovimbundu, the largest ethnic group in Angola with 30 to 40 per cent of the population. As Heywood notes, despite the accusations of his detractors that he possessed a personality cult, had no commitment to democracy and had been involved in witchcraft, support for UNITA and admiration for Savimbi remained high among significant elements of Angola's rural population throughout. An understanding of Ovimbundu political ideology as it has transformed from the pre-colonial period goes a long way to explain this continued political support.[127]

Nevertheless, as Minter's analysis of the 1992 election results shows, labeling the Angolan conflict as simply 'ethnic' would have been a mischaracterization. In both the presidential and legislative elections the MPLA (supported predominantly by the Mbundu ethnic group) and UNITA had won at least a significant minority of voters in every province, including their opponent's ethnic home ground. For Minter this was proof that the majority of Angolans from all backgrounds, profoundly weary of war, had strongly endorsed national unity and reconciliation. Within each ethnic group, people had opted for a variety of political viewpoints.[128] So, although the FAA may have been overly optimistic in its hopes of totally eradicating UNITA in late 1994 and despite the fact that its military defeat would definitely not have ensured national reconciliation, the UN may have inadvertently lost an opportunity to severely limit Savimbi's influence and bargaining position.

Obviously, having given Savimbi the benefit of the doubt the UN, as the neutral guarantor of the peace process, then had a responsibility to ensure that he could not take advantage of it. However, although the UN had imposed an arms and petroleum embargo on UNITA as far back as September 1993, it had failed to do the same on its trade in diamonds until July 1998. Even then the sanctions were poorly monitored. When asked about the general failure of the sanctions system UN and US officials insisted that there was little that could be done. As Paul Hare, US Special Envoy to Angola acknowledged:

> Without military force to back up the arms embargo, the two-way flow of diamonds and arms between UNITA territory and neighboring Zaire was impossible to stop. But the sanctions did have political and psychological effects; they have increased UNITA's international isolation.[129]

The latter effects may have been felt more by the international community than by Savimbi, who in Anstee's opinion thrived on international prominence, whether positive or negative.[130] Regardless of its increasing diplomatic isolation UNITA was still able to spend much of the $1.72 billion it had earned through diamond sales during the Lusaka process on arms, petroleum products, food and medicines.[131] In fact the greatest setback to UNITA's smuggling came in May 1997, not from the UN, but from the fall of his neighboring ally Mobutu in Zaire. As Hare had identified, Zaire had long acted as a conduit for UNITA's diamond sales, as the entry point for equipment and as the way in and out from its headquarters in Bailundo. Exacerbated by the fall of Lissouba in the Congo the following October, for the first time in 30 years Savimbi had found himself isolated.[132] Even so, UNITA was still able to sell its diamonds on the black market and the UN had received insufficient help from the international diamond trading companies in stopping the trade by the time UNAVEM III's mandate had expired. Thus, UNITA's diamond sales had been reduced by 1998–1999, but it was still earning more than $200 million per year.[133]

The Government, it has to be said, did not always help in applying sanctions against UNITA. Throughout the Lusaka process Government officials regularly bought diamonds from it, passing them off as diamonds mined from Government controlled areas through a rather lax Certificates of Origin system.[134] In 1997 the Government had even allowed private companies to negotiate directly with UNITA over future mining concessions. This was a means to ensure UNITA an income even if it relinquished the territory in which the mines were located. Thus, when the Government placed all the blame on the UN for allowing UNITA the means to rearm and prepare for war it was being more than a little disingenuous.

6   Conclusion

As he watched the Angolan peace process collapse despite his best efforts, the Secretary-General could only conclude in his January 1999 report that 'history will, of course, pass judgment on the reasons for which this unique opportunity was missed. In the meantime, however, the parties and their leaders must assume full and direct responsibility for the suffering of their people'. Defending his organization's efforts he reiterated the inability of the UN to impose its presence on the Angolan parties, or to play an effective role without their cooperation.[135]

In the fateful words of SGSR Diallo, 'the finish line was there. We wanted to cross it, but we didn't cross it'.[136] The important question is, of course, why the parties did not cross that metaphorical finish line. After all, as the previous sections have made clear, the Lusaka process was a definite improvement on its predecessor. The most obvious answer appears to be that Savimbi was interested more in gaining absolute power than he was in peace. The parties therefore existed in an intersubjective understanding of aggression. However, as Savimbi was actually determined to use violence there were no true security dilemmas present. Transforming the shared understanding between the parties was thus impossible without a basic change in Savimbi's and UNITA's identities and interests. Though this was not possible in the limited timeframe of both UNAVEM operations, the creation of the Renovation Committee of UNITA suggests that the UN's intervention was not without effect.

Nevertheless, as it was dealing with at least one predatory actor, the UN required the ability to control the conflict environment in order to make its intervention as effective as possible. Unfortunately, the lack of an effective arms embargo on either Angolan party left it unable to maintain strategic control of the peace process. As Vines asserts, 'what the UN failed to address was that uninterrupted arms imports greatly contributed to the lack of confidence on the ground'.[137] It also allowed each party to feel that the status quo could continue, or even that total victory could be achieved. In these conditions the UN's disarmament process simply became a sideshow to both parties' continuing preparations for a return to war.

The lack of effective Track 1 diplomacy at the level of ex-combatants and the general population also made general disarmament unlikely. By the end of the operation the ANP was actively fighting alongside regular FAA units and had become increasingly implicated in human rights abuses during its attempts to unilaterally disarm civilians living in former UNITA held areas. The country's judicial and penal systems also remained under-staffed and under-funded. Without a more successful reform of Angola's whole justice system, therefore, the degree of security required to sustain the disarmament of ex-combatants and begin a comprehensive disarmament of the general population could not be created.

Of course, with the failure of the peace process and the continued forced recruitment and conscription being conducted by the parties, there was never any hope that the soldiers demobilized by the UN would remain unarmed.[138] This was also the case for the general population. Even though the UN had brought four years of relative peace to Angola, the failure of public security reform, together with UNAVEM III's initial lack of attention to human rights abuses, had left the general population with little sense of fundamental change. Depressingly, despite the UN's best efforts, the life expectancy of the average Angolan remained as low as 42 years. One-third of all children were dying before the age of five and one out of every 133 Angolans was maimed. Fifty per cent of men and 70 per cent of women were also illiterate: high even by African standards.[139] The return to war had also left nearly two million Angolans in need of international food deliveries. Therefore, despite obvious improvements in the organization and conduct of the UN's third Angolan operation, the security required for general disarmament was simply not present.

Conclusion

In the literature of the [Cold War] period there was little, if any, discussion of a disarmed world, despite a great deal of discussion on disarmament.
John W. Burton, *Peace Theory: Preconditions for Disarmament*, 1962[1]

I don't know when I'm going to be demobilized. After being demobilized, I really want support, some assistance to support me in the first stage of being a civilian. We need some training to enter tomorrow's life.
Sebastiao Chiwisse, 28-year veteran of the Angolan civil war, 2002[2]

This book has sought to achieve two objectives. The first is to provide an historical account of the major disarmament processes conducted by the UN in intra-state conflicts during the 1990s. In doing so it has also tried to highlight the major lessons that the UN's experiences have taught, many of which will be discussed in this conclusion. The second objective is to provide an explanation for the variation in success that the UN has witnessed in implementing its disarmament mandates. Thus, from a Constructivist theoretical foundation it has argued that the UN's success has depended (and depends) on its ability to transform the existing social structures in war-torn societies through the application of a twin-track approach to the provision of security at three levels of such societies: the warring parties, ex-combatants and the general population.

As the preceding case studies have demonstrated, at the first level of the warring parties both Neo-Realism and Neo-Liberalism have made significant contributions to our understanding of the impediments that exist to the implementation of disarmament agreements. In this sense both traditions have highlighted the effects of the security dilemma on parties existing in social structures of aggression and competition. However, whilst they explain a great deal of the behavior of actors caught in certain types of intersubjective understanding, they each tell us only part of the story and thus 'must be assimilated into a constructivist framework'.[3] As rationalist theories, both Neo-Realism and Neo-Liberalism are limited in their ability to fully explain behavior due to their failure to take account of the mutually constitutive effects of actors' identities and the social structures in which they are embedded. As Alexander Wendt explains:

> The rationalist strategy treats identities and interests as exogenously given and constant, and focuses on the factors shaping actors' expectations about each other's behavior. Structural change occurs when the relative expected utility of normative vs. deviant behavior changes. The constructivist strategy treats identities and interests as endogenous to interaction and thus a dependent variable in process. Structural change occurs when actors redefine who they are and what they want. The strategies are not mutually exclusive, but they are different with different ideas about what is going on in structural change and what causes it to happen.[4]

This leaves scholars in both traditions struggling to explain cases in which the former warring parties have behaved in ways that their basic assumptions would suggest to be unlikely. As this text has highlighted, and Mark Peceny and William Stanley have previously argued, Barbara Walter's Neo-Realist analysis cannot account for cases like those of El Salvador (and also Guatemala in Peceny's and Stanley's study) in which the security dilemmas of the parties were overcome without either externally provided security guarantees or internal power sharing arrangements.[5] It also struggles to account fully for cases like Mozambique, in which the UN helped transform the intersubjective understanding between the parties, thereby lowering their security dilemmas and enabling them to accept the outcome of democratic elections without significant internal guarantees for the future.[6]

As in international relations theory in general, the application of Neo-Liberalism to sub-state group relations has expanded the explanatory power of the rationalist approach. Rather than relying on the concept of externally provided security guarantees, Neo-Liberalist scholars like Caroline Hartzell and Matthew Hoddie have concentrated on the potential for cooperation generated by costly signaling and third party monitoring and verification of the parties' compliance with their agreements. Hartzell and Hoddie are therefore able to account for instances in which peace agreements have been implemented and peace has endured without the presence of a third-party.[7] However, even Hartzell and Hoddie recognize that their theory does not provide a ready answer for the fact that half of the cases in their study that did not see full implementation of the military provisions agreed to by the parties still succeeded in maintaining peace for at least five years.[8] And this result does not even include the case of Mozambique, which in their analysis is included under fully implemented military agreements.

This suggests that, as in Mozambique and El Salvador, social structures can change though parties may retain forces outside of their disarmament processes. Therefore, just as the Cold War ended when the superpowers no longer believed each other to be serious military threats, and not when they destroyed their nuclear and conventional arsenals, the relations of sub-state groups can also change without the need for full disarmament. What truly matters is not that parties to agreements retain arms, but the degree to which they each believe they will be used. In Mozambique the threat posed by retained weapons was low enough for SRSG Aldo Ajello to have sufficient confidence to allow the elections to proceed. The evidence therefore suggests (and as the Mozambican case study in this text has already argued) that the shared understanding between the parties had already transformed from one of aggression to one of competition by the time of the elections. The transformation in El Salvador was even more evolved, with the parties coming even closer to a shared understanding of cooperation.

If the threat weapons pose thus depends on the social structures in which they exist then maybe the premise of complete disarmament before elections should be questioned. This is especially so given the UN's obvious inability to verify that all weapons and forces belonging to former civil warring parties have been declared. This was evident in Angola, Cambodia, Mozambique and El Salvador. All these operations suffered from a lack of personnel, tactical mobility, advanced technologies and investigative powers that could have made the location and destruction of hidden arms caches and ammunition dumps possible.[9] The UN's impotency in this regard was exacerbated by its reliance on the parties themselves to supply it with information on their weapons and troops strengths (which often did not materialize for months after they were due and were generally inaccurate). It is not surprising to find, therefore, that following the completion of a questionnaire compiled by UNIDIR all UN respondents seemed to agree that an independent intelligence and information gathering system should be established to assist them in accomplishing their disarmament and demobilization missions. As Paulo Wrobel concluded in the case of El Salvador:

> The existence of hundreds of additional weapon caches could have been uncovered through the analysis of intelligence instead of by an accidental explosion…[Wrobel suggests that]…One member country could take responsibility for the collection, analysis and dissemination of all-source intelligence to support disarmament and demobilization efforts during a UN operation. This 'force multiplier' would go a long way in providing the UN with some 'measures of success' that could be demonstrated and verified. Currently, the UN asks all the parties to turn in all their weapons but no verification mechanism to determine compliance exists.[10]

Attempting to disarm parties completely in the limited timeframes of UN peacekeeping operations may therefore only exacerbate already heightened insecurity unnecessarily. As Fred Tanner has asserted, what may be more appropriate is for peace agreements to strive towards normative balancing, a concept that 'rests on a controlled and clearly prescribed military adjustment process, which allows the various parties to retain "fail-safe" or residual forces during the transition period'.[11] After an agreed confidence-building time-span (maybe after the formation of a new government) these forces could be disarmed or assimilated into the newly created armed forces.[12] In principle the UN applied this approach of stability through arms control in both Cambodia and Mozambique, with the parties able to retain 30 per cent of their forces until elections in the former and the unofficial acknowledgment of retained forces in the latter.[13] However, whilst the Cambodian operation faltered on political grounds, the failure of the UN to maintain a presence after the elections in Mozambique, in order to ensure the disarmament of residual forces and the general population, meant the disarmament process as a whole was left open-ended.

Though the importance of disarmament may thus be overrated in the Neo-Liberal explanation, its advocacy of a limited role for third parties underestimates the potential function of such actors in the transformation of social structures. By limiting third parties to a monitoring and verification role Neo-Liberalism precludes the manipulation of the economic, political and personal incentives that actors possess to cooperate in peace processes, as to do so would only undermine the confidence built through voluntary interaction. However, the need for more intrusive external intervention is evident in the recent work of a number of scholars who have all highlighted the rationality of violence that persists beyond the point at which it would seem to be in the best interests of the belligerents in civil wars to continue fighting.[14] For example, David Keen's study of civil wars found that they have 'persisted not so much despite the intentions of rational people, as because of them'. This, as Mats Berdal and David Malone concur, is because 'war is not simply a breakdown in a particular system, but a way of creating an alternative system of profit and power and even protection.'[15]

Violence in these alternative systems has generally manifested itself in two basic forms: 'top-down violence' perpetrated by political and military leaders and 'bottom-up violence' perpetrated by civilians and low ranking soldiers.[16] Stephen John Stedman has paid particular attention to the first type in his study of 'spoilers' in peace processes, who he defines as 'leaders and parties who believe that the emerging peace threatens their power, worldview, and interests and who use violence to undermine attempts to achieve it'.[17] He notes that the international community has tended to pursue three major strategies in its attempts to manage such spoilers. The first strategy is coercion, the second is inducement and the third is socialization. Whilst coercion involves punishing the spoiler for bad behavior by reducing their capacity to destroy the peace process, inducement is essentially providing the spoiler with what they desire. He defines socialization as attempts to convince the spoiler to adhere to established norms of behavior through material and intellectual persuasion.[18] These strategies thus have a close resemblance to the three levels of socialization described in Chapter 1.

Stedman is of course correct to argue that the first step in dealing effectively with a spoiler is to diagnose the type of spoiler that they are. This involves an assessment of both the spoiler's goals and their determination to achieve them. Stedman's own typology includes three types of spoiler, all of which have been prominent in recent peace processes: total spoilers, greedy spoilers and limited spoilers. Whilst limited spoilers have limited goals, their commitment to achieving these goals may vary. Total spoilers, on the other hand, see the world in all-or-nothing terms and pursue total power. The greedy spoiler lies between these two and holds goals that expand or contract based on calculations of cost and risk.[19] Once this diagnosis is made the key to success is to match the spoiler's type with the appropriate strategy. For Stedman this means coercion for total spoilers, socialization for greedy spoilers and inducement for limited spoilers.[20]

As Stedman acknowledges, however, making accurate diagnoses of spoilers can be a difficult enterprise in the complex and uncertain conditions of peace processes. Nor will there always be a consensus as to the type each spoiler represents. For example, in Stedman's opinion Pol Pot and the Khmer Rouge were total spoilers, whereas this study would argue that they were at most greedy spoilers. Nevertheless, Stedman's work is important for at least three reasons. Firstly, it stresses the need for coherent strategies when third parties like the UN are forced to deal with spoilers. Secondly, it highlights the tendency of UN personnel to constrain attempts to challenge spoilers due to their devotion to the values of traditional peacekeeping: consent and impartiality.[21] And thirdly, it shows that even when the UN is willing to apportion blame, as it eventually did in the case of UNITA in Angola, it remains relatively impotent to stop such parties trading in diamonds, oil and weapons unless there also exists an 'external coalition for peace' composed of the countries with the resources and consensus necessary to constrain the parties.[22] Unfortunately, as Berdal and Malone have noticed, such coalitions remain elusive because 'the motivations of key international actors conflict, the governments of major powers often [display] a mercantilist bent where conflict threatens or rages, and there is understandable although excessive reluctance by leading governments to focus on the role of multinational companies in the drama.'[23]

Nevertheless, though Neo-Liberalism may overestimate the role of disarmament in peace processes and underestimate the potential role of third parties in helping to transform social structures, Hartzell is correct to emphasize the importance of internal security guarantees for parties existing in social structures of aggression and competition, as it is only these that can effectively assure their survival in the post-implementation period. However, at this point it is important to remember that just as externally provided security guarantees become less important as parties transition from social structures of aggression to those of competition, institutional guarantees also become less important as they transition from social structures of competition to those of cooperation. As one might expect, social structures of the latter kind have not been particularly prevalent at the end of civil wars and so institutional guarantees have proven to be consistently important ingredients of comprehensive agreements.

As explained in Chapter 1, Hartzell's study has already proven that those negotiated settlements likely to experience the greatest stability are the ones that have incorporated the most extensive institutional guarantees in three areas: the distribution of political power, the distribution of economic resources and the new State's use of coercive force.[24] As she suggests herself, awareness of the importance of institutional guarantees in these areas can contribute to the improved success of UN operations by allowing it to design and promote more effective agreements, especially when the internal parties themselves are unaware of the efficacy of such guarantees.[25] However, as the account of the UN's involvement (or lack thereof) in the negotiations leading to the agreements for Angola and Cambodia in the early 1990s testify, the Organization was itself insufficiently aware of the need to incorporate greater institutional guarantees in the distribution of political and economic power at that time. Instead, the UN acquiesced to agreements that expected the parties to determine the distribution of these commodities through the holding of democratic elections, a policy that encouraged the parties to perceive them as winner-take-all competitions.

Despite the failure of elections to maintain the commitment of major signatory parties in both Angola and Cambodia, the UN did not give up on the idea of liberal social reconstruction as a strategy of conflict resolution. Rather, it has continued to rely on the strategy, with 25 of 33 UN peacekeeping missions initiated between 1989 and 1998 involving at least some effort to promote liberal democracy.[26] In conducting elections the UN hopes to achieve two mutually reinforcing goals: democratization and conflict resolution. The strategy of peace through democratization is obviously based on the logic of the Kantian democratic peace thesis, in which states with democratic electoral systems, shared moral values and economic interdependence are believed less likely to go to war with one another. In the same vain, it is hoped that democratic transitions from civil wars will help institutionalize bargaining as a permanent, durable alternative to violence.[27] They also provide opportunities for parties to signal their beliefs in tolerance and mutual respect. Greater economic interdependence between former combatants can also act as an incentive for cooperation and as a barrier to renewed war.[28]

However, as SGSR Aldo Ajello realized in Mozambique, the tendency of elections to polarize political discourse and highlight social cleavages can work to undermine the goals of confidence-building peace processes.[29] Despite this, Andrew Reynolds and Timothy Sisk still believe that if sequenced, structured and conducted properly, elections can be appropriate instruments of conflict resolution through democratization, as in their view:

> democratization and conflict resolution are not inevitably trade-offs, [nor should] conflict resolution be promoted as a short-term alternative to democratization. Rather the critical question for both research and policy is how democratization can be conceived to achieve both aims concurrently. We do not agree with a dichotomy that juxtaposes democratic elections and social stability. On the contrary, elections can help create an environment that promotes social stability through the creation of legitimate, inclusive, representative governments.[30]

Reynolds and Sisk thus place particular emphasis on the role of institutional design and constitutional engineering in efforts to promote inclusivity and power sharing in deeply divided societies. Though they reject the notion that there exists a perfect generic package that can be applied to all societies, they do believe that, on the whole, electoral systems based on proportional representation are more favorable than majoritarian systems, as the latter tend to induce more competitive, confrontational and exclusionary politics.[31]

Providing for appropriate constitutional checks and balances is also important. As the UN realized belatedly in Angola, parliaments elected by proportional representation mean little in systems that concentrate the vast majority of political power in directly elected presidencies. Despite UNITA's impressive showing in the 1992 parliamentary elections, therefore, the loss of the presidential election left Savimbi and UNITA relatively powerless in the new state.[32]

Other constitutional means of distributing political and economic power include the design of territorial federations. However, as Harvey Glickman explains, though federalism can provide regionally concentrated minorities with greater security through the devolution of power, it also 'risks the entrenchment of recalcitrant minorities in regional enclaves, threatens to dissatisfy new subminorities seeking institutional expression of emerging group identities, invites struggle over control of resources, especially taxing powers, and, at the extreme, can create constant concern over secession'.[33]

The allocation of administrative positions is another means of promoting inclusiveness and power sharing through institutional design. As in the case of the Angolan Lusaka Protocol, parties can be allocated positions in government on the basis of the proportion of votes cast for them in elections (even if the elections themselves did not originally include the provision).[34] Of course, power-sharing deals that include the allocation of administrative positions can be negotiated before elections are held, so as to reduce the uncertainty of the electoral outcome. However, as Sisk warns, the international community's promotion of such pre-election pacts is riddled with normative considerations, especially the potential to reward aggression or appease extremists.[35] There is also the difficulty of gauging the relative strength of parties before elections are held. Just as UNITA's loss in Angola shocked many, so too did RENAMO's healthy showing in the polls in Mozambique.[36] Allocating positions on the basis of presumed popularity therefore risks over-rewarding some and unfairly depriving others.

How quickly democratic institutions should be introduced to post-war societies and whether pre-election pacts should be promoted as interim solutions are thus case specific decisions. Along with the institutional and constitutional design of the political system, it is a decision that should be based on a careful analysis of the social, cultural, political and military conditions on the ground. Accurate assessments of the parties' commitment to, and readiness for, the democratic process are particularly important. As the proceedings following Angola's 1992 elections showed, sometimes parties will willingly accept early elections due to their perception of certain victory at the ballot box, only to later complain that they were given insufficient time to prepare. UN negotiators must therefore be aware that 'ripe moments' in Track 1 diplomacy can also 'come from the paradoxical situation in which both sides believe a settlement will produce a victory for them'.[37]

The need for the UN to take account of the contextual rationality operating in distinct cultures has been a consistent theme of this study. Culture is both the means through which security is sought and the prism through which reality is perceived. Raymond Cohen describes the importance of culture well when he stresses that:

> From characterizing culture as a shared body of meaning, it is but a short step to realizing that a boundary that contains may also be a barrier that excludes...culture constructs reality; different cultures construct reality differently; communication across cultures pits different constructions of reality against each other.[38]

As discussed in Chapter 2, it is therefore imperative that the UN promotes respect for non-western socio-cultural institutions when designing its democratic transitions whilst at the same time appreciating the resistance to change they pose.[39] There can be no better example of this than Cambodia, where the demise of the Khmer Rouge and a coup in 1997 has left Prime

Minister Hun Sen once again in complete political and military control. Thus, despite the façade of continued elections, the general feeling in Cambodia is that the UN's attempts at democratization have failed.[40] Though this outcome provides credence to the socio-institutionalist argument that Cambodian culture was simply incompatible with western style democracy, the socializing effects of the UN's intervention are still evident. As Seth Mydans reported in June 2000, the greatest transformation in Cambodian society has come through the birth of a nascent civil society and a culture of human rights:

> At the start of the last decade there were just 12 local non-governmental organizations [in Cambodia]. Today there are 360, a sort of shadow government that provides services ranging from the protection of women to the digging of wells to the provision of legal aid. Many of those involved are young Cambodians who received their first education in political and civil rights during the period of United Nations control. The greatest challenge to the old power structure is the growth of local groups that protect human rights.[41]

The UN's sensitivity to local culture and its recognition that the parties were ill prepared to compete in democratic elections did play a critical part in the success of liberal social reconstruction in Mozambique. Firstly, by providing RENAMO's leader, Dhlakama with a substantial monthly allowance, the UN and international donors protected his status as an African chief and discouraged his potential return to a more meager lifestyle. Secondly, delaying the elections and establishing a Trust Fund provided RENAMO with both the time and resources required to transform itself into a viable political party. And thirdly, extending the peace process also provided additional time for the parties to communicate their commitment to peace through a more extensive implementation of the other elements of the agreements. Through financial inducements and the establishment of new norms the UN was thus able to 'socialize RENAMO into the rules of democratic competition'.[42]

Of course, elections held in the midst of UN operations are in essence only the beginning of a democratization process that may take many years to consolidate. In the words of Donald Rothchild, what is really needed is 'more attention focused on second and third elections and the maintenance process that keeps democratic systems going'.[43] And showing that she is not adverse to constructivist logic, Barbara Walter quotes Larry Diamond's observation that 'over time, citizens of a democracy become habituated to its norms and values, gradually internalizing them. The risk is for democracies to survive long enough – and function well enough – for the process to occur'.[44] Unfortunately, given the limited timeframes of its operations, the most the UN can ever hope to achieve is the creation of the best possible conditions for the birth of democracy. As in the case of Mozambique (where a second round of national elections in 1999 enjoyed an 80 per cent voter turnout) this will involve 'demilitarizing' politics to the greatest extent possible through strengthening the interim institutions that provide the context for post-settlement elections; establishing electoral administrations that can ensure free and fair elections; and engaging in programs to transform militarized factions into political parties.[45]

Nevertheless, liberal social reconstruction is not the only conflict resolution mechanism available. Nor, if the pressing aim is to stop continued fighting, will it always be the most appropriate. For example, holding elections in Somalia might only have exacerbated tribal rivalries.[46] Local traditions and culture may therefore provide a more immediate method to stop the violence and even an alternative means to promote democracy.[47] However, in Somalia both the US and UN (after SRSG Sahnoun) missed the opportunity to engage properly with traditional sources of authority and instead heightened the prestige of those whose interest lay in continued violence.

This brings us to the issue of Track 1 diplomacy at the second and third levels of war-torn societies; demobilizing soldiers and the general population. As the twin-track framework outlined in Chapter 1 suggests, Track 1 diplomacy for both these groups involves the provision of adequate public security through what is sometimes referred to as the 'tripod' of the justice system: the police, judiciary and prison system.[48] Only through prioritizing the reform of these three elements can the UN ever hope to implement the 'security first' approach that its Malian mission in the mid-1990s concluded was essential to its disarmament operations (including inducement-based disarmament such as 'buy-back' programs). As Paddy Ashdown acknowledged of the international community's approach in Bosnia, 'we thought that democracy was the highest priority and we measured it by the number of elections we could organize...In hindsight, we should have put the establishment of the rule of law first, for everything else depends on it: a functioning economy, a free and fair political system, the development of civil society, public confidence in police and the courts.[49] The provision of security is thus the key to a whole new 'social contract' between the governments and populations of post-war societies.[50]

As one-half of the coercive arm of the State, along with the military, the reform of the police provides a number of opportunities to encourage peaceful transitions from civil wars. Firstly, the police forces of war-torn societies are generally larger than that required in peaceful environments and are normally staffed with officers who reflect the ideology of the incumbent government. Structural reforms can therefore reduce their size and allow for the incorporation of former adversaries (or recruits who had no affiliation with any party to the conflict). As well as reflecting the new mood of reconciliation, these reforms can also provide the former warring parties with institutional guarantees over the State's future use of coercive force. Secondly, behavioral reforms through reeducation and training can help produce a neutral police force respectful of human rights. Altogether, these reforms will help negate the security value of weapons and promote confidence in the consolidation of peace.[51]

The UN's failure to ensure sufficient structural and behavioral reforms of local police forces thus goes a long way to explain its inability to achieve general disarmament. In cases like Angola and Mozambique the UN's mandate did not even include a role in the area of public security reform (at least initially). However, as its experiences in Cambodia, El Salvador, Angola (after Lusaka) and the former Yugoslavia proved, even when it was provided with an extensive role the UN's CIVPOL components remained incapable of fulfilling their required tasks. Although this was to a great extent due to the refusal of the parties and their police forces to accept reform, it was also due to the failure of UN member-States to ensure the Organization was supplied with properly trained personnel and appropriate levels of funding.

However, police forces are only one element of a justice system and to operate as desired they must be integrated with equally impartial and effective judicial and penal systems. As Annika Hansen has observed, for a long time these latter elements of the justice system were regarded as distinct from the establishment of police forces, a view that was reflected in the manner in which the international community has approached civilian sector reform.

> Accordingly, the legal assistance that was provided in post-settlement reconstruction tended to be the result of bilateral initiatives and was seldom linked to civilian police monitors that were dispatched under UN auspices. Cases such as Haiti, El Salvador and to a lesser degree in Bosnia – where work on the court system almost appears as an afterthought in civilian security sector reform – have contributed to the realization that police, judicial and penal reform are closely interrelated.[52]

Of course, as this study has elucidated, Angola, Cambodia and Mozambique could also be added to Hansen's list of countries in which this lesson has been taught.

Failing to protect human rights has had negative consequences for both the affected population and the UN. As Gareth Evans stated after the Cambodian operation, the 'point is simply that if a peacekeeping operation is given a mandate to guard against human rights violations, but there is no functioning system to bring violators to justice – then not only is the UN force's mandate to that extent unachievable, but its whole operation is likely to have diminished credibility, both locally and internationally'.[53] The UNTAC Special Prosecutor Mark Plunkett's own suggestion was that future operations required a 'judicial package – a systematic, prepared combination of prosecutorial, police and judicial capacities, together with a mandate to train.'[54] Though this proposal has not been formally adopted, the Panel on United Nations Peace Operations of 2000 (more commonly referred to as the Brahimi Report) recommended both the organization of enhanced CIVPOL reserves through the United Nations Stand-By Arrangements System (UNSAS) and 'similar arrangements for judicial, human rights and other relevant specialists who with specialist CIVPOL [can] make up collegial "rule of law" teams'.[55]

This still leaves open the question of how culturally sensitive the UN should be to local standards of human rights and the degree to which the rule of law should be enforced. Rami Mani argues that the 'minimal legal framework' that the UN and other international organizations usually attempt to construct, though understandably motivated by a need to be culturally sensitive, is insufficient to ensure that justice and human dignity are respected in war-torn societies. In her opinion, such a minimalist approach will not suffice 'as it is too easily manipulated in a vulnerable political situation, and too easily infused with the intent and content that suit the ruling regime'.[56] Tonya Putnam, on the other hand, believes that an approach designed to enforce individual accountability and redress human rights violations is entirely unsuited to the early stages of a peace process, not only because it may act as a stumbling block to settling the conflict, but also because it assumes the functionality of the very justice systems that these processes are designed to bring into existence. Enforcing the rule of law through external agencies is not the answer either, she believes, as this will only tend to create dependence by undermining local capacities, thus spurring a return to practices of the past when the agencies inevitably leave. Putnam recommends that agencies like the UN concentrate on introducing new norms through helping to build and train local justice systems; by implementing other elements of comprehensive agreements that affect human rights (such as ending the war, disarmament, democratic elections and the reform of the military); and by encouraging the growth of local NGOs whose protection of human rights is more 'context-driven' and permanent.[57]

Thus, deciding on the standard of human rights to be enforced is yet another difficult dilemma facing UN representatives. As with the socialization of all new norms, local cultural sensitivities and political considerations do need be taken into account. Still, providing ordinary citizens and NGOs with greater security will embolden those who wish to challenge local cultural practices and government policies that violate basic rights. This was the apparent realization of the SGSR in Angola, Alioune Blondin Beye, who in 1998 reversed UNAVEM III's policy of ignoring human rights abuses committed by the parties to the agreements, thus acknowledging that cultures of impunity can also work to undermine the prospects for peace. Nevertheless, as stressed by Putnam, the UN and international human rights organizations deployed during transitory peace processes must remain cognizant of the need to strengthen local capacities if the benefits of their presence are to be felt in the long-term.

As this conclusion has so far elucidated, when using Track 1 diplomacy the UN and international community must deal with both the security and economic value of weapons if general disarmament is to be achieved. They must also take account of the cultural (weapons as an integral part of an individual's identity and status) value of weapons when deciding on the appropriate level of disarmament to be sought. At the same time, as the analytical framework created for this study suggests, Track 2 diplomacy can also contribute to the success of UN disarmament mandates. However, whereas Track 1 diplomacy involves official negotiations with the internal parties and the suppression of conflict (or crime) through the threat or use of force, Track 2 diplomacy involves a problem-solving approach that seeks to resolve the antagonisms still existing within war-torn societies. Herbert Kelman explains the importance of Track 2 approaches when he states that to resolve rather than simply suppress conflict:

> What is required, in short, is a gradual process conducive to change in structures and attitudes, to reconciliation, and to the transformation of [relationships] – the development of a new relationship that recognizes the interdependence of the conflicting [groups] and is open to cooperative, functional arrangements between them.[58]

Track 1 and Track 2 approaches are therefore to a great extent mutually reinforcing, as the former can create an environment conducive to the success of the latter. In turn, the success of Track 2 approaches can consolidate the peace achieved through Track 1 approaches. Or, as John Prendergast and Emily Plumb express the relationship: 'for peace agreements between warring parties to lead to durable peace, there needs to be, alongside the top-down implementation of the peace agreement, concurrent bottom-up processes aimed at constructing a new social contract and healing societal divisions'.[59]

A major goal of Track 2 diplomacy is thus to generate a robust civil society that can contribute to societal reconciliation and actively participate in the search for solutions to problems lingering from the civil war. As Nat Colletta, explains, 'revitalizing civil society entails the promotion of local associations, community participation and peer accountability – all of which reduce individual fear, enable collective condemnation of violence and strengthen local security.'[60] Prendergast and Plumb reiterate this point when they note that:

> since the early 1990s civil society organizations have become involved in important, innovative projects to address issues of long-term peace-

building, including addressing trauma, organizing problem-solving workshops, training for conflict management, creating peace media, assembling peace committees, resurrecting indigenous mechanisms for conflict management, encouraging collaborative community activities and supporting democracy and human rights.[61]

One of the central contributions that the UN can make to the restoration of civil societies is to help with the orderly demobilization and reintegration of former military personnel and the peaceful return to civilian life of hitherto destabilizing forces.[62] Such help also has a direct bearing on the goal of sustainable disarmament. As the UN's own study into the issue acknowledged, 'disarmament alone has no long-term benefits if not accompanied by the demobilization and reintegration of ex-combatants into civil society through economically viable alternative lifestyles, as well as overall socio-economic development in the target country as a whole'.[63]

Though both groups are equally dependent on national socio-economic development for their long-term well being, this study has separated ex-combatants from the general population in recognition of their need for special consideration. Ex-combatants are generally uneducated, unskilled and many of them may feel insecure outside of the normal camaraderie associated with military life. This insecurity will only be exacerbated by the fear of being rejected by the communities to which they wish to return.[64] Convincing ex-combatants to adopt constructive lifestyles thus requires well-planned and resourced programs to ensure their full reintegration into society.

Of course, one alternative to reintegration is to allow as many ex-combatants as possible to continue in military service through their participation in newly unified armed forces. As mentioned earlier, the police and military together compose the coercive arm of the state and, therefore, just as structural and behavioral reforms of the police can encourage peaceful transitions from civil wars, so too can similar reforms of the armed forces. In fact, one of the most important structural reforms is to clearly distinguish the role of the military in *external* security from that of the police in the provision of *internal* security. All too often in the midst of civil wars the organizational independence of these two organizations is corrupted as the military is called upon to conduct policing operations. Other structural reforms of the military include downsizing and incorporating members of former enemy groups, as well as recruiting civilians that played no active part in the war. Again, as in the case of the police, these reforms will add to the new mood of societal reconciliation and also act as an institutional guarantee for the former warring parties over the State's future use of coercive force. Finally, behavioral reforms fostered through reeducation and training can make the armed forces more respectful of human rights and more accepting of the democratic norm of civilian control.[65]

However, as the cases in this text have proven, the reform of the military was awarded far too little attention in the design of peace agreements during the 1990s. In early examples, like those of Angola and Cambodia, the issue of military reform was treated more as a peripheral concern to the peace process rather than as an integral part of general disarmament. Only after learning the consequences of these experiences did the UN begin to adopt a more central role in overseeing the creation of these bodies. Nevertheless, as the operation in Mozambique taught those involved, only the promise of adequate pay and conditions will lure sufficient numbers of ex-combatants to volunteer for continued service when most of them will already be greatly disillusioned by their previous experiences of military life. This will require significant funding from the international community and international NGOs, many of whom have previously been reluctant to donate time and resources to the formation of military forces.

Given the size of modern professional armies, however, continued military service will only ever be an alternative for a minority of ex-combatants. The vast majority will always need to be disarmed, demobilized and reintegrated into society. Fortunately, the UN's unparalleled experience in peacekeeping operations has allowed it to accumulate a substantial degree of knowledge in the implementation of these processes, which it has set out in both the UN Department of Peacekeeping Operation's (DPKO) 1999 document, 'Disarmament, Demobilization and Reintegration of Ex-Combatants in a Peacekeeping Environment: Principles and Guidelines' and the 'Report of the Secretary-General on The Role of United Nations Peacekeeping in Disarmament and Reintegration' of 2000. The UN's learning process has been augmented by the excellent work of organizations such as the World Bank's Post-Conflict Unit, the Bonn International Center for Conversion and its own Geneva based Institute for Disarmament Research (UNIDIR). Mats Berdal's 1996 paper, 'Disarmament and Demobilization After Civil Wars', written for the International Institute for Strategic Studies, is another notable contribution.[66]

A conclusion such as this can therefore provide only a very basic outline of the lessons elucidated in both the comprehensive work of the organizations and scholars listed above and of those learnt from this study. Perhaps the most important lesson learnt from the UN's experiences so far has been the need to treat disarmament, demobilization and reintegration as a continuum in peace processes, with all three phases requiring comprehensive, integrated and coordinated planning.[67] And as Ball and Campbell have noted, the UN's experiences in operations like those of Mozambique and El Salvador, in which the planning for demobilization and reintegration was conducted separately, have proven the need to locate their planning in one civilian entity. This allows trust built during demobilization between the entity and demobilizing soldiers to be more easily transferred into the reintegration process: 'Having worked with the soldiers during demobilization the entity would [also] have a better understanding of their needs during reintegration. And finally, if one entity has supervisory responsibility for the entire planning process it can more effectively identify gaps and develop strategies for moving forward in a timely fashion.' [68] Nat Colletta also believes that 'the central coordination of demobilization and reintegration by one civilian agency with overall responsibility – balanced by decentralization of implementation authority to districts and communities through existing organizational structures – makes for a powerful institutional arrangement'. [69]

Of course, building trust requires that ex-combatants awaiting demobilization and reintegration be treated with dignity and respect. It is thus essential to ensure that the demobilization camps are capable of accommodating all who enter them and that they can be adequately supplied. One way of improving on the UN's past experiences in this regard would be to elicit the geographical locations of the demobilization camps before peace agreements are signed. As the UN has found to its detriment, former warring parties consistently seek to locate their forces in remote areas under their own control, either to ensure their protection from attack or to circumvent the UN's verification mechanisms. This makes their logistical supply a nightmare. Early designation of the sites would allow the UN additional time to either negotiate for more appropriate sites or plan for the extra requirements involved. However, regardless of the timing of designation, it is clear that the UN cannot continue to rely on the parties themselves to supply these camps. There are two reasons for this. Firstly, past experience has taught that political leaders of former warring parties tend not to take their own organization's capabilities (or lack thereof) into account when they commit themselves to do so. And secondly, the UN accepts, in good faith, that the parties will not use the logistical supply of encamped troops for their own political advantage. With so much at stake, it is not surprising to find that the UN's trust has often been misplaced.[70]

Requiring ex-combatants to build their own demobilization camps is also no way to start such an important process. As former SGSR Aldo Ajello noted, this requirement is symptomatic of the conflict between the culture of peacekeeping and the cultures of development and humanitarian aid. Whilst the latter seeks to develop indigenous capacities and has no time restrictions, the former requires political momentum and the most precipitous end to what is a very costly process.[71] However, whilst employing a civilian contractor will help solve this problem, contingency planning will always be required. As Mats Berdal emphasizes, disarmament, demobilization and reintegration are not simply managerial or administrative challenges to be overcome. Rather, they are intensely political processes.[72] Delays will, therefore, always occur. Obvious mistakes like those made in Mozambique, in which the soldiers were provided with huts designed to last days rather than months, should be avoided.[73] So too should the failure to formulate a clear policy regarding the inevitable congregation around the demobilization camps of soldiers' families.[74]

Ensuring a speedy demobilization phase is in the interest of everyone seeking peace. Not only does it reduce the costs of the peacekeeping operation, but it also prevents ex-combatants from becoming frustrated and restless. As already noted, however, delays will always occur and even the fastest demobilization process will require some time to complete. It is therefore an excellent opportunity to provide ex-combatants with training, education and health care (including psychological assistance). Nevertheless, as the Director of the US Agency for International Development (USAID) has argued, 'devising ways to educate soldiers in the assembly areas is less important than figuring out ways to get them into, through, and processed out of the camps as quickly as possible'.[75] This makes the design of demobilization packages particularly important. As Colletta notes, staggered cash entitlements have several advantages over in-kind provisions, including reducing transaction costs, stimulating local economies and allowing the beneficiaries to make more flexible use of their entitlement.[76] These cash handouts can then be linked with community-based training and education. Of course all this requires funding and organizational capacities that war-torn societies do not possess. Unfortunately, though disarmament is covered by the UN's assessed budget, demobilization and reintegration are both dependent on voluntary contributions which, if they arrive at all, are generally slow in forthcoming. There can be no surprise therefore, that the Secretary-General requested in 2000 that at least the initial stages of both processes be brought under the UN's assessed budget, a request supported by the Brahimi report of the same year.[77]

Compared to demobilization, reintegration is a relatively long-term process. In planning for reintegration the UN now advises that funding and staff be committed for a minimum of three years (the same period is advised for child soldiers).[78] The broader requirements of reintegration are stressed by Hoffman and Richter when they argue that despite the importance of training for ex-combatants, 'such training…would be incomplete if it were not embedded in an overall effort to rebuild the infrastructure, restore the national economy, create or recreate a "social net'"and fight unemployment'.[79] The interconnected needs of ex-combatants and the general population are therefore obvious. This is especially so given the usual existence of thousands of paramilitary forces and militia members who do not fit neatly into either category. Although greater planning would enable more of these forces to be accommodated in demobilization programs, the difficulty of identifying their existence will mean they will generally be left reliant on an improvement in the overall economy and civil society.

The demobilization and reintegration of ex-combatants is thus a contributor to, and a beneficiary of, the emergence of a vibrant civil society. As

John Prendergast and Emily Plumb note, while disarmament, demobilization and reintegration will always depend on the support of international organizations, local civil society organizations 'can be ideal in implementing them and seeing them through to the more advanced stages of reintegration. For instance they can help former combatants find new employment, teach them marketable skills, treat post-traumatic stress disorder cases, and meet the special needs of former child and female soldiers'. They are also better equipped to understand the needs of the community and more sensitive to cultural norms. [80] It is therefore essential for the UN and international NGOs to dedicate themselves to enhancing local civil society organizations and for civil society to participate to the maximum extent possible in the design and execution of the UN's disarmament, demobilization and reintegration programs.[81]

Finally, the UN's success in implementing its mandates will always depend on the international community's willingness to provide it with the resources and capabilities it needs. As the cases in this text have shown, the UN's personnel shortages, together with its weaknesses in planning, procurement and funding, have all contributed to the difficulties it has faced. Sustainable disarmament also requires that the international community remain engaged, even in those cases like Angola, where disarmament has failed in the past. With the death of Jonas Savimbi in April 2002 the former warring parties have finally negotiated an end to the war and the disarmament, demobilization and reintegration of UNITA's forces. Democratic elections are due to be held in 2004 or 2005. A new civil society also seems to be growing, with 300 local NGOs having registered since it became legal to do so in 1991. Nevertheless, hundreds of thousands of troops remain encamped as of early 2003 without food, medicine or water.[82] As the quote of Sebastiao Chiwisse at the beginning of this chapter attests, the problems faced by UNITA's soldiers today are the same as those they faced over a decade ago.

Perhaps, therefore, it is fitting to give the last word to the former UN Secretary-General, Boutros Boutros-Ghali, who after years of striving to implement disarmament mandates provided by the world's most powerful states (and greatest purveyors of light and heavy arms) on the Security Council, expressed the continuing irony of his Organization's predicament, when he stated that:

> The world is witnessing amazing contradictions. Arms are manufactured in rich countries for sale to poor ones at a healthy profit. These same wealthy states later spend much greater sums on relief for the victims of the wars their arms made possible and on clearing the mines they sold from the lands they were designed to destroy.[83]

Notes

Introduction

1. R. Licklider, quoted in T.D. Mason and P.J. Fett, 'How Civil Wars End', *Journal of Conflict Resolution*, Vol. 40, No. 4 (1996) pp. 547.
2. S. Croft, *Lessons from the Disarmament of Factions in Civil Wars*, Paper presented at the BISA Conference, Southampton, 1995.
3. Stern and Druckman explain that 'structured, focused case comparisons differ from the traditional case study approach in that cases are selected and case descriptions developed with particular theory-guided questions or conceptual issues in mind. The method requires that an analytical protocol be developed before the case studies are conducted that defines the variable of interest and some of the researcher's key questions about them. This allows the researcher to compare the cases on the central issues of interest. See P.C. Stern and D. Druckman, 'Evaluating Interventions in History: The Case of International Conflict Resolution', in P.C. Stern, and D. Druckman (eds), *International Conflict Resolution after the Cold War* (Washington: National Academy Press, 2000) pp. 72–3.

Chapter 1

1. H.J. Morgenthau, *Politics Among Nations: The Struggle for Power and Peace* (New York: Alfred A. Knopf, 1948) p. 327.
2. E. Azar, 'Protracted International Conflict: Ten Propositions' in H. Starr (ed.), *The Understanding and Management of Global Violence* (New York: St. Martin's Press, 1999) p. 32.
3. A. Ajello, 'Mozambique: Implementation of the 1992 Peace Agreement', in C. Crocker, F.O. Hampson and P. Aall (eds), *Herding Cats: Multi-Party Mediation in a Complex World* (Washington D.C.: USIPP, 1999) p. 639.
4. *The Blue Helmets: A Review of United Nations Peacekeeping* (New York: United Nations, 1990) p. 4.
5. For an account of the evolution of UN peacekeeping during the Cold War see A. James, *Peacekeeping in International Politics* (London: Macmillan Press, 1990) or S. Hill and S. Malik, *Peacekeeping and the United Nations* (Aldershot: Dartmouth Press, 1996). The 13 operations were the UN Special Commission on the Balkans (1947–51); the UN Truce Supervision Organization (1948–present); the UN Military Observer Group in India and Pakistan (1949–present); the UN Emergency Force (1956–67); the UN Observation Group in Lebanon (1958); the UN Operation in the Congo (1960–64); the UN Temporary Executive Authority (1962–63); the UN Yemen Observation Mission (1963–64); the UN Force in Cyprus (1964–present); the UN India-Pakistan Observer Mission (1965–66), the UN Emergency Force II (1974–79); the UN Disengagement Force (1979–present); and the UN Interim Force in Lebanon (1978–present).
6. B. Boutros-Ghali, 'UN Peacekeeping in a New Era: A New Chance For Peace', *World Today*, (1993) 66.
7. *United Nations Press Release, SG/SM/95/147, 3 July 1995.*

8. Boutros-Ghali, op. cit., p. 67.
9. B. Boutros-Ghali, *Agenda for Peace* (New York: United Nations, 1992) pp. 26–7.
10. A. James, 'Is There a Second Generation of Peacekeeping?', *International Peace-keeping*, Vol. 1, No. 4 (1994) 10–11. Presumably James would have the same problem with the term coined by Boutros-Ghali himself: that of 'expanded peacekeeping'. As Boutros-Ghali includes the possibility of the use of force in his conception, it is reasonable to assume that James would argue this was more than an 'expansion' of peacekeeping as legally conceived. See B. Boutros-Ghali, 'An Agenda for Peace, One Year Later', *Orbis*, Vol. 37, No. 3 (1993) p. 328.
11. In line with James' determination many of the principal UN peacekeeping contributors have conceptually separated 'peace enforcement' from 'peacekeeping' in their military doctrines. See, for example, US Army doctrine *FM 100-23: Peace Operations* and UK Army doctrine *Wider Peacekeeping*.
12. The UN Security Council had already recognized the possibility of this when, after the experience of peacekeeping in the Congo, it changed the rules of engagement for its peacekeepers in 1973 to include the use of force against anyone preventing the UN from implementing its mandate.
13. M.W. Doyle, 'War Making, Peace Making, and the United Nations', in C. Crocker, F.O. Hampson and P. Aall (eds), *Turbulent Peace: The Challenges of Managing International Conflict* (Washington: USIPP, 2001) p. 532.
14. They are also sometimes called 'light arms'.
15. The UN Panel of Governmental Experts on Small Arms in its 1997 report included 'clubs, knives and machetes' in its definition. Landmines are often treated as a separate and individual category of 'light weapons', especially in the context of international agreements. Other definitions of light weapons include weapons that can be carried by an infantry soldier or perhaps a small vehicle or pack animal and weapons that do not need elaborate logistical and maintenance capability and can therefore be employed by insurgent groups and paramilitary formations. The best categorization of 'heavy weapons' is the UN Register of Conventional Weapons, which lists seven categories of heavy weapons as battle tanks; armored combat vehicles; large caliber artillery; combat aircraft; attack helicopters; warships; and missiles/launchers. See A. Latham, 'Taking the Lead? Light Weapons and International Conflict', *International Journal*, 318 and E.J. Laurance, 'Surplus Weapons and the Micro-Disarmament Process', *Disarmament: A Periodic Review by the United Nations*, Vol. 19, No. 2 (1996) p. 59 and *Small Arms*, Study Series 28 (New York: United Nations, 1999) p. 11.
16. The UN Register of Conventional Weapons is an attempt to increase the transparency of international conventional arms flows and to highlight destabilizing accumulations of weapons. Former UN Secretary-General, Boutros Boutros-Ghali, recommended as far back as 1994 that small arms and light weapons be included as a category. However, a lack of consensus among member States has prevented such action being taken as of 2002.
17. H. Wulf, 'Disarming and Demobilizing Ex-Combatants: Implementing Micro-Disarmament', *Disarmament: A Periodic Review by the United Nations*, Vol. 19, No. 2 (1996) p. 55.
18. In one instance the newly unified German government donated 304,000 AK-47s and 5,000 RPG-7 grenade launchers to the Turkish military. M.T. Klare, 'The International Trade in Light Weapons: What Have We Learned', in J. Boutwell and M.T. Klare (eds), *Light Weapons and Civil Conflict: Controlling the*

Tools of Violence (Lanham: Rowman and Littlefield, 1999) p. 17 and Latham, op. cit., p. 326.

19. Global arms exports declined in real terms by 61 per cent between 1987 and 1995. See N. Cooper, 'The Arms Trade and Militarized Actors in Internal Conflicts', in P.B. Rich (ed.), *Warlords in International Relations* (London: Macmillan Press, 1999) p. 18 and P. Lock, 'Armed Conflicts and Small Arms Proliferation: Refocusing the Research Agenda', *Policy Sciences*, Vol. 30, No. 3 (1997) p. 120 and J. Van der Graaf, 'Proliferation of Light Weapons in Africa', *Policy Sciences*, Vol. 30, No. 3 (1997) p. 140.

20. Latham, op. cit., p. 325 and B. Urquart, 'The United Nations in 1992: Problems and Opportunities', *International Affairs*, Vol. 68, No. 2 (1992) p. 315. Cooper notes that the market share of non-traditional military suppliers (those outside Russia, the US and Europe) had increased from 3 per cent in 1981 to 13 per cent in 1995. Cooper, op. cit., p. 18.

21. Spear, op. cit., p. 396. M. Phythian, 'The Price of Success', *The World Today* (2001). For example, in 1996 the US Congress passed an amendment to the 1976 Arms Control Export Act that requires American arms brokers anywhere in the world and foreign nationals living or working in the US to register and obtain licenses for all arms deals they make, whether on or off American soil. Despite being heralded as one of the best legislative instruments in the world for controlling arms middlemen, not a single broker had been prosecuted for failing to register deals under the statute as of 2001. 'Arms Traffickers', *International Herald Tribune*, 3 July 2001.

22. J. Spear, 'Arms Limitations, Confidence-Building Measures and Internal Conflict', in M. Brown (ed.), *International Dimensions of Internal Conflict* (Massachusetts: MIT Press, 1996) pp. 382–3.

23. M. Phythian, op. cit.

24. United Nations document, S/2002/1053, 20 September 2002. 60 per cent of these weapons are believed to be legally held by civilians.

25. In February 2002 US and European law enforcement officials claimed that they had scored an important advance in breaking what some officials called the 'biggest weapons-trafficking network in the world' responsible for supplying the Taliban and terrorist groups from Al Qaeda in Afghanistan to the Abu Sayyaf in the Philippines, as well as rebel forces in Africa. However, many of the weapons that supplied this network were manufactured in the very countries trying to break it. For instance, as recently as 2001 Al-Qaeda supporters are believed to have bought American- made missiles and small arms in the Pakistani city of Peshawar. See R. Norton-Talyor, 'Arms deals hinder war on terror, says Amnesty', *The Guardian*, 24 June 2002 and D. Farah, 'Arrest Aids Pursuit of Weapons Network', *The Washington Post*, 26 February 2002.

26. Many observers note that the supply network for light weapons is virtually identical to that of drugs. Lock, op. cit., p. 120 and M. Goulding, 'Expanding the Disarmament Agenda', *Disarmament: A periodic Review by the United Nations*, Vol. 19, No. 2 (1996) p. 35–6.

27. Cooper, op. cit., p. 22.

28. Spear, op. cit., p. 389 and Ajello, op. cit., p. 639.

29. Klare notes that Edward Laurance uses the term 'circulation', whilst he prefers the term 'diffusion'. Proliferation denotes only the spread of one type of weapon from one or two States to many. See, Klare, op. cit., p. 21.

30. According to the UN 500,000 people continue to die every year as a result of small arms use. *United Nations document*, S/2002/1053, op. cit.

31. Spear, op. cit., p. 378.
32. For evidence of disarmers being concerned by the security dilemma and an excellent overview of the development of arms control see T. Salmon, 'The Nature of International Security' and M. Sheehan, 'Arms Control and International Security', both in R. Carey and T. Salmon (eds), *International Security in the Modern World* (New York: St. Martin's Press, 1992).
33. Small Arms, op. cit., pp. 15–6.
34. Spear, op. cit., pp. 380, 396.
35. Sislin and Pearson, op. cit., p. 60.
36. J.H. Herz, 'Idealist Internationalism and the Security Dilemma', *World Politics*, Vol. 2, No. 2 (1950) pp. 157–80.
37. B. Posen, 'The Security Dilemma and Ethnic Conflict', *Survival*, Vol. 35, No. 1 (1993).
38. J. Sislin and F.S. Pearson, *Arms and Ethnic Conflict* (Lanham: Rowman and Littlefield, 2001) pp. 60, 65. Latham, op. cit., p. 320.
39. Latham, op. cit. p. 321 and K. Krause, 'Multilateral Diplomacy, Norm Building, and UN Conferences: The Case of Small Arms and Light Weapons', *Global Governance*, Vol. 8 (2002) 251 and *Small Arms*, op. cit., p. 16.
40. S. Croft, *Strategies of Arms Control* (Manchester: University of Manchester Press, 1996) p. 195.
41. Ibid.
42. B. Boutros-Ghali, 'Global Leadership after the Cold War', *Foreign Affairs*, Vol. 75, No. 2 (1996) p. 93.
43. *Small Arms*, op. cit., p. 19. According to Fung the Secretary-General had already concluded an in-house study that had reached the same conclusion. See I.R. Fung, 'Control and Collection of Light Weapons in Sahel-Sahara Subregion: A Mission Report', *Disarmament*, Vol. 19, No. 2 (1996) p. 45.
44. *Small Arms*, op. cit., p. 58. In October 1998 the DDA created a home page on the Internet devoted to conventional arms, in particular small arms (http://www.un.org/Depts/dda/CAB/index.htm).
45. Idem. Other notable events in the evolution of international action on the issue of small arms and light weapons include the meeting of 21 States in Oslo, Norway, in July 1998, to discuss appropriate action. The meeting's final document was entitled, *An International Agenda on Small Arms and Light Weapons: Elements of a Common Understanding*. In October 1998 an *International Conference on Sustainable Disarmament for Sustainable Development* was also held in Brussels, Belgium. Another significant development was the first meeting of 'The Group of Interested States in Practical Disarmament Measures (GIS)' in March 1998. The GIS meets on a regular basis and provides financial, technical and political support for disarmament projects. For more information on the work of the GIS go to http://www.disarmament.un.org/cab/pdm-gis.html. *Small Arms*, op. cit., pp. 5, 60.
46. Idem.
47. B. Boutros-Ghali, 'Address of the Secretary-General to the Advisory Board on Disarmament Matters', *Disarmament*, Vol. 19, No. 2 (1996) p. 5.
48. Fung, op. cit., p. 47.
49. *Small Arms*, op. cit., p. 23.
50. The *Program of Action to Prevent, Combat and Eradicate the Illicit Trade in Small Arms and Light Weapons in all its Aspects* includes a number of commitments made by the conference participants at the national, regional and global levels. These include commitments to enhance national legislation to regulate the

production and transfer of small arms and light weapons; to support and establish regional moratoria on their manufacture and transfer; and to encourage States to promote safe, effective stockpile management and security, in particular physical security measures for their small arms and light weapons. The Conference has been criticized by some States and NGOs for failing to negotiate an international mechanism to trace illicit small arms (only a UN feasibility study was agreed); for failing to regulate the civilian possession of weapons (the US was the principal state opposing such action); for failing to increase transparency in the production, stockpiling and trade in small arms and light weapons; and for failing to agree on specific criteria (that is, a code of conduct) governing exports; or negotiate agreements to regulate arms brokering. K. Krause, Multilateral Diplomacy, Norm Building and UN Conferences: The Case of Small Arms and Light Weapons, *Global Governance*, Vol. 8 (2002) 251. For a discussion of the limitations and achievements of the conference see also A. Karp, 'Laudable Failure', *SAIS Review*, Vol. 22, No. 1 (2002) and O. Greene, 'The 2001 UN Conference: A Useful Step Forward?', *SAIS Review*, Vol. 22, No. 1 (2002). Copies of the *Program of Action* are available at http://www.disarmament.un.org/cab/poa.html

51. *United Nations document, S/2002/1053*, 20 September 2002.
52. *Small Arms*, op. cit., p. 59. The DDA also convened meetings of relevant experts in 1999 in order to help curb the illicit manufacture and trade in small arms.
53. *United Nations document*, S/2002/1053.
54. Idem.
55. *United Nations document, S/200/101*, 11 February 2000.
56. The first UN operation to undertake both disarmament and demobilization was ONUCA. All the other 13 operations also undertook at least both these processes except UNOSOM II, which only assumed forceful disarmament, and MINURCA, in which the UN was mandated only to disarm and destroy weapons. Idem.
57. These studies are listed in the bibliography.
58. The *Report of the Group of Experts on the Problem of Ammunition and Explosives* was also produced in June 1999.
59. This report is *UN document S/2000/101*, 11 February 2000.
60. T.D. Mason and P.J. Fett, 'How Civil Wars End', *Journal of Conflict Resolution*, Vol. 40, No. 4 (1996) p. 546.
61. S.J. Stedman, 'Negotiation and Mediation in Internal Conflict', in *The International Dimensions of Internal Conflict*, op. cit., p. 343 and R. Licklider, 'The Consequences of Negotiated Settlements in Civil Wars 1945–1995', *American Political Science Review*, Vol. 89, No. 3 (1995).
62. H.J. Morgenthau, *Politics Among Nations: The Struggle for Power and Peace* (New York: Alfred A Knopf: 1954) p. 384.
63. R.K. Betts, 'The Delusion of Impartial Intervention', *Foreign Affairs*, Vol. 73, No. 6 (1994). E.N. Luttwak, 'Give War a Chance', *Foreign Affairs* (1999).
64. E.N. Luttwak, 'Give War a Chance', *Foreign Affairs*, Vol. 78, No. 4 (1999) 38.
65. S.J. Stedman, 'Spoiler Problems in Peace Processes', in P.C. Stern and D. Druckman (eds), *International Conflict Resolution After the Cold War* (Washington D.C.: National Academy Press, 2000) p. 182.
66. J. Snyder and R. Jervis, 'Civil War and the Security Dilemma', in B.F. Walter and J. Snyder (eds), *Civil Wars, Insecurity and Intervention,* (New York: Columbia University Press, 1999) p. 28.

67. B.F. Walter, 'Designing Transitions from Civil War' in B.F. Walter and J. Snyder (eds), *Civil Wars, Insecurity and Intervention*, Ibid, p. 46. See also B.F. Walter, *Committing to Peace* (Princeton, Princeton University Press, 2002).

68. C.A. Hartzell, 'Explaining the Stability of Negotiated Settlements of Intra-State Wars', *Journal of Conflict Resolution*, Vol. 43, No. 1 (1999) p. 7.

69. Idem, p. 6.

70. M. Hoddie and C.A. Hartzell, 'Civil War Settlements and the Implementation of Military-Power-Sharing Arrangements', *Journal of Peace Research*, Vol. 40, No. 3 (2003) p. 312.

71. Idem. pp. 304–306. Hartzell's Neo-Liberalism is also evident in her assessment of the implementation of the Esquipulas II Accords for Central America in which she asserts that ' [c]entral to the successful implementation of the Nicaraguan peace accords was the creation by the Central American presidents of an implementation regime focused on monitoring and verification of progress towards peace. That the Central American parties acknowledged their limitations, and were willing to divide implementation responsibilities accordingly, strengthened this regime and helped surmount difficulties faced by the peace process'. See C.A. Hartzell, 'Peace in Stages: The Role of an Implementation Regime in Nicaragua', in S.J. Stedman, D. Rothchild and E.M. Cousens (eds), *Ending Civil Wars: The Implementation of Peace Agreements* (London: Lynne Rienner, 2002) p. 354.

72. Hoddie and Hartzell, op. cit., p. 316.

73. A. Wendt, 'Constructing International Politics', *International Security*, Vol. 20, No. 1 (1995) pp. 71–2.

74. Ibid., p. 73.

75. A. Wendt, *Social Theory of International Politics* (Cambridge: Cambridge University Press, 1999) p. 141.

76. Ibid., pp. 165–6 and A. Wendt, 'Identity and Structural Change in International Politics', in Y. Lapid and F. Kratochwil (eds), *The Return of Culture and Identity in IR Theory* (Boulder, Colo.: Lynne Rienner, 1996) p. 51.

77. Wendt, *Social Theory of International Politics*, op. cit., pp. 169–70. For an explanation of the limitations of Neo-Realism and Neo-Liberalism as rationalist theories, as well as the recognition of these limitations by preeminent theorists in each tradition, see P.J. Katzenstein, 'Introduction: Alternative Perspectives on National Security', in P.J. Katzenstein (ed.), *The Culture of National Security* (New York: Columbia University Press, 1996) pp. 11–7.

78. Wendt, *Social Theory of International Politics*, op. cit., p. 250.

79. Ibid., p. 342.

80. Ibid., p. 250.

81. R.L. Jepperson, A. Wendt and P.J. Katzenstein, 'Norms, Identity and Culture in National Security' in P.J. Katzenstein (ed.), *The Culture of National Security*, op. cit., pp. 43–4.

82. B. Arfi, 'Ethnic Fear: The Social Construction of Insecurity', *Security Studies*, Vol. 8, No. 1 (1998) p. 160. Arfi's three 'social identities' do not correspond exactly to Wendt's. The principle difference seems to be Arfi's refusal to accept that a security dilemma can exist in a competitive culture. This is only possible if force is never expected to be used, which is not the definition used by Wendt. Arfi does not quite explain why groups who do not perceive each other as possible threats would still be concerned with relative gains.

83. Wendt, *Social Theory of International Politics*, op. cit., p. 265.

84. Ibid., p. 282.

85. This is a paraphrase of Wendt's most famous statement. See A. Wendt, 'Anarchy is What States Make of it: The Social Construction of Power-Politics', *International Organization*, Vol. 46 (1992).
86. A. Wendt, 'Identity and Structural Change in International Politics', in Lapid and Kratochwil (eds), *The Return of Culture and Identity in IR Theory*, op. cit., p. 50.
87. Went, *Social Theory of International Politics,* op. cit., p. 327.
88. Idem.
89. Katzenstein, op. cit., p. 25.
90. Went, *Social Theory of International Politics*, op. cit., p. 186.
91. Ibid., p. 188.
92. Idem.
93. Idem.
94. Ibid., p. 210.
95. S. White quoted in D.L. Jones, Ibid., p. 650.
96. For excellent overviews of the development of third party participation in conflict settlement and resolution see H. Maill, O. Ramsbotham and T. Woodhouse, *Contemporary Conflict Resolution* (Oxford: Polity Press, 1999) and L. Kreisberg, 'The Development of the Conflict Resolution Field', in I.W. Zartman and J.L. Rasmussen (eds), *Peacemaking in International Conflict: Methods and Techniques* (Washington D.C.: USIPP, 2002).
97. D.G. Pruitt, 'The Tactics of Third-Party Intervention', *Orbis*, Vol. 44, No. 2, (2000) 245 and P. Terrence Hopmann, 'Bargaining and Problem-Solving: Two Perspectives on International Negotiation', in Crocker et al., *Turbulent Peace*, op. cit., p. 448.
98. D.L. Jones, 'Mediation, Conflict Resolution and Critical Theory', *Review of International Studies*, Vol. 26 (2000) p. 649.
99. S. White, quoted in Ibid., p. 650.
100. M. Hoffman, 'Third-Party Mediation and Conflict Resolution in the Post-Cold War World', in J. Bayliss and N.J. Renegger, *Dilemmas of World Politics* (Clarendon Press, 1992) p. 266.
101. A mutually hurting stalemate is defined as a feeling of stalemate or deadlock between the warring parties; a situation in which each party realizes it is locked in a painful conflict from which it cannot escalate to victory. However, as Zartman makes clear, the stalemate may not necessarily be equally painful to each party or be so for the same reasons. Though the combination of a mutually hurting stalemate and the feeling that continued conflict will only lead to significantly greater pain is conducive to successful mediation, the latter is neither necessary for the definition or the existence of a mutually hurting stalemate. I.W. Zartman, 'Ripeness: The Hurting Stalemate and Beyond', in Stern and D. Druckman, op. cit., p. 228.
102. S.J. Stedman, *Peacemaking in Civil War* (London: Lynne Rienner, 1991) p. 25.
103. J. Bercovitch and A. Houston, 'The Study of International Mediation: Theoretical Issues and Empirical Evidence', in J. Bercovitch (ed.), *Resolving International Conflicts* (Boulder Colo.: Lynne Rienner, 1996) p. 26.
104. H.C. Kelman, 'The Interactive Problem-Solving Approach', in C.A. Crocker, F.O. Hampson and P. All, *Managing Global Chaos: Sources and Responses to International Conflict* (Washington D.C.: USIPP, 1996) p. 503. E. Azar, 'Protracted International Conflict: Ten Propositions' in H. Starr (ed.), *The Understanding and Management of Global Violence* (New York: St Martin's Press, 1999) p. 25. John Burton refers to the human needs of identity, recognition and autonomy,

which he believes are inherent in all individuals regardless of culture. He therefore argues that if his human needs theory is correct then there are some behaviors that cannot be either deterred by coercion or altered through socialization. Jurgen Habermas, on the other hand, in a more critical analysis, refers to 'need interpretations' which emphasizes their cultural variability. See Burton, op. cit., pp. 4–5, 36 and Jones, op. cit., p. 656.

105. M. Hoffman, quoted in Jones, op. cit., p. 654.
106. M. Hoffman in 'Third-Party Mediation and Conflict Resolution in the Post-Cold War World', op. cit., p. 271.
107. Kelman, op. cit., p. 507.
108. C.L. Yordan, *Negative Peacemaking in Bosnia: The Failure of the State-Building Program*, Paper presented at the ISA Conference, Los Angeles, USA (2001).
109. V. Jabri, 'Agency, Structure, and the Question of Power in Conflict Resolution', *Paradigms*, Vol. 9, No. 2 (1995) p. 66.
110. J.W. Burton, *Conflict: Resolution and Provention*, (London: Macmillan, 1990) pp. 2–3 and Yordan, op. cit.
111. Burton, op. cit., p. 121.

Chapter 2

1. K. Somerville, 'The Failure of Democratic Reform in Angola and Zaire', *Survival*, Vol. 35, No. 3 (1993) pp. 59–60.
2. The head of the US negotiation team, Chester Crocker, claimed that US insistence on a linkage was based on the belief that the prospects of reconciliation and negotiated political change within states was directly affected by the climate of security (or insecurity) between them. Nevertheless, the UN rejected this linkage calling the presence of troops in Angola an 'irrelevant and extraneous' issue to the independence of Namibia. C. Crocker, in D. Wendt, 'The Peacemakers: Lessons of Conflict Resolution for the Post-Cold War World', *Washington Quarterly*, Vol. 17, No. 3 (1994) p. 167. See also UNSC Resolution 566 (1985).
3. A. Parsons, *From Cold War to Hot Peace* (London: Penguin, 1995) p. 118.
4. C. Crocker quoted in J. Hamill, 'Angola's Road from Under the Rubble', *World Today*, Vol. 50, No. 1 (1994) p. 8.
5. Hamill states that all reference to 'parity', which had been central to Soviet requirements during negotiations in the 1970s, had disappeared by the beginning of the 1990s. Hamill, op. cit., p. 8. In March 1991 Somerville was told by an Angolan diplomat based in East Africa that the MPLA was being forced to accept a deal more favorable to UNITA because the US still supported UNITA steadfastly, while the USSR was pushing the MPLA to accept 'any deal' because of Moscow's desire to curry favor with Washington. Somerville, op. cit., footnote 11, pp. 76–7.
6. Ibid, p. 54.
7. Hamill, op. cit., p. 8.
8. G. Wright, *The Destruction of a Nation-US Policy Toward Angola Since 1945* (London: Pluto Press, 1997) pp. 142–7.
9. The MPLA was concerned by the Portuguese President Mario Soares' support for UNITA, yet he had maintained fairly good relations with the Angolan government. Although UNITA believed Portuguese business interests with the Angolan government might jeopardize its neutrality, it also perceived Portugal

244   *Notes*

(as a democracy) to be in support of UNITA's goal of a multi-party state. See P.F. Fortna, 'United Nations Angola Verification Mission II', in W. Durch (ed.), *The Evolution of UN Peacekeeping* (New York: St. Martin's Press, 1993).

10. Wright, op. cit., p. 156.
11. Ibid., p. 157.
12. Ibid., p. 158.
13. Ibid., pp. 158–9.
14. S. R. Ratner, *The New UN Peacekeeping* (New York: St. Martin's Press, 1995) pp. 139–40.
15. Ibid., p. 141.
16. Although China remained the only country directly supplying the Khmer Rouge, US overt and covert aid to its partners in the CGDK amounted to nearly $30 million per year. W.S. Turley, 'The Khmer War: Cambodia After Paris', *Survival*, Vol. 32, No. 5 (1990) p. 438.
17. Only 7,000 to 8,000 of these troops were believed to be 'hard core' troops, unquestionably loyal to their leader Pol Pot.
18. Turley, op. cit., p. 443.
19. J. Chopra in T. Findlay, *Cambodia and the Lessons of UNTAC*, SIPRI Research Report No. 9 (Oxford: Oxford University Press, 1995) p. 3.
20. Turley, op. cit., pp. 443–4.
21. P. Lizee, 'Peacekeeping, Peace-Building and the Challenge of Conflict Resolution in Cambodia', in D. Charters (ed.), *Peacekeeping and the Challenge of Conflict Resolution* (Canada: University of New Brunswick, 1994) p. 138.
22. Turley, op. cit., p. 439.
23. Idem and Ratner, op. cit., p. 143.
24. *The Comprehensive Settlement Plan for Cambodia* (CSPC), 23 October 1991.
25. M. Hong, 'The Paris Agreement on Cambodia: In Retrospect', *International Peacekeeping*, Vol. 2, No. 1 (1995) p. 93.
26. Findlay, op. cit., pp. 5–6.
27. Turley, op. cit., p. 441.
28. Ratner, op. cit., p. 145.
29. J. Wang, *Managing Arms in Peace Processes: Cambodia* (Geneva: UNIDIR, 1996) p. 10.
30. Idem.
31. Ratner, op. cit., p. 145.
32. President of the SoC quoted in Wang, op. cit., p. 11.
33. Idem.
34. CPSC, op. cit., and Findlay, op. cit., p. 10.
35. Peace Accords for Angola, 1 May 1991
36. The FAA was also to include a 6,000 strong Air Force and a 4,000 strong Navy. However, UNITA did not have Naval or Air Force personnel and therefore its participation in these forces was delayed until they could be adequately trained.
37. The three observer States did include a declaration in the Accords requesting that the elections be held by 1 October 1992, so as 'to reduce the high costs that the international community will have to bear in monitoring the cease-fire'.
38. Somerville, op. cit., p. 61.
39. Fortna, op. cit., p. 352.
40. CSPC, op. cit.
41. The SRSG was to make this determination.

42. Idem.
43. M. Doyle and N. Suntharalingham, 'The UN in Cambodia, Lessons for Complex Peacekeeping', *International Peacekeeping*, Vol. 1, No. 2 (1994) p. 124.
44. Somerville, op. cit., p. 59.
45. Quoted in Ibid., p. 62.
46. The other defector was the former UNITA Secretary-General, Miguel N'Zau Puna. Hamill, op. cit., p. 10 and Somerville, op. cit., p. 62.
47. Ibid., p. 63.
48. Fortna, op. cit., p. 400. UNITA also claimed that up to 30,000 MPLA troops that had supposedly been demobilized had actually been transferred into the Government's anti-riot police, or 'Ninjas'. M. Chaka quoted in K. Hart and J. Lewis, *Why Angola Matters* (Cambridge: University of Cambridge, 1995) p. 38.
49. Only 8,000 troops had been trained for the new army.
50. Wright, op. cit., p. 168.
51. J. Campino in *Why Angola Matters*, op. cit., p. 89.
52. Anstee made her statement at 4.00 pm on 17 October. F.O. Hampson, *Nurturing Peace-Why Peace Settlements Succeed or Fail* (Washington: USIP, 1996) p. 114.
53. *The Situation in Angola* (New York: United Nations, 1993) p. 4.
54. These officials included UNITA's Vice-President, Jeremias Chitunda and UNITA's chief representative on the JPMC (a close relative of Savimbi), Salupeto Pena. Idem.
55. *Why Angola Matters*, op. cit., p. 11.
56. *United Nations document, S/24826*, 14 July 1992.
57. To ensure no military advantage was accrued, all subsequent regroupments and cantonments took place in areas were there was no military confrontation. The Secretary-General also stipulated that some cantoned troops might be allowed to retain their weapons until the situation with the PDK had been clarified. Idem.
58. Although some PDK soldiers had shown an interest in demobilizing, their commanding officers had maintained tight control of their actions. However, by November 1992, 200 PDK personnel had 'spontaneously presented themselves to UNTAC'. *United Nations documents, S/24800*, 15 November 1992, and *S/24286*, 14 July 1992.
59. 'Letter dated 27 July 1992, from the SRSG for Cambodia, concerning the situation in Cambodia', *The UN and Cambodia*, op. cit., p. 206
60. The exact number cantoned was 52,292. All forces given agricultural leave had to first hand in their weapons and identification card. They were also subject to recall at two weeks notice to ensure 100 per cent cantonment before the process of formal demobilization began. *United Nations documents, S/24578*, 21 September 1992 and *S/24800*, 15 November 1992.
61. Idem.
62. *United Nations document, S/25913*, 10 June 1993.
63. *The UN and Cambodia*, op. cit., p. 46.
64. D. Roberts, 'More Honoured in the Breech: Consent and Impartiality in the Cambodian Peacekeeping Operation', *International Peacekeeping*, Vol. 4 No. 1 (1997) p. 13
65. The secession was short-lived, however, ending with Chakrapong's exile to Vietnam three days later. Ibid., p. 11 and The UN and Cambodia, op. cit., p. 47.
66. Roberts notes that the US tried to prevent Sihanouk from assuming the position of Head of State, even after the internal parties had elected him to the position in the Cambodian Assembly. Ibid., pp. 15–16.

67. See B. Boutros-Ghali, *Agenda for Peace* (New York: United Nations, 1992).

68. B. Boutros-Ghali, 'UN Peacekeeping in a New Era: A New Chance for Peace', *World Today* (1993) p. 67.

69. W. Durch, 'Paying the Tab: Financial Crises' in *The Evolution of UN Peacekeeping*, op. cit., p. 41.

70. M. Berdal, *UN Peacekeeping at a Crossroads: The Challenges of Management and Institutional Reform*, IFS Info, No. 7 (1993) p. 10.

71. M.J. Anstee, *Orphan of the Cold War* (London: Macmillan Press, 1996) p. 192.

72. Berdal, op. cit., p. 10

73. Fortna, op. cit., pp. 395, 398.

74. 'Unclear', *The Economist*, February 29, 1992.

75. P. Lewis, 'UN sets June deadline in Cambodia', *The International Herald Tribune*, 11 May 1992.

76. S. Awanohara and R. Delfs, 'Travelling Salesman', *Far Eastern Economic Review*, 9 April 1992, p. 12.

77. N. Thayer, 'Biding their time', *Far Eastern Economic Review*, 27 February 1992, p. 27.

78. Lewis, op. cit. The US also owed $112 million for past operations.

79. *United Nations document*, S/23613, 19 February 1992.

80. *United Nations document*, S/24578, September 1992.

81. J.A. Schear quoted in T. Findlay, op. cit., p. 113.

82. T. Findlay, 'UNTAC: Lessons to be Learned', *International Peacekeeping*, Vol. 1, No. 1 (1994) p. 7.

83. *United Nations document. S/23780*, 1 May 1992.

84. Berdal, op. cit., p. 6.

85. Ibid., p. 114.

86. Findlay, *Cambodia: The Lessons and Legacy of UNTAC*, op. cit., p. 117–18.

87. The DPKO was headed by an Under-Secretary-General and consisted of four divisions (Europe and Latin America, Asia, the Middle East, Africa and Electoral Assistance). It also included an Office of Planning and Support, which consisted of a Planning Division and a Field Administration and Logistics Division.

88. J.M. Sanderson, 'UNTAC: Successes and Failures', in H. Smith (ed.), *International Peacekeeping, Building on the Cambodia Experience* (Canberra: Australian Defence Studies Centre, 1994) p. 18.

89. With only six military officers (donated by member states) and six civilian personnel the military survey mission was also unable to evaluate the modalities for the control of the cease-fire and the cessation of outside military assistance. *United Nations document, S/23097*, 30 September 1991.

90. Findlay, *The Legacy and Lessons of UNTAC*, op. cit., p. 117.

91. Ibid., p. 124.

92. One of Sanderson's major frustrations had been the inability to put the administrative aspects of the UNTAC operation into place as quickly as he believed necessary. Idem.

93. 'Demobilization After Civil Wars' in *Strategic Survey* (London: Brassey's for the International Institute of International Studies, 1993–94) p. 26.

94. Anstee, op. cit., p. 533.

95. Roberts, op. cit., p. 7. A shortage of qualified personnel for UNTAC's civil component (caused by competition with five other on-going operations) had contributed significantly to its inability to exert sufficient control over the local administrations. See Findlay, op. cit., p. 115 and M. Hiebert, 'Draining the Swamp', *Far Eastern Economic Review*, 11 June 1992, p. 25.

96. Although as a simple observer of proceedings the UN could argue that this type of assessment was not its responsibility, there is surely an expectation that essential commitments like these are not just taken for granted. Luckily, as a temporary solution, the US was able to fly more than 450,000 Meals-Ready-to-Eat, as well as tents and other supplies to assembly areas in Angola. In addition, a six-month, $27.5m UN special relief program began in early October 1991 to deliver food and other supplies to assembled troops. Since a UN disaster relief program had been in Angola for several years, there was a pre-existing structure that could be used to distribute the food. The UN World Food Program made an exception to its rule of not supplying military forces and agreed to take over the job of feeding Angolan troops whilst UNICEF provided non-food items. Fortna, 'Angola Verification Mission II' op. cit., p. 398.

97. Somerville, op. cit., p. 63. The first peacekeeping operation to suffer the consequences of a lack of preparation for assembly areas was not a UN mission. Rather, it was the Commonwealth Monitoring Force (CMF), which deployed in Zimbabwe/Rhodesia in December 1979 to demilitarize the 15-year-old civil war between the nationalist guerilla forces and the Rhodesian government. Although assured that the areas could be supplied with sufficient food and water, the CMF in fact found that many of the areas were not readily accessible and suffered from inadequate water supplies and sanitation. This had serious repercussions for the security of the demobilizing troops and their monitors. See J. Ginifer, *Managing Arms in Peace Processes: Rhodesia/Zimbabwe* (Geneva: UNIDIR, 1995) pp. 35–6.

98. General Sanderson has argued that the UN's detailed reconnaissance and standard operating procedures for the cantonment and disarmament of the parties' forces made both processes achievable. However, he also acknowledged that inadequate support to the troops and their families in the cantonments, which had not been budgeted by the UN and was not a priority for the parties, would have been the most serious difficulty arising from the success of the cantonment process. The parties themselves had the responsibility for the provision of food and medical care, but none of them had the normal military logistic or medical capabilities to undertake the task. D. Cox, 'Peacekeeping and Disarmament: Peace Agreements, Security Council Mandates and the Disarmament Experience', in *Managing Arms in Peace Processes: The Issues* (Geneva: UNIDIR, 1996) pp. 103–4.

99. M. Berdal, 'Demobilisation and Disarmament After Civil Wars', *Adelphi Paper*, No. 303 (London: Brassey's for the International Institute for Strategic Studies, 1996) p. 47.

100. Ibid., p. 47

101. The staff officer also stated that '[an] enquiry has shown that about 60% [of the soldiers to be demobilized] wished to go back to family and village and to start farming. This leaves 56,000 others. In conjunction with the ILO, UNESCO and UNDP and NGOs, UNTAC had planned training and educational programs. However, due to budget capacity problems, UNTAC could only offer short training to 25,000 men, not at one time but phased. There have been speculations how many not immediately successful farmers and other jobless would again have taken a Kalajnikov to survive'. Cox, op. cit., p. 106.

102. Cox, op. cit., p. 107.

103. Ibid., p. 64.

104. *United Nations document, S/23613*, 19 February 1992.

105. UNTAC also trained police officers, judges and prosecutors in the Penal Code adopted by the SNC in September 1992.
106. R.B. Oakley, M.J. Dziedzic and E.M. Goldberg (eds.), *Policing the New World Disorder: Peace Operations and Public Security* (Washington D.C.: National Defense University Press, 1998) p. 88.
107. M. Plunkett, 'Reestablishing Law and Order in Peace Maintenance', *Global Governance*, Vol. 1, No. 1 (1998). Findlay, 'Cambodia: The Legacy and Lessons of UNTAC', op. cit., p. 106. Doyle, M., *UN Peacekeeping in Cambodia: UNTAC's Civil Mandate*, International Peace Academy, Occasional Paper Series (London: Lynne Rienner, 1995) pp. 44, 49.
108. Anstee, op. cit., pp. 69–76.
109. Ibid., p. 529
110. M. Liefer quoted in P. Sorpong, *Conflict Neutralization in the Cambodian War: From Battlefield to Ballot Box* (Oxford: Oxford University Press, 1997) p. 3.
111. Lizee, op. cit., pp. 135–48.
112. Findlay, *Cambodia: The Lessons and Legacy of UNTAC*, op. cit., p. 110.
113. Lizee, op. cit., p. 143.
114. Anstee, op. cit., p. 534.
115. Jeffrey Millington, the most senior US official in Angola, quoted in V. Brittain in *Why Angola Matters*, op. cit., p. 69.
116. Hampson, op. cit., p. 115.
117. Somerville, op. cit., p. 74.
118. Hamill, op. cit., p. 10.
119. Brittain claims that many junior UNTAC members were privately warning of hidden UNITA armies, but were reluctant to do so publicly for fear of losing their jobs. V. Brittain in *Why Angola Matters*, op. cit., pp. 69, 77.
120. Peou argues that if the Khmer Rouge had intended to derail the operation from the start they would have attacked UNTAC during its most vulnerable period; its initial deployment. He also cites testimony from a former right-hand man of the Khmer Rouge, General Ta Mok, that the group was serious about taking part in the elections. Also, Cambodian expert Nate Thayer argues that internal Khmer Rouge documents show clearly that the party intended to implement the CPSC when they signed it. Peou, op. cit., p. 269.
121. G.L. Munck and C. Kumar, 'Civil Conflicts and the Conditions for Successful International Intervention: A Comparative Study of Cambodia and El Salvador', *Review of International Studies*, Vol. 21 (1995) p. 178.
122. Evans, op. cit., pp. 24–7.
123. Ethnic Vietnamese were obviously presumed to be a natural electoral catchment for the CPP. However, the Khmer dislike of resident Vietnamese was not based solely on their likelihood to vote for the CPP. In fact there exists a long history of antagonism between the two nations, probably emanating from the imbalance of power between them. Vietnam has a population size approximately eight times that of Cambodia. There is also historical animosity caused by the Vietnamese annexation of Kampuchea Krom, or southern Cambodia, which is now part of southern Vietnam. Roberts, op. cit., pp. 8–9.
124. Ledgerwood in Roberts, op. cit., p. 9.
125. Ibid., p. 10.
126. Munck and Kumar, op. cit., p. 178.
127. Peou, op. cit., p. 268.
128. Idem.
129. Anstee, op. cit., p. 47.

Chapter 3

1. Alden and Simpson believe that FRELIMO, unlike its Angolan counterpart, was not actually pro-Marxist. C. Alden and M. Simpson, 'Mozambique: A Delicate Peace', *Journal of Modern African Studies*, Vol. 31, No. 1 (1993) pp. 110–11. Most scholars, including Hall, Vines and Minter, concur in the belief that RENAMO was not a genuine Mozambican resistance movement but rather the external creation of first, Rhodesia, and then South Africa. Hoile, however, disagrees. See W. Minter, *Apartheids Contras* (Witwatersand University Press, 1994) p. 156 and D. Hoile, *Mozambique: Resistance and Freedom* (The Mozambique Institute, 1994) p. x. See also M. Hall, 'The Mozambican National Resistance (RENAMO): A Study in the Destruction of an African Country', *Africa*, Vol. 60, No. 1 (1990) and H. Anderson, *Mozambique: A War Against the People* (London: Macmillan, 1992).
2. A. Vines, *RENAMO: From Terrorism to Democracy in Mozambique?* (Villiers Publications, 1996) p. 120.
3. It was feared that the re-occupation of many Mozambican towns by these rebel soldiers might split the country in two. E. Berman, *Managing Arms in Peace Processes: Mozambique* (Geneva: UNIDIR, 1996) p. 15.
4. Ibid., p. 18.
5. Alden and Simpson, op. cit., pp. 115–16. Unlike its Angolan counterpart, FRELIMO could not rely on revenue from oil and precious stones to bolster its flagging international support. Mozambique does, however, contain large coal reserves, iron ore and some of the world's largest deposits of tantalite. There are, of course, vast tracks of arable land. W. Finnegan, *A Complicated War: The Harrowing of Mozambique* (University of California Press, 1992) p. 197 and Anderson, op. cit., p. 163.
6. Berman, op. cit., pp. 51–3.
7. Two prominent reports written by Robert Gersony and William Minter in 1988 and 1989 respectively, both condemned RENAMO's treatment of refugees and civilians. Gersony was, at the time, a consultant to the US State Department's Bureau for Refugee Programs.
8. Vines, op. cit., pp. 42–50 and Minter, op. cit., p. 165.
9. Hume, op. cit., p. 28.
10. Vines, op. cit., pp. 124–5.
11. *Sant' Egidio* had become familiar with the Mozambican conflict through its long association with Fr. Jaime Gonclaves, who had become Archbishop of Beira in 1977. Gonclaves had helped facilitate negotiations and relations between FRELIMO, RENAMO and the Vatican throughout the 1980s. See Vines, op. cit., pp. 126–7 and *The United Nations and Mozambique 1992–1995* (New York: United Nations, 1995) p. 12.
12. Vines, op. cit., pp. 129, 132.
13. Of eight cease-fire violations investigated by the JVC between December and 10 January, six of them were found to be the fault of RENAMO. RENAMO continued to protest that Zimbabwean troops were active outside the corridors to which they should have been confined. Ibid., pp. 133–4.
14. *The United Nations and Mozambique*, op. cit., p. 16.
15. Such a role would also obviously have required the consent of the Government, which given its stance on other issues was hardly likely. Vines, op. cit., p. 135.
16. *The United* Ibid *Nations and Mozambique*, op. cit., p. 17.

17. Vines, op. cit., p. 136.
18. *The United Nations and Mozambique*, op. cit., pp. 16–17.
19. Ibid., p. 18. The observers joined the proceedings to offer expert advice on election and cease-fire monitoring. Berman states that UN involvement only became significant with the arrival of the Political Affairs Officer, Tayeb Merchoug. Berman, op. cit., p. 26.
20. Vines, op. cit., p. 136.
21. *The United Nations and Mozambique*, op. cit., p. 19.
22. The technical team sent to assess requirements for monitoring a cease-fire subsequently reported that the UN operation would be faced with a situation including an estimated 3 million internally displaced persons, 1.5 million refugees, millions of unmarked landmines and the possibility of soldiers waiting for demobilization drifting into banditry. Idem. and Hume, op. cit., pp. 118, 130, 131, 141–2.
23. *The United Nations and Mozambique*, op. cit., p. 20.
24. The General Peace Agreement for Mozambique (GPA), 4 October 1992.
25. This second ballot was to be held within three weeks of the announcement of the results of the first ballot.
26. Non-portable military facilities, which were to be verified *in situ,* were also to be designated within seven days of the GPA's signing.
27. It was to be composed of 24,000 army, 4,000 air-force and 2,000 navy personnel.
28. *The United Nations and Mozambique*, op. cit., p. 22.
29. Ajello's appointment was approved by the Security Council only two days before his deployment. *United Nations document, S/24642*, 9 October 1992 and A. Ajello, ' Mozambique: Implementation of the 1992 Peace Agreement', in C. Crocker, F.O. Hampson and P. Aall (eds), *Herding Cats: Multi-Party Mediation in a Complex World* (Washington D.C.: USIPP, 1999) p. 620.
30. *United Nations document, S/24724*, 28 October 1992.
31. *United Nations document, S/24892*, 3 December 1992. The lack of CSC meetings before this meant that the UN was unable to investigate the previous cease-fire violations of both parties.
32. 'Document 24', *The United Nations and Mozambique*, op. cit., pp. 147–8. Dhlakama changed his mind after a meeting with Mugabe on 11 December. However, he immediately began to insist that the UN deploy at least 65 per cent of its forces before demobilization process could begin.
33. *United Nations document, S/24892*, 3 December 1992.
34. Idem.
35. Idem.
36. *Security Council Resolution 797*, 16 December 1992.
37. Berman, op. cit., pp. 37–9.
38. 'Document 29', *The United Nations and Mozambique*, op. cit., p. 170.
39. *United Nations document, S/25518*, 2 April 1993.
40. *United Nations document, S/26034*, 30 June 1993.
41. This delay also took account of the time required for the Government to procure sophisticated equipment it had demanded for the electoral registration process and the obstacle of the rainy season, which was due to last between November and March.
42. *United Nations document, S/26385*, 30 August 1993.
43. *United Nations document, 26385/Add. 1*, 10 September 1993.
44. *United Nations document, S/26666*, 1 November 1993.

45. Idem.

46. Idem.

47. *United Nations document, S/1994/89*, 28 January 1994.

48. Idem.

49. The Secretary-General blamed the expectations of RENAMO soldiers on their commanders who had made unrealistic promises concerning the possible benefits of demobilization.

50. *United Nations documents, S/1994/89*, 28 January 1994 and *S/1994/511*, 28 April 1994.

51. Idem.

52. *United Nations document, S/1994/803*, 7 July 1994.

53. 'Mutinees endanger Maputo peace plans', *The Daily Telegraph*, 29 July 1994 and 'Looting troops spread unease', *The Guardian*, 1 August 1994.

54. Idem.

55. *United Nations document, S/1994/1009*, 29 August 1994.

56. *United Nations document, S/1994/1002*, 26 August 1994.

57. *United Nations document, S/1994/1449*, 23 December 1994.

58. V. Brittain, 'Rebel Group Strangles Quarter of Mozambique', *The Guardian*, 3 August 1994.

59. *United Nations document, S/1994/1196*, 21 October 1994.

60. RENAMO claimed 8.3 million cards had been printed, when only 6.4 million people had registered to vote. 'RENAMO Promises No More Fighting', *The Times*, 26 October 1994. Mozambique Poll Bedeviled By Sabotage Claims', *The Times*, 24 October 1994.

61. Ajello, op. cit., p. 635.

62. 'RENAMO Withdrawal Confuses Voters', *Financial Times*, 28 October 1994.

63. With only half the population having access to a radio, the news of RENAMO's boycott spread only on the first morning of voting, causing inevitable confusion. When asked what Dhlakama had received for his reinstatement, Ajello declared 'a cup of coffee'. *International Herald Tribune*, 29 October 1994.

64. 5,402,940 Mozambicans voted.

65. The CNE had accepted 12 presidential candidates and accredited 14 political parties and coalitions to partake in the legislative elections.

66. *United Nations document, S/1994/1449*, 23 December 1994.

67. The UN's total deficits for its general and peacekeeping budgets in 1994 reached $2.7 billion. The US and Russia owed $288 and $507 million to the peacekeeping budget respectively. G. Kostakos, 'UN Reform: The Post-Cold War Organization', in D. Bourantonis and J. Wienner (eds), *The United Nations in the New World Order* (London: Macmillan, 1995) p. 70.

68. L. Elliot, 'Debts Fetter World's Police Force', *The Guardian*, 13 May 1994.

69. D.J. Puchala, 'Outsiders, Insiders and UN Reform', *Washington Quarterly*, Vol. 17, No. 4 (1994) p. 168.

70. *United Nations document, S/25518*, 2 April, 1993. The Secretary-General explained that the formulation of a budget, given the uncertain political situation in the country, 'proved to be a very complex task and required considerable internal consultations'.

71. Due to the prevarications of the Mozambican government the UN was unable to acquire a Status of Forces agreement until 14 May 1993. This hampered the deployment of ONUMOZ, for without such an agreement the UN is required to abide by Mozambican laws (including the need to obtain authorization for all its flights, pay airport duties and register its vehicles locally), as well as pay

local taxes and duties that are levied in accordance with national practice. The ONUMOZ approved budget did not of course account for such unforeseen expenditure. *United Nations documents, S/25518*, 2 April 1993 and *S/26034*, 30 June 1993.

72. Idem.
73. Idem.
74. *United Nations document, S/26034*, 30 June 1993. The final withdrawal of foreign forces did not take place until 9 June 1993.
75. United Nations document, S/25518, 2 April 1993.
76. F. Bridgland, 'Shoestring Peace About to Snap', *Sunday Telegraph*, 21 February 1993.
77. In November 1993 the Secretary-General complained that only 13 of the 18 helicopters required by the operation had been authorized. *United Nations documents*, S/26666, 1 November 1993 and *S/1994/511*, 28 April 1994.
78. Anstee's expectation that she might be asked to transfer to the operation in Mozambique had caused her to take steps to ensure that the UN was assigned the chairs of the supervisory commissions; that the timing of the elections was flexible and made conditional on the prior fulfillment of key provisions; and that early steps were taken to accommodate the losers within a framework of national reconciliation. M.J. Anstee, *Orphan of the Cold War* (London: Macmillan Press, 1996) pp. 534–5.
79. C. Alden, 'The UN and the Resolution of Conflict in Mozambique', *Journal of Modern African Studies,* Vol. 33, No. 1, 114–15.
80. Supplied by the UN to the parties in August 1992 this timetable was subsequently incorporated into the GPA.
81. *United Nations document, S/24892*, 3 December 1992.
82. Berman, op. cit., p. 83.
83. Hume, op. cit., p. 131.
84. 'Document 10', *The United Nations and Mozambique*, op. cit., p. 103. Even with this added preparation the UN found that the whole pace of disarmament in Angola was slowed due to the process of getting UNITA and MPLA troops to their assigned assembly points running behind schedule. This was in part due to logistical problems being exacerbated by a severely damaged infrastructure, especially in remote areas. Keeping the forces in their assembly areas was also found difficult due to the sever shortages of food which the Angolan parties were incapable of supplying to these remote areas. With the infrastructure of Mozambique equally as devastated, if not worse, and the logistical planning for assembly areas dependent on their location, their designation surely should have been addressed by the time the GPA was signed. See V.P. Fortna, 'Success and Failure in Southern Africa: Peacekeeping in Namibia and Angola', in H. Bradd and D. Donald (eds), *Beyond Traditional Peacekeeping* (London: Macmillan) p. 290.
85. *United Nations document, S/25518*, 2 April 1993.
86. *United Nations document, S/26666*, 1 November 1993.
87. Hume, op. cit., pp. 132 and 136–7.
88. *United Nations document, S/1995/511*, 28 April 1994.
89. Alden, 'The UN and the Resolution of Conflict in Mozambique', op. cit., p. 117.
90. M. Hamlyn, 'Poll Raises Mozambican Fears', *The Times*, 21 October 1994.
91. *United Nations document, S/26034,* 30 June 1993. Although not supported by the GPA, the disbandment of irregular forces before the assembly of regular troops may have had beneficial confidence-building effects. It could have acted as a

test of the parties' willingness to allow peacekeeping personnel into their areas of control.

92. Negotiations over the next two months allowed the parties to agree on a number of 49,638. Officials in the Ministry of Defense were found to have purposefully overestimated the number of troops in order to pocket the redundant salaries of non-existent soldiers. This fraud also slowed the demobilization process and the selection of troops for the FADM.

93. 69 and 79 of these locations were undeclared by the Government and RENAMO respectively. *United Nations document, S/1994/1449*, 23 December 1994.

94. Alden, 'The UN and the Resolution of Conflict in Mozambique', op. cit., pp. 112–4.

95. The Government's unilateral action was spurred on by the need to reduce military expenditure in the wake of the IMF structural adjustment program it had adopted in 1987. The Government had first proposed a unilateral reduction of the FAM in December 1991 and had planned for a substantial reduction with help from the SDC. Although a hesitancy to supply FRELIMO with funds whilst negotiations for the peace process were on-going meant that support for the process was not forthcoming, the Government presented a revised and more modest plan in May 1992. By the signing of the GPA the Government was claiming to have demobilized 16,000 soldiers, although they remained armed, salaried and resident in barracks. After signing the GPA, however, the Government did unilaterally demobilize 15,087 FAM troops under UN supervision. The process of registering and resettling these personnel in areas of their choice began on 17 April 1993. Berman, op. cit., p. 59 and *United Nations document, S/26034*, 30 June 1993.

96. However, as UNOHAC was established by the UN Department of Humanitarian Affairs it did earn the resentment of the UN Development Program, which believed that UNOHAC had usurped the mandate of its resident representative. It was also resented by much of the bi-lateral donor community, which viewed UNOHAC as an unnecessary layer of bureaucracy. See N. Ball, 'The Challenge of Rebuilding War-Torn Societies' in C. Crocker, F. Hampson and P. Aall (eds), *Managing Global Chaos* (Washington D.C.: USIP, 1997) p. 614 and Ajello, op. cit., pp. 637–8.

97. C. Alden, 'Swords into Ploughshares? The UN and Demilitarization in Mozambique', *International Peacekeeping*, Vol. 2, No. 2 (1995) pp. 179–80.

98. On the day of departure from the assembly areas each soldier received civilian clothing, a demobilization card, a cash sum equivalent to three months pay and a voucher for an additional three months subsidy to be paid in the former soldier's district of residence. In addition to this each former soldier received transport subsidies, rations for two weeks and packages containing seeds and agricultural tools. Transport was provided for the demobilized soldiers, their dependents and belongings. Humanitarian assistance was also provided to the dependents that had encamped around the assembly areas during the demobilization phase. *United Nations document, S/1994/511*, 28 April 1994.

99. *United Nations documents, S/1994/89*, 28 January 1994 and *S/1994/1002*, 26 August 1994.

100. Ajello, op. cit., p. 631.

101. The Secretary-General also noted the expected need of those refugees and displaced persons who would 'inevitably gather around the assembly areas and [that would] also require food assistance'. *United Nations document, S24892*, 3 December 1992.

102. Berman, op. cit., p. 61 and Alden, op. cit., p. 107.

103. *United Nations document, S/26385*, 30 August 1993. As early as April 1993 the Secretary-General had reported that although the worst drought in 70 years of Mozambican history had finally broken, a lack of seeds and tools during the growing season would mean the 1993 crop of staple cereals would be much less than normal. *United Nations document, S/25518*, 2 April 1993.

104. *United Nations document, S/S/1994/1449*, 23 December 1994.

105. *United Nations document, S/1994/1009*, 29 August 1994.

106. *United Nations document, S/26385*, 30 August 1993.

107. ONUMOZ was also represented on a task force created to oversee and co-ordinate the rehabilitation of the training centers, which the Government claimed it could not undertake. *United Nations document, S/1994/89*, 28 January 1994.

108. Hamlyn, op. cit.

109. Alden, op. cit., p. 120. A least one key Mozambican opposition figure expressed the view that the lack of sufficient volunteers for the new army would correct itself after the elections. In his opinion, having exercised their option to demobilize and thereby collect their severance pay and 18 month subsidy at salary level, these ex-soldiers would still be free to return after elections to resume their military careers. *United Nations document, S/1994/1009*, 29 August 1994.

110. *United Nations document, S26666*, 1 November 1993.

111. *United Nations document, S/1994/511*, 28 April 1994.

112. Ajello states that the influence of the CIVPOLS was 'marginal'. Ajello, op. cit., p. 622.

113. *United Nations document, S/1994/1449*, 23 December 1994.

114. R.B. Oakley, M.J. Dziedzic and E.M. Goldberg (eds), *Policing the New World Disorder: Peace Operations and Public Security* (Washington D.C.: National Defense University Press, 1998) p. 166.

115. Most writers on Mozambique, such as Minter, Vines and Anderson argue that RENAMO had little if no independent political platform before the peace process started. See Vines, Minter and Anderson, op. cit.

116. Hoile, op. cit., p. 50. The Court's decision was a ruling on whether RENAMO was a political movement or simply a creation of Rhodesia and South Africa. When RENAMO had attacked the Zimbabwean oil pipeline the oil companies had invoked insurance policies for the losses incurred. However, Lloyds of London had refused to pay out citing exclusion clauses for losses incurred by civil war, insurrection or rebellion. The oil companies argued that because RENAMO was a foreign creation without a Mozambican popular base, it could not therefore be classed as a civil war, insurrection or rebellion.

117. Tom Young quoted in Idem.

118. Hume, op. cit., p. 138.

119. Before the end of 1992 the Secretary-General had acknowledged that all the commissions would require technical support from the UN, including legal advice, translators, information and security services and transport. *United Nations document, S/24892*, 3 December 1992.

120. United Nations document, S/25044, 7 January 1993.

121. 'Document 31', *The United Nations and Mozambique*, op. cit., p. 172.

122. 'Document 32', Idem.

123. V. Brittain, 'Fear of War Clouds Poll', *The Guardian*, 23 September 1994.

124. 'Document 54', *The United Nations and Mozambique*, op. cit., p. 215.

125. C. Crawford, 'Mozambique's Fragile Peace Process Risks Too Easy Derailment', *Financial Times*, 25 January 1994.

126. D. Beresford, 'Final Lap for UN's Man in Maputo', *The Guardian*, 26 October 1994.
127. *The Guardian*, 11 July 1994.
128. Brittain, 'A State Made to the UN's Design', op. cit.
129. Idem.
130. *The Telegraph*, 18 November 1994.
131. B.F. Walter, 'Designing Transitions from Civil War', in B.F. Walter and J. Snyder (eds), *Civil Wars, Insecurity and Intervention* (New York: Columbia University Press, 1999) p. 57.
132. Ajello, op. cit., p. 636
133. Walter, op. cit., p. 57.
134. Ajello, op. cit., p. 636
135. Walter argues that the international communities commitment to ensure free and fair elections for Mozambique in 1999 also provided RENAMO with post-election security guarantees. However, she provides no evidence to suggest the international community felt so committed. Certainly, after the events of Somalia in 1993 and Rwanda in 1994 one would have to question any assumptions of international commitment to African conflicts. Walter, op. cit., p. 57.
136. T. Kurzidem, 'ONUMOZ- How To Make A Successful Peacekeeping Operation', *International Peacekeeping*, Vol. 1, No. 4 (1994) p. 133.
137. *United Nations document, S/1994/89*, 28 January 1994. Alden notes that the FADM was not short of officers, who had all been offered higher salaries than their subordinates. Alden also suggests full demobilization before the formation of new armies. This would solve the problem of benefit discrepancies and reduce the complications that arise from the reluctance of governments to disband the organizational structures and resources of present armies and transfer them to new ones. Ibid., p. 186.

Chapter 4

1. C. Adibe, *Managing Arms in Peace Processes: Somalia* (Geneva: UNIDIR, 1995) pp. 6, 8.
2. M. Sahnoun, *Somalia: The Missed Opportunities* (Washington: USIP, 1994) p. 5.
3. Adibe, op. cit., p. 9.
4. R.G. Patman, 'The UN Operation in Somalia', in R. Thakur and C.A. Thayer (eds), *A Crisis of Expectations: UN Peacekeeping in the 1990s* (Boulder, Colo: Westview Press, 1995) p. 86 and Sahnoun, op. cit., p. 6.
5. Sahnoun, op. cit., p. 8.
6. Patman, op. cit., p. 87.
7. Ibid., pp. 87, 88.
8. Sahnoun, op. cit., p. 8.
9. *The United Nations and Somalia 1992–1996*, The UN Blue Book Series, Vol. 8 (New York: United Nations, 1996) p. 15.
10. *United Nations document, S/RES/733*, 23 January 1992.
11. *United Nations document, S/RES/751*, 24 April 1992.
12. *United Nations document, S/23829*, 21 April 1992.
13. *United Nations document, S/23693*, 11 March 1992.
14. *United Nations document, S/24343*, 22 July 1992.
15. Ibid. The Security Council approved the creation of the four zones on 27 July 1992, pursuant to Resolution 767. The Council also 'strongly supported' the

dispatch of a technical team to examine the feasibility of an 'arms-for-food' exchange program.

16. *United Nations document, S/RES/794*, 3 December 1992.
17. *United Nations document, S/24868*, 30 November 1992.
18. *Letter dated 8 December 1992 from the UN Secretary-General to US President Bush* and *UN document, S/24992*, 19 December 1992.
19. R.G. Patman, 'Disarming Somalia: The Contrasting Fortunes of United States and Australian Peacekeepers During United Nations Intervention, 1992–1993', *African Affairs*, Vol. 96 (1997) p. 512.
20. President Bush quoted in J.R. Bolton, 'Wrong turn in Somalia', *Foreign Affairs* (1994) p. 60. Bolton, Assistant Secretary of State for International Organization in the Bush administration claims that Boutros-Ghali made no mention of any nation-building projects, including disarmament, when Eagleburger met him in late November and early December.
21. T. Farrell, 'Sliding into War: the Somalia Imbroglio and US Army Peace Operations Doctrine', *International Peacekeeping*, Vol. 2, No. 2 (1995) p. 197.
22. President Bush quoted in W. Clarke and J. Herbst, 'Somalia and the Future of Humanitarian Intervention', *Foreign Affairs*, Vol. 75, No. 2 (1996) pp. 74–5.
23. J.L. Hirsch and R.B. Oakley, *Somalia and Operation Restore Hope* (Washington: USIP, 1995) pp. 44–5.
24. *United Nations document, S/24992*, 19 December 1992.
25. Idem.
26. *United Nations document, S/25354*, 3 March 1993.
27. *United Nations document, S/RES/814*, 26 March 1993.
28. *United Nations document, S/1994/653*, 1 June 1994.
29. Adibe, op. cit., p. 40.
30. *United Nations document, S/23839*, 21 April 1992.
31. Sahnoun, op. cit., p. 17.
32. Idem.
33. Ibid., p. 18.
34. Ibid., p. 32.
35. Aideed's suspicions had arisen following the recognition, by default, of Ali Mahdi's position of Interim President by Under-Secretary-General, James Jonah, on a visit to Somalia in January 1992. Aideed had even wanted the observers to wear civilian attire with only berets and arm bands for recognition as UN personnel. This was, of course, unacceptable to the UN. Patman, 'The UN Operation in Somalia', op. cit., pp. 86, 90.
36. *United Nations document, S/24343*, 22 July 1992.
37. Sahnoun quoted in J. Stevenson, 'Hope Restored in Somalia?', *Foreign Policy*, No. 91 (1993) p. 145.
38. Patman, 'The UN Operation in Somalia', op. cit., p. 91.
39. *United Nations documents, S/24480*, 24 August 1992 and *S/RES/775*, 28 August 1992. Also see 'UN Chief Wants 3,500 Troops to Guard Somalia Aid', *The Financial Times*, 26 August 1992. Sahnoun, who recommended the action to prevent an over-concentration of UN action on Mogadishu, supported the creation of the four zones.
40. Sahnoun, op. cit., pp. 38–39.
41. *United Nations document, S/24480*, 24 August 1992.
42. *Letter dated 24 November 1992 from the Secretary-General to the President of the Security Council, S/24859*, 27 November 1992.
43. Adibe, op. cit., p. 73.

44. Hirsch and Oakley, op. cit., p. 57.
45. The agreement also included the registration of all weapons in the hands of civilians and the return of property unlawfully taken during previous hostilities. See R.G. Patman, 'Disarming Somalia: The Contrasting Fortunes of United States and Australian Peacekeepers During United Nations Intervention, 1992–1993', op. cit., p. 513.
46. Farrell, op. cit., p. 200.
47. Adibe, op. cit., p. 74.
48. Farrell, op. cit., p. 200.
49. The receipts also conferred a 'good-guy status' upon a holder. Adibe, op. cit., p. 76.
50. Idem.
51. K. Kennedy, 'The Relationship between the Military and the Humanitarian Organizations in Operation Restore Hope', *International Peacekeeping*, Vol. 13, No. 1 (1996) pp. 104–5.
52. Duties, fees and commissions were also levied. $4150 for the landing of every small plane, $500 for cargoes, $10,000 for every boat entering the post, plus $100 per ton unloaded. This was all paid whilst 40 per cent to 80 per cent was stolen. A UN official provided these prices. See E. Augelli and C. Murphy, 'Lessons of Somalia for Future Multilateral Humanitarian Assistance Operations', *Global Governance*, Vol. 1 (1995) p. 347.
53. A. Natsios, 'Humanitarian Relief Interventions in Somalia: The Economics of Chaos', *International Peacekeeping,* Vol. 3, No. 1 (1996) p. 77.
54. Idem.
55. Oakley and Hirsch, op. cit., p. 68.
56. J. Prendergast, *The Bones of Our Children Are Not Yet Buried* (Center for Concern, 1994) pp. 28–9.
57. Adibe, op. cit., p. 78. The ability to distinguish between official and unofficial agency guards was hampered by the issuing of permits or 'pink cards' that failed to include photographs or even the names of holders. Even UNITAF confidence in these cards was reduced following a number of abuses by illegal holders. A new ID card was produced later that included a photograph together with the serial number of the weapon, but poor support for the program from UNITAF limited its effectiveness together with a variety of ever stricter interpretations by the units enforcing the policies. See K. Kennedy, op. cit., p. 106.
58. Adibe, op. cit., pp. 78–9.
59. Patman, 'The UN Operation in Somalia', op. cit., p. 95.
60. Robert Oakley believes that had UNITAF pursued a policy of full-scale disarmament it would have required a much greater force and it would have become embroiled in a series of clashes, both large and small scale, with the SNA and other groups. He also quotes Lt. General Johnston as having questioned the possibility of such action, asking how disarmament of that magnitude could be carried out when it would require 'house to house, hut to hut searches... [in]...the lawless conditions prevailing in Somalia'. Oakley and Hirsch, op. cit., p. 105.
61. A 'cantonment' was defined as a location where heavy weapons would be stored. A 'transition site' was a location where the factional forces would be given temporary accommodation while they turned in their small arms and registered for future non-governmental and governmental support. They were also to receive guidance and training for their eventual reintegration into civilian life.

258 *Notes*

62. Oakley and Hirsch, op. cit., p. 99.
63. *Text of the Addis Ababa Agreement – First Session of the Conference on National Reconciliation in Somalia*, 27 March 1992.
64. Oakley and Hirsch, op. cit., p. 49.
65. *The United Nations and Somalia*, op. cit., p. 49.
66. Adibe, op. cit., p. 88.
67. Idem.
68. The relief community accepted the four-stage plan when it was presented to them at the end of May because it recognized that disarmament was to take place in an 'unresourced environment'. For greater detail see Adibe, op. cit., pp. 88–91.
69. *United Nations document, S/26351*, 24 August 1993.
70. *United Nations document, S/1994/653*, 1 June 1994.
71. *The United Nations and Somalia*, op. cit., p. 49.
72. *United Nations document, S/26351*, 24 August 1993.
73. *United Nations document, S/RES/837*, 6 June 1993.
74. *United Nations document, S/26022*, 1 July 1993.
75. Idem.
76. *The United Nations and Somalia*, op. cit., p. 58.
77. Idem.
78. *United Nations document, S/26317*, 17 August 1993.
79. Adibe, op. cit., pp. 107–8.
80. *United Nations document, S/26738*, 12 November 1993.
81. *United Nations document, S/RES/897*, 4 February 1994.
82. T. Weiss, 'Overcoming the Somalia Syndrome: Operation Rekindle Hope', *Global Governance*, Vol. 1 (1995) p. 178.
83. C. Crocker, 'The Lessons of Somalia: Not Everything Went Wrong', *Foreign Affairs*, Vol. 74, No. 3 (1995) p. 5.
84. Sahnoun, op. cit., p. viii.
85. Idem.
86. Ibid., p. 38.
87. Sahnoun also criticizes the UN agencies for a number of failures and missed opportunities. For details see Idem.
88. J. Hillen, *Blue Helmets: The Strategy of UN Military Operations* (Washington D.C.: Brassey's, 1998) p. 194.
89. Ibid., p. 26.
90. Ibid., p. 36.
91. *United Nations document, S/25168*, 26 January 1994.
92. Oakley and Hirsch, op. cit., p. 65.
93. Ibid., pp. 105–6.
94. B. Boutros-Ghali, *An Agenda for Peace* (New York: United Nations, 1992) pp. 26–7.
95. Patman, 'Disarming Somalia', op. cit., p. 519.
96. Ibid., p. 523.
97. A police force of over 200 had been recruited and deployed in Baidoa by May 1993. Ibid., p. 525.
98. Idem.
99. Ibid., p. 526.
100. The good relationship maintained between the Australians and the NGOs working in the Baidoa HRS also helped affect local attitudes as the people who were feeding them, educating them and looking after them, were also telling them that the Australians were competent and even-handed. See Ibid., p. 524.

101. Ibid., p. 526.
102. Ibid., pp. 527–530.
103. *United Nations document*, S/RES/837, 6 June 1993.
104. L. Mackensie, quoted in R. Thakur, 'From Peacekeeping to Peace-Enforcement: the United Nations Operation in Somalia', *Journal of Modern African Studies*, Vol. 32, No. 3 (1994) p. 396.
105. T. Montgomery, quoted in Farrel, op. cit., p. 203. The decision to offer the reward was also perceived as culturally insensitive because it was seen as insulting and reminded the Somalis of their previous experiences under colonialism.
106. 170 others were also injured in the raid. M. Berdal, 'Fateful Encounter: the United States and UN Peacekeeping', *Survival,* Vol. 36, No. 1 (1994) p. 42. The increasing use of violence also led UN contingents from Islamic countries to seek clearance from their home governments before carrying out their orders. Italy, Ireland, the Vatican, World Vision and the OAU also called for a review of UN policy after 12 July. Thakur, op. cit., p. 398.
107. Bradbury quoted in J. Prendergast, *The Gun Talks Louder Than the Vote* (Center for Concern, 1994) p. 42.
108. Patman, 'The UN Operation in Somalia', op. cit., p. 97.
109. Oakley and Hirsch, op. cit., p. 123.
110. G.A. Anderson, 'UNOSOM II: Not Failure, Not Success', in D. Daniel and B. Hayes (eds), *Beyond Traditional Peacekeeping*, op. cit., p. 270.
111. M. Mazarr, 'The Military Dilemmas of Humanitarian Intervention', *Security Dialogue*, Vol. 24, No. 2 (1993) p. 158.
112. Ken Menkhaus, 'International Peacebuilding and the Dynamics of Local and National Reconciliation in Somalia', *International Peacekeeping*, Vol. 3, No. 1 (1996) p. 63.
113. *United Nations documents, S/26317*, 17 August 1993 and *S/26738*, 12 November 1993.
114. Sahnoun, op. cit., p. 29
115. M.P. Ganzglass, 'The Restoration of the Somali Justice System', *International Peacekeeping*, Vol. 3, No. 1 (1996) p. 115.
116. Ibid., p. 116 and Clarke and Herbst, op. cit., p. 78.
117. Ganzglass, op. cit., pp. 117, 121. A fledgling judicial committee was also formed at this time, composed of equal numbers of magistrates and judges nominated by Aideed and Ali Mahdi. However, given that neither group would allow the prosecution of their own faction members, the independence of the committee was, not surprisingly, 'fundamentally compromised'. See Patman, 'Disarming Somalia', op. cit., p. 517.
118. Ganzglass, op. cit., p. 125.
119. Menkhaus, op. cit., p. 63.
120. Oakley and Hirsch, op. cit., p. 92.
121. *United Nations document, S/26738*, 12 November 1993. Despite the US donations international support remained poor. Out of an estimated cost of $19.08 million for the Somali police program only $8.08 million had been donated by October 1994. The Secretary-General expected the shortfall to have reached $11 million by March 1995.
122. Report of the Life and Peace Institute quoted in J. Prendergast, *Crisis Response: Humanitarian Band-Aids in Sudan and Somalia* (London: Pluto Press, 1997) p. 120.
123. John Prendergast also criticizes the UN for negotiating with the warlords for the deployment of peacekeepers during 1992, as it provided them with a false

legitimacy. However, it would have been equally a mistake to have excluded them completely and at that stage they had not been allowed to consume all the political space. Prendergast, *The Gun Talks Louder than the Vote*, op. cit., p. 2. Prendergast, *Crisis Response*, op. cit., p. 120. Menkhaus, op. cit., p. 52.

124. Natsios, op. cit., p. 79.
125. Menkhaus, op. cit., p. 62.
126. Prendergast, *The Bones of Our Children Are Not Yet Buried*, op. cit., p. 18.
127. R. Betts, 'The Delusion of Impartial Intervention', *Foreign Affairs*, Vol. 37, No. 6 (1994) p. 26.
128. I.S. Spears, 'Building Confidence Amidst Africa's Civil Wars: The Opportunities and Constraints', *Civil Wars*, Vol. 3, No. 2 (2000) pp. 29–30.
129. M. Berdal, 'Lessons not Learned: The Use of Force in "Peace Operation" in the 1990s', *International Peacekeeping*, Vol. 7, No. 4 (2000) p. 70.
130. Patman, 'Disarming Somalia', op. cit., p. 533.
131. Berdal, op. cit., p. 67.
132. F.E. Stiftung, *Comprehensive Report of Lessons-Learned From United Nations Operation in Somalia April 1992–March 1995* (New York: United Nations, 1995) p. 12.
133. Natsios, op. cit., p. 79.
134. Sahnoun, op. cit., p. 35. As he stated of monetization, '[There] is so much hesitation and lack of motivation when I bring up the subject that I now despair of seeing this very important operation ever implemented…It will provide jobs to Somalis and involve them more inn the process of re-establishing market activities throughout the country'.
135. One instance occurred after the Secretary-General had accepted that national reconciliation would be better fostered through the 'framework of the traditional structures' of Somali society and had supported the Imam of Harib's attempts to convene a Hawiye clan reconciliation conference as a prelude to a national reconciliation conference. The Imam and other members of the Hawiye clan were surprised by Aideed when he announced that following a preliminary agreement on disarmament by the political subcommittee of the Hawiye conference, he felt the actual Hawiye reconciliation conference to be unnecessary. *United Nations documents, S/1994/977*, 19 August 1994 and *S/1994/1166*, 14 October 1994.

Chapter 5

1. Also in 1993 the UN deployed troops as part of the UNPROFOR operation to the Former Yugoslavian Republic of Macedonia, to prevent Serbia spreading the conflict over their shared border.
2. J.G. Stoessinger *Why Nations go to War* (New York: St. Martin's Press, 2001) p. 217.
3. M. Glenny, *The Fall of Yugoslavia: The Third Balkan War* (London: Penguin, 1996) p. 142.
4. Ibid., p. 13.
5. Stoessinger, op. cit., p. 218.
6. L. Silber and A. Little, *Yugoslavia: Death of a Nation* (London: Penguin, 1996) p. 31.
7. D. Owen, *Balkan Odyssey* (New York: Harcourt Brace and Company, 1995) p. 37.
8. Silber and Little, op. cit., p. 29. The presidency of the federal presidency rotated annually amongst its members. As Head of State the president was also commander-in-chief of the armed forces.

9. Ibid., pp. 75–6.
10. S. Stankovic, *The End of the Tito Era: Yugoslavia's Dilemmas* (Stanford: Hoover Institution Press, 1981) p. 51.
11. Fearing a similar invasion to that suffered by Hungary in 1956 Tito organized the TOs as a civil army that could aid the JNA in defeating an occupational force through the conduct of a costly guerilla war. TO and JNA forces were highly integrated, with officers swapping between them throughout their careers. However, only the highest ranking TO officers were full-time soldiers (the rest were reservists), whilst most JNA units were fully active. Silber and Little, op. cit., pp. 106, 118.
12. Ibid., pp. 106–7.
13. Idem.
14. Of the ethnic Serbs living in Croatia around 200,000 did so in Serb dominated areas. Another 400,000 lived in Croatian dominated areas. Footnote 2. Ibid., p. 153.
15. Ibid., pp. 96–7.
16. Though a secret meeting in March 1991 between Milosevic and Tudjman at Tito's old hunting lodge at Karadjordjevo appeared to end with a gentleman's agreement on the division of Bosnia between them, the issue of the Krajina Serbs was to be the thorny issue on which the two leaders were to continue to differ. While Milosevic never divulged the details of this secret meeting, Tudjman bragged afterwards of the impending doubling of Croatia's territory. Ibid., pp. 113–4, 131.
17. Ibid., pp. 137.
18. Ibid., pp. 137, 147.
19. Gow asserts that the EC's quick response was primarily due to the fact that its Prime Ministers and Foreign Ministers were all meeting at the Luxembourg summit as the Slovenian conflict began. The EC's response, therefore, was reactionary and ill-conceived. J. Gow, *Triumph of the Lack of Will* (New York: Columbia University Press, 1997) pp. 47, 50.
20. Ibid., p. 18.
21. Ibid., pp. 19–20.
22. R. Holbrooke, *To End a War* (Random House, 1999) op. cit., p. 27.
23. Silber and Little, op. cit., p. 161.
24. Gow, op. cit., pp. 50–53. Around 200 EU monitors were eventually deployed.
25. Silber and Little, op. cit., p. 191.
26. Gow, op. cit., p. 55.
27. Ibid., p. 57.
28. Silber and Little, op. cit., p. 196.
29. Ibid., p. 185.
30. Ibid., p. 196.
31. S.M. Hill, and S. Malik, *Peacekeeping and the United Nations* (Aldershot: Dartmouth Press, 1996) p. 106.
32. *United Nations document, S/RES/743*, 21 February 1992.
33. M. Berdal, 'UN peacekeeping in the Former Yugoslavia', in D. Donald, and B. Hayes eds, *Beyond Traditional Peacekeeping* (London: Macmillan Press, 1995) p. 229.
34. B. Ekwall-Uebelhart and A. Raevsky, *Managing Arms in Peace Processes: Croatia and Bosnia-Herzegovina* (Geneva: UNIDIR, 1996) p. 26.
35. These local police forces were to carry only side arms and were to be responsible to the existing *opstina* councils in the UNPAs. B. De Rossanet, *Peacemaking and Peacekeeping in Yugoslavia* (Kluwer Law International, 1996) p. 64.

36. Ekwall-Uebelhart and Raevsky, op. cit., pp. 34–5.
37. United Nations, 'The United Nations and the situation in the former Yugoslavia', *Reference paper revision 4* (New York: United Nations) p. 4.
38. Ekwall-Uebelhart and Raevsky, op. cit., p. 33.
39. A. Bair, 'What happened in Yugoslavia? Lessons for Future Peacekeepers', *European Security*, Vol. 3, No. 2 (1994) p. 343.
40. Fetherston, et al., op. cit., p. 182.
41. According to an interview conducted by Misha Glenny with General Mladic in 1991 '90 per cent of the [JNA] in Krajina were local people' who would stay behind if the JNA were to withdraw from Croatia. Glenny, op. cit., p. 29.
42. Ekwall-Uebelhart and Raevsky, op. cit., p. 31.
43. The US also did not support early recognition.
44. The first major breakthrough was to occur at talks held in Lisbon between 22–23 February.
45. M. Glitman, 'US Policy in Bosnia: Rethinking a Flawed Approach', *Survival*, Vol. 38, No. 4 (1996–97) p. 70, and N. Malcolm, 'Faulty History', *Foreign Affairs*, Vol. 74, No. 6 (1995).
46. *United Nations document, S/RES/757*, 30 May 1992.
47. This was despite the fact that both requirements were officially prerequisites for the opening of the airport itself. Ekwall-Uebelhart and Raevsky, op. cit., pp. 62–4.
48. A. Fetherston, O. Ramsbotham, and T. Woodhouse, 'UNPROFOR: some observations from a conflict resolution perspective, *International Peacekeeping*, Vol. 1, No. 2 (1994) pp. 185–6. See also R. Mauther, 'Boutros-Ghali attacks EC peace plan', *The Financial Times*, 22 July 1992. Boutros-Ghali was apparently so annoyed with Carrington that he agreed to chair the London Conference only on the condition that he resign as EC Envoy. See Glenny, op. cit., p. 215.
49. Ramet, op. cit., p. 248.
50. Ekwall-Uebelhart and Ravesky, op. cit., pp. 65–6.
51. Idem.
52. Ibid., p. 67.
53. Until this time UNPROFOR's role in Bosnia was limited to the provisions in Resolution 743 (the Vance Plan) that had mandated UN military observers to patrol certain limited areas in Bosnia following the demilitarization of the UNPAs in Croatia. Idem.
54. Ramet, op. cit., p. 248.
55. Ekwall-Uebelhart and Raevsky, op, cit., pp. 34–5.
56. Fetherston, op. cit., p. 184.
57. *The UN and the situation in the Former Yugoslavia*, op. cit., p. 17.
58. Ibid., p. 4.
59. The three strategic sites concerned were the Maslenica bridge, the Zadar airport and the Peruca Dam. Ekwall-Uebelhart and Raevsky, op. cit., pp. 37–42.
60. Silber and Little, op. cit., p. 276.
61. Idem.
62. Control measures included the declaration of forces in being, including the location of minefields; the monitoring of front lines; the declaration of heavy weapons in separation areas; the establishment of agreed lines on which forces might be located; and the staged withdrawal of forces culminating in their relocation to designated provinces. Ekwall-Uebelhart, op. cit., p. 72.
63. Idem.
64. Izetbegovic, by his own admission, also accepted the plan because he believed the Serbs never would. Silber and Little, op. cit., pp. 276–7.

65. *United Nations document, SC/5564*, 3 March 1993.
66. Silber and Little, op. cit., p. 273.
67. Fetherston, op. cit., p. 188.
68. *United Nations document, S/RES/836*, 4 June 1993.
69. *United Nations document, S/RES/842*, 18 June 1993. Also see 'Ex-Yugoslavia: proposals by Boutros-Ghali for implementation of Resolution 836 – New London conference', *Atlantic News*, No. 2535, 16 June 1993.
70. Burg and Shoup, op. cit., pp. 251–4.
71. Silber and Little, op. cit., p. 288. Owen notes that the one redeeming feature of the JAP was its proposal to establish a Yugoslav War Crimes Tribunal. Owen, op. cit., p. 173.
72. The Bosnian Army also had 2,500 Muslim guerillas operating hit-and run raids on the model of Tito's partisans. Ramet, op. cit., p. 252.
73. Idem.
74. Silber and Little, op. cit., pp. 303–5.
75. Ekwall-Uebelhart and Raevsky, op. cit., p. 79.
76. Ibid., p. 81.
77. Silber and Little, op. cit., p. 316.
78. Ekwall-Uebelhart and Raevsky, op. cit., pp. 88–90.
79. The Croats and Muslims had also benefited from a large infusion of weapons from Iran. Ramet, op. cit., p. 257.
80. Ibid., p. 46 and *United Nations document, S/1994/1067*, 17 September 1994.
81. *United Nations document, S1994/1067*, 17 September 1994.
82. Ekwall-Uebelhart and Raevsky, op. cit., pp. 47–8.
83. *United Nations document, S/1994/1067*, 17 September 1994.
84. C. De Jonge Oudraat, 'Bosnia' in D.C.F. Daniel and B.C. Hayes, *Coercive Inducement and the Containment of International Crises* (Washington: USIP, 1999) p. 63.
85. *United Nations document, S/1994/600*, 19 May 1994.
86. De Jonge Oudraat, op. cit., p. 63.
87. *United Nations document, S/1994/600*, 19 May 1994.
88. Idem.
89. R. Cohen, 'Map blocks a Bosnian peace', *The International Herald Tribune*, 8 November 1994.
90. 'The Balkan Battlefields', *Strategic Survey*, Brassey's for the International Institute for Strategic Studies, 1994/95, p. 95.
91. Ibid., p. 98. These sanctions were lifted pursuant to Security Council Resolution 943 of 23 September 1994.
92. Clinton remained under pressure from Congress to lift the embargo. Ibid., p. 100.
93. The US had initially advocated air strikes at ammunition dumps and supply bases throughout Bosnia, not just Serb weapons in the neighborhood of Bihac. De Jonge Oudraat, op. cit., p. 65.
94. Ekwall-Uebelhart, op. cit., p. 100, *United Nations document, S/1994/1389*, 1 December 1994 and Ramet, op. cit., p. 263.
95. De Jonge Oudraat, op. cit., p. 65.
96. US interests in maintaining European support for NATO expansion seemed to be the determining factor in its decision to back down from its previously more belligerent policies. In the words of De Jonge Oudraat, 'Atlantic unity became more important than Bihac'. Ibid., p. 66.
97. Ekwall-Uebelhart and Raevsky, op. cit., p. 102.

98. J. Pomfret, 'If UN troops go, can Croatia avoid war with Serbs', *The International Herald Tribune*, 21 February 1995.

99. *United Nations document, S1995/222*, 22 March 1995.

100. *The UN and the situation in the former Yugoslavia*, op. cit., p. 37.

101. Ibid., p. 44.

102. *United Nations document, S/1995/320*, 18 April 1995.

103. The attack was ostensibly to restore order after a spate of killings following the stabbing of a Serb by a Croatian refugee on 28 April.

104. *United Nations document, S/1995/467*, 9 June 1995.

105. *Information notes on the former Yugoslavia*, No. 8, August 1995, Office of the Special Envoy for the former Yugoslavia, p. 1.

106. *United Nations document, S/1995/987*, 23 November 1995.

107. *United Nations document*, 30 May 1995. A further 224 UN personnel were in locations where access and movement were being denied by Serb forces.

108. R. Cohen, 'Serbs to keep hostages to deter new UN force', *The International Herald Tribune*, 13 June 1995.

109. S. Helm, 'Zagreb likely to be winner under US plan', *The Independent*, 22 August 1995.

110. R. Cornell, 'Clinton rebuilds his Yugoslav team', *The Independent*, 22 August 1995.

111. De Jonge Oudraat, op. cit., p. 70.

112. The NATO strikes themselves had been carefully designed to avoid altering the strategic balance between the Serb and Muslim-led government forces too dramatically. NATO leaders also insisted that the strikes would stop as soon as the heavy weapons surrounding Sarajevo were removed. See Ibid., p. 71.

113. Stoessinger, op. cit., pp. 230–1.

114. M. Berdal, 'United Nations Peacekeeping in the former Yugoslavia' in D. Donald and H. Brad, *Beyond Traditional Peacekeeping* (London: Macmillan Press, 1995) p. 235.

115. Berdal also notes three other factors that adversely influenced UNPROFOR's logistic situation. The first was UNPROFOR's difficulty in obtaining logistics and engineering units from member states. The second was UNPROFOR's acute lack of spare parts, maintenance facilities and stocks of peacekeeping equipment. And thirdly, the rapid changes in UNPROFOR's mandate, which further contributed to the unsatisfactory logistics arrangements. Ibid., p. 236.

116. Ibid., p. 235.

117. Ekwall-Uebelhart and Raevsky, op. cit., p. 25.

118. All the principal troop contributors, including the UK, France, Spain and the Nordic countries occasionally either refused to carry out orders issued by the Force Commander, or imposed their own conditions on them. Berdal, 'United Nations Peacekeeping in the former Yugoslavia', op. cit., p. 238.

119. S. Peou, *Conflict Neutralization in the Cambodia War* (Oxford: Oxford University Press, 1997) pp. 293–4.

120. Berdal, 'United Nations Peacekeeping in the former Yugoslavia, op. cit., p. 242.

121. Ekwall-Uebelhart and Raevsky, op. cit., p. 30.

122. Although under UNPROFOR control, all weapons remained the property of the parties, who retained the right to carry out maintenance work on them. Once demilitarization was complete UNPROFOR conducted joint search operations with UN CIVPOLS and the local police in order to seize any illegally held weapons. The only weapons authorized by UNPROFOR in Sector West were

side arms for the local police. The wearing of military uniforms was also out-
lawed. Idem.

123. Ibid., p. 106.

124. Idem.

125. The services UNPROFOR offered to provide included meetings on demarcation
lines, a 'village visitation program', the distribution of humanitarian aid and
repairs to the civilian infrastructure. Idem.

126. Ekwall-Uebelhart and Raevsky, op. cit., p. 31.

127. Glenny mentions that as he was not carrying a gun on his travels through the
Krajina the Serb militias allowed him to pass as if he were a 'member of some
harmless sub-human species'. For the Krajina Serbs 'a man who has no gun is
no man'. Glenny, op. cit., pp. 6, 10.

128. Ibid., p. 7.

129. The Security Council's willingness to tolerate this clear breach of the Vance
Plan is cited by Owen as one of the factors behind Tudjman's repeated threats
to end the UN's mandate. Owen, op. cit., pp. 43–4.

130. The Secretary-General noted in September 1994 that UNPROFOR did not have
the means or the mandate for enforcement action. *United Nations document,
S/1994/1067*, 17 September 1994.

131. See Glenny, p. 283 and Owen p. 70.

132. A. Wohlstetter, 'Bosnia as Future', in Z.M. Khalilzad (ed.), *Lessons from Bosnia*
(Santa Monica CA: RAND, 1993) p. 30.

133. Owen, op. cit., pp. 141–2.

134. B. de Rossanet, *Peacemaking and Peacekeeping in Yugoslavia* (The Hague: Kluwar
Law International, 1996) p. 43.

135. Owen, op. cit., p. 349. The Secretary-General had warned as such in his
September 1994 report, in which he stated that the lifting of the arms embargo
'would be tantamount to fanning the flames that the UN [was] deployed to
extinguish...the result would be a fundamental shift from the logic of peacekeeping to the logic of war and would require the withdrawal of UNPROFOR
from Bosnia. *United Nations document, S/1994/1067*, 17 September 1994.

136. See De Rossanet, op. cit., pp. 43–5.

137. In his report of July 1993 the Secretary-General recommended that an additional
10,000 troops would be required to fulfill the Security Council's request to add
border monitoring to UNPROFOR's mandate so as to facilitate the implementation of the arms embargo and reduce interference from outside forces. Only two
of the ten member states asked to supply resources were willing to donate even a
limited number of observers. Resolution 838 (1993), which called for the addition of border monitoring to UNPROFOR's mandate, was therefore never implemented. *United Nations document, S/1995/444*, 30 May 1995.

138. Owen, op. cit., pp. 120, 349.

139. A.F. Fogelquist, 'Turning Points in Bosnia and the Region', in Khalilzad,
op. cit., p. 17.

140. Holbrooke, op. cit., p. 50. When the Croat-Muslim war erupted in the spring of
1993 the Croats stopped supplies to the Muslims completely until it ended a
year later. Owen, op. cit., p. 347.

141. Owen had also pressured for a no-fly zone to prevent scenarios like an Iranian
aircraft landing at Tuzla angering the Serbs to such an extent that they might
put all humanitarian efforts at risk. Ibid., p. 52

142. De Jonge Oudraat, op. cit., p. 50. A French proposal to deploy an intervention
force along with the embargo's adoption in 1992 had already been dropped for

lack of support See Steinberg, J.B., 'Turning Points in Bosnia and the West', in Khalilzad, op. cit., p. 6.

143. De Jonge Oudraat, op. cit., p. 50. Ironically the US Joint Chiefs of Staff actually softened their previous support for the embargo to avert the need to deploy US troops. See Owen, p. 142.

144. Owen, op. cit., p. 178.

145. *United Nations document, S/25939*, 14 June 1993.

146. Two of the contingents lacked extensive supplies, ranging from armored personnel carriers to winter clothing. The UN had to first acquire these supplies and then train the contingents in their use. *United Nations document, S/1994/1389*, 1 December 1994.

147. UNPROFOR was also restricted by its mandate, which allowed it to use force only in self-defense and as a last resort when defending the UNSAs. Once having opened fire, it was also to adhere to the principle of minimum force and stop firing when their opponent did. Retaliatory fire was prohibited. De. Jonge Oudraat, op. cit., p. 56.

148. Idem.

149. Silber and Little, op. cit., p. 316.

150. Idem and De Jonge Oudraat, op. cit., p. 60.

151. *United Nations documents, S/1994/1389*, 1 December 1994 and *S/1995/444*, 30 May 1995.

152. Ekwall-Uebelhart and Raevsky, op. cit., p. 127 and *United Nations document, S/1995/444*, op. cit.

153. The failure to properly delineate the borders of the UNSAs also seems to have contributed to UNPROFOR's problems. For instance, the Secretary-General reported in late 1994 that most of the offensives conducted by Muslim forces from the Bihac pocket were not actually launched from within the Safe Area as it was defined by UNPROFOR. Although he had already stressed the need for a clearer delineation of UNSA boundaries in his earlier reports that year, the Security Council had not acted upon his recommendations. Referring to the Muslim surprise at UNPROFOR's refusal to defend them against Serb counter-attacks, he noted that the 'non-existence of clearly defined boundaries seems to have led to a certain confusion as to the size and configuration of the Bihac Safe Area and created false expectations on the part of the Government of [Bosnia] as to the extent of the responsibilities of UNPROFOR'. Similar problems were experienced in the other UNSAs. Idem.

154. Some believe Ganic was genuinely concerned that demilitarization would increase the permanence of the confrontation line dividing the city. Others speculate that he was holding out for the incoming Clinton administration in the hope of US intervention. Owen also notes that even as late as 1994 the Americans remained wary of committing themselves to the demilitarization of Sarajevo as they felt it might put them in conflict with the Muslim leadership. Owen, op. cit., pp. 85, 256.

155. Ibid., p. 131.

156. Ukwall-Uebelhart and Raevsky, op. cit., p. 127.

157. Srebrenica was located just ten miles from the Serbian border and would have remained a thorn in the side of the Serbians had they allowed it to stay under Muslim control. Gorazde, the largest of the three eastern UNSAs, was also better armed than the others. It also held greater strategic importance as it straddled the main road between two large Serb-held towns in the Drina Valley. Silber and Little, op. cit., pp. 324, 359. Following the fall of Srebrenica

and Zepa one UN commander was quoted as saying that 'nobody in their right minds can believe that Gorazde can remain as a Muslim enclave. It is indefensible.' S. Helm, 'Zagreb likely to be winner under US plan', *The Independent*, 22 August 1995.

158. M.J. Driedzic and A. Blair, 'Bosnia and the International Police Task Force' in *Policing the New World Disorder,* op. cit., p. 262.

159. Silber and Little, op. cit., pp. 107–8.

160. Glenny, op. cit., p. 13.

161. Fetherston, op. cit., pp. 183–4.

162. *United Nations document, S/1995/222*, 22 March 1995 and Driedzic and Blair, op. cit., p. 254.

163. Ibid., pp. 264–7.

164. *United Nations document, S/1994/1067*, 17 September 1994.

165. Fewer than half of all CIVPOLS deployed in early 1992 met the DPKO's minimum standards. In July 1992 a complete Colombian contingent was repatriated as a consequence. Holm also highlights the difficulties caused by CIVPOL's reliance on interpreters that were only available during the day. This meant CIVPOL would only be notified after the local police had finished a job, thus making it impossible for them to monitor their activities. See T.T. Holm, 'CIVPOL Operations in Eastern Slavonia, 1992–1998', *International Peacekeeping*, Vol. 6, No. 4 (1999) pp. 138–142.

166. Ibid., pp. 139, 142.

167. This is one of Gow's major explanations for the failure of the international community to prevent the violent dissolution of the Yugoslav state. Gow, op. cit., p. 300.

168. Holbrooke describes the dichotomy of views that existed within the administration. Whilst former Ambassador to Yugoslavia, Lawrence Eagleburger, and National Security Advisor, Brent Scowcroft (the two most knowledgeable individuals on the issue), were the most concerned, Secretary of State Baker and President Bush remained disinterested, not least because of the imminent Presidential election and the aftermath of the Gulf War. However, US Ambassador to Yugoslavia, Warren Zimmerman, together with Burg and Shoup, paint a picture of a more assertive Baker, claiming that he not only favored the selective bombing of Serbian targets (including Belgrade) in mid-1992, but that he continued to support increases in humanitarian aid (despite opposition from the US military) and a greater EC involvement in the crisis. See, Holbrooke, op. cit., pp. 26–7. W. Zimmerman, 'The Last Ambassador, A Memoir of the Collapse of Yugoslavia', *Foreign Affairs*, Vol. 75, No. 2 (1995). Silber and Little op. cit., p. 151. Burg and Shoup, op. cit., pp. 201–6.

169. Silber and Little, op. cit., p. 159.

170. Gow, op. cit., pp. 63–4.

171. Owen, op. cit., p. 12.

172. Zimmerman, op. cit.

173. This obstacle is emphasized particularly by Silber and Little who describe the Lisbon Agreement as one of the 'most misrepresented' agreements of the whole war.

174. Significantly, Malcolm notes that the JNA's war plans included places of strategic importance, whether or not they were in Serb-majority areas, and were in many cases either occupied or ringed by JNA forces before the war began. Malcolm, op. cit.

175. When Warren Zimmerman was told by Izetbegovic that he no longer accepted the agreement, his response was to tell the Bosnian president that he was under no obligation to sign an agreement he did not agree with, although he also told him that he should fulfill any obligations he had committed himself to. This, at the very most, represents lukewarm support for an agreement that, for Glenny at least, could potentially have averted war. Glenny, op. cit., p. 195.

176. Gow, op. cit., p. 314.

177. Owen, 'Balkan Odyssey', op. cit., p. 354.

178. Fogelquist asserts that the territory was distributed deliberately to gain Croatian support, leaving the Muslims controlling 15 per cent less than they did before the war started. Glitman notes that the incentive for the groups to merge with their ethnic kindred in adjoining countries was still present. Holbrooke believed the VOPP would not solve the Bosnian problem, only perhaps let the world think it was solved for a while. Glenny believed the VOPP was an exceptionally good document if seen as only an interim political solution. Few however go as far as Ramet in asserting that the VOPP was little more than the private notions of both co-chairmen. See Ramet, op. cit., p. 249, Glenny, op. cit., p. 224, Holbrooke, op. cit., p. 52, Fogelquist, op. cit., p. 15, and Glitman, op. cit., p. 71.

179. Silber and Little, op. cit., p. 287.

180. Burg and Shoup, op. cit., p. 255.

181. Owen, op. cit., p. 121.

182. The US also criticized the VOPP for being unenforceable, an opinion shared by Milosevic, who attempted to persuade the Bosnian Serbs to sign it on the basis that they would never have to implement it. However, Karadic feared that only 10,000 troops deployed in Zvornik and the Posavina corridor would effectively neutralize them as a fighting force and therefore refused to endorse it until heavily pressured to do so. Though this in itself does not prove that the VOPP was enforceable, it at the very least intimates the probable effectiveness of a credible international force had it been deployed in 1993. Silber and Little, op. cit., p. 279.

183. Burg and Shoup, op. cit., p. 257.

184. M. Wesley, *Casualties of the New World Order* (London: Macmillan Press, 1997) p. 63.

185. See Glitman, op. cit., S.L. Woodward, 'Bosnia and Herzegovina: How Not to End Civil War' in B.F. Walter and J. Snyder (eds), *Civil Wars, Insecurity and Intervention* (New York: Columbia University Press, 1999) and C.D. Kaufman, 'When All Else Fails', *International Security*, Vol. 23, No. 2 (1998).

186. The Economist argued for just such an arrangement back in August 1992. See 'Reinventing Bosnia', *The Economist*, 22 August 1992.

187. 'Peace at last, at least for now', *The Economist*, 25 November 1995.

188. Y. Akashi, 'The Limits of UN Diplomacy and the Future of Conflict Mediation', *Survival*, Vol. 37, No. 4 (1995–96) p. 93.

189. Through OpPlan 40–104 the US had committed itself to deploy 20,000 US troops to help UN soldiers evacuate Bosnia, a commitment Clinton only learned of in June 1995. Whilst the operation was expected to end in casualties, a decision not to help the UN troops withdraw would have left the US-European security relationship in tatters. Thus, as Holbrooke admits, 'we had to find a policy that avoided a disastrous UN withdrawal'. See Holbrooke, op. cit., pp. 65–8.

190. P. Roe, 'Former Yugoslavia: The Security Dilemma That Never Was?', *European Journal of International Relations*, Vol. 6, No. 3 (2000).

191. N. Cigar, 'False Relativism', *Foreign Affairs*, Vol. 74, No. 6 (1995) p. 150.
192. Woodward, op. cit., p. 86.
193. Idem.

Chapter 6

1. For a detailed account of the causes of the Salvadoran civil war see H. Bryne, *El Salvador's Civil War: A Study of Revolution*, (London: Lynne Reinner, 1996) and T.S. Montgomery, *Revolution in El Salvador: From Civil Strife to Civil Peace* (Boulder, Colo: Westview Press, 1992).
2. Byrne, op. cit., p. 20.
3. This was to be the first time that the US had become directly involved in Salvadoran politics.
4. Montgomery, op. cit., p. 127.
5. General Assembly Resolution 35/192. *The United Nations and El Salvador 1990–1995*, Blue Book Series Vol. 4 (New York: United Nations, 1995) p. 6.
6. The five constituent groups were the *Partido de Conciliacion Nacional* (PCN), the *Fuerzas Populares de Liberacion-Farabundo Mari* (FPL), the *Partido Revolucionario de Trabajadores Centroamericanos*, the *Ejercito Revolucionario del Pueblo* (ERP) and the *Fuerzas Armadas de Resistencia Nacional* (FARN). These groups were sufficiently distinctive through ideology and structure to prevent integration or cooperation further than coordination at the top level of their general command.
7. P.S. Wrobel, *Managing Arms in Peace Processes: Nicaragua and El Salvador* (Geneva: UNIDIR, 1995) p. 124. At its height US funding reached $1.2 million per day.
8. These offers included a letter addressed to President Reagan and signed by all five FMLN group commanders.
9. Montgomery, op. cit., p. 199.
10. The US even persuaded Costa Rica, Honduras and El Salvador to reject a draft treaty prepared by the Group, on the basis that the verification mechanisms were inadequate. The US reaction followed its surprise at the decision of Nicaragua to sign the document. Montgomery, op. cit., pp. 174–5. See also L.C. Wilson and R.G. Diaz, 'United Nations Peacekeeping in Central America' in R. Thakur and C.A. Thayer (eds). *A Crisis of Expectations: United Nations Peacekeeping in the 1990's* (Boulder, Colo: Westview Press, 1995) p. 142 and C. Equizabal, 'Regional Leadership and Universal Implementation in El Salvador's Quest for Peace', in T.G. Weis (ed.), *The United Nations and Civil Wars* (London: Lynne Reinner, 1995) pp. 173–6 and A.H. Moss Jr., 'Peace in Central America', *Survival*, Vol. 32, No. 5 (1990).
11. Duarte was inaugurated as the first elected President of El Salvador in 53 years on 1 June 1984.
12. Equizabal, op. cit., pp. 178–9 and T.L. Karl, 'El Salvador's Negotiated Revolution', *Foreign Affairs*, Vol. 71, No. 2 (1992) pp. 149–150.
13. Moss, op. cit., p. 421.
14. The FMLN also proposed negotiations on its willingness to accept the existence of the military. Acceptance was based, however, on the conditions that that the size of the military be reduced, that its officers responsible for human rights abuses be punished and the police place under civilian control.
15. Eguizabel, op. cit., p. 180 and Wilson and Diaz, op. cit., p. 145.

16. Equizabel, op. cit., p. 180 and Montgomery, op. cit., p. 215.
17. For an account of the ONUCA operation and its eventual involvement in the disarmament of the Nicaraguan resistance see S.M. Hill and S. Malik, *Peacekeeping and the United Nations* (Aldershot: Dartmouth Press, 1996) pp. 59–91.
18. Karl, op. cit., p. 152 and Montgomery, op. cit., p. 219.
19. Planning for the offensive had begun as early as 1987, but senior FMLN personnel have stated that it could have been averted if negotiations had proceeded. Montgomery, op. cit., p. 214.
20. Ibid., p. 219.
21. Moss, op. cit., p. 431.
22. Karl, op. cit., p. 153.
23. The FMLN had made its first diplomatic approaches to the UN during its 1989 offensive and the Central American Presidents had already requested it to act as a mediator. Ibid., p. 154.
24. *The United Nations and El Salvador*, op. cit., p. 12.
25. Karl, op. cit., p. 155.
26. Montgomery, op. cit., p. 220.
27. ONUSAL was created pursuant to SC Resolution 693. For an account of the unprecedented nature of ONUSAL, see Flores, T., 'ONUSAL – A Precedent for Future United Nations Missions?', *International Peacekeeping*, Vol. 2, No. 1 (1995).
28. Karl, op. cit., p. 156.
29. Cristiani had requested that the UN monitor these elections. However, without a negotiated settlement and lacking a cease-fire, the Secretary-General informed him that the conditions did not exist at that time for such a role.
30. Sullivan, op. cit., pp. 93, 94.
31. Karl, op. cit., p. 158.
32. The Secretary-General's invitation was initiated by the joint request of the US Secretary of State and the Soviet Minister for Foreign Affairs, for him to take personal leadership of the negotiation process. See *The United Nations and El Salvador*, op. cit., p. 20.
33. Idem.
34. Sullivan, op. cit., p. 44.
35. Some observers believed a 50 per cent cut was too small for a country without any apparent international threat.
36. Emphasis added. See Flores, op. cit., p. 5.
37. Resolution 729, 14 January 1992.
38. ONUSAL also included 15 military liaison officers, 27 police advisors and 36 administrative and support staff.
39. Troops belonging to units destined to be abolished were to be redeployed in the FAES when it was compatible with its intended reduction and after vetting by the Ad Hoc Commission. Compensation for discharge was to be one year's wages together with Government reintegration packages. *United Nations document, A/46/864–S/23501*, 30 January 1992.
40. The presence of military officers on the Commission was a compromise between the preferred options of the FAES and FMLN. Whilst the former wanted to conduct a 'self-purge', the FMLN wanted foreigners as commissioners. In the end the FMLN accepted the compromise solution on condition that it, and the UN, had a say in the selection of the commissioners. See I. Johnstone, *Rights and Reconciliation: United Nations Strategies in El Salvador*, IPA Occasional Paper Series (London: Lynne Reinner, 1995) p. 32.

41 ONUSAL would deploy at any installations required and use random, mobile checks. *United Nations document, S/23402,* 13 January 1992.

42. *United Nations document, S/25006,* 23 December 1992.

43. *United Nations document, S/23999,* 26 May 1992.

44. Although the Agreements contained special conditions in policing and land tenure for former zones of conflict, the term 'zone of conflict' was nowhere defined. The PAT was to be composed of PNC recruits deployed for short periods of time after a 15-day preparatory course. The delay in creating a 'special regime for the maintenance of public security in the zones of former conflict' had led residents of those areas to form 'public security committees'. *United Nations document, S/24833,* 23 November 1992.

45. Equizabel, op. cit., pp. 184–5 and *United Nations document, S/25812/Add.2,* 25 May 1993.

46. This was much less than the nine and six months postponements Cristiani had sought.

47. *United Nations document, S/25812,* 21 May 1993.

48. These agreements were reached on 22 December 1992 and 4 February 1993.

49. The SIU and UEA were renowned for their connection to the death squads. The longer tenure for the hard-line military leadership prevented swifter military reform. *United Nations documents, S/25006,* 23 December 1992 and *S/25078,* 9 January 1993.

50. *United Nations document, S/25812,* 21 May 1993.

51. *The United Nations and El Salvador,* op. cit., p. 39 and *United Nations document, S/25812,* 21 May 1993.

52. *United Nations document, S/26005,* 29 June 1993.

53. Of the 30 per cent, two-thirds were found as a consequence of the 23 May explosion and the constituent groups handed in the final third. Idem and *United Nations document, S/26371,* 30 August 1993.

54. *United Nations document, S/26790,* 23 November 1993.

55. The Electoral Division was created pursuant to SC Resolution 832.

56. *United Nations document, S/26790,* 23 November 1993.

57. *United Nations document, A/49/59–S/1994/47,* 18 January 1994.

58. *United Nations document, S/1994/561,* 11 May 1994. The number that had received titles by this time was 6,261.

59. *The United Nations and El Salvador,* op. cit., p. 521.

60. *United Nations document, S/26790,* 23 November 1993.

61. Johnstone, op. cit., p. 53.

62. *United Nations document,* S/1994/375, 31 March 1994.

63. Death Squads Still Cast Shadow Over El Salvador', *The Guardian,* 2 June 1994.

64. *United Nations document, S/1994/561,* 11 May 1994.

65. The Secretary-General did agree for more former PN personnel to join the PNC, but only with the agreement of the FMLN.

66. *United Nations document, S/1994/886,* 28 July 1994.

67. By October only 32 per cent of the potential beneficiaries of the land-transfer program had received land. *United Nations document, S/1994/1212,* 31 October 1994

68. Idem.

69. *United Nations document, S/1995/143,* 17 February 1995.

70. *United Nations document, S/1995/220,* 24 March 1995.

71. *Security Council Resolution 143.*

72. *United Nations document, S/1995/220,* 24 March 1995.

73. The Chapultepec Agreements stipulated that this was only to occur 'in exceptional circumstances and for the time strictly necessary'. See Annex II, Art. 21.

74. *United Nations document, S/1995/220*, 24 March 1995.

75. *United Nations document, A/50/517*, 6 October 1995.

76. *United Nations document, A/50/935*, 23 April 1996.

77. *United Nations document, A/51/917*, 1 July 1997.

78. Ibid.

79. E.J. Laurance, 'Surplus Weapons and the Micro-Disarmament Process', *Disarmament: A Periodic Review by the United Nations*, Vol. 19, No. 2 (1996) p. 61.

80. *United Nations document, S/25812*, 21 May 1993.

81. *The United Nations and El Salvador*, op. cit., p. 26.

82. After the explosion the UN conducted a more 'realistic' assessment of the FMLN's inventory. These new estimates were based on information provided by renowned international and national research institutions; the number of demobilization certificates issued by ONUSAL to former FMLN combatants; and acquisition and operative plans disclosed. *United Nations document, S/23671*, 30 August 1993.

83. Wilson and Diaz, op. cit., p. 154.

84. *United Nations document, 2/25812*, 21 May 1993.

85. Y. Grenier and J. Daudelin, 'Foreign Assistance and the Market Place of Peacemaking: Lessons from El Salvador', *International Peacekeeping*, Vol. 2, No. 3 (1995).

86. Wrobel, op. cit., p. 202.

87. Grenier and Daudelin, op. cit., p. 354.

88. R. Stahler-Sholk, op. cit., p. 13 and F.O. Hampson, *Nurturing Peace: Why Peace Settlements Succeed or Fail* (Washington: USIP, 1996) p. 145.

89. See the Chapultepec Agreements, Chap. 1, Art. 3A.

90. Johnstone, op. cit., p. 32. Nevertheless, ONUSAL showed great determination to ensure the Commission's recommendations were implemented. The importance of implementation was expressed by the Secretary-General, who believed that the Commission's report was not just a substantive issue in the process of restructuring the FAES, but also had a 'direct bearing on the armed force's obedience and constitutional subordination to civilian authority'. It was also, therefore, ' a test of the development and consolidation of the rule of law in El Salvador'. *United Nations document*, A/47/912–S/25521, 5 April 1993.

91. *United Nations document, S/1995/220*, 24 March 1995.

92. G. Costa, 'The United Nations and Reform of the Police in El Salvador', *International Peacekeeping*, Vol. 2, No. 3 (1995) p. 372.

93. The PNC itself uncovered a major arms cache in August 1995 that included an array of machineguns, anti-tank weapons and grenade launchers. The lawyers of the illegal gang held responsible claimed that military officials were the principal suppliers of the weapons. 'PNC Scores Success in Crime Fight', *Latin American Monitor*, August 1995.

94. Statement by P. Sollis, Washington Office on Latin America, quoted in Montgomery, op. cit., p. 230.

95. De Soto, A., and Del Castillo, G., 'Implementation of Comprehensive Peace Agreements: Staying the Course in El Salvador', *Global Governance*, Vol. 1 (1995) 195.

96. Ibid., p. 196.

97. W. Stanley and D. Holiday, 'Peace Mission Strategy and Domestic Actors: UN Mediation, Verification and Institution-Building in E Salvador', *International Peacekeeping*, Vol. 4, No. 2 (1997) p. 47.
98. *United Nations document, S/1995/220*, 24 March 1995.
99. Wrobel, op. cit., pp. 216–7.
100. Grenier and Daudelin, op. cit., p. 358.
101. Ibid., p. 357.
102. *United Nations document, A/50/455*, 23 October 1995.
103. Hampson, op. cit., p. 146.
104. US Aid, the World Bank and other international donors had helped the Government's preparations. United Nations document, S/24833, 23 November 1992. Hampson, op. cit., p. 146 and Sullivan, op. cit., p. 94.
105. *The UN and El Salvador*, op. cit., p. 27.
106. *United Nations document, A/51/917*, 1 July 1997.
107. *United Nations document, S/26790*, 23 November 1993.
108. *United Nations document, A/50/455*, 23 October 1995. As De Soto and Del Castillo point out this situation also highlighted a lack of coordination and transparency in the UN system. Whilst the IMF and World Bank failed to keep the UN abreast of the economic programs they had sponsored, the UN neglected to inform the Bretton Woods institutions of the peace agreements. See De Soto and Del Castillo, op. cit., p. 168.
109. *United Nations document, A/50/455*, 23 October 1995.
110. *United Nations document, A/50/517*, 6 October 1995. ONUSAL criticized the FMLN for not supplying comprehensive lists of potential beneficiaries earlier in the process. However it was recognized that the FMLN was still distrustful of the Government and armed forces and feared the names would not be kept confidential. *United Nations document, S/1994/1000*, 26 August 1994.
111. *United Nations document, A/51/917*, 1 July 1997.
112. *United Nations document, S/1995/220*, 24 March 1995.
113. *United Nations document, A/51/917*, 1 July 1997.
114. *United Nations document, S/1995/220*, 24 March 1995.
115. Some of the greatest setbacks for the PNC were to occur through 1993 following the appointment of Oscar Pena Duran as the PNC's first Deputy Director of Operations. As the Director-General at this time was a former businessman with no police experience, Duran subsequently became *de facto* head of the force. As an army captain and former head of the UEA, Duran used his position to transfer former military personnel into the force without passing them through the PNSA; denied ONUSAL information on public security personnel; created an intelligence network of former UEA members to monitor the activities of former FMLN members in the PNC; and refused ONUSAL's offers of technical assistance. Paradoxically, Duran had supposedly been handpicked by the US for his administrative skills and his willingness to prosecute officers who might violate human rights. He was replaced in May 1994. Montgomery, op. cit., p. 240.
116. 'Pressure Grows For Police Purge', *Central America*, November 1995. Some analysts even suggested that the UN was watering down reports of human rights abuses by the PNC in order to present more favorable conditions for the conduct of the elections. Stanley and Holiday, op. cit., p. 35.
117. Stanley and Holiday, op. cit., p. 30.
118. Ibid., p. 39 and Oakley et al., op. cit., p. 111.

119. R. Stahler-Sholk, 'El Salvador's Negotiated Transition: From Low-Intensity Conflict to Low-Intensity Democracy', *Journal of Interamerican Studies and World Affairs*, Vol. 36, No. 4 (1994) p. 16.

120. Stanley and Holiday assert that the second ONUSAL Chief of Mission made numerous positive pronouncements of progress in implementing the Agreements that not only contradicted reality, but also undercut the position of those within ONUSAL (as well as the FMLN) pushing for more rigorous compliance. Stanley and Holiday, op. cit., p. 35.

121. The Government's new commitment was evident in its account to ONUSAL that it had collected 2,000 such weapons in the first three months of 1995 alone. A plan to establish buy-back programs was presented to the Government by the UN in August 1995. Laurance, op. cit., pp. 64–5.

122. M.W. Chernick, 'Peacemaking and Violence in Latin America' in M.E. Brown (ed.), *The International Dimensions of Internal Conflict*, (Massachusetts: MIT Press, 1996) pp. 288–9.

123. G.L. Munck and C. Kumar, 'Civil conflicts and the conditions for successful international intervention: a comparative study of Cambodia and El Salvador', *Review of International Studies*, Vol. 21 (1995) p. 178.

124. The commitment of the FMLN to democracy was also evident in its willingness to abide by the electoral result despite some of its members expressing deep disappointment that it had sacrificed a great deal for the election of 21 Deputies and 15 Mayors in the 1994 elections. Montgomery, op. cit., p. 269.

125. *United Nations document, A/51/917*, 1 July 1997.

126. M. Peceny and W. Stanley, *Liberal Social Reconstruction and the Resolution of Civil Wars in Central America, International Organization*, Vol. 55, No. 1 (2001) pp. 163–4.

127. Even the Nicaraguan resistance had demanded a UN battalion for protection.

128. Oakley, et al., op. cit., p. 122.

129. Peceny and Stanley, op. cit., pp. 168–9.

130. *United Nations document, S/25812*, 21 May 1993.

131. *United Nations document, S/25901*, 8 June 1993.

132. *United Nations document, S/2999*, 26 May 1992.

133. Stanley and Holiday, op. cit., p. 28.

134. W. Stanley, 'Building New Police Forces in El Salvador and Guatemala: Learning and Counter-Learning, *International Peacekeeping*, Vol. 6, No. 1 (1999) p. 118.

135. Stahler-Sholk, op. cit., pp. 12–3.

136. *United Nations document, S/1995/220*, 24 March 1995.

137. S.N. MacFarlane and T.G. Weiss, The United Nations, Regional Organizations and Human Security: Building Theory in Central America, *World Third Quarterly*, Vol. 15, No. 2 (1994) p. 289.

Chapter 7

1. *United Nations document, S/25840*, 25 May 1993.

2. Security Council Resolution 804, 29 January 1992, *The Situation in Angola* (New York: United Nations, 1994) p. 6.

3. The transitional government had included posts for 5 UNITA dissidents.

4. G. Wright, *The Destruction of a Nation – US Policy Towards Angola Since 1945* (London: Pluto Press, 1997) p. 173 and *United Nations document, S/25840*, 25 May 1993.

5. Hampson, op. cit., p. 118.
6. Wright, op. cit., p. 175.
7. *United Nations document, S/25840*, 25 May 1993.
8. Idem.
9. Wright, op. cit., p. 184.
10. *The Situation in Angola*, op. cit., p. 8.
11. *United Nations document, S/26872*, 14 December 1993.
12. UNITA demanded five ministerial posts, including Defense, Finance and Foreign Affairs. The Government, however, offered only those of Geology and Mines, Health and Tourism, Trade and the Hotel Industry. It also offered UNITA a number of vice-ministerial posts, including those of Defense, Interior and Finance.
13. The Government also recognized that the list of governorships requested by UNITA represented a *de facto* partition of the country. UNITA's official spokesperson, Jorge Valentin, had actually proposed a partition of the country as a constitutional solution to the crisis.
14. K. Maier, 'UN Toils for Peace as Angolan Rebels Create a Capital', *The Independent*, 19 February 1994.
15. Smith, op. cit., p. 162.
16. 'No Relief', *The Economist*, 18 June 1994.
17. T.W. Lippman, 'UN Hoping for Angola Settlement, Delays on New Savimbi Sanctions', *International Herald Tribune*, 9 August 1994.
18. *United Nations document, S/1994/1069*, 17 September 1994.
19. Idem. and Smith, op. cit., p. 163.
20. *United Nations documents, S/1994/1197*, 20 October 1994.
21. Under UN auspices and with the observer states present, these talks were intended to establish the technical modalities of the cessation of hostilities *in situ* for such tasks as the disengagement of forces; the setting up of verification mechanisms; the specific numbers and types of forces; and the quartering areas for UNITA forces. *United Nations document, S/1994/1441*.
22. S. Kiley, 'Peace Deal Halted as Angolan Offensive Drives Back Rebels', *The Times*, 15 November 1994.
23. 'Angola Orders Its Troops to Stop Shooting', *International Herald Tribune*, 17 November 1994.
24. 'Angola Peace Shaky as Treaty is Signed Without 2 Leaders', *International Herald Tribune*, 21 November 1994.
25. *United Nations document, S/1994/1376*, 4 December 1994.
26. *United Nations document, S/1994/1441*.
27. Idem.
28. Idem.
29. The four Ministerial positions offered to UNITA were those for Geology and Mines, Trade, Health and Hotel Business and Tourism. Deputy-Ministerial positions were provided for Home Affairs, Finance, Agriculture, Public Works, Social Reintegration and Mass Communication. UNITA was also awarded three provincial governorships and six ambassadorial positions. At the levels below provincial governor, UNITA was awarded positions for 30 Municipal Administrators, 35 Deputy Municipal Administrators and 75 Administrator of Communes. Idem.
30. This included the actions of the Polling Station Officers; the design, manufacture and storage of voting material; and the preparation of the electoral registration rolls.

31. 'Both Sides Ignore Cease-Fire in Angola', *International Herald Tribune*, 23 November 1994.
32. 'Fingers Crossed', *The Economist*, 29 April 1995 and 'Inside the Tent', *Africa Confidential*, Vol. 36, No.14 (1995) p. 5.
33. Ibid., p. 6.
34. *United Nations document, S/1995/842*, 4 October 1995.
35. Wright, op. cit., p. 198.
36. *United Nations document, S/1995/842*, 4 October 1995.
37. *United Nations document, S/1996/75*, 31 January 1996.
38. UNITA was also to supply the Air Force with 200 troops and the Navy with 100.
39. *United Nations document, S/1996/75*, 31 January 1996.
40. *United Nations document, S/1996/171*, 6 March 1996.
41. *United Nations document, S/1996/960*, 4 October 1996.
42. 'Quartering of UNITA troops', *Angola Peace Monitor*, Vol. 3, No. 1, 27 September 1996. UNITA had also failed to relinquish any of its heavy weapons or communications equipment.
43. The caliber of the generals that had arrived, coupled with those that were noticeably absent led some analysts to question whether Savimbi was simply using the process to 'clear out some dead wood' and keep his best officers in the field. 'UNITA Generals Arrive in Luanda, But Progress Slow', *Angola Peace Monitor*, op. cit.
44. *United Nations document*, 4 October 1996.
45. *United Nations document, S/RES/1075*, 11 October 1996.
46. *United Nations document, S/1996/960*, 19 November 1996.
47. 'Military Tasks "75 per cent to 100 per cent" Completed by Deadline Date', *Angola News*, No. 37 (1996).
48. *United Nations document, S/1996/960*, 19 November 1996.
49. *United Nations document, S/1997/115*, 7 February 1997.
50. Idem.
51. *United Nations document, S/1996/1000*, 2 December 1996.
52. *United Nations document, S/RES/1098*, 27 February 1997.
53. *United Nations document, S/1997/239*, 19 March 1997.
54. *United Nations document, S/1997/304*, 14 April 1997.
55. *United Nations document, S/1997/438*, 5 June 1997.
56. *United Nations document, S/1997/640*, 13 August 1997.
57. UNITA's first estimate was only 3,000.
58. United Nations document, *Weekly update on humanitarian activities: Period covered 21–25 July 1997*, Department of Humanitarian Affairs, 1 August 1997.
59. *United Nations document, S/1997/640*, 13 August 1997.
60. *United Nations document, S/RES/1127*, 28 August 1997.
61. *United Nations document, S/1998/17*, 12 January 1998.
62. A. Vines, *Angola Unravels: The Rise and Fall of the Lusaka Peace Process*, Human Rights Watch, 1999, p. 25.
63. Ibid., p. 26.
64. *United Nations document, S/1998/117*, 12 June 1998.
65. *United Nations document, S/1998/723*, 6 August 1998.
66. *United Nations document, S/1998/838*, 7 September 1998
67. *United Nations document, S/1998/110*, 23 November 1998.
68. *United Nations document, S/1999/49*, 17 January 1999.
69. *United Nations documents*, S/1998/110, 23 November 1998, S/1999/202, 24 February 1999.

70. 'Albright Says UN Peacekeeping Reduces the Risks in Crises', *Official Text*, 9 May 1994, p. 1.
71. PDD25 also addressed the reform of UN management of peacekeeping operation, the improvement of US management of its own forces deployed in UN operations and the cooperation required between the US Executive, Congress and the American public.
72. R. Jones, et al. (eds), *International Peacekeeping News*, 19 July 1995.
73. B. Boutros-Ghali, 'Secretary-General Calls for Burden Sharing in Peacekeeping', *United Nations document, SG/SM/5589*, 22 March 1995.
74. S. Ogata and P. Volcker, et al., *Financing an effective United Nations: A Report of the Independent Advisory Group on UN Financing* (New York: Ford Foundation, 1993) p. 17.
75. *United Nations document, S/1999/49*, 17 January 1999.
76. This phased deployment envisaged the immediate deployment of UNAVEM's planning and support elements, the deployment of the logistical elements within two months and the deployment of six infantry battalions within three months. See Wright, op. cit., p. 193.
77. Ibid., p. 195.
78. For the Secretary-General's criticisms of troop contributing countries see *United Nations document, S/1995/588*, 17 July 1995.
79. Vines, op. cit., p. 2.
80. 'Peace, Maybe', *The Economist*, 18 February 1995.
81. N. Ball and F. Campbell, *Complex Crisis and Complex Peace* (New York: United Nations Office for the Coordination of Humanitarian Affairs, 1998) p. 44. The Secretary-General recognized the unsettling effect a lack of agreement on the FAA was having on demobilization in his 6 March 1996 report, warning that many UNITA troops and particularly their officers remained uncertain of their futures. *United Nations document, S/1996/171*, 6 March 1996.
82. Ball and Campbell, op. cit., p. 44.
83. Idem.
84. United Nations troops were not even originally expected to help UNITA construct the quartering sites. *United Nations document, S/1996/75*, 31 January 1996.
85. Ball and Campbell, op. cit., p. 47.
86. As NGO's are frequently wary of working with ex-combatants they were thought to be more likely to participate if the processes were clearly overseen by a civilian agency. Equally, many organizations have restrictions on providing funding to members of armed forces and they were thought more likely to donate funds if the demobilization process was clearly lodged within a civilian entity. See Ibid., pp. 38–39.
87. Ball and Campbell note that there existed a certain degree of tension between the DRO and UNDP starting with UCAH's well-founded concerns that the UNDP could not develop the Community Referral Service program in time for demobilization. Ibid., p. 49.
88. Ibid., p. 46 and *United Nations document, A/52/563*, 3 November 1997.
89. V. Brittain, *Death of Dignity: Angola's Civil War* (London: Pluto Press, 1998) p. 91.
90. The Secretary-General supported the idea of 'reconstruction teams' as a way to help the demobilization and reintegration of ex-combatants. He believed that such teams, supported by both the Government and international community, would be an important means of promoting social reintegration as well as the country's overall economic rehabilitation. *United Nations document, S/1996/503*, 27 June 1996.

91. Ibid., p. 92.
92. Idem. Nevertheless, there were incentives for both internal parties in global incorporation. The plan would have denied UNITA trained manpower and complicated its efforts to return to war. On the other hand, it would also have provided UNITA with greater leverage within the FAA. Ball and Campbell, op. cit., p. 51.
93. *United Nations document, S/1996/503*, 27 June 1996.
94. Ball and Campbell, op. cit., p. 46 and *United Nations document, A/52/563*, 3 November 1997.
95. In addition, the Special Subsidy to Support Reinsertion included $125 to support a second relocation for a family of five should they choose not to settle in the first choice location. Ball and Campbell, op. cit., p. 52.
96. Ball and Campbell, op.cit., pp. 48–49, 51–52.
97. *United Nations documents, S/1996/248*, 4 April 1996 and *S/1996/328*, 30 April 1996. He also noted that the health of those troops that had arrived was generally poor. Between 5 February and 25 March 1996 over 25,000 different pathologies had been diagnosed in the first four quartering areas alone. Health workers resident in the areas were already treating many of these and mobile medical teams were being set up to help.
98. Brittain, op. cit., p. 90.
99. The UN did persuade UNITA to accept primary responsibility for its soldiers' dependents, but in the circumstances this could be considered little more than a pyrrhic victory.
100. Ball and Campbell, op. cit., pp. 47, 52.
101. Ibid., pp.49–50. One experienced NGO that refused to adopt a similar role to that which it had adopted in Mozambique and El Salvador was *Medicine Sans Frontiers*.
102. Idem.
103. *United Nations document, S/1998/17*, 12 January 1998.
104. *United Nations document, S/1997/640*, 13 August 1997. Ball and Campbell, op. cit., p. 42.
105. *United Nations document, S/1998/524*, 17 June 1998.
106. The fall in oil prices to a new low of $11 a barrel in 1998 played a significant role in the government's lack of money. The Angolan government had also sold rights to oil exploration and mortgaged the potential revenue for a number of years to come in order to buy arms. The Secretary-General remarks in his report of 13 March 1998 that progress in demobilization and reintegration was being achieved despite the lack of government subsidies.
107. Ball and Campbell, op. cit., p. 74 and personal interview at DPKO, UN Headquarters, November 1996.
108. Wright, op. cit., p. 94.
109. A. Dev Sen, 'Not Such a Fashionable War', *New Statesman*, 30 August 1999.
110. The Secretary-General had called for such assistance in mid-1996. *United Nations document S/1996/503*, 27 June 1996.
111. *United Nations document, S/1997/640*, 13 August 1997.
112. *United Nations document, S/1997/115*, 7 February 1997.
113. *United Nations document, S/1998/1110*, 23 November 1998.
114. *United Nations document, S/1998/524*, 17 June 1998.
115. Vines, op. cit., pp. 174–176.
116. Heywood, op. cit., p. 148.
117. M. Anstee, 'The Fight Goes On', *The World Today*, Vol. 54, No. 10 (1998) p. 256.

118. 'Trying', *The Economist*, 15 July 1995. When questioned by Western journalists, the day after the Security Council voted to create UNAVEM III, Savimbi reassured them that he was personally committed to the peace process, but that hardline military commanders were putting him under intense pressure to reject it. 'Peace Maybe', *The Economist*, 18 February 1995.
119. Brittain, op. cit., p. 67.
120. Anstee, 'The Fight Goes On', op. cit., p. 256.
121. Brittain, op. cit., p. 79.
122. D. Shearer, 'Outsourcing War', *Foreign Policy*, No. 112 (1998) 76.
123. Brittain, op. cit., p. 89.
124. *United Nations document, S/1998/931*, 8 October 1998.
125. *United Nations document, S/1998/1110*, 23 November 1998.
126. N. McQueen, 'Peacekeeping by Attrition: The UN in Angola', *The Journal of Modern African Studies*, Vol. 36, No. 3 (1998) p. 402.
127. L.M. Heywood, 'Towards an Understanding of Modern Political Ideology in Africa: the Case of the Ovimbundu of Angola', *The Journal of Modern African Studies*, Vol. 36, No. 1 (1998) pp. 144–5, 148. In Heywood's opinion the African-influenced nationalism that UNITA has promoted will present formidable obstacles to the full integration of the Ovimbundu and other rural populations into a modern Angolan state.
128. W. Minter, *Apartheid's Contras* (Witswatersrand University Press, 1994) p. 105.
129. Vines, op. cit., p. 111.
130. Anstee, 'The Fight Goes On', op. cit., p. 258.
131. Vines, op. cit., p. 135.
132. Brittain, op. cit., p. 100.
133. Vines, op. cit., p. 134.
134. Ibid., pp. 142–3.
135. *United Nations document, S/1999/49*, 17 January 1999.
136. V. Brittain, 'UN Mission to Pull Out of Angola Says Annan', *The Guardian*, 18 January 1999.
137. Idem.
138. 'On and On They Fight', *The Economist*, op. cit.
139. B. Harden, 'Angolan Paradox: Oil Wealth Only Adds To Misery', *New York Times*, 9 April 2000.

Conclusion

1. J.W. Burton, *Peace Theory: Preconditions for Disarmament* (New York: Alfred A Knopf, 1962) p. 35.
2. Quoted in H.E. Cauvin, 'Rebels Without a War Wait for Help in Angola', *New York Times*, 29 September 2002.
3. A. Wendt, *Social Theory of International Politics* (Cambridge: Cambridge University Press, 1999) p. 115.
4. Ibid., pp. 336–7.
5. M. Peceny and W. Stanley, 'Liberal Social Reconstruction and the Resolution of Civil Wars in Central America', *International Organization*, Vol. 55, No. 1 (2001) pp. 175–6.
6. See Chapter 2
7. M. Hoddie and C.A. Hartzell, 'Civil War Settlements and the Implementation of Military-Power-Sharing Arrangements', *Journal of Peace Research*, Vol. 40,

No. 3 (2003) p. 316. In their study these cases included South Africa and the Philippines.

8. Ibid., p. 314.

9. 'Demobilization After Civil Wars', *Strategic Survey* 1993–4 (London: Brasssey's for the IISS, 1994) p. 29.

10. P.S. Wrobel, *Managing Arms in Peace Processes: Nicaragua and El Salvador* (Geneva: United Nations, 1995) pp. 186–7. The need for independent sources of information, including technical reconnaissance and information from Member States is also recognized in the UN study, 'Disarmament, Demobilization and Reintegration of Ex-Combatants in a Peacekeeping Environment' (New York, United Nations, 1999) p. 20.

11. F. Tanner, 'Bargains for Peace: Military Adjustments During Post-War Rebuilding', in M. Pugh (ed.), *Regeneration of War-Torn Societies* (London: Macmillan, 2000) p. 80.

12. As the soldiers retained would almost certainly be the finest soldiers under their command, given adequate incentives many of them would be prime candidates for newly formed armed forces.

13. Interestingly, in her 1999 study of the stability of negotiated agreements Caroline Hartzell also suggests that retained forces might contribute to the maintenance of peace. Hartzell cites the fact that two negotiated settlements in her study that included such provisions proved to be stable: the settlement to end the Yemini civil war and the Managua Protocol on Disarmament for Nicaragua. Though Cambodia and Mozambique are included in her study she fails to mention the first and does not include the second because her study does not analyze the degree of implementation. C.A. Hartzell, 'Explaining the Stability of Negotiated Settlements to Intrastate Wars', *Journal of Conflict Resolution*, Vol. 43, No. 1 (1999) p. 8.

14. C. King, 'Ending Civil Wars', *Adelphi Paper 308* (London: Brassey's for the IISS, 1997) p. 57.

15. D. Keen, 'The Economic Functions of Violence in Civil Wars', *Adelphi Paper 320* (London: Brassey's for the IISS, 1998) p. 11 and M. Berdal and D.M. Malone, 'Introduction', in M. Berdal and D.M. Malone (eds), *Greed and Governance: Economic Agendas in Civil Wars* (Boulder, Colo.: Lynne Rienner, 2000) p. 4.

16. Keen refers to economic violence in his study. Keen, op. cit., p. 12.

17. S.J. Stedman, 'Spoiler Problems in Peace Processes' in P.C. Stern and D. Druckman (eds), *International Conflict Resolution After the Cold War* (Washington D.C.: National Academy Press, 2000) p. 178.

18. Ibid., p. 184.

19. Ibid., pp. 182–3.

20. The strategy of coercion actually has several variations, including coercive diplomacy, the use of force, withdrawal and the 'departing train'. As the political will of the international community to follow through on threats is often lacking and spoilers have a tendency to call the bluff of those who threaten them, Stedman advises against the use of coercive diplomacy. His primary prescription is therefore the 'departing train' approach, a metaphor that implies the peace process is like a train leaving the station at a preordained time and that once set in motion anyone not aboard will be left behind. See Ibid., pp. 185–6, 189.

21. Ibid., p. 215.

22. Ibid., p. 180.

23. Berdal and Malone, op. cit., p. 14.

24. Hartzell, op. cit.

25. Ibid., p. 19–20.
26. Peceny and Stanley, op. cit., p. 153.
27. T.D. Sisk and A. Reynolds, 'Elections and Electoral Systems' in T.D. Sisk and A. Reynolds (eds), *Elections and Conflict Management in Africa* (Washington D.C.: USIPP, 1998) p. 15.
28. Peceny and Stanley, op. cit., p. 153.
29. D. Beresford, 'Final lap for UN's man in Maputo', *The Guardian*, 26 October 1994. Ajello, was quoted as saying that the confidence-building process had been a nightmare because it was incompatible with electioneering.
30. Reynolds and Sisk, op. cit.,, p. 13.
31. Ibid., p. 5.
32. Ibid., p. 34.
33. H. Glickman, 'Ethnicity, Elections and Constitutional Democracy in Africa', in Ibid., p. 51.
34. Hartzell, op. cit., p. 9.
35. T.D. Sisk, *Power Sharing and International Mediation in Ethnic Conflict* (Washington D.C.: USIPP, 1997) p. xii.
36. T. Lyons, 'The Role of Postsettlement Elections' in S.J. Stedman, D. Rothchild and E.M. Cousens (eds), *Ending Civil Wars* (Boulder, Colo.: Lynne Rienner, 2002) p. 220.
37. S.J. Stedman, *Peacemaking in Civil War* (London: Lynne Rienner, 1991) p. 237.
38. R. Cohen, 'Cultural Aspects of International Mediation' in J. Bercovitch (ed.), *Resolving International Conflicts* (Boulder, Colo.: Lynne Rienner, 1996) pp. 109, 111.
39. It is also important to recognize that culture can also be a source of conflict. For example, in the case of Mozambique, Keen explains that the attractiveness of joining RENAMO was increased for young men who were prevented from obtaining a secondary education or from upward mobility within their society because the control of their villages had fallen into the hands of the dominant lineage's elders. RENAMO not only offered alternative income and excitement, but also the potential for authority denied them in their villages. Keen, op. cit., p. 49.
40. S. Mydans, 'Fragile Stability Slowly Emerges in Cambodia', *New York Times*, 25 June 2000.
41. Idem.
42. S.J. Stedman, 'Spoiler Problems in Peace Processes', *International Security*, Vol. 22, No. 2 (1997) p. 41.
43. D. Rothchild quoted in T.D. Sisk, 'Elections and Conflict Management in Africa', op. cit., p. 161.
44. L. Diamond quoted in B.F. Walter, 'Designing Transitions from Civil War', *International Security*, Vol. 24, No. 1 (1999) pp. 139–40.
45. Lyons, op. cit., p. 216.
46. J. Prendergast, *Crisis Response* (London: Pluto Press, 1997) p. 132.
47. For an explanation of how local cultural traditions can be utilized to encourage democratic transitions see B. Pouligny, 'Promoting Democratic Institutions in Post-Conflict Societies: Giving Diversity a Chance', *International Peacekeeping*, Vol. 7, No. 3 (2000).
48. R. Mani, 'The Rule of Law or the Rule of Might? Restoring Local Justice in the Aftermath of Conflict', in M. Pugh (ed.), *Regeneration of War-Torn Societies*, op. cit., p. 92.
49. P. Ashdown, 'What I Learned in Bosnia', *New York Times*, 28 October 2002.

50. A.S. Hansen, 'International Security Assistance to War-torn Societies', in M. Pugh (ed.), *Regeneration of War-Torn Societies*, op. cit., p. 35.
51. Hansen, op. cit., pp. 47–9.
52. Ibid., p. 50.
53. G. Evans, 'Peacekeeping in Cambodia – Lessons Learned', *NATO Review*, Vol. 42, No. 4 (1994) p. 27.
54. M. Doyle, *UN Peacekeeping in Cambodia: UNTAC's Civil Mandate*, International Peace Academy Occasional Paper Series (London: Lynne Rienner, 1995) pp. 45, 49.
55. *United Nations document, A/55/305–S/200/809*. Much of the problem in establishing such reserves is that current missions outstrip the number of officers made available by Member States. For discussion of this and other issues related to CIVPOL recruitment see E.J. Latham, 'CIVPOL Certification: A Model for Recruitment and Training of Civilian Police Monitors', *World Affairs*, Vol. 163, No. 4 (2001). For an overview of the suggestions of the Brahimi report with respect to criminal justice and the success registered in their implementation, see W. Lewis, E. Marks and R. Perito, 'Enhancing International Civilian Police in Peace Operations', *USIP Special Report*, 22 April 2002.
56. Mani, op. cit., pp. 106.
57. T.L. Putnam, 'Human Rights and Sustainable Peace', in S.J. Stedman, D. Rothchild and E.M. Cousens (eds), *Ending Civil Wars*, op. cit. pp. 237–71.
58. H.C. Kelman, Social-Psychological Dimensions of International Conflict, in I.W. Zartman and J.L. Rasmussen (eds), *Peacemaking in International Conflict: Methods and Techniques* (Washington D.C.: USIPP, 2001) p. 201.
59. J. Prendergast and E. Plumb, 'Building Local Capacity: From Implementation to Peacebuilding', in S. J. Stedman et al. (eds), *Ending Civil Wars*, op. cit., p. 327.
60. N.J. Colletta, 'The World Bank, Demobilization and Social Reconstruction', in J. Boutwell and M. Klare (eds), *Light Weapons and Civil Conflict* (Lahnam, M.D.: Rowman and Littlefield, 1999) p. 209.
61. Prendergast and Plumb, op. cit., p. 334.
62. Ibid., p. 212.
63. *Disarmament, Demobilization and Reintegration of Ex-Combatants in a Peacekeeping Environment: Principles and Guidelines* (New York: United Nations, 1999) p. 1.
64. OXFAM reported that some UNITA soldiers in Angola had been rejected by their own communities. See R. Carroll, 'Peace Brings UNITA Only Humiliation', *The Guardian*, 21 February 2003.
65. For a guide to the constituent processes involved in military reform see Hansen, op. cit., p. 47.
66. During interviews at UN Headquarters in 1996 Berdal's paper and the publications of UNIDIR were mentioned most frequently to me.
67. *Disarmament, Demobilization and Reintegration of Ex-Combatants in a Peacekeeping Environment: Principles and Guidelines*, op. cit., p. 1.
68. N. Ball and F. Campbell, *Complex Crisis and Complex Peace* (New York: United Nations Office for the Coordination of Humanitarian Affairs, 1998) p. 49.
69. Colletta, op. cit., p. 208.
70. Even in the 1979 CMF operation animosity had been sown amongst the guerilla forces who began to believe that the poor conditions and lack of proper food was designed to force them to leave the assembly areas, thereby allowing the Rhodesian forces to claim that they had reneged on their commitment to regroup. See Chapter 2 footnote 97.
71. In the case of Mozambique the soldiers were also upset because they were supplied with the raw material to build African huts rather than military tents.

There was thus a general feeling that they were being treated as peasant farmers rather than soldiers. A. Ajello, 'Mozambique: Implementation of the 1992 Peace Agreement', in C. Crocker, F.O. Hampson and P. Aall (eds), *Herding Cats: Multi-Party Mediation in a Complex World*, (Washington D.C.: USIPP, 1999) p. 629.

72. M. Berdal, 'Disarmament and Demobilization After Civil Wars', *Adephi Paper 303*, (London, IISS, 1996) pp. 5–6.

73. Ajello, op. cit., p. 629.

74. This is noted in *Disarmament, Demobilization and Reintegration of Ex-Combatants in a Peacekeeping Environment: Principles and Guidelines,* op. cit., p. 38.

75. Quoted in K.M. Clark, 'The Demobilization and Reintegration of Soldiers: Perspectives from US Aid', *Africa Today* (1995) 55.

76. Colletta, op. cit., p. 207.

77. *United Nations documents, S/2000/101*, 11 February 2000 and *A/55/305–S/2000/809*. The Secretary-General suggests that the assessed budget can be reimbursed as voluntary contributions arrive.

78. *Disarmament, Demobilization and Reintegration of Ex-Combatants in a Peacekeeping Environment: Principles and Guidelines,* op. cit., p. 29.

79. W. Hoffman, and W. Richter, 'The Proliferation of Light Weapons, Small Arms and Land-mines', *Disarmament*, Vol. 19, No. 2 (1996) 15.

80. Prendergast and Plumb, op. cit., pp. 329, 336.

81. *Disarmament, Demobilization and Reintegration of Ex-Combatants in a Peacekeeping Environment: Principles and Guidelines,* op. cit., p. 6. One example of this would be for the UN to allow the SGSR in each operation to distribute some percentage of a mission's budget to support projects undertaken by local populations. See *United Nations document, S/2000/101*. Another is for the UN to employ more local staff during its peacekeeping operations.

82. See R. Carroll, 'Peace Brings UNITA Only Humiliation', *The Guardian*, 21 February 2003 and B.D. De Klerk, 'Moving From War to Peace: Building Democracy in Post-Conflict Angola', *Conflict Trends*, Vol. 4 (2002) 9–11.

83. B. Boutros-Ghali, 'Global Leadership After the Cold War', *Foreign Affairs*, Vol. 75, No. 2 (1996) 93.

Selected Bibliography

Primary Sources: United Nations Documents

S/20338, 17 December 1988; S/23097, 30 September 1991; S/23402, 13 January 1992; S/RES/733, 23 January 1992; A/46/864–S/23501, 30 January 1992; S/23613, 19 February 1992; S/23693, 11 March 1992; S/23829, 21 April 1992; S/RES/751, 24 April 1992; S23870, 1 May 1992; S/23999, 26 May 1992; A/46/935–S/24066, 5 June 1992; S/24090, 12 June 1992; S/23999 Add. 1, 19 June 1992; S/24286, 14 July 1992; S/24343, 22 July 1992; A/46/955–S/24375, 12 August 1992; S/24480, 24 August 1992; SC RES 775, 28 August 1992; S/24578, 21 September 1992; S/24635, 8 October 1992; S/24642, 9 October 1992; S/24688, 19 October 1992; S/24719, 27 October 1992; S/24724, 28 October 1992; S/24800, 15 November 1992; S/24892, 3 December 1992; S/RES/794, 3 December 1992; S/24992, 19 December 1992; S/25006, 23 December 1992; S/25044, 7 January 1993; S/25078, 9 January 1993; S/25200, 29 January 1993; S/25241, 4 February 1993; S/25354, 3 March 1993; S/RES/814, 26 March 1993; S/25518, 2 April 1993; A/47/912–S/25521, 5 April 1993; S/25719, 3 May 1993; S/25812, 21 May 1993; S/25812/Add. 2, 25 May 1993; S/RES/837, 6 June 1993; S/25901, 8 June 1993; S/25913, 10 June 1993; S/26005, 29 June 1993; S/26034, 30 June 1993; S/26022, 1 July 1993; S/26052, 8 July 1993; S/26317, 17 August 1993; S/26351, 24 August 1993; S/26385, 30 August 1993; S/26371, 30 August 1993; S/26385/Add. 1, 10 September 1993; S/26581, 14 October 1993; S/26606, 20 October 1993; S/26666, 1 November 1993; S/26689, 3 November 1993; S/26738, 12 November 1993; S/26790, 23 November 1993; A/49/59–S/1994/47, 18 January 1994; S/25168, 26 January 1994; S/1994/89, 28 January 1994; S/RES/897, 4 February 1994; S/1994/361, 30 March 1994; S/1994/375, 31 March 1994; A/49/116–S/1994/385, 5 April 1994; S/1994/511, 28 April 1994; S/1994/561, 11 May 1994; S/1994/612, 24 May 1994; S/1994/653, 1 June 1994; S/1994/803, 7 July 1994; S/PRST/1994/35, 19 July 1994; S/1994/886, 28 July 1994; S/1994/977, 19 August 1994; S/1994/1002, 26 August 1994; S/1994/1009, 29 August 1994; S/1994/1166, 14 October 1994;

S/1994/1196,
21 October 1994;
S/1994/989,
22 October 1994;
S/1994/1212,
31 October 1994;
S/1994/1449,
23 December 1994;
S/1995/143,
17 February 1995;

Economic and Social
Council document,
E/AC. 51/1995/2,
17 March 1995;
SG/SM/5589, 22 March
1995; S/1995/220,
24 March 1995;
SG/SM/95/82, 3 April
1995; SG/SM/95/147,
3 July 1995;

A/50/517, 6 October
1995; A/50/455, 23
October 1995;
A/50/455,
30 October 1995;
A/50/935, 23 April
1996; A/51/917,
1 July 1997;
S/2000/101,
11 February 2000.

Secondary Sources: United Nations Publications

Adibe, C., *Managing Arms in Peace Processes: Liberia* (Geneva: UNIDIR, 1996).

Adibe, C., *Managing Arms in Peace Processes: Somalia* (Geneva: UNIDIR, 1995).

Berman, E., *Managing Arms in Peace Processes: Mozambique* (Geneva: UNIDIR, 1996).

Boutros-Ghali, B., *An Agenda for Peace* (New York: United Nations, 1992).

Cox, D., 'Peacekeeping and Disarmament: Peace Agreements, Security Council Mandates and the Disarmament Experience', in *Managing Arms in Peace Processes: The Issues* (Geneva: UNIDIR, 1996).

Disarmament, Demobilization and Reintegration of Ex-Combatants in a Peacekeeping Environment: Principles and Guidelines (New York, United Nations, 1999).

Ekwall-Uebelhart, B. and Raevsky, A., *Managing Arms in Peace Processes: Croatia and Bosnia-Herzegovina* (Geneva: UNIDIR, 1996).

Financing an Effective United Nations: a Report of the Independent Advisory Group on UN Financing (New York: Ford Foundation, 1993).

Gamba, V. and Potgieter, J., 'Concluding Summary: Multinational Peace Operations and Enforcement of Consensual Disarmament', in *Managing Arms in Peace Processes: The Issues* (Geneva: UNIDIR, 1996).

Gamba, V., Potieter, J., Tiihonen, I., Carrai, B., Querner, C., and Tulliu, S., *Managing Arms in Peace Processes: Training* (Geneva: UNIDIR, 1998).

Ginifer, G., *Managing Arms in Peace Processes: Rhodesia/Zimbabwe* (Geneva: UNIDIR, 1995).

The United Nations and Cambodia 1991–1995, Blue Book Series, Vol. II (New York: United Nations, 1995).

The United Nations and El Salvador 1990–95, Blue Book Series Vol. IV (New York: United Nations, 1995).

The United Nations and Somalia 1992–1996, Blue Book Series, Vol. VIII (New York: United Nations, 1996).

Wang, J., *Managing Arms Processes: Cambodia* (Geneva: UNIDIR, 1996).

Wrobel, P.S., *Managing Arms in Peace Processes: Nicaragua and El Salvador* (Geneva: UNIDIR, 1995).

Zowels, E.A., *Managing Arms in Peace Processes: The Issues* (Geneva: UNIDIR, 1996).

Secondary Sources: Books

Anderson, H., *Mozambique: A War Against the People* (London: Macmillan, 1992).

Anstee, M.J., *Orphan of the Cold War* (London: Macmillan, 1996).

Azar, E., 'Protracted International Conflict: Ten Propositions' in H. Starr (ed.) *The Understanding and Management of Global Violence* (New York: St. Martin's Press, 1999).

Bercovich, J., *Resolving International Conflicts*, (Boulder, Colo: Lynne Rienner, 1996).

Berdal, M. and Malone, D.M. (eds), *Greed and Grievance: Economic Agendas in Civil Wars* (Bolo. Colo.: Lynne Rienner, 2000).

Bert, W., *The Reluctant Superpower: United States' Policy in Bosnia 1991–95* (New York: St Martin's Press, 1997).

Bourantonis, D. and Wiener, J., (eds), *The UN in the New World Order* (London: Macmillan, 1994).

Boutwell J. and M.T. Klare (eds), *Light Weapons and Civil Conflict: Controlling the Tools of Violence*, (Lanham: Rowman and Littlefield, 1999).

Brittain, V., *Death of Dignity: Angola's Civil War* (London: Pluto Press, 1998).

Brown, M. (ed.), *International Dimensions of Internal Conflict* (Cambridge Mass: MIT Press, 1996).

Burton, J.W., *Peace Theory: Preconditions for Disarmament* (New York: Alfred A Knopf, 1962).

Burton, J.W., *Conflict Resolution and Provention* (London: Macmillan, 1990).

Byrne, H., *El Salvador's Civil War: A Study of Revolution* (London: Lynne Rienner, 1996).

Carey, R. and Salmon T. (eds), *International Security in the Modern World* (New York: St. Martin's Press, 1992).

Charters, D., *Peacekeeping and the Challenge of Conflict Resolution* (University of New Brunswick, 1994).

Collier, P., 'Economic Causes of Civil Conflict and their Implications for Policy' in *Turbulent Peace: The Challenges of Managing International Conflict* (Washington D.C.: USIPP, 2001).

Crocker, C.A., Hampson, F.O., and Aall, P., (eds), *Managing Global Chaos: Sources of and Responses to International Conflict* (Washington D.C.: USIPP, 1998).

Crocker, C.A., Hampson, F.O., and Aall, P., (eds), *Turbulent Peace: The Challenges of Managing International Conflict* (Washington D.C.: USIPP, 2001).

Crocker, C.A., Hampson, F.O., and Aall, P., (eds), *Herding Cats: Multiparty Mediation in a Complex World* (Washington D.C.: USIPP, 2001).

Croft, S., *Strategies of Arms Control: A History and Typology* (Manchester: Manchester University Press, 1996).

Deng, F.M. and Zartman, I.W. (eds), *Conflict Resolution in Africa* (Washington D.C: Brookings Institution Press, 1991).

Diehl, P.F., *International Peacekeeping* (John Hopkins University Press, 1994).

Donald D. and Hayes, B., *Beyond Traditional Peacekeeping* (London: Macmillan, 1995).

Doyle, M., *UN Peacekeeping in Cambodia: UNTAC's Civil Mandate*, IPA Occasional Paper Series (London: Lynne Rienner, 1995).

Durch, W.J., (ed.), *The Evolution of UN Peacekeeping* (New York: St. Martin's Press, 1993).

Evans, G., *Co-operating for Peace* (Allen and Unwin, 1993).

Findlay, T., *Cambodia: The Legacy and Lessons of UNTAC*, SIPRI Research Report No.9 (Oxford: Oxford University Press, 1995).

Finnegan, W., *A Complicated War: The Harrowing of Mozambique* (University of California Press, 1992).

Gardenker, L. and Baehr, P., *The United Nations in the 1990's*, 2nd ed., (London: Macmillan, 1990).

Hampson, F.O., *Nurturing Peace: Why Peace Settlements Succeed or Fail* (Washington D.C.: USIP, 1996).

Hart, K. and Lewis, J., *Why Angola Matters* (Cambridge: University of Cambridge, 1995).

Hill, S.M., 'Negotiating Within Cultures: The United Nations and the Resolution of Civil Conflict', in Goodwin, D. (ed.) *Negotiation in International Conflict: Understanding Persuasion* (London: Frank Cass, 2001).

Hill, S.M. and Malik, S., *Peacekeeping and the United Nations* (Aldershot: Dartmouth Press, 1996).

Hillen, J., *Blue Helmets: The Strategy of UN Military Operations* (Washington D.C.: Brassey's, 1998).

Hirsch, J. and Oakley, R., *Somalia and Operation Restore Hope* (Washington: USIPP, 1995).

Hoile, D., *Mozambique: Resistance and Freedom* (The Mozambique Institute, 1994).

James, A., *Peacekeeping in International Politics* (London: Macmillan, 1990).

Jett, D.C., *Why Peacekeeping Fails* (New York: St. Martin's Press, 1999).

Johnstone, I., *Rights and Reconciliation: United Nations Strategies in El Salvador*, IPA Occasional Paper Series (London: Lynne Rienner, 1995).

Licklider, R. (ed.), *Stopping the Killing* (New York: New York University Press, 1993).

Liu, F.T., *United Nations Peacekeeping and the Non-Use of Force* (London: Lynne Rienner, 1992).

Mearsheimer, J., *The Tragedy of Great Power Politics* (New York: W.W. Norton and Co., 2001)

Metz, S., *Reform, Conflict and Security in Zaire* (Strategic Studies Institute Publication, 1996).

Minter, W., *Apartheids Contras* (Witwaters and University Press, 1994).

Montgomery, T.S., *Revolution in El Salvador: From Civil Strife to Civil Peace*, (Boulder, Colo: Westview Press, 1995).

Morgenthau, H.J., *Politics Among Nations: The Struggle for Power and Peace*, (New York: Alfred A. Knopf, 1948).

Murray, K., *El Salvador: Peace on Trial* (Oxford: Oxford University Press, 1997).

O'Balance, E., *Civil War in Bosnia 1992–94* (London, St. Martin's Press, 1995).

Oakley, R.B., Dziedzic, M.J., and Goldberg, E.M., (eds), *Policing the New World Disorder: Peace Operations and Public Security* (Washington D.C.: National Defense University Press, 1998).

Parsons, A., *From Cold War to Hot Peace* (London: Penguin, 1995).

Prendergast, J., *The Bones of Our Children Are Not Yet Buried*, Centre of Concern, January 1994.

Prendergast, J., *Crisis Response*, (London: Pluto Press, 1997).

Pugh, M. (ed.), *Regeneration of War-Torn Societies* (London: Macmillan, 2000).

Ratner, S.R., *The New UN Peacekeeping* (New York: St. Martin's Press, 1995).

Rich P.B. (ed.), *Warlords in International Relations* (London: Macmillan Press, 1999).

Sahnoun, M., *Somalia: The Missed Opportunities* (Washington: USIPP, 1994).

Sandole, D. and Van der Merwe, H., *Conflict Resolution Theory and Practice* (Manchester: Manchester University Press, 1993).

Sisk, T.D., *Power Sharing and International Mediation in Ethnic Conflict* (Washington D.C.: USIPP, 1997).

Sislin, J. and Pearson, F.S., *Arms and Ethnic Conflict* (Lanham: Rowman and Littlefield, 2001).

Smith, H., *International Peacekeeping, Building on the Cambodian Experience* (Canberra: Australian Defense Studies Center, 1994).

Snow, D.M., *UNCIVIL WARS: International Security and the New Internal Conflicts* (London: Lynne Rienner, 1996).

Sorpong, P., *Conflict Neutralization in the Cambodian War: From Battlefield to Ballot Box* (Oxford: Oxford University Press, 1997).

Starr, H., (ed.), *The Understanding and Management of Global Violence* (New York: St Martin's Press, 1999).

Stedman, S.J., 'Negotiation and Mediation in Internal Conflict', in *The International Dimensions of Internal Conflict*, Brown, B.E. (ed.), (Cambridge Mass.: MIT Press, 1996).

Stedman, S., *Peacemaking in Civil War*, (London: Lynne Rienner, 1991).

Stedman, S.J., Rothchild, D. and Cousens, E.M. (eds), *Ending Civil Wars: The Implementation of Peace Agreements* (London: Lynne Rienner, 2002).

Stern, P.C and Druckman, D. (eds.), *International Conflict Resolution After the Cold War* (Washington: National Academy Press, 2000).

Thakur R. and Thayer, C.A. (eds), *A Crisis of Expectations: United Nations Peacekeeping in the 1990's* (Boulder, Colo: Westview Press, 1995).

Touval, S. and Zartman, I.W. (eds), *International Mediation in Theory and Practice* (Boulder, Colo: Westview Press, 1985).

Vines, A., *RENAMO: From Terrorism to Democracy in Mozambique?* (Villiers Publications, 1996).

Walter, B.F. and Snyder, J. (eds), *Civil Wars, Insecurity and Intervention* (New York: Columbia University Press, 1999).

Walter, B.F., *Committing to Peace* (Princeton, Princeton University Press, 2002).

Weiss, T.G. (ed.), *The United Nations and Civil Wars* (London: Lynne Rienner, 1995).

Wendt, A., *Social Theory of International Politics* (Cambridge: Cambridge University Press, 1999).

White, N.D., *Keeping the peace: The United Nations and the Maintenance of International Peace and Security* (Manchester: Manchester University Press, 1993).

Wright, G., *The Destruction of a Nation – US Policy Toward Angola Since 1945* (London: Pluto Press, 1997).

Lapid, Y. and Kratochwil, F. (eds), *The Return of Culture and Identity in IR Theory* (Boulder, Colo.: Lynne Rienner, 1996).

Zartman, I.W., 'Ripeness: The Hurting Stalemate and Beyond', in Stern, P.C. and Druckman, D. (eds), *International Conflict Resolution After the Cold War* (Washington D.C.: National Academy Press, 2000).

Zartman, I.W., 'The Unfinished Agenda: Negotiating Internal Conflicts', in Licklider, R. (ed.), *Stopping the Killing* (New York: New York University Press, 1993).

Zartman, I.W. (ed), *Negotiating to End Civil Wars* (Washington D.C.: Brookings Institution Press, 1996).

Zartman, I.W., *Ripe for Resolution* (New York: Oxford University Press, 1989).

Zartman, I.W. and Touval, S., 'International Mediation in the Post-Cold War Era', in Crocker, C.A., et. al., *Managing Global Chaos: Sources of and Responses to International Conflict* (Washington D.C.: USIPP, 1998).

Zartman, I.W. and Rasmussen J.L. (eds), *Peacemaking in International Conflict: Methods and Techniques* (Washington D.C.: USIPP, 2002).

Secondary Sources: Articles

Alden, C. and Simpson, M., 'Mozambique: A Delicate Peace', *Journal of Modern African Studies* Vol. 31, No. 1 (1993).

Alden, C., 'Swords into Ploughshares? The UN and Demilitarisation in Mozambique', *International Peacekeeping*, Vol. 2, No. 2 (1995).

Alden, C., 'The UN and the Resolution of Conflict in Mozambique', *Journal of Modern African Studies*, Vol. 33, No.1

Akashi, Y., 'The Limits of UN Diplomacy and the Future of Conflict Mediation', *Survival*, Vol. 37, No. 4 (1995–1996).

Anstee, M., 'The Fight Goes On', *The World Today*, Vol. 54, No. 10 (1998).

Arfi, B., 'Ethnic Fear: The Social Construction of Insecurity', *Security Studies*, Vol. 8, No. 1 (1998).

Augelli, E. and Murphy, C., 'Lessons of Somalia for Future Multilateral Humanitarian Assistance Operations', *Global Governance*, Vol. 1 (1995).

Berdal, M., 'Disarmament and Demobilization After Civil Wars', *Adelphi Paper*, No. 303 (London: Brassey's for the International Institute for Strategic Studies, 1996).

Berdal, M., 'Fateful Encounter: the United States and UN Peacekeeping', *Survival*, Vol. 36, No. 1 (1994).

Berdal, M., *UN Peacekeeping at a Crossroads: The Challenges of Management and Institutional Reform*, IFS Info, No.7 (1993).

Berdal, M., 'Whither UN Peacekeeping', *Adelphi Paper*, No. 281 (London: Brassey's for the International Institute for Strategic Studies, 1993).

Berridge, G., 'Diplomacy and the Angola/Namibia Accords', *International Affairs*, Vol. 65, No. 3 (1989).

Betts, R.K., 'The Delusion of Impartial Intervention', *Foreign Affairs*, Vol. 73, No. 6 (1994).

Bolton, J.R., 'Wrong Turn in Somalia', *Foreign Affairs* (1994).

Boutros-Ghali, B., 'Agenda for Peace One Year Later', *Orbis*, Vol. 37, No. 3 (1993).

Boutros-Ghali, B., 'Empowering the United Nations', *Foreign Affairs*, Vol. 72, No. 5 (1992).

Boutros-Ghali, B., 'Global leadership after the Cold War', *Foreign Affairs*, Vol. 75, No. 2 (1996).

Boutros-Ghali, B., 'UN Peacekeeping in a New Era: A New Chance for Peace', *World Today*, (1993).

Clarke, W. and Herbst, J., 'Somalia and the Future of Humanitarian Intervention', *Foreign Affairs*, Vol. 75, No. 2 (1996).

Colletta, N.J., Kostner, M., and Wiederhofer, I., *The Transition from War to Peace in Sub-Saharan Africa* (Washington D.C.: World Bank 1996).

Cooper, R. and Berdal M., 'Outside Intervention in Ethnic Conflicts', *Survival*, Vol. 35 (1993). Costa, G., 'The United Nations and Reform of the Police in El Salvador', *International Peacekeeping*, Vol. 2, No. 3 (1995).

Crocker, C., 'The Lessons of Somalia: Not Everything Went Wrong', *Foreign Affairs*, Vol. 74, No. 3 (1995).

Croft, S., 'Lessons from the Disarmament of Factions in Civil Wars', Paper presented at the BISA Conference, Southampton (1995).

'Demobilisation After Civil Wars' in *Strategic Survey 1993–94*, (London: Brassey's for the International Institute of International Studies, 1993–1994).

De Soto, A. and Del Castillo, G., 'Implementation of Comprehensive Peace Agreements: Staying the Course in El Salvador', *Global Governance*, Vol. 1 (1995).

Doyle, M. and Suntharalingham, N., 'The UN in Cambodia, Lessons for Complex Peacekeeping', *International Peacekeeping*, Vol. 1, No. 2 (1994).

Duke, S., 'The UN and Intra-State Conflict', *International Peacekeeping*, Vol. 1, No. 4 (1994).

Evans, G., 'Peacekeeping in Cambodia – Lessons Learned', *NATO Review*, Vol. 42, No. 4 (1994).

Farrell, T., 'Sliding into War: the Somalia Imbroglio and US Army Peace Operations Doctrine', *International Peacekeeping*, Vol. 2, No. 2 (1995).

Findlay, T., 'UNTAC: Lessons to be Learned', *International Peacekeeping*, Vol. 1, No. 1 (1994).

Fisher, R.J. and Keashley, K., 'The Potential Complementarity of Mediation and Consultation Within a Contingency Model of Third Party Intervention', *Journal of Peace Research*, Vol. 28, No. 1 (1991).

Flores, T., 'ONUSAL – A Precedent for Future United Nations Missions?', *International Peacekeeping*, Vol. 2, No. 1 (1995).

Fung, I.F., 'Control and Collection of Light Weapons in the Sahel-Sahara Subregion: A Mission Report', *Disarmament*, Vol. 19, No. 2 (1996).

Ganzglass, M., 'The Restoration of the Somali Justice System', *International Peacekeeping*, Vol. 3, No. 1 (1996).

Goulding, M., 'The Use of Force by the United Nations', *International Peacekeeping*, Vol. 3, No. 1 (1996).

Grenier, Y. and Daudelin, J., 'Foreign Assistance and the Market Place of Peacemaking: Lessons from El Salvador', *International Peacekeeping*, Vol. 2, No. 3 (1995).

Griffiths, R.J., 'Democratisation and Civil-Military Relations in Namibia, South Africa and Mozambique', *Third World Quarterly*, Vol. 17, No. 3 (1996).

Hall, M. 'The Mozambican National Resistance (RENAMO): A study in the destruction of an African country', *Africa*, Vol. 60, No.1, 1990.

Hamill, J., 'Angola's Road From Under the Rubble', *World Today*, Vol. 50, No. 1 (1994).

Hartzell, C.A., 'Explaining the Stability of Negotiated Settlements of Intra-State Wars', *Journal of Conflict Resolution*, Vol. 43, No. 1 (1999).

Herz, J.H. 'Idealist Internationalism and the Security Dilemma', *World Politics*, Vol. 2, No. 2 (1950).

Heywood, L.M., 'Towards an Understanding of Modern Political Ideology in Africa: the Case of the Ovimbundu of Angola', *The Journal of Modern African Studies*, Vol. 36, No.1 (1998).

Hill, S.M., 'Disarmament in Mozambique: Learning the Lessons of Experience', *Contemporary Security Policy*, Vol. 17, No. 1 (1996).

Hill, S.M., 'Creating an Analytical Framework for Disarmament in UN Peacekeeping Operations', *Civil Wars*, Vol. 2, No. 4 (1999).

Hoddie, M. and Hartzell, C.A., 'Civil War Settlements and the Implementation of Military Power-Sharing Arrangements', *Journal of Peace Research*, Vol. 40, No. 3, (2003).

Hoffman, W. and Richter, W., 'The Proliferation of Light Weapons, Small Arms and Land-mines', *Disarmament*, Vol. 19, No. 2 (1996).

Hong, M., 'The Paris Agreement on Cambodia: In Retrospect', *International Peacekeeping*, Vol. 2, No. 1 (1995).

Howe, J.T., 'Somalia: Learning the Right Lessons', *The Washington Quarterly*, Vol. 18, No. 3 (1995).

James, A., 'Internal Peacekeeping: A Dead End for the UN?', *Security Dialogue*, Vol. 24, No. 4 (1994).

James, A., 'Is There a Second Generation of Peacekeeping?', *International Peacekeeping*, Vol. 1, No. 4 (1994).

James, A., 'Problems of Internal Peacekeeping', *Diplomacy and Statecraft*, Vol. 5, No. 1 (1994).

James, A., 'The History of Peacekeeping: An Analytical Perspective', *Canadian Defence Quarterly*, Vol. 23, No. 1 (1993).

Jennar, R.M., 'UNTAC: "International Triumph" in Cambodia?', *Security Dialogue*, Vol. 28, No. 2 (1994).

Johansen, R., 'The Future of United Nations Peacekeeping and Enforcement: A Framework for Policymaking', *Global Governance*, Vol. 2 (1998).

Karl, T.L., 'El Salvador's Negotiated Revolution', *Foreign Affairs*, Vol. 71, No. 2 (1992).

Kaufman, C., 'Possible and Impossible Solutions to Ethnic Civil Wars', *International Security*, Vol. 20, No. 4 (1996).

Kaufman, S.J., 'An "International" Theory of Inter-Ethnic War', *Review of International Studies*, Vol. 22, No. 2 (1996).

Keefe, J.M., 'The Operational Art of Peace Enforcement', *Low Intensity Conflict & Law Enforcement*, Vol. 5, No. 1(1996).

Keen, D., 'The Economic Functions of Violence in Civil Wars', *Adelphi Paper*, No. 320 (London: Brassey's for the International Institute of Strategic Studies, 1998).

Kennedy, K., 'The Relationship between the Military and the Humanitarian Organizations in Operation Restore Hope', *International Peacekeeping*, Vol. 13, No. 1 (1996).

Kennedy, P. and Russet, B., 'Reforming the United Nations', *Foreign Affairs*, Vol. 74, No. 5 (1995).

King, C., 'Ending Civil Wars', *Adelphi Paper*, No. 308 (London: Brassey's for the Institute of Strategic Studies, 1997).

Krause, K., 'Multilateral Diplomacy, Norm Building, and UN Conferences: The Case of Small Arms and Light Weapons', *Global Governance*, Vol. 8 (2002).

Krska, V., 'Peacekeeping in Angola (UNAVEM I and II)', *International Peacekeeping*, Vol. 4, No. 1 (1997).

Laurance, E., 'Surplus Weapons and the Micro-Disarmament Process', *Disarmament: A Periodic Review by the United Nations*, Vol. 19, No. 2 (1996).

Licklider, R., 'The Consequences of Negotiated Settlements in Civil Wars 1945–1995', *American Political Science Review*, Vol. 89, No. 3 (1995).

Lock, P., 'Armed Conflicts and Small Arms Proliferation: Refocusing the Research Agenda', *Policy Sciences*, Vol. 30, No. 3 (1997).

Lyons, G.M., 'A New Collective Security: The United Nations and International Peace', *The Washington Quarterly*, Vol. 17, No. 2 (1994).

MacFarlane, S.N. and Weiss, T.G., The United Nations, Regional Organisations and Human Security: Building Theory in Central America, *Third World Quarterly*, Vol. 15, No. 2 (1994).

Makinda, S., 'Security in the Horn of Africa', *Adelphi Paper*, No. 269, (London: Brassey's for the International Institute of Strategic Studies, 1992).

Mason, T.D. and Fett, P.J., 'How Civil Wars End', *Journal of Conflict Resolution*, Vol. 40, No. 4 (1996).

Mazarr, M., 'The Military Dilemmas of Humanitarian Intervention', *Security Dialogue*, Vol. 24, No. 2 (1993).

McQueen, N., 'Peacekeeping by Attrition: The UN in Angola', *The Journal of Modern African Studies*, Vol. 36, No. 3 (1998).

Menkhaus, K., 'International Peacebuilding and the Dynamics of Local and National Reconciliation in Somalia', *International Peacekeeping*, Vol. 3, No. 1 (1996).

Moss, A.H. Jr., 'Peace in Central America', *Survival*, Vol. 32, No. 5 (1990).

Munck, G.L. and Kumar, C., Civil Conflicts and the Conditions for Successful International Intervention: a Comparative Study of Cambodia and El Salvador, *Review of International Studies*,Vol. 21 (1995).

Natsios, A.S., 'Humanitarian Relief Interventions in Somalia: The Economics of Chaos', *International Peacekeeping*, Vol. 3, No. 1 (1996).

Peceny, M. and Stanley, W., 'Liberal Social Reconstruction and the Resolution of Civil Wars in Central America', *International Organization*, Vol. 55, No. 1 (2001).

Plunkett, M., 'Reestablishing Law and Order in Peace-Maintenance', *Global Governance*, Vol. 1, No. 1 (1998).

Posen, B.R., 'The Security Dilemma and Ethnic Conflict', *Survival*, Vol. 35, No. 1 (1993).

Plunkett, M., 'Reestablishing Law and Order in Peace Maintenance', *Global Governance*, Vol. 1, No. 1 (1998).

Pouligny, B., 'Promoting Democratic Institutions in Post-Conflict Societies: Giving Diversity a Chance', *International Peacekeeping*, Vol. 7, No. 3 (2000).

Puchala, D.J., 'Outsiders, Insiders and UN Reform', *The Washington Quarterly*, Vol. 17, No. 4 (1994).

Roberts, A., 'From San Francisco to Sarajevo: the UN and the Use of Force', *Survival*, Vol. 37, No. 4 (1995).

Roberts, A., 'The Crisis in UN Peacekeeping', *Survival*, Vol. 26, No. 3 (1994).

Roberts, A., 'The UN and International Security', *Survival*, Vol. 35, No. 2 (1993).

Roberts, D., 'More Honoured in the Breech: Consent and Impartiality in the Cambodian Peacekeeping Operation', *International Peacekeeping*, Vol. 4, No. 1 (1997).

Roe, P., 'Former Yugoslavia: The Security Dilemma That Never Was', *European Journal of International Relations*, Vol. 6, No. 3 (2000).

Russel, B. and Sutterlin, J.S., 'The UN in a New World Order', *Foreign Affairs*, Vol. 70, No. 2 (1991).

Sadowski, Y., 'Ethnic Conflict', *Foreign Policy*, No. 11 (1998).

Sammaruga, C., 'Land-Mines: From Global Negotiations to National and Regional Initiatives', *Disarmament: A Periodic Review by the United Nations*, Vol. 19, No. 2 (1996).

Shearer, D., 'Outsourcing War', *Foreign Policy*, No. 112 (1998).

Somerville, K., 'The Failure of Democratic Reform in Angola and Zaire', *Survival*, Vol. 35, No. 3 (1993).

Stanley, W., 'Building New Police Forces in El Salvador and Guatemala: Learning and Counter-Learning', *International Peacekeeping*, Vol. 6, No. 1 (1999).

Stedman, S.J., 'Spoiler Problems in Peace Processes', *International Security*, Vol. 22, No. 2 (1997).

Stevenson, J., 'Hope Restored in Somalia?', *Foreign Policy*, No. 91 (1993).

Sullivan, J.G., 'How Peace Came to El Salvador', *Orbis*, Vol. 38, No. 1 (1994).

Thakur, R., 'From Peacekeeping to Peace-Enforcement: The United Nations Operation in Somalia', *Journal of Modern African Studies*, Vol. 32, No. 3 (1994).

Tickell, C., 'The United Nations: Pressures For Change', *Global Society*, Vol. 12, No. 1 (1998).

Turley, W.S., 'The Khmer War: Cambodia after Paris', *Survival*, Vol. 32, No. 5 (1990).

Urquart, B., 'Beyond the Sheriff's Posse', *Survival*, Vol. 32, No. 3 (1990).

Urquart, B., 'The United Nations in 1992: Problems and Opportunities', *International Affairs*, Vol. 68, No. 2 (1992).

Urquart, B., 'The United Nations System and the Future', *International Affairs*, Vol. 65, No. 2 (1989).

Van der Graaf, J., 'Proliferation of Light Weapons in Africa', *Policy Sciences*, Vol. 30, No. 3 (1997).

Walker, J., 'International Mediation and Ethnic Conflicts', *Survival*, Vol. 35, No. 1, 1993.

Washington, J.L., 'United Nations Relations with the United States: The UN Must Look Out for Itself', *Global Governance*, Vol. 2 (1996).

Webb, K., 'Third Party Intervention and the Ending of Wars – A Preliminary Approach', *Paradigms*, Vol. 9, No. 2 (1995).

Weiss, T.G., 'Humanitarian Shell Games: Whither UN Reform?', *Security Dialogue*, Vol. 29, No. 1 (1998).

Weiss, T., 'Overcoming the Somalia Syndrome: Operation Rekindle Hope', *Global Governance*, Vol. 1 (1995).

Weiss, T.G., 'The United Nations and Civil Wars', *The Washington Quarterly*, Vol. 17, No. 4 (1994).

Wendt, A., 'Constructing International Politics', *International Security*, Vol. 20, No. 1 (1995).

Whitman, J. and Bartholemew, I., 'Collective Control of UN Peace Support Operations: A Policy Proposal', *Security Dialogue*, Vol. 25, No. 1 (1994).

Wulf, H., 'Disarming and Demobilising Ex-Combatants: Implementing Micro-disarmament', *Disarmament: A Periodic Review by the United Nations*, Vol. 19, No. 2 (1996).

Yordan, C.L., *Negative Peacemaking in Bosnia: The Failure of the State-Building Program*, Paper presented at the ISA Conference, Los Angeles, USA (2001).

Zartman, I.W., 'Mediating Conflicts of Need, Greed and Creed', *Orbis* (2000).

Secondary Sources: Newspapers

Far Eastern Economic Review
Newsweek
The Daily Telegraph
The Economist
The Financial Times
The Guardian
The Independent
The International Herald Tribune
The New York Times
The Sunday Telegraph
The Times
The Washington Post

Index